IN LIGHT
OF ALL
DARKNESS

ALSO BY KIM CROSS

What Stands in a Storm
The Stahl House

IN LIGHT
OF ALL
DARKNESS

*Inside the Polly Klaas Kidnapping
and the Search for America's Child*

KIM CROSS

GRAND
CENTRAL

NEW YORK BOSTON

Grand Central Publishing
Hachette Book Group
1290 Avenue of the Americas, New York, NY 10104
grandcentralpublishing.com
twitter.com/grandcentralpub

First Edition: October 2023

Grand Central Publishing is a division of Hachette Book Group, Inc. The Grand Central Publishing name and logo is a trademark of Hachette Book Group, Inc.

The publisher is not responsible for websites (or their content) that are not owned by the publisher.

The Hachette Speakers Bureau provides a wide range of authors for speaking events. To find out more, go to hachettespeakersbureau.com or email HachetteSpeakers @hbgusa.com.

Grand Central Publishing books may be purchased in bulk for business, educational, or promotional use. For information, please contact your local bookseller or the Hachette Book Group Special Markets Department at special.markets@hbgusa.com.

Library of Congress Cataloging-in-Publication Data

Names: Cross, Kim (Kimberly Hisako), 1976- author.
Title: In light of all darkness : inside the Polly Klaas kidnapping and the
    search for America's child / Kim Cross.
Description: First edition. | New York : Grand Central Publishing, 2023. |
    Includes bibliographical references and index.
Identifiers: LCCN 2023020949 | ISBN 9781538725061 (hardcover) |
    ISBN 9781538725085 (ebook)
Subjects: LCSH: Klaas, Polly Hannah, 1981–1993. |
    Kidnapping—Investigation—California—Case studies. |
    Murder—California—Petaluma—Case studies. | Kidnapping
    victims—California—Petaluma—Case studies. | Murder
    victims—California—Petaluma—Case studies.
Classification: LCC HV6603.K46 C76 2023 |
    DDC 363.25/9540979418—dc23/eng/20230607
LC record available at https://lccn.loc.gov/2023020949

ISBNs: 9781538725061 (hardcover), 9781538725085 (ebook)

Printed in the United States of America

LSC-C

Printing 1, 2023

For there is always light,
if only we're brave enough to see it.
If only we're brave enough to be it.

—AMANDA GORMAN

"You can't grow a new heart. But when you have a big piece torn away,
you can either fill it with anger and rage, or you can fill it with love.
I just have to try and choose love."

—EVE NICHOL, POLLY'S MOTHER

For Polly

and for those
who tried to save her

Contents

Part III: The Turning Point

Author's Note

ONE SUNDAY IN JULY 2021, I USHERED TWO RETIRED FBI SPECIAL AGENTS INTO my living room in Boise, Idaho. We'd never met in person, but I had been studying their work for more than six years. One of them lifted the kidnapper's latent palm print from Polly Klaas's bedroom. The other interrogated the killer, who confessed to the murder of Polly Klaas and led him to her body. These two investigators played key roles in one of the most famous kidnappings in true-crime history. But their names were missing from everything I'd seen published about the case.

We settled into my living room to study the videotaped confession, pausing the tape repeatedly to analyze interrogation techniques and signs of deception. For me, it was like a live "director's cut," narrated by deep insiders.

Larry Taylor, the agent interviewing Richard Allen Davis on the tape, was now eighty years old, a barrel-shaped Texan with a dry sense of humor and a Dallas drawl. He had not seen this tape in almost three decades. Tony Maxwell, a lead forensic agent on the case, had never seen the confession.

I'd spoken to Tony by phone for years. But I had never been able to locate Larry. Tony easily found him—living right across town from me.

When I first interviewed Tony on Skype in 2016, he wept openly, recalling the impact Polly Klaas had made on his profession, his career, and his heart. Over the subsequent seven years, he supported my quest to ensure this narrative was comprehensive and accurate. He sent me primary sources, helped me understand documents, and tracked down other insiders, convincing them to help me.

"Tony, you've never talked to the press before," I said one day. "Why are you talking to me?"

He smiled. "Because you're family."*

(༼ ༽)

I AM THE daughter-in-law of Eddie Freyer,† the FBI case agent in charge of the Polly Klaas investigation. Because of Eddie's blessing, people like Tony and Larry—deep FBI insiders who rarely speak to reporters—not only went on the record with me, but went out of their way to help me. They provided unrestricted access to themselves and their primary source materials, but never presumed editorial control. Without them, this book would not have been possible.

About seven years ago, after I finished my first book, my husband, Eddie Freyer, Jr., suggested I write the book of record on the Polly Klaas investigation. This would never have occurred to me. True crime is not my natural habitat. I don't consume it and have never felt drawn to it as a writer. Even though "Polly Klaas" is a name that comes up every time we gather as a family, I didn't think this was my kind of story. The central themes of my work are resilience and redemption. Polly's fate was tragic and horrific. I didn't want to write a book that glorified a killer or exploited the pain of others.

Then I did some research and realized the educational value and historical significance of this case. Unfolding at the dawn of the internet age, it harnessed new technology in pioneering ways, setting precedents that would be useful to future investigators and searchers. The

---

* Also, he'd put me through a background check and thorough vetting, as Tony later admitted. "Old habits die hard."

† I made conscious efforts to check myself for bias and fact-check Eddie's recollections as thoroughly as I did with every other source.

case turned into a testing ground for new forensic tools, techniques, and procedures. As Tony put it, "It changed the way the FBI does business."

I was intrigued to learn how relevant this thirty-year-old case remains today. As a case study, it has been used to train thousands of investigators in skills ranging from latent fingerprinting techniques to interview and interrogation methods. Eddie Freyer, Sr., now seventy-two, has given his Polly Klaas presentation hundreds of times, from Iraq to Macedonia. After three attempts to retire, he still teaches it at least once a month.

Eddie felt strongly that the case ought to be formally documented—comprehensively and accurately—while the people who lived it were alive and able to remember. Months before going to press, we lost two of them. FBI Special Agent Frank Doyle, who played a key role in the creation of the FBI's first Evidence Response Team, died in December 2022. In February 2023, I went to Frank's memorial with Eddie and former SWAT team leader Tom LaFreniere. Polly Klaas was mentioned in the service and the program. The day after Frank's funeral, we lost Lillian Zilius, his supervisor and supporter. Polly Klaas meant so much to Lillian that her husband and daughter decided to forego a formal funeral and donate the cost of a service instead to the Polly Klaas Foundation.

Like Frank and Lillian, most agents and police officers who worked to save Polly were deeply and personally affected, in meaningful, life-long ways. Many were also scarred. Their pain doesn't compare to that of Eve Nichol, Marc Klaas, and every member of Polly's family. But I was struck by how many cops and agents wept in their interviews, surprising even themselves with the magnitude of their emotions and the persistence of long-suppressed trauma. Some, like Petaluma detective Andy Mazzanti, found catharsis and healing in telling stories they had never before shared, with the press or even with family.

This book interweaves the point of view of investigators like Eddie, Andy, Tony, Larry, Frank, Lillian, and Tom, who worked for sixty-five days to assess 60,000 tips and investigate 12,000 active leads. The focus of the book is the investigation and the lessons learned—investigative insights shared and used to solve future crimes.

The story is based entirely on facts from verifiable sources. I minimized journalistic attributions for the sake of narrative flow, but I've listed all sources in the end notes, along with a brief explanation of how each chapter was reported. The manuscript was fact-checked by investigators for accuracy, and peer-reviewed by journalists to help me detect reportorial blind spots or bias toward law enforcement. I made great efforts to fact-check and "triangulate the truth" by corroborating key facts—particularly recollected dialogue—with multiple sources.

Most of the details, facts, and dialogue came from primary sources documented in 1993—police reports, FBI records, recorded interviews, public records, and VHS tapes. Lengthy dialogue in interview scenes was captured in audio and video recordings and/or transcripts. What appears on the page is very close to verbatim, with minor cuts for length and clarity. Witnesses' and investigators' thoughts (and quotes) were largely recorded in 1993 investigative reports or recounted three years later, during the 1996 trial. In a few scenes, brief, quippy exchanges were recounted to me in interviews many years after the fact.

All sources were obtained legally and without the need for a Freedom of Information Act (FOIA) request. Greg Jacobs, the Sonoma County assistant district attorney who prosecuted the murder trial, entrusted me with 12,000 pages of trial transcripts and seven banker's boxes of primary sources, many of which are not easy to obtain through public records requests. Defense attorney Barry Collins lent me the original folder he was handed when he accepted the case. Other detectives and agents dug boxes of original case files out of their attics and garages and loaded them in my car.

Thoughts, quotes, analysis, and emotional impressions came from more than 300 interviews with detectives, FBI agents, and volunteers who searched for Polly, as well as subject-matter experts who could add insight and perspective. I mined some quotes, dates, and atmospheric details from hundreds of newspaper stories, mindful that errors are likely in anything reported on deadline in the middle of a crisis fraught with misinformation. Many of these news stories are missing in online databases; most were physical newspaper clippings saved by sources.

Of the twenty-nine FBI agents I reached out to, twenty-four agreed to help me (including Director Louis Freeh). Of the twenty-five police officers, sheriff's deputies, and other local law-enforcement agents, only one opted out. They all spoke candidly and let me call them as often as

I needed. Most let me interview them at least twice; some more than a dozen times.

I approached various members of Polly's family to see if they wanted to participate in the writing or fact-checking of this book. Polly's mother, Eve Nichol, wished me luck, but said she couldn't help—it was too painful. After meeting Marc Klaas in person at a KlaasKids event, I reached out to him in 2016 and 2022, but he never responded. (Eddie, who knows Marc, made sure he knew about this book.) Since Eve and Marc were integral to the story, I represented their point of view and voice through dialogue recorded by others in newspapers, magazines, and TV shows, as well as public records existing in the case files. Polly's sisters, Annie and Jessica, did not want to be involved. Polly's best friend, Annette Schott, also declined. I respect their choices.

Gillian Pelham and Kate McLean—Polly's twelve-year-old friends who witnessed her abduction—chose to help me. Gillian, a lawyer in Manchester, England, committed to accuracy, spent hours with me on Zoom, helping me check not only my facts but my assumptions. Gillian read and fact-checked every chapter in which she or Kate appeared.

Kate McLean agreed to talk with me—strictly on background, with clear boundaries—preferring not to be interviewed or quoted, but willing to help me understand these events with greater nuance and context. She asked me not to reveal anything about her adult life. I honor her wish, and I hope that other journalists will respect her desire for privacy. Kate and Gillian both granted me permission to answer a question I expected readers would wonder: *Are they okay?* Not only are they mentally and physically healthy and resilient, they are kind, well-grounded, intelligent, and professionally successful. Yes, they are still close friends.

I sent two handwritten letters to Richard Allen Davis on Death Row in San Quentin. He never responded.

While my narratives are always aimed at delivering a fascinating and fast-paced read, my goal for this book was to present a story that would be useful: to investigators who can learn from a nuanced case study, or to readers who want a fact-based, realistic account of the inner workings of an investigation. My greatest hope is that this story helps someone I may never meet in ways I can hardly imagine.

Locard's Exchange Principle: Every contact leaves a trace.

—Edmond Locard, 1934

"Wherever he steps, whatever he touches, whatever he leaves—even unconsciously—will serve as a silent witness against him. Not only his fingerprints and his shoeprints, but also his hair, the fibers from his clothes, the glass he breaks, the tool mark he leaves, the paint he scratches, the blood or semen he deposits or collects—all of these and more bear mute witness against him. This is evidence that does not forget. It is not confused by the excitement of the moment. It is not absent because human witnesses are. Physical evidence cannot be wrong; it cannot perjure itself; it cannot be wholly absent. Only in its interpretation can there be error. Only human failure to find, study, and understand it can diminish its value."

—Paul Leland Kirk, criminologist, 1953

PART I

SOMEWHERE OUT THERE

chapter one

THE SLEEPOVER

⌒⌒

October 1, 1993, 3 p.m.—Petaluma, California

ON THE FIRST FRIDAY OF OCTOBER 1993, A TWELVE-YEAR-OLD GIRL WITH A dimpled grin burst out of the week's final class at Petaluma Junior High. Polly Klaas was dressed in a turquoise T-shirt and loose patterned shorts, her purple backpack stuffed with seventh-grade textbooks, crumbs, and a three-ring binder. Polly scanned the carpool lane for her mother. At breakfast, she had asked her mom if a friend could spend the night.

"Well, maybe," her mother told her. "But you have to clean your room."

It was a deal. She'd even vacuum. Polly and her friends, Kate and Gillian, planned the details at lunch, conspiring to make it a sleepover. They'd dress up, play games, and probably find some new way to prank one another. Last weekend, sleeping over at Gillian's house, they had stayed up until five a.m. Polly brought a tape of Gregorian chants to play while telling scary stories in the dark. They enlisted Gillian's brother to rap on the door on cue to make it even more eerie.

Sleepovers were on Polly's list of all-time favorite things. She loved theater, ice cream, music, jokes, pizza, costumes, Broadway musicals (especially *Phantom of the Opera*), and novels (*Little Women* and mysteries). She had a kitty named Milo, who came after Spooky, who was run over by a car. Her favorite color was purple. She knew by heart the lyrics to her favorite song, "Somewhere Out There," and she sang it a cappella. She enjoyed playing Super Nintendo games, recording skits with friends on audio cassettes, and renting movies from Kozy Video. She hated history, show-offs, strangers, snobs, long hikes, and being alone in the dark. She still called her parents Mommy and Daddy and wished they were still married.

Three months from her thirteenth birthday, Polly was on the cusp between cute and beautiful. Four-foot-ten and eighty pounds, she still had the body, unblemished skin, and baby teeth of a child. But she had recently started to ask her mother, "How do I look? How's my hair?" and "What should I wear with these pants?" Everyone said how pretty she was, and she had done a bit of modeling for a children's clothing catalog. But when someone paid her a compliment, she didn't know what to say, so she would look down and whisper, "Thank you." Lately, she'd caught her mother glancing up from the morning paper and gazing at her wistfully.

"What are you looking at, Mom?"

Her mother would smile. "Oh, nothing."

Polly could be sassy, but she adored and admired her mother. Until recently, she had preferred her mom to pick out her outfit every day. This fall, back-to-school shopping was a major event. They went to Mervyns and Ross so Polly could choose her own seventh-grade wardrobe: Converse high-tops, loose-fitting jeans, and baggy hoodies. She wasn't exactly into grunge, though she liked leggings with oversize flannel shirts—nothing sleek or skimpy. Sometimes she wore skirts around the house, but rarely in public. What if she had to bend over? She and her friends played around with makeup, but she never left the house wearing it.

Polly had been anxious about going to junior high, about leaving middle school classes with a few dozen kids to enter a school with 700 or 800 students and a schedule of changing classes. What if she couldn't find her locker? What if she forgot where to go? Could she keep up with all the homework? Would she get lost in a sea of kids?

The middle-school years had been difficult. Polly went to three different schools in fifth grade before moving to Petaluma at the start of sixth. She was extremely shy, especially around new people, and it was hard to make friends. Because she was pretty, some peers mistook her shyness for standoffishness and labeled her a snob. But at Cherry Valley Elementary school, things had gotten better. Other sixth-graders were drawn to her charm and wit, and a few went out of their way to befriend her. There was a bit of middle-school drama—cliques and jealous mean-girl stuff—but she'd found a circle of close friends.

Now, a month into seventh grade, Polly was finding her place in the world and in the halls of Petaluma Junior High. Built on a hill over-looking the valley, it was a classic California school: outdoor lockers and a courtyard where kids could gather for lunch. Polly was making straight A's and was recognized as one of the best clarinet players in the band.

One of the best things about junior high was that it had an actual drama class. On stage, Polly's shyness melted away. A year ago, she had played the lead role of the Chief in a sixth-grade play, *Where in the World Is Carmen Sandiego?* To give the crew time to change sets mid-scene, she learned to stall and improvise. In one such moment, she inspected a phone that might have been "bugged." Out popped rubber insects and spiders, surprising her drama teacher and making the audience roar. This year, she was crushed when laryngitis prevented her from audition-ing. She dreamed of becoming an actress like Winona Ryder, who grew up in Petaluma.

⌒⌒⌒

A LITTLE BEFORE three p.m. Polly saw her mother's Colt Vista wagon pull into the carpool lane. Polly bounded over to the car and climbed in. She greeted her mother and her blue-eyed, six-year-old half sister, Annie.

Their mother, Eve Nichol, was forty-four years old, a gentle, slender brunette with a narrow face and sad brown eyes. Born in Brooklyn, she was the only child of Austrian Jews who had survived the Holo-caust in Austria and the Nazi bombing of London. Eve's father, Eugene Reed, was a PhD and an engineer elected to the National Academy of

Sciences. He spoke with Polly on the phone every week, and they had a routine: She'd tell him jokes and make him laugh with skits in various accents. (She could do a hilarious Elvis impression.) He and Eve's mother, Joan, had retired in Pebble Beach, 160 miles south of Petaluma on the Monterey Peninsula. Polly visited them often and enjoyed long summer days roller-skating on their deck and having picnics on the beach. Eugene and Joan spent Mother's Day on the shore with Eve and the girls, watching Polly and Annie romp through the surf and dig in the sand.

Eve worked in sales and marketing for Bio Bottoms, a local catalog company that sold cloth diapers and children's clothing. It was the source of many of Polly and Annie's clothes, and Polly had modeled a jumper in their catalog. Eve was allowed to take a late lunch break to pick up the girls from school and drive them home. Polly was old enough to look after Annie now, so Eve could go back to the office a few blocks away and finish her workday.

Eve had been divorced for nine years from Polly's father, Marc Klaas, who ran a Hertz rental car franchise at the Fairmont Hotel. They'd had, as Marc liked to put it, "a lousy marriage and a great divorce," and now they shared custody of their only child. Polly spent weeknights at her mother's house, but often spent weekends at her father's condo in Sausalito, where she had her own room. Marc was a doting and protective dad who nurtured his daughter's mistrust of strangers and bristled when he learned that a boy at her school had a crush on her and was calling several times a week.

Polly's half-sister, Annie, was the daughter of Eve and her third husband, Allan Nichol, an architect who had three children from a previous marriage. Eve and Allan had separated, but were still married and in close touch. They had different parenting styles and were getting counseling, trying to patch things up. Allan lived around twenty miles north, in Santa Rosa, where Polly and Annie spent time with their stepsiblings, though they never used the word "step." Polly and twelve-year-old Jessica shared a deep bond.

After picking Polly up from school, Eve drove downtown to treat the girls. Polly craved an Icee, and Annie wanted stickers. Afterward,

Eve dropped them off at home around three-thirty p.m. and drove back to work a few blocks away. Polly called and begged her to let a second friend sleep over. Eve agreed, as long as she kept her end of the bargain. Polly promised to clean her room before her friends came over.

Their home at 427 Fourth Street was a two-bedroom Victorian cottage, light gray with white trim, four blocks from downtown Petaluma. It sat one block from the corner of Fourth and G Street, catty-corner to Wickersham Park and its trellis-shaded benches. The 1906 rental had a small front porch where the girls parked their bikes, a bay window that overlooked the street, and a wooden deck in the back. The neighborhood was filled with modest homes, closely spaced.

It was a quiet part of west Petaluma, then a city of 45,000 residents. Though it was only forty miles north of San Francisco, Petaluma felt like a small town from a simpler time. It had the double distinction of being the "egg capital of the world" and also the wrist-wrestling capital, with statues erected in honor of both. George Lucas and Francis Ford Coppola had chosen Petaluma's iconic main drag for the filming of *American Graffiti* (1973), a coming-of-age film about drag racing, muscle cars, and teenage love in the 1950s and '60s. It later became the set for *Peggy Sue Got Married* and TV commercials for Ronald Reagan's 1984 presidential campaign. The historic downtown embodied an age of innocence Reagan sought to capture with his "Come Home, America" theme. Like many parts of Sonoma, Petaluma felt like the kind of place where bad things didn't happen. Maybe it was the fresh ocean air that slid across the Pacific and over the Marin headlands, or how the light there always looked golden.

Eve returned home from work around five-thirty p.m. and parked on Fourth Street, leaving the driveway open for Aaron Thomas, a nineteen-year-old tenant who rented a mother-in-law unit behind the house. The tiny dwelling had a kitchen but no bathroom, so to use the toilet or take a shower, he had to walk out his front door, climb onto Eve's deck, and go through a service porch, which led to a small bathroom. The service porch shared a door with Eve's kitchen, and that door was almost always locked.

Eve ordered a pizza from Domino's while Polly did her chores. She made her bed, tucking floral sheets into place on the top mattress of the wooden bunk bed she shared with her sister. (Annie would sleep with Eve that night so the big girls could have fun.) She hung her pink robe on the corner of the bed and returned bright-haired trolls and books to her shelves. Not exactly tidy, but enough to pass inspection.

Polly walked to the back of the kitchen and unlocked the door to the service porch, where the vacuum cleaner was stored, and brought it back to her room. The roar of its suction filled her ears as she swept it across the blue floral area rug that covered the hardwood floor. She vacuumed around a keyboard and chair, a toy shopping cart, and bins of stuffed animals. When she was finished, she flipped the off switch and brought the vacuum cleaner back to the service porch, closing the door behind her.

She might have forgotten to lock it.

AROUND SEVEN P.M. a white Toyota Tercel pulled up to the house and twelve-year-old Gillian Pelham hopped out. Gillian and Polly had met in sixth grade at Cherry Valley Elementary, where they got to know each other in band class. Gillian played the flute and Polly the clarinet. Now they made music together in the junior high band. Gillian brought her sleeping bag, a Monopoly game, and a plastic bag filled with clothes. She'd packed a brand-new long-sleeved nightgown, white flannel with red stripes and tiny hearts, a gift from her grandparents.

Gillian's mother spoke briefly with Eve as the girls ran off to Polly's room. Their other friend, Kate McLean, wouldn't be there for another hour or so—her family was going out for pizza—so the girls played Super Nintendo games and fiddled with Gak, a gooey slime toy. They were happy that Kate would be able to join them after all. She'd left her soccer game that day with a stomachache, and her mother had thought about keeping her home. But Polly had gotten on the phone to persuade Kate's mother. Polly could be quite charming.

Polly and Gillian wanted to get ice cream, so Eve gave the girls money for Starnes Market, a neighborhood store about a block from the house. Polly had been there many times to buy treats with Annie or milk for her mom. The girls were back in less than five minutes, still eating their cups of mint chocolate chip.

Eve was taking a bath with Annie when Kate's mother dropped her off around 8:15 p.m. Polly had put on Mickey Mouse ears, and Gillian was wearing a hood with antlers. When Kate arrived, they were perched on either side of the front porch, poised like two stone lions. Kate got out of the car dressed like a hippie, in floppy pants and a tie-dyed shirt, carrying a stuffed dragon and her sleeping bag. The girls greeted one another and went inside.

As Alice McLean was backing her van out of the driveway around eight-thirty p.m., she noticed a man walking down the sidewalk. He was dressed in black and was carrying a bag. Her van was blocking the sidewalk, directly in his path, and he was walking toward it, not appearing to alter his pace or slow down. She jerked the van forward to get out of his way. She only saw him in profile and noticed his hair had a swept-back look.

In Polly's room, the girls messed around with clothes and makeup. Polly changed into a hot pink samba top with a little tie at the waist and a white denim miniskirt, a hand-me-down from her father's girlfriend, Violet Cheer. Halloween was just a few weeks away, and she wanted her friends to make her up "so she looked dead." Gillian and Kate whitened Polly's face, applied a slash of red lipstick, and used dark eye shadow to make her eyes ghoulish. Polly looked at herself in the mirror, initially pleased with the effect, but then something made her recoil.

"Get it off me! Get it off me!"

She ran to the bathroom and washed her face. Then she felt better.

Sprawled on the floor of Polly's room, they played a board game called Perfect Match, a funny spoof on dating, though none of them had ever been on a date. Boys were barely on their radar. They had recently gone to the first junior-high dance, where Gillian and Kate had witnessed Polly's first slow dance. At the end of the song, the boy surprised Polly by leaning in for a little kiss. It was her first, and Polly looked mortified, but her friends believed she was secretly pleased.

Eve popped in around ten p.m. and told them to keep it down. She was fighting a migraine, and Annie was already asleep. She said they could stay up a little while longer, but not past eleven. Before going to bed, Eve checked the front door to make sure it was locked.

"Good night," Eve said.

"Good night, Mommy," Polly said.

Eve closed both doors to the Jack-and-Jill bathroom that separated her bedroom from Polly's and crawled into bed next to Annie. She could still hear muffled laughter through the walls. At least they were having fun. Eve took a sleeping pill, read for a while, and sank into sleep.

⌒⌒

AROUND 10:30 P.M., Kate was lying on her belly on Polly's rug, chin propped on her hands. Gillian was sitting facing the door. Polly stood up from the board game to go and get the sleeping bags from the family room. She opened her bedroom door.

In her hallway stood a stranger. It was a man they had never seen before, dressed in all black. Black eyes. Black hair. His beard was charcoal gray, peppered with white streaks. In his right hand, he carried a black duffel bag. In his left, a kitchen knife.

"Don't scream," he said, "or I'll slit your throats."

chapter two

THE STRANGER

⌒⌒

Friday, October 1, 10:30 p.m.

THE MAN IN BLACK ENTERED POLLY'S ROOM, SO BIG HE FILLED THE WHOLE DOOR-way. The knife in his hand was long and thin, with a wooden handle and three steel rivets.

"Get down on the floor," the stranger said. His voice was calm and clear.

He told them not to look at him, to lie facedown, heads toward the wall, with their hands behind their backs. They did what he said.

"Don't be scared," he said. "Just stay calm."

Gillian, facedown on the carpet, wondered if this was real. *This must be a joke*, she thought. She giggled. This sort of thing only happened in the movies.

"Don't worry, I won't hurt you," he said. "I'm just doing this for the money."

Polly was an avid prankster. Maybe this was her latest ruse. This guy was really convincing. Scary. But he also looked kind of normal. Not like someone she should fear. Maybe he was a friend of the family. An uncle in on the joke.

"Why are so many people here?" the man said. "There shouldn't be so many people."

It was a sleepover, the girls explained.

"Who lives here?" he said.

"I do," Polly said.

"Where are the valuables?"

Polly told him she had thirty dollars in a pink jewelry box. It was on the top shelf of her dresser. He made no effort to find it.

"Please," Polly said, "don't hurt my mom and my sister."

They were lying facedown in a row, like dolls. Polly, then Kate, then Gillian. One by one, they felt their hands being bound behind their back, tightly, first with some kind of silky cloth, and then with electrical cord. That's when Gillian felt a stab of fear. Polly would never take a joke this far.

"Oh, it's too tight!" Gillian said. "That hurts!"

The stranger loosened the knot.

"Don't turn around," he said. "Don't look at me."

He pulled a pillowcase over each of their heads and tied a gag around it. The gag hurt, and the floor was hard. Kate, who had a cold, found it difficult to breathe.

He wanted to know where the valuables were.

"Stand up," he said.

Kate moved to stand.

"Not you," he said, pressing her firmly back into the floor. She couldn't tell if he was using his fist or maybe the butt of the knife.

Polly rose.

"I won't touch you," he said.

"Count to one thousand," he told Gillian and Kate. By the time they finished counting, he said, Polly would be back, and he would be gone. They couldn't see anything, but they heard footsteps growing softer. Under the pillowcases, through the gags, Gillian and Kate counted aloud, softly.

One.

Two.

Three...

The footsteps seemed to grow fainter.

Fourteen.

Fifteen.

Sixteen...

They counted slowly, starting and stopping, unable to see through the pillowcases.

Twenty-seven.

Twenty-eight.

Twenty-nine...

They wondered if he was still in the room, watching.

Forty-four.

Forty-five.

Forty-six...

They kept losing count, stopping and restarting. Somewhere in the hundreds, they felt sure he was gone. Maybe ten minutes had passed. Kate and Gillian wriggled back-to-back and tried to untie each other. It only seemed to make things worse. Kate scrambled to her feet, still bound and hooded, and searched blindly for the door. She found a door but wound up in the closet.

Gillian, a gymnast, sat on the bottom bunk, tucked her knees to her chest and pulled her legs through her arms. Once her hands were in front of her, she removed the gag and the pillowcase and bit at the ligatures binding her wrists, working the knot loose with her teeth. After freeing her own hands, Gillian untied Kate.

Gillian ran through the house, then out the back door and down the driveway on the side of the house, looking for Polly. It was so dark, and she was scared the man could be lurking in the shadows, so she didn't shout or raise too much alarm.

Meanwhile, Kate dashed through the kitchen and into Eve's room, where she flicked on the light and stood in the doorway.

"Eve, wake up!" Kate blurted. "Eve!"

Eve startled out of a sound sleep.

"A man broke into the house," Kate said. "He had a knife. He tied us up. He threatened to kill us. And I think he took Polly!"

Eve blinked up at her, groggy and disoriented.

"Kate, you just woke me up," she said. "You've got to be kidding me."

"Eve, it's not a joke!" Kate said. "There was a guy. He tied us up. We just got ourselves free."

Irritation turned into confusion. Confusion bled into fear. Eve was on her feet now.

"Where's Polly?"

"He took her."

"Who took her?"

"The man!"

chapter three

THE FIRST HOUR

༄

Friday, around 11 p.m.—Polly's House

"POLLY!" GILLIAN DARTED FROM ROOM TO ROOM, CRYING AND LOOKING FOR HER friend. "*Polly!*"

It didn't take long to search the five-room house. No sign of Polly. Nothing seemed to be missing or disturbed. Kate and Gillian flung open the front door and ran onto the porch, yelling into the darkness.

"POLLY!"

No answer. They ran back inside.

"Eve!" they cried. "She's not here!"

At 11:03 p.m., Eve dialed 911. Not quite thirty minutes had passed since the man had left with Polly.

"911 Petaluma." A woman's voice. Calm.

"Yeah, um, I'm sorry..." Eve began, her voice brittle.

"What's the problem?" the dispatcher said. "Hello?"

"I just woke up," Eve said. "I'm at 427 Fourth near G. Apparently a man just broke into our house and—and they said he took my daughter!"

"Do you know this man?"

"No, I just woke up and these two girls that spent the night—I spent the night with my other daughter—they just woke me up and said someone just broke into the house..."

"How old is your daughter?"

"She's twelve and a half. She's not here."

"Okay. What's your name?"

"Eve Nichol. Her name is Polly Klaas."

"It's what?"

"Polly P-O-L-L-Y Klaas. K-L-A-A-S."

"Did they say why they took her?"

"I didn't even hear anything! I was sleeping. They said a man came into the house and he tied them up and he ransacked the house, although I don't see anything gone ..."

"Are the other girls still there?"

"Yes! And Polly. And he took Polly!"

"Okay, I want you to stay on the phone with me. I'm going to get some officers over there. Did they see what kind of car they left in?"

"No, I got nothing from them."

"Okay. Can I talk to one of the other girls?"

"Yeah." Eve called for Kate, handed her the phone.

"Hi," Kate said.

"Hi. This is the police. What happened?"

"Okay," Kate said, her voice soft but steady. "We were in her room, and we were talking. She was sitting on the bed. And Gillian and I were sitting on the floor. And then this guy came in—I thought it was a joke. He had a knife."

"He had a knife?"

"Yeah. He had a big knife. And he said, 'Nobody move or I'll slit your throat.'"

"How did ... Where did he come in at?"

"We saw there's a window open ... so I guess he came in through a window."

"Okay. Did you see a car or anything?"

"No. Then he took Polly away and then we heard the screen door bang shut. What happened was, so we were sitting there and he came in and he told us to be quiet and don't scream—"

"When did this happen?"

"We don't know. We weren't...it was an hour...at least thirty...at a half an hour ago."

"Is he a white male?"

"Yeah, and he has a dark beard."

"About how old?"

"I don't know, thirties or forties maybe."

"How old are you?"

"I'm twelve. Like everyone else here."

"Okay. And he was alone?"

"Yeah, he was alone. And he tied us up and put pillowcases over our heads."

"He tied—"

"He used some sort of silky little thing to tie us up with."

"Do you still have that stuff?"

"Yeah. Have it all. We got it off because our hands were starting to swell up and turn purple or something."

"What is your name?"

"I'm Kate McLean."

"How do you spell your last name, Kate?"

"Capital M, lowercase C, capital L, lowercase E-A-N."

"Do you need an ambulance or anything like that?"

"No, our hands are just swollen and red."

"Have you ever seen this man before?"

"Never."

"Did he leave in a car—you don't know. Did you hear anything else?"

"We heard the screen door bang shut. He kept telling us, 'It's okay. I'm not going to hurt you. It's okay. Don't cry now. I'm not going to hurt you. I'm not going to touch you. I just want money. Show me where your valuables are.'"

"Okay."

"He said, 'You get up,' and I started to get up, then he tapped me on the back and said, 'Get down, I meant her.' He took Polly outside. We heard the screen door bang shut. We didn't know what was going on. He kept saying stuff to her like, 'I'm not going to touch you. It's gonna be okay.'"

"Okay, what was he wearing?"

"I didn't see."

"Hold on . . . Okay, do you remember what he was wearing?"

"No, he made us lie facedown on the floor. I didn't see anything but his face and the knife."

"Have you called your mother yet?"

"No."

"There's another girl with you, too?"

"Yeah, Gillian." Kate's voice began to rise with emotion.

"Okay. Okay," the dispatcher said. "I want you guys to stay in the house, okay?"

"Okay," Kate whimpered.

"Did you get yourself loose? Is that what happened?"

"What happened was, he told us to count to one thousand.* And then he said we could get up because he'd be gone by then."

"Okay. We've got officers coming, okay?"

"There they are."

"Do you see them now?"

"Yeah." Another whimper.

"It's going to be okay."

Kate's voice became small. "Can I call my mom?"

"Why don't you wait, because the officer's going to want to talk to you. Ask the officer, okay? Because it's real important that he gets this information as fast as he can."

"Of course. I'll tell them everything I know."

"But you talk to him about calling your mom, okay?"

"All right."

"Is he there now?"

"He's on the steps."

"Okay, I'm gonna hang up. Bye-bye."

---

* On the recorded 911 call, Kate says "ten thousand," but in every subsequent interview, Kate and Gillian consistently said "one thousand." Quote edited here for clarity.

THE FIRST COP on the scene was Danny Fish, a twenty-seven-year-old officer four years on the job at the Petaluma Police Department. Fish had been on patrol, cruising in a black-and-white Crown Victoria a few blocks away, turning onto D Street from Lakeville. Friday nights were usually busy, but it was still early enough to be quiet. That's when the radio barked his call number.

Lincoln 21, respond to a possible 207 at 427 Fourth Street.

A kidnapping—in Petaluma? They always said this job would be 99 percent boredom, 1 percent terror. Without turning on his lights or siren, he accelerated toward Fourth Street. Close behind was Vail Bello, the detective sergeant, who was pulling an overtime shift as the supervisor of the graveyard team.

At 11:15 p.m., twelve minutes after Eve dialed 911, eight minutes after being dispatched, Bello and Fish knocked on Polly's door. Polly's mother opened it. Dark hair. Dark eyes. Narrow face. Eve Nichol appeared disoriented, confused, perhaps groggy from the sleeping pill. Her voice was reedy and tremulous.

"Polly's gone," she said. "Polly's been taken!"

chapter four

THE TRESPASSER

꙯

Friday, 11 p.m.—Pythian Road, Sonoma County

AROUND TWENTY-SIX MILES NORTH OF PETALUMA, IN A SECLUDED HOUSE IN THE Sonoma hills, a twelve-year-old girl was getting ready for bed. Kelila Jaffe was at home with her babysitter, nineteen-year-old Shannon Lynch, in a house she shared with her mother on 192 acres of forested land surrounded by parks and vineyards. Her home had a swimming pool, no neighbors in sight, and a web of overgrown fire roads to hike. The nearest neighbor was Sonoma State's botany lab.

Kelila's mother, Dana Jaffe, worked as a chef for John Ash & Co., an upscale restaurant in Santa Rosa known for wine country fare, locally sourced foods served at peak season and paired with the perfect vintage. She typically left for work in the afternoon and came home between ten p.m. and midnight. A few months ago, she had hired Shannon, a student at Santa Rosa Community College, to pick Kelila up from Herbert Slater Middle School and drive her to their home in the woods. Sometimes they'd stop for snacks. Then Shannon would cook dinner, wash dishes, and see that Kelila finished her homework before she played Nintendo.

Dana Jaffe's twenty-five-minute drive home from Santa Rosa took her down Highway 12, a two-lane country highway that connected the town of Sonoma to the vineyards. A mile or two past the community of

Oakmont, she turned onto Pythian Road, which led past the turnoff for Los Guilicos Training Center, a juvenile detention center. At the county line, the road pinched into a poorly maintained one-lane private road that snaked through stands of oak and madrone. At the edge of her property, she passed through a gate that, more often than not, remained open. From here, the road—a mile-long driveway that ended at the house—steepened into a hill that required down-shifting into second gear. Her woods had grown so thick that she had needed to hire woodcutters to thin them before fire season. When she got home around 10:45 p.m., Kelila was still up. Jaffe chatted with Shannon for about fifteen or twenty minutes, wrote her a check, and said good night.

A LITTLE AFTER eleven p.m., Shannon Lynch climbed into a 1986 Ford Escort and drove down the hill. Less than a mile from the house, inside the open gate, something unusual appeared in her headlights: a white Ford Pinto. The back end was angled diagonally off the road, the rear bumper against the embankment. It appeared to be stuck in a ditch.

Then she saw the man. He was standing near the trunk of the car, hunched over. As Shannon approached, the man looked up, rose, and turned toward her, seemingly surprised to encounter another car on this road at this time of night.

He's not supposed to be here, Shannon thought. She immediately worried about Jaffe and Kelila, just up the road in a house by themselves. She braked to a stop. The man walked over to speak to her, so she rolled down her window, but only an inch. Her door was locked.

"What the fuck are you doing up here?" Shannon hissed through the crack in the window.

"I'm stuck," he said. "I need some rope."

"Are you illiterate?" she said. "Can you read?"

There were signs all over the place. *Not a Through Road. Private Property. No Trespassing.*

He told her to get out of the car. He said it "like he wanted to overpower the situation," Shannon would later say, "like he wanted to be in control." As he spoke, he leaned in and leered at her, his fingers snaking through her open window. So close she could smell him.

He smelled like he looked—as if he hadn't showered in days. His beard was unruly, and his shoulder-length hair looked matted and greasy. He was wearing blue jeans, a dark sweatshirt, and tennis shoes. Shannon noticed his sweatshirt was inside out. Leaves and bits of brush were tangled in his hair.

"What's up the road?" he demanded. "What's up the road?"

Up the road, she said, were people who would call the cops. Then she pressed the gas and sped away as fast as the road would allow. At Highway 12, she turned right, toward Santa Rosa, and drove to the nearest pay phone she knew of, at Melita Road.

She shoved in a quarter. The call didn't go through. She dialed 0.

"The phone ate my quarter," she told the operator, begging to connect her with Jaffe. "This is an emergency."

The operator told her to call the police.

"I don't have time!" Shannon said.

She hung up, pulled out her parents' calling card, and dialed Jaffe's number.

It was 11:24 p.m. From the encounter to the call, maybe seven minutes had passed. This guy could be on his way up the hill. He might be approaching the house.

⌒⌒⌒

KELILA AND JAFFE were already undressed and ready for bed when the phone rang. They were planning to sleep in the living room, by the fire, where it was warmer. Shannon sounded terrified.

"There's a scary guy on the hill," she blurted. "I think you need to call the cops."

"How long ago did you see him?" Jaffe asked.

"He should still be there now. He's walking toward your house."

Jaffe quickly calculated the risks of being found alone with a young girl in the house, isolated, in the dark woods. Levelheaded under pressure, she didn't feel afraid, although her instincts said they were in danger.

"Get dressed," she told Kelila.

There was a stranger on their property, Jaffe told her daughter. They'd be safer in the car. Instead of being stalked, they'd confront him on their own terms. Kelila dressed quickly and grabbed a baseball bat and a can of mace. Out of the house in less than a minute, they didn't waste time putting on any shoes. They got in Jaffe's car, a red Toyota Corolla hatchback with Utah plates, and immediately locked the doors.

Jaffe drove slowly down the hill, expecting to encounter a silhouette in her headlights, a stranger walking up her road. He never appeared.

"If he's supposed to be on the road," she said to her daughter, "where is he?"

There was the car—a white Pinto—on her right, just inside the gate. It was obviously stuck. But where was the man? That's when she decided to call the cops. She slowed down to look for the stranger and kept scanning the road all the way to Highway 12. *He must be off in the woods*, Jaffe thought. *What is he doing?*

She drove a couple of miles down Highway 12 to an adult retirement community where she knew of a pay phone outside Oakmont Market.

She shoved a quarter in. No dial tone. *Shit!* She only had one more.

She got back in the Corolla and drove until she found another pay phone at a gas station less than a mile away. At 11:42 p.m., Jaffe dialed 911 and spoke with a Santa Rosa police dispatcher.

"I just got home from work and my babysitter left," she said. "She called me up about five minutes later and told me that there was some guy up on my road and the car is stuck. I got in the car with my daughter, because we live in a really isolated place. Nobody has any business being up there. I see the car, but I don't see the guy, and she said he was, like, walking towards the house."

"Okay," the dispatcher said.

"I'd like to have somebody else come and check [it] out. She said he was kinda scary looking."

"And where are you right now?" the dispatcher asked.

"I'm at a pay phone at Oakmont. I thought I'd wait for the sheriff at Los Guilicos on Pythian Road."

The dispatcher took her name, her car make, model, and color.

It was a Friday night, and the dispatcher warned it might take a while to get an officer there. Jaffe didn't feel comfortable going back to the house with a stranger somewhere out there in the woods. She said she'd wait for the officers at the intersection of Highway 12 and Pythian Road.

⌒⌒⌒

EIGHT MINUTES AFTER midnight, a Ford Taurus and a Crown Victoria turned onto Pythian Road, both marked with the green-on-white stripe and yellow star of the Sonoma County Sherriff's patrol cars. Two deputies, Thomas Howard and Michael Rankin, emerged in uniform: khaki shirt, dark green nylon pants, boots. They found Jaffe and her daughter waiting in their car.

Jaffe explained that she had seen the Pinto, but not the occupant, and she didn't feel safe going home alone. They agreed to follow her up the road to investigate. If she wanted to press charges, she could have this man arrested for trespassing. She said she didn't want him arrested, just escorted off her property. She led them to the Pinto, slowing at the bottom of the hill to warn them to downshift.

The man was leaning against his car, smoking a cigarette, as if he'd been expecting them.

Jaffe slowed, and he walked over to her car window. She thought he looked "swarthy, almost Mediterranean." She rolled down her window slightly to talk to him, and his scent crept into her car. She would never forget how he smelled. "Like fear."

"You're on private property," she said.

"I know." He said he had seen the signs and tried to turn around. That's how the Pinto had gotten stuck.

Jaffe said the two officers would assist him. He nodded and watched her taillights disappear up the hill.

Deputy Howard parked about fifteen feet downhill from the Pinto. He left the car running, headlights on, as he got out and approached the trespasser. Deputy Rankin pulled in behind him, turned on his spotlight, and aimed it at the Pinto. The reflective paint on Howard's patrol car lit up in the dark. The scanner muttered in the background.

The trespasser appeared to be in his mid-forties, with black-and-white hair that fell in waves to his shoulders. His salt-and-pepper beard obscured his chin and neck. He wore a long-sleeved cotton shirt with yellow-and-blue horizontal stripes.

As Howard approached, the man looked around a few times and took a couple of steps away from his car. He appeared agitated—black eyes narrowed, face crumpled in frustration.

"I was wondering when somebody was going to get here," he said. "Some lady just drove past without stopping."

Howard informed the man he was trespassing and asked him what he was doing in the area.

The man said he was "sightseeing" and thought it was "a beautiful area" to check out. He said he was a welder in the Bay Area, and he was passing through on his way to visit his brother-in-law, who lived in Redwood Valley, just east of Ukiah. He said he'd pulled off the road to view the scenery.

"I don't believe you," Howard said, noting that it was pitch black.

Howard smelled the faint odor of alcohol on the man's breath. He moved the beam of his Kel-Lite, a fourteen-inch black metal flashlight, over the man's face, to see how his pupils would react to the outer beam. They didn't appear blown or dilated, and they quickly constricted in the light. His balance seemed fine. His speech wasn't slurred or rapid. Other than the smell of alcohol, the usual signs of intoxication were absent. But as they spoke, the man nervously ran his fingers through his hair, which was filled with twigs and bits of brush.

Deputy Rankin, in his backup role, sized up the scene before approaching. There was something off—the time of night, the situation, the way the trespasser looked—that made him grab his baton and slip it into the ring on his duty belt. Like Howard, he had a Glock .45 holstered on his hip. He viewed the Pinto's California license plate from an angle and radioed it to dispatch: "Seven nine nine yellow Robert Ida." He wouldn't realize until months later that he'd read the first digit wrong. That seven was really a two.

After calling in the license plate, Rankin walked over to conduct a routine pat-search while the two men talked. He started at the top, walking his hands down the trespasser's body in a systematic pattern, working from one side to the other, front to back, feeling for bulges that might be knives or guns. As he got to the trespasser's waistband, he noticed the pants were wet. From sweat or urine, he couldn't be sure. He paused to pull on a pair of leather gloves before completing the procedure. No weapons. No drugs. No contraband. Just a small flashlight in his left rear pocket. Rankin noticed the twigs and leaves in his hair. They looked consistent with the roadside vegetation. Perhaps they were from his attempts to push the car out of the ditch.

But things weren't adding up. The man said he'd tried to place some dirt and brush under his tires to get traction. They didn't see much evidence of brush or dirt under the car. He mentioned he'd had to change his shirt, because it had gotten soiled from attempting to push his vehicle out of the ditch.

They hadn't asked about his shirt.

Something about the way he walked and moved suggested to the deputies that this man had been in prison. They asked if he was on parole.

"No," he said.

They ran a check on his license but found no outstanding warrants. The name on the vehicle registration did not match the name on the driver's license, because Rankin had misread the license plate number. The mismatch might have raised red flags, but the Pinto wasn't listed as stolen.

Legally, they needed probable cause to conduct a search of his car. An odd story about sightseeing at midnight wasn't probable cause. The only law they could tell he was breaking was trespassing. So they asked permission.

"Do you have a problem if we take a look in your vehicle?" Howard said.

"No," the man said. "Go ahead."

On the floorboard of the front passenger seat, they found a small brown paper bag containing three or four unopened cans of Budweiser beer, loose. In the back seat, they found a miscellaneous assortment of clothing. A brown paper bag with more clothing. A light blue athletic duffel bag with still more clothing. None of it looked suspicious. They opened the hatchback and saw a spare tire. After they'd searched the car, the trespasser reached for one of the cans of Bud, cracked it open, and began drinking it.

That wasn't illegal on private property, but a twelve-ounce can of anything, wielded with skill and force, could be a surprisingly effective weapon. So they asked him to get rid of the beer, and he tossed it in the bushes. They made him retrieve it, pour it out, and toss the empty can in his car.

By now, the man's behavior strongly suggested that something wasn't right. But their options for dealing with him were limited. They couldn't arrest him for an open container, because he was technically on private property—even though it wasn't his. Trespassing was a misdemeanor, but the law required the property owner to issue a citizen's arrest before the deputies could arrest him. Dana Jaffe didn't want this man arrested—she just wanted him off her property.

Having no legal means to detain him, the deputies refocused their efforts on freeing his car. They just wanted to get him out of here. There had been a drive-by shooting elsewhere in the county that night, and they might be needed.

"Why don't you take your push bumpers and push my vehicle out of the ditch?" the man said.

"We can't do that," Howard replied. It might damage the patrol car.

"Well, why don't you try to push me out?"

Howard and Rankin got behind the car and heaved while the man pressed on the gas. The wheels spun, and the Pinto didn't budge. They suggested calling a tow truck. The man pulled out his wallet to see if he had enough cash to pay for one. It contained about thirty dollars. Not enough.

Rankin decided to drive up the hill to Jaffe's house to see if she had a rope or chain they could use to pull the car out. His instincts prickled, and he felt nervous about leaving Deputy Howard alone with this man.

"Code four," Howard told him. Situation under control.

Deputy Rankin drove Howard's car up the hill and knocked on Jaffe's door. He asked her if she had AAA. She did, but she didn't think her membership should pay for this stranger's tow truck. If she didn't want to file a citizen's arrest and have him spend the night in jail, the alternative would be for the man to come back and retrieve his car at some point in the future. Jaffe just wanted him gone, so she looked in her garage and found a suitable chain for towing. Rankin took it and drove back down the hill. The deputies hooked the chain to the Pinto and the push bumper of Howard's patrol car, which was pointing downhill after Rankin's return. Backing the patrol car up the hill, they managed to free the Pinto.

The Pinto was facing uphill, and the man asked if he could drive up the road to turn around. They wouldn't allow it. He would have to reverse down the driveway. It was steep and curved, but he showed no difficulty backing out. The man stopped, got out of his vehicle, and started walking toward Rankin's car, as if he wanted to speak to him further. Rankin turned on the PA system and told him over the loudspeaker that he had to leave or be subject to arrest.

The trespasser shrugged, got into his car, and left. It was 12:46 a.m.

As the deputies left Pythian Road, they noticed the white Pinto parked on the side of Highway 12, just a few hundred yards down the road. He wasn't breaking any laws, so they did not attempt to reengage.

IN ALL, HOWARD and Rankin spent thirty-eight minutes engaged on the trespassing call. Six minutes into the encounter, at 12:14 a.m., Petaluma Police Department had sent out an all points bulletin via teletype, an electronic dispatch printed out by local terminals in surrounding law enforcement agencies. The APB reported a stranger abduction and described the suspect as a white man driving a dark gray Toyota Tercel—a make and model reported to the police by a thirteen-year-old neighborhood witness. These details would turn out to be inaccurate.

Howard and Rankin never heard the bulletin—which their dispatcher never broadcast.

Petaluma PD had tagged its APB with the heading "Not for Press Release," hoping to avoid tipping off local news reporters, who were known to monitor police-radio channels. Seeing this instruction, the Sonoma sheriff's dispatcher made sure not to announce the kidnapping over the radio.

chapter five

THE CASE AGENT

༄

Saturday, October 2, just past midnight—Windsor, California

WHILE THE TWO SONOMA COUNTY SHERIFF'S DEPUTIES WERE RESPONDING TO A trespasser near Pythian Road, a ringing phone stirred an FBI agent awake in Windsor, a wine-country town about thirty miles north of Petaluma. It was a clerk from the San Francisco FBI office calling about a bulletin that had come across the transom.

"Looks like you've got a kidnapping in Petaluma," the clerk said.

Eddie Freyer jumped out of bed and dressed quickly. There wasn't much to go on yet—the kidnapping report might turn out to be a false alarm, a runaway, or a girl sneaking off with her boyfriend. But if this was real, he'd have to cancel his weekend plans.

Freyer had spent that Friday afternoon abalone diving at Salt Point, swimming down through frigid waters into the shadowy kelp beds, hunting for mollusks the size of salad plates attached to the rocky Pacific floor. It was not easy to skin-dive ten or fifteen feet down, find a legal-size shell, and pry it off its rock with an abalone iron before running out of breath. But he thrived on physical and mental extremes. He loved shucking the mollusks from their mother-of-pearl shells, beating the tough muscles with a baseball bat to tenderize the meat, and sautéing thin strips of the shellfish in butter, white wine, and garlic. His wife and three young children feasted on his catch.

Freyer was the senior resident agent for the FBI's Santa Rosa office, one of four hundred agents in northern California and 11,000 nation-wide. He had worked bank robberies, extortions, kidnappings, and the occasional missing person. For a few years his job called for undercover surveillance, and he lived on a houseboat in Sausalito with an alternate identity and grew a beard that made his kids gawk and giggle when they visited "Edward Reardon." He was now a member of the SWAT team, which he enjoyed not only because it kept him involved in all sorts of cases, but because the training—rappelling, shooting, and hostage simulations—was strenuous and fun.

He was an athlete, a serious runner, though he didn't discover this until his mid-thirties. Before that, he was a smoker with a pack-and-a-half daily habit. One rainy night, after running out of Marlboros, he pulled on a jacket and grabbed his keys to head out into the storm for more smokes. He opened the door, squinted into the wind and spitting rain, and thought: *Who the hell is in charge here?* He closed the door, ripped his raincoat off, and never smoked again. The next day, he laced on a pair of running shoes and went on a jog. Six months later, with a book called *The Self-Coached Runner*, he started training to run 10K races at a 5:20 pace. Running tamped down the stress of the job. It also fed his competitive streak. In the Police Games, a sort of Olympics for cops and agents, he won medals in the biathlon (running and shooting), cross-country, and 5,000-meter and 10,000-meter runs. His twelve-member team had won the Hood to Coast, an overnight relay race from Oregon's Mount Hood to the Pacific, just a few months ago, averaging a 5:32 pace for 197 miles.

Now forty-two, Freyer was approaching the prime years of his career. After two decades with the Bureau, he was the top agent in his office, overseeing an average load of twenty-five to thirty different cases. He served as a liaison between the FBI and local law enforcement agencies, and he was well respected by his peers, many of whom were his closest friends. His best friend, Tom LaFreniere, was an FBI agent who lived in Petaluma and worked on the narcotics squad in San Francisco. They had met while working together on the bank robbery squad. Now they trained together three to six days a month as members of the SWAT team. They started abalone diving together and shared a love of the outdoors. This off-duty weekend they had planned a backpacking trip in the Trinity Alps.

With his second wife, Sue, a fitness instructor with a sunny disposition, Freyer had a five-year-old son and two daughters, ages three and one. He had two older kids from his first marriage, twenty-two-year-old Eddie Jr., his namesake and spitting image, and a seventeen-year-old daughter named Tina, who had given him two grandsons. Freyer and Sue had been married for six years, and Sue was accustomed to the long hours and erratic schedule of the occasional big cases. Life had been fairly consistent of late, and Freyer was usually home for dinner. The family was his sanctuary, and when he walked in the door every night, he was able to leave his work behind. Off duty for the weekend, with his backpacking gear packed and ready to go, Freyer had watched the ten o'clock news before settling into bed.

He was asleep when the phone rang a little after midnight. News of a kidnapping triggered a spurt of adrenaline that brought him to instant alert. He jumped out of bed, pulled on a dress shirt, slacks, and tie. As he dressed, the phone rang again.

"I've got the father of the kidnapping victim on the phone," the dispatcher said. "Want to talk to him?"

"Yeah, patch him through."

It was Polly's father, Marc Klaas. He was screaming in panic.

"I'll be there in thirty minutes," Freyer told him.

Before leaving the house, he called Tom LaFreniere, who lived in Petaluma.

"Get your ass out of bed," Freyer said, explaining the situation. "I'll pick you up."

Around one-thirty a.m., they pulled up to 427 Fourth Street, already buzzing with crime scene chaos. The Petaluma Police had set up a roadblock and cordoned off the small Victorian house with yellow crime scene tape, protecting the outer perimeter. Flashing blue lights drew neighbors onto their porches and lawns, where they blinked in bleary-eyed disbelief at the cops swarming in every direction, the heli-copters thundering overhead, and the sounds of voices echoing through the shadows. Inside the house, lights blazed behind the sheer lace cur-tains, and silhouettes moved through every room. Freyer and LaFreniere flashed their FBI badges at a cop, who waved them up the steps and through the front door.

A familiar face stepped forward to brief him. Sergeant Vail Bello was a detective on the force. Freyer had met him at a brass badge retirement dinner, and they'd chatted at interagency lunches designed to foster relations between the feds and the local cops.

"What do you have?" Freyer asked.

"The girls were having a slumber party," Bello said. "They say a man came and took her."

Bello loved patrol, the thrill of the chase, and he'd been rotated to investigations "kicking and screaming" a year and a half before. He had worked a whodunnit homicide—the body found in a dumpster—and an assault-with-a-deadly-weapon case in which the victim had been beaten within a centimeter of his life. But, like most of the guys on the force, he had never worked a kidnapping case. And certainly never a stranger abduction. That sort of thing didn't happen in a town that averaged less than one murder a year.

Bello found the circumstances of Polly's disappearance disturbing. He'd grown up here. It was a town with the usual crime. But things like stranger abductions didn't happen in Petaluma. There had to be some logical explanation.*

"The parents are divorced," Bello said.

Divorce suggested the possibility—the overwhelming statistical probability, in fact—that the child had been taken by an estranged par-ent.† While exact numbers of child abductions have always been con-troversial (and sometimes dramatically inflated as a result of multiple

---

* Though investigators didn't think this was the case with Polly, 65 percent of miss-ing children reported to the National Center for Missing and Exploited Children (NCMEC) in 1993 were runaways.

† In 1993, the National Center for Missing and Exploited Children reported that 30 percent of its missing-child cases over the past three years were family abductions.

reporting systems), the most rigorous dataset available at the time found that more than three-quarters of the children abducted were taken by either a non-custodial parent or family acquaintance.*

But in this case, Marc Klaas was cooperating fully. His voice rang with the timbre of panic. Eve believed the stranger abduction was real.

Bello said the cops had already scoured the house and searched yard to yard. They were knocking on doors and waking the neighbors.

Freyer had spoken briefly with Bello during his drive to Petaluma. Cell phones, relatively new and shaped like bricks, were notoriously insecure. Any reporter with a scanner could intercept the call. They'd been brief, avoiding any sensitive details about the crime.

"What do you need?" Freyer had wanted to know.

"I need a hundred guys here now," Bello said.

"I'll have you fifty by tomorrow."

When the Federal Kidnapping Act was signed into law in 1932—on what would have been Charles Lindbergh, Jr.'s second birthday—it compelled the FBI to get involved after seven days, at which point it was presumed that state lines had been crossed. By 1993, that wait time had decreased to twenty-four hours—the window of time in which many missing kids were found or came back on their own.

But evidence suggested that even twenty-four hours was too long to wait. In cases where kidnapped children were murdered by their abductors, 89 percent of the victims were dead within twenty-four hours of disappearing, and 76 percent of the victims died within three hours.

Since a missing person case falls under the jurisdiction of local law enforcement, cops have to request help from the FBI, which has multi-state jurisdiction. Because kidnappers often flee across state lines, investigators must operate with the assumption of an interstate crime.

When he had reached for the phone to call Freyer, Bello knew what the feds could offer. Polygraphers. Profilers. Evidence Response Teams with better technology. SWAT teams. Plenty of backup. From that moment on, Freyer and Bello would be partners in charge of the case.

---

* As research methods became more sophisticated, the number of estimated stranger abductions dwindled to less than 1 percent, the current figure cited by the National Center for Missing and Exploited Children.

Bello would direct the Petaluma police. Freyer would make decisions on behalf of the FBI. It would be a joint investigation, feds paired with local law enforcement agents at every level in the chain of command. Teamwork would be critical to bringing Polly home.

As the case agent, Freyer must make a very important decision. If he designated this as a kidnapping, they would get federal resources, lots of them, fast. But if he summoned the feds in full force and Polly turned up the next day, the error would be costly. The fallout could include his professional reputation and increased criticism from a public already unhappy with the rising count of missing children.

This was Freyer's first time in charge of an abduction case, but the Bay Area's unsolved kidnappings lingered over him. So many kids were still missing: ten-year-old Kevin Collins, who disappeared from a San Francisco bus stop in 1984. Amber Swartz-Garcia, a seven-year-old kidnapped in 1988 while jumping rope in her yard in Pinole. Thirteen-year-old Ilene Misheloff, who vanished in 1989 while walking home from middle school in Dublin. Jaycee Dugard, an eleven-year-old who went missing in 1991 while walking to the bus stop in Meyers.

The vast majority of kidnapped kids were taken by someone they knew, a family friend, an acquaintance, or someone who encountered them in the community.

Stranger abductions were incredibly rare—200 or 300 a year, according to the National Center for Missing and Exploited Children. Since August, there had been fewer than three dozen in a population of 260 million Americans. Most of the kids and teens kidnapped by strangers had been taken from a public place: a bus stop, in a store, or while walking home from school. That was the case for Kevin, Amber, Ilene, and Jaycee. All such cases resulted in media coverage and scrutiny, though it's worth noting that almost all of the missing children who got enough press to become household names*—then and now—were white, with middle- to upper-class backgrounds.

---

* Elizabeth Smart. Samantha Runnion. Natalee Holloway—the trend would lead to the coining of a term for the phenomenon—Missing White Woman Syndrome—when journalist Gwen Ifill remarked at a 2004 journalism conference: "If it's a missing white woman, you're going to cover *that*, every day."

Stranger abductions *from the home* were rarest of all. Over the previous three years, there had been only about twenty such instances, according to NCMEC. Sometimes an adult was home, sometimes not. But the facts of Polly's abduction broke logic. For a stranger to walk into someone's house, with a parent present, and kidnap a girl in full view of two witnesses...The most experienced kidnapping experts in the Bureau had never encountered such a circumstance.

Less than two hours into the emergency, there wasn't nearly enough information to make a confident call. But a decision had to be made, and it would alter the course of everything that came after. Freyer took stock of the totality of the circumstances, considering all of the factors, trying not to weigh any one thing too lightly or heavily. As unfathomable and illogical as the situation appeared, he had to believe it was real.

Freyer called Lillian Zilius, the Supervisory Special Agent (SSA) who oversaw the Evidence Response Team (ERT).

"Hey, Lillian," he said, "I think I've got a kidnapping up here in Petaluma."

"What do you think it is, Freyer?" she said.

"I'm calling it a stranger abduction."

"Okay. We'll call up the ERT," she said. "Let me call the troops and see who's available, and we'll get some people up there."

As he waited for the ERT to arrive, Freyer approached Eve, who was curled around six-year-old Annie in a papasan chair. He leaned in.

"Eve," he said softly, "we will do everything humanly possible to find your daughter."

chapter six

THE EYEWITNESSES

༄

Saturday around 1:30 a.m.—Petaluma PD

AS EDDIE FREYER AND VAIL BELLO SUMMONED HELICOPTERS AND BLOODHOUNDS, two Petaluma investigators were preparing to interview Kate and Gillian at the Petaluma PD, a few miles north of Polly's house. They needed to talk to the girls—immediately and separately—away from the chaos of the crime scene. Kate and Gillian were, so far, the only witnesses, and the images, noises, smells, and sensations impressed in their memory would be integral to the investigation.

The girls were stunned and eerily calm. They were probably still processing, trying to make sense of what had just happened, wondering if it was real. But their calmness triggered doubts in investigators who were themselves wondering if this was real, who didn't believe—or want to believe—such a thing could occur in Petaluma. Many of them had grown up here, some in Polly's neighborhood.

Andy Mazzanti, thirty-three, a cop with a dozen years on the street, was a gentle Italian giant, six-foot-two, built like a lineman, with warm eyes, a square jaw, and a chevron mustache. His size and the eyebrows that knit themselves together on his forehead inspired his colleagues to nickname him "Mongo," after the super-size outlaw who knocks out a horse with a single punch in the Mel Brooks comedy *Blazing Saddles*.

Gillian Pelham (left) and Kate McLean, photographed by investigators on the night of the abduction.
(Courtesy of Greg Jacobs)

Those same colleagues described Mazzanti as "one of the best cops I've ever known." He was the kind of cop who sent sympathy cards and stayed in touch with victims who needed moral support. He was earnest and took things to heart.

Newly assigned to investigations, Mazzanti was "just hours" out of a three-week course on sexual assault, child abuse, and homicide. This was his first call-out after deep training in interview and interrogation, and he hadn't expected to put his new techniques and skills to use so immediately. While Kate McLean was ushered into a nearby room by another detective, Mazzanti led Gillian Pelham into the primary interview room, where a mirrored window allowed outside observation. At 1:45 a.m., he turned on the tape recorder and began the official interview.

"You can call me Andy," he told Gillian.

Mazzanti built rapport by finding common ground. This was easy to do with Gillian, who giggled when she and Mazzanti discovered their birthdays were two days apart. A soft-spoken, intelligent girl with dark brown hair cut in a bob, Gillian mentioned she was a gymnast, still recovering from a recent hip surgery that inhibited her ability to run or jump. Mazzanti figured out they both saw the same orthopedist, a small coincidence that seemed to put her at ease. When Gillian seemed relaxed, Mazzanti explained the interview process.*

"I'm going to ask you some questions," Mazzanti said gently. "I'm going to have you tell me the story of what happened, then later I'm going to have you tell me the story as if you were in a different position in the room." Sometimes this subtle shift in point of view helped jog free a detail that otherwise might not surface.

In a small, sweet voice, with a pitch that made her sound younger than twelve, Gillian recounted her Friday, which began at six-thirty a.m. when she crawled out of bed and went downstairs to have a cup of tea and a Carnation instant breakfast bar, then grabbed her flute and boarded the school bus to Petaluma Junior High. After a typical seventh-grade day—history, English, math, lunch, science, and PE—she rode home in the front seat of the bus, let herself in through the back gate, practiced her flute, and phoned Polly around four p.m. to finalize their sleepover plans. She recounted how the evening began, with games and a dress-up session.

"Kate came over and we put makeup on Polly and made her look really weird, and then she washed it off and changed into a different outfit and then..."

"What was Polly wearing when you first put makeup on?"

"Um, I'm not quite sure."

"When you say you made her look weird, what did you do to her?"

"Well, we made her face really white and put on dark lipstick and put dark stuff around her eyes so she'd look dead."

"And after you guys did that, what happened?"

"She just washed it off and then we were just reading some sort of trivia questions—by then it was ten or eleven—and we were going to go into the living room. That's when Polly opened the door and the guy with the knife was there."

---

* Today, the FBI would bring in child and adolescent forensic interview (CAFI) specialists to interview young witnesses or victims, usually in a "soft room" with residential furniture, art on the walls, and other familiar comforts. But the practice didn't emerge until 1996, when the American Professional Society on the Abuse of Children (APSAC) held the first forensic interviewing clinic to train people in interviewing children and adolescents. Today, the FBI employs more than two dozen CAFIs nationwide.

"Tell me in your own words what happened, and try to remember what you were feeling, if you smelled anything, if you heard anything... all your senses and anything you were thinking about."

"When he tied our hands up, he tied it pretty tight," Gillian said. "But when we complained about how tight it was, he said, 'Oh, I'm sorry,' and he just seemed like he didn't really want to hurt us. He said, 'I don't want to hurt you. I just want some money and the valuables, so if you keep quiet no one will get hurt.' Then he put pillowcases over our heads and gagged us. He asked us who lived there and why there were so many people and we explained to him that it was a sleepover."

"Was there anything about his face that you noticed?"

"He had a really thick, dark gray beard, and it was sort of fluffy, and I think he had dark eyes, I don't know. He was dressed in all black, I know that. And he was pretty tall. He looked like he was about thirty or forty."

"When you say he had a dark gray beard, does that mean it was all one color, or was it more than one color?"

"It was sort of like a couple of different grays, like dark gray, and medium gray, and something between."

"Do you know what kind of clothes he had on?"

"I think he was wearing a black turtleneck. Then it might have been just black jeans, I don't know."

"What about his shoes? Did you notice what kind of shoes he had on?"

"No."

"What about smell? Did you smell anything in the room when he came in the room?"

"No."

"His face, was there anything about his face that you remember besides the beard?"

"It was sort of round."

"What about his nose?"

"It just seemed like a normal average nose. And he was pretty tall, too."

"How tall do you think he was?"

"Um, somewhere in six feet."

IN ANOTHER ROOM, Kate McLean was talking to lead investigator Dennis Nowicki, a grizzly bear of a man, six-foot-two like Mazzanti but a stouter 275 pounds, with a belly laugh and a bushy beard. A methodical investigator, Nowicki was a second-career cop, a former juvenile probation officer who often worked undercover, a workhorse who would take on any assignment. Nowicki was known for practical jokes, and he deployed sarcasm as an instrument of brotherly affection as well as a means of deflecting praise for his quiet acts of kindness.

Kate's light brown hair fell past her shoulders in loose waves, and thick bangs brushed her forehead. Her freckled cheeks were flushed, her brown eyes red from crying. She had a deeper voice than Gillian, delivering facts in an assertive, no-nonsense tone. She spoke with measured self-confidence, thoughts spilling out in paragraphs punctuated by sighs that sounded like exasperation but might have been nervous energy. She described how she was positioned on the floor when the stranger entered the room.

Nowicki looked down at the written statement she had given and signed an hour or so after the kidnapping. It described, in seventh-grade cursive and spelling, the details she recalled.

We were sitting and Polly started to open the door. A man with a full balck beard, black hair, a round face and a neon yellow bandana wick a knife stuck his head and the knife in. He told us to lay face down on the floor and be quiet. He bound our hands with cloth and wire cord. He coverd our heads with pillows caces. He would apoligise if we told him our binding was to tight and loosen it a little. He asked who lived in the house. He kept telling us it would be allright. He told Polly to stand up. She whimpered and he appeared to be loosing his patience. He told her it was allright and he was not going to touch her anywhere. He lead her out reasuruing her all the way. He said he didn't want to hurt anyone and just wanted money. We herd the door slam.

"It says, 'We were sitting...'" Nowicki noted. "Who's 'we'?"

"Polly, Gillian, and I were in her room. Polly was seated on—"

"About what time was this?" Nowicki interrupted.

"Ah, I don't know. I'd say around eleven o'clock. Maybe ten thirty, eleven o'clock."

"Okay. And it says a man with a full black beard."

"Full, yes. Like, thick..."

"You see my beard, okay?" said Nowicki. It was gray and close-trimmed.

"Uh, yeah. About that full."

"Okay, was it bigger? As far as further away from the face?"

"Yes, it was. It was longer."

"How much longer?"

"About two or three inches."

"So its overall length—it was about yea big?"

"Yeah."

"About three inches. Okay. And you mention here that he had a neon yellow bandana."

"Yes. It was just like a length of cloth tied around his head."

This yellow bandana, which Kate so clearly recalled, would be one of the inconsistencies that caused investigators to doubt the girls' accounts. Gillian didn't recall it.

"Now when this person talked, did he have an accent?"

"No, he had a calm voice. It was kind of soothing. I could recognize it but I find it difficult to describe. I wasn't really paying attention to the voice. I was more paying attention to what he was saying, which was, 'Calm down, calm down. If anybody talks, I'll slit your throats.'"

There was a knock at the door. Someone needed to speak with Nowicki. The detective paused the tape recorder, excused himself, and left the room. When he returned, he explained that a police sketch artist was on the way. He'd ask them more questions and draw a composite sketch of the man in the bedroom.

Nowicki reviewed Kate's description of the suspect. Big guy. Full black beard, about three inches long. Black shoulder-length hair. Kate confirmed these details with confidence.

"I could recognize him," she said, even though "I was facedown on the floor with a pillowcase over my head for the most part."

"When you first see him, where are you exactly in the room?"

"I was on the floor, seated."

"Uh-huh."

"Next to Gillian. If the door was here," she said, gesturing, "the bed was here. And I would be seated right about here."

"Were you seated, sitting just like that?"

"Well, a little bit farther."

"Were your feet straight out?"

"I was laying down with my head on my hands like this," Kate said. She got down on the floor on her stomach and propped her chin in her hands.

"Okay," Nowicki said, "and then you look up."

"Polly is starting to open the door to go get something. I look up—"

"Go ahead and have a seat," Nowicki interrupted.

Kate ignored him and went on.

"And suddenly this strange man has popped his head and his hand with a knife through the door. He says, 'Anybody says anything...' or he says, 'You're alone, right? If anybody says anything then I'll slit your throats.'"

"Okay."

"'Now roll over and lay flat on your faces.' I thought he was some odd relation of Polly's playing a joke."

"Okay."

"And after that, he started to cuss, and..."

"What did he say?"

"He said, 'Fuck.' And, um, he seemed to calm down and everybody was starting to whimper and get scared."

"Go ahead and have a seat," Nowicki repeated.

"I'd rather stand," Kate said. "He started to bind our hands behind our backs. He used a silky length of cloth and some cord—we think it had wire in it. It was brown, some of the cord was brown, and some of it was black. After he finished doing our hands, he left our feet alone and got a pillowcase. First he put one over my head. I think it was because I was talking the most."

"Okay." Nowicki. said. As an interviewer, he shifted into an active-listening approach with open-ended questions and minimal interruption.

"Then once he had got it over my head, he gagged me and then he did the same to Gillian, and he asked, 'Who lives here?' And Polly said, 'I do.' He ransacked the room for a while, and I think he gagged her. I heard him gagging her, I think."

"Uh-huh."

"But he didn't put a pillowcase over her head, like he had to me and Gillian."

"Okay."

"I heard her say, 'Ouch!' as he was ransacking the room and something he was throwing around had dropped on her back. She said, 'My mom and my sister are in the next room in their bed—please don't hurt them, leave them alone.'"

"Uh-huh."

"And he said, 'You're lying to me.' And she said, 'No, I swear, they're in the next room, please leave them alone.' And he said, 'No, they aren't supposed to be here. Why are they here?' Then Polly pointed out there was money in her jewelry box, which was up there. And he said, 'I'm just here for your money. I'm not here to hurt anybody.' He kept repeating that, over and over again when one of us would start to whimper or sound scared. He tapped Polly and he said, 'You come with me. I want you to show me where the valuables are.'"

"Uh-huh."

"He took her away. I heard her door close and then I heard another door close. I think that was their front door."

"Okay."

"As he was taking her away, he kept saying over and over again, 'It's okay. I'm not going to touch you anywhere.' So then when they were out the door Gillian and I waited. He had told us to count to a thousand."

"Uh-huh."

"And when we had counted to a thousand it would have been ten minutes and he would be gone. So we counted and about fifty we lost count, so for a while we just laid there and we waited. We were afraid that he would kill Polly if he came back to find that we had taken off our gags or anything so we waited and we waited and when we felt sure that he was gone, we counted to five hundred just to make sure. Our hands were starting to get swollen and turn purple. From the binding being too tight. Oh, and by the way, whenever you told him your binding was too tight, he would loosen it."

"Huh."

"But not so much that you could get free. He'd just sort of reach over and tug on it."

"Uh-huh."

"Enough to loosen it a bit. Anyway, Gillian after a while started to struggle out of her, out of her stuff, and she and I stood back to back and worked on each other and after a while finally she was able to step over her hands and get them in front of her instead of in back of her and finally she got her binding untied, took off her pillowcase and her gags and she, um, took off mine also."

"Okay."

Kate exhaled. "By then we were positive that Polly had been left in another room of the house while he left us with all the stuff."

"Uh-huh."

Kate coughed. "And he, well, we got up and we looked around for a while and then I realized we'd better tell Polly's mom. I went in without Gillian..."

"If I can interrupt, Kate," Nowicki said, "what I want you to do is remember exactly everything you did."

"Okay, Gillian and..."

"No, no, no, no—just continue after you went and talked to Polly's mom."

"I went out into the kitchen and looked around. We realized that Polly wasn't there, and that Gillian and I also checked in the living room and all the rooms in there. We checked the back porch. We unlocked that door, so yes, it was locked that evening.* But we unlocked it to search for Polly."

"Okay."

---

* This was later disputed.

"We couldn't find her anywhere and we were horrified. That's when I went in to wake up her mom without Gillian and so her mom woke up and she thought I was playing some sort of joke on her for a while."

"Okay."

"She said, 'Are you kidding me? You've got to be kidding me.' Finally she got up and she seemed pretty shocked and so she called the police and that's where the rest of the weirdness started."

"In the beginning . . . Let me see your wrists."

"This is the one that was bad. See? You can see some marks there and there."

"Okay. Let me see your other wrist. Just relax your hand. Now, were your wrists tied in front of you or behind you?"

"They were tied behind us, with one wrist on top of the other, like I said, with two different things, and he'd loop it around one wrist and then he'd tie a knot and hook it around the other wrist, and he went on like that and used a lot of cord. See right there, it's kind of reddish . . ."

"Uh-huh."

". . . still."

"Now, where do you think he got the cord from?"

"I'm not sure. It looks sort of like cut . . . electrical appliance cord. You can feel that there, you can feel that there was wire in there and it was coated with plastic on the outside. It was shaped like electrical appliance cord, but it was thick."

"Uh-huh. Okay."

"It's still back there in the sacred room that no one can enter."

She was referring to Polly's room, which had been cordoned off to protect trace evidence. Later in the interview, Kate called it "the forbidden room."

"Just call it Polly's room," Nowicki said. "It's not the forbidden room. It's a crime scene, okay?"

"I understand," Kate said.

"They're there to collect every bit of evidence to solve this crime."

chapter seven

THE CRIME SCENE

∽

Saturday, October 2, 1:45 a.m.—Polly's House

MEANWHILE, BACK ON FOURTH STREET, PETALUMA DETECTIVES WERE PROCESSING Polly's house. Sergeant Mike Meese and Detective Larry Pelton began with a thorough walk-through, taking in the big picture before zeroing in on the details. The house looked lived-in, but not ransacked. They walked through each room with Eve, asking if she noticed anything different—items missing or repositioned, an object moved from one part of the house to another. They found nothing disturbed outside Polly's room. The living room stereo was where it should be. Eve's purse sat on the kitchen table, exactly as she'd left it. Her wallet, her keys—everything still there.

They inspected every window and door. On the front porch, the screen door was propped open by Polly's and Annie's bicycles. The front door had an older doorknob without a deadbolt, but the lock had not been jimmied. The window screens were all intact, and the windows on the front of the house wouldn't even open. A kitchen window was propped open with a vase. The windows on the south side—Polly's bedroom and the sunroom—showed no signs of forcible entry. Meese noticed cobwebs intact between the sunroom windows and the bushes. Polly's bedroom window was cracked, just barely, maybe enough for a cat to squeeze through. Standing outside, they noticed scuff marks on

Polly's house in a crime scene photo taken on the night of the abduction.
(COURTESY OF TONY MAXWELL)

the white paint beneath her window, and a little dirt on her window-sill. Pelton looked closely and believed them to be animal paw prints. They checked the attic and the crawl space under the house. Nothing unusual. They studied the dirt between the back porch and the rental unit behind the house. No footprints or evidence of any value.

They moved on to Polly's room. The venetian blinds were lowered and closed, and the window was partially blocked by a TV set on top of a chest. The Nintendo box was missing the cords that linked the controllers to the console. One control pad was resting on top of a Monopoly box, its cord sliced by something sharp. Larry Pelton reached for this and recorded the first piece of official evidence, marking it P-1. He bagged the Nintendo box, the other controller, and the severed cords, which had been used to bind Kate's and Gillian's wrists.

On the floor, Pelton found a small brown purse. Eve said it belonged to Polly. It contained a few coins, some lipstick, and a movie ticket stub. The purse strap had been sliced off. Near the closet he found a pillowcase, knotted and torn. On the inside were brownish stains that he gathered to be makeup. On the floor lay a pair of red-and-black polka-dotted girls' tights, the legs tied in a knot.

All of these things belonged in Polly's room. That suggested the kidnapper had improvised, using whatever he found on hand to bind and gag the girls. One thing stood out as an item brought in from else-where: two strips of a silky, stretchy, off-white fabric, knotted and tied into bindings. They appeared hastily cut, with jagged, fraying edges. The fabric looked consistent with that of a women's nylon slip. The kidnapper must have brought this in. Had he cut it on site? Or before, in a moment of premeditation? They couldn't be sure.

Meese and Pelton began gathering evidence, working quickly as a team. Meese identified probable evidence, and Pelton photographed each item as it lay, before it was touched or moved. Then he handled the "bagging and tagging"—placing each item in a plastic bag, assigning it an ID number, and recording its number, description, and location in an official evidence log.

Meese dusted for latent fingerprints, delicately brushing each sur-face with standard-issue black powder. He dusted the wood floors, the wooden bed frame, and any surfaces on which he'd had previous expe-rience in finding prints. He made some lifts.

When the first FBI agents arrived around midnight, Meese walked Eddie Freyer and Tom LaFreniere through the house, giving them the rundown. Freyer had offered to call in the FBI Evidence Response Team, which had more sophisticated equipment. Everyone agreed. But the Petaluma police didn't want to wait for the FBI to arrive, so they'd started the crime scene processing.

After Meese finished dusting for prints—which were of little use[*] until they had a suspect—he stood in Polly's doorway, scanning the

---

[*] At the time of Polly's kidnapping, fingerprints lifted at a crime scene were only of use when a suspect was identified—for comparison with fingerprints already on file, or obtained from a suspect under arrest, or provided voluntarily. In July 1999, the FBI's Integrated Automated Fingerprint Identification System (IAFIS) would be implemented, allowing an unidentified fingerprint to be compared with the FBI's mas-sive database of known fingerprints.

room for something he'd missed, anything he could take as possible evidence. They had the bindings, the hoods, the sliced purse strap, and the severed Nintendo cords. *Such a pittance,* he thought.

"Let's take the rug," Meese said.

"Why?" Pelton asked.

"I don't know why," Meese said. "Let's just take the rug. We just don't have enough evidence."

⌒⌒⌒

FBI FORENSIC SPECIALIST Tony Maxwell awoke to a ringing phone in his Clayton home at the foothill of Mount Diablo. It was Lillian Zilius, who supervised the Evidence Response Team.

"Have you had anything to drink?" she said.

"No," Maxwell said. "I can respond. What's going on?"

"Eddie Freyer is asking for an ERT callout."

"I'm on my way."

After eighteen years of responding to calls that often came in the middle of the night, Maxwell always went to sleep with his Smith & Wesson .357 Magnum revolver tucked next to the bed and his clothing and gear staged for a grab-and-go. His bug-out bag contained a handheld radio, a magazine of ammunition, and his FBI credentials. The keys to his Suburban—the FBI-issued vehicle for evidence technicians—were clipped to the bag. He always filled the gas tank before coming home from work. Standard practice.

"The police have secured the scene," Zilius said. "Get there as quickly as you can. The mother is beside herself. We don't have a lot of details, but it looks like a bona fide child abduction."

"Where exactly is the location?" he said.

"Petaluma. Dispatch will give you the details. Call if you need something."

Tony rolled over and woke his wife, Elvira.

"We have a child kidnapping," he whispered. "A twelve-year-old girl."

She knew what that meant. Their son, Steven, was also twelve.

"Go find her," she said. "I know you can do it."

TONY MAXWELL WAS part of a new group of FBI agents working in small local squads called Evidence Response Teams. As the first generation of ERT members, they were pioneering the latest forensic tools and forging a new model for crime scene investigation by the Bureau.

Historically, FBI crime scene investigations were conducted by forensic experts dispatched from the Laboratory Division at headquarters in Washington, DC. But during the time it took to get to the crime scene—twenty-four hours or more in some cases—trace evidence could deteriorate, disappear, or become contaminated.

A different approach had bubbled up from the ranks over the past few years, initiated by field agents who saw the need for "a new way of doing business." Outside FBI headquarters, agents in field offices were assembling local forensic squads that could arrive at a crime scene within hours or even minutes. Maxwell was one of three team leaders on the San Francisco ERT, the Bureau's first field ERT, formed in 1990.

In the top-down culture of the FBI, these mavericks were initially considered rogues. Their decentralized approach and immediate response often required acting outside of the traditional chain of command. They encountered considerable resistance within the Bureau, an institution that prized and guarded protocol. "This new team concept was not received warmly by either the Laboratory Division nor the agents in the field," Maxwell said. "We had to win the support of our colleagues one by one, case by case."

They were also experimenting with new forensic tools, methods, and procedures, many of which concerned the recovery of trace evidence: hair and fibers, fingerprints and DNA. "The evidence we can't see," as Maxwell liked to say. "Before, you'd want the gun. Now you want the *smoke* from the gun."

New technology had given him increasingly precise ways to apply Locard's Exchange Principle, which holds that whenever a perpetrator leaves a crime scene, he or she always takes something and leaves something behind. Developed in the 1920s by Edmond Locard, a forensic pioneer often referred to as "the Sherlock Holmes of France," the concept holds that "every contact leaves a trace." A person cannot come into contact with another person or a place without a cross-transfer of evidence. Whatever is found—on either side—can serve as physical evidence of that contact. Bits of soil on the sole of a shoe. A human hair clinging to a woolen coat. A few fibers from an orange polyester couch attached to denim jeans.

Paul Kirk, a 1950s criminologist from the University of California at Berkeley, articulated the concept memorably in a quote often misattributed to Locard: "Wherever he steps, whatever he touches, whatever he leaves, even unconsciously, will serve as a silent witness against him. Not only his fingerprints or his footprints, but his hair, the fibers from his clothes, the glass he breaks, the tool mark he leaves, the paint he scratches, the blood or semen he deposits or collects."

The key was to gather the evidence quickly, before it could vanish or spoil, and to record and preserve it painstakingly with the best tools and skills in the business. In a case where eyewitness accounts were already being called into question, trace evidence would offer incontrovertible facts. "There are only two ways a guy goes to jail: witnesses and evidence," Maxwell liked to say. "If witnesses are compromised, it all comes down to evidence."

AFTER AN HOUR'S drive, Maxwell turned onto Fourth Street around five-thirty a.m. Police waved his Suburban through the barricade so he could park in front of the house and unload. FBI agent David Alford, the ERT leader for the North Bay office, met him on the lawn and briefed him. It was still dark, but as they walked up the steps, every light in the house was burning and the TV blared in the background. As he entered the house, he carefully sidestepped the area where the kidnapper might have left footprints.

Maxwell was surprised to find that Eve and her husband, Allan Nichol—separated but amicable—had been allowed to remain in the house with Annie. This was outside of normal protocol, which called for vacating the crime scene to protect trace evidence. But in this case, the family was told to stay in the house, just in case there was a ransom call. Everyone was hoping for a ransom call. That would mean Polly was still alive. They waited in the living room, where tension hung thick as woodsmoke. Maxwell introduced himself and quickly got to work. The Petaluma detectives who had done the first round of processing were elsewhere. Maxwell had questions but no time for answers. *You go to war with the information you have.*

Evidence collection by the FBI officially began at 6:58 a.m. ERT members Tracey Zucker and David Alford collected the following: the plastic front door mat from the front porch, tagged FP-1; the entry rug from the entry foyer, tagged EF-1. From the living room, near a table by the front window, they collected Polly's purple-and-black vinyl school bag, which contained schoolbooks, notebooks, and miscellaneous items. Polly's clarinet, inside a brown case, was in the entry foyer. Around 7:25 a.m. Eve offered them a large comb used by Polly, found in the bottom of a laundry basket.

Meanwhile, Maxwell photographed the crime scene. If this case ever came before a jury, they would need to see exactly how everything looked that night in the dark. He documented the interior and exterior of the house from different angles, paying close attention to the doors, windows, and back porch. Outside the front door, standing on the front porch, he aimed his lens at Wickersham Park. After sunrise, he would recapture every shot and angle in the light.

The agents needed to figure out the suspect's point of entry and departure. For this, the ERT had a new forensic tool the size and shape of a small suitcase. It was an electrostatic dust lifter, which could lift latent shoeprints from a hard floor. The technique used static electricity to draw particles of dirt and dust onto a sheet of Mylar film. They spread the shiny film, black side down, silver side up, over the floor in spots where the kidnapper might have stepped.

To create the electrostatic charge, Maxwell clipped positive and negative electrodes—which looked and worked like jumper cables—onto the Mylar film. He placed a metal alligator clip on his ear to ground himself, protection against getting shocked. Then he turned the machine on and, using a rubber roller, gently removed any air bubbles between the paper and the floor. He carefully peeled back the Mylar, hoping to see a pattern that might define the bottom of a certain shoe. No clear shoeprints emerged from the floor inside the front or back doors.

They moved on to the next possible entry point: Polly's bedroom window. They stood outside in the driveway that led to the detached cottage occupied by tenant Aaron Thomas. He was home with guests—his girlfriend and another friend—and they had been told to stay inside the cottage while investigators worked. Maxwell stood outside Polly's window and shined his flashlight obliquely over the sill, where he noticed smudges, as if someone had leaned on their fingers there, trying to peer inside. Maxwell made a note to go back and lift those later. The top priority was a meticulous processing of Polly's room.

It was fortuitous that Polly had vacuumed her room that night before the sleepover. That meant that any dust, fibers, or other trace evidence would be fresh. Some of it might be embedded in the rug that the Petaluma detectives had rolled up, bagged, and removed. Now Maxwell and Alford worked methodically over every inch of her bare wood floor. Maxwell made an electrostatic lift, folded up the Mylar with any contents attached, and bagged it. Alford then went over the same area using a vacuum with a filter attachment to collect hairs, fibers, and loose particles. They worked their way across the floor: Lift. Vacuum. Lift. Vacuum.

The next step was fingerprinting. Mike Meese and Larry Pelton had already dusted the room with standard-issue black powder, a mixture of rosin, black ferric oxide, lampblack, and various inorganic compounds. Along with silver powder, which produced better contrast on dark surfaces, it was the variety most police departments used.

That was good, but Maxwell had something better: fluorescent powder, which was a hundred times more sensitive. It contained tracers, chemicals that would fluoresce under an alternate light source (ALS), a forensic tool so new that the FBI didn't yet own one. A fourteen-pound unit the size of a small microwave, the ALS (later called a forensic light) generated light through a fiber-optic cable that resembled a small hose. It could be tuned to produce different nanometers of light—precise hues across the color spectrum from ultraviolet to infrared. Beamed at a surface under inspection, the colored light would cause latent fingerprints to fluoresce, often without the use of powder.

Early ALS use focused on fingerprints until technicians at crime scenes noticed other types of trace evidence glowing in the background: gunshot fibers; traces of paint, cosmetics, and body fluids. Blood, semen, urine, saliva, and perspiration lit up like neon paint under a blacklight. So did non-incriminating substances—Tide detergent, vitamin B, even animal fats from a greasy cheeseburger. It wasn't an evidence technician's job to determine what the substance was. Anything that glowed would be sent to the FBI lab in Quantico for that purpose.

In the 1990s, an ALS cost around $8,000. FBI headquarters could be slow to approve big expenditures on new and unproven technology, so Maxwell had borrowed one of the first models—the Omniprint 1000—from Omnichrome, the manufacturer. Maxwell had taught himself to use it, practicing in his living room, where his wife ran a children's day care. Children's fingerprints were smaller and harder to lift, because their oils had a more delicate viscosity. They didn't absorb the powder as well, and they could be wiped away by the act of brushing the powder on. His wife's day care kids peppered every knee-high surface with fingerprints and deposited all kinds of bodily fluids. He was able to develop his skills in the comfort of his own living room.

Maxwell unpacked his fingerprinting kit, closed the door, and turned off the lights. The darker the room, the better the light would fluoresce. The trick was finding the right combination of light color and goggle lens for a particular crime scene. Different combinations worked in different situations and on different types of materials. He pulled on orange goggles, the first lens color he would test, and tuned the ALS to emit a cool blue light. He began with a preliminary scan, working the hoselike light over the room, covering every inch of every object, like a painter spray-painting a room. He could see dark smudges that indicated where the detectives had already dusted.

After scanning the room, he decided to target the bunk bed. It was a matter of proximity and logic: it was the biggest object in the room, and it would have been within arm's reach of where the kidnapper stood. Maybe he had leaned on it while tying up the girls. If he wasn't wearing gloves, the friction skin on his fingers and palms would have left a ridge-detail imprint. Friction skin—which exists only on the fingers,

Polly's bunk bed in a crime scene photo taken on the night of the abduction. (COURTESY OF TONY MAXWELL)

palms, and soles of the feet—has no hair follicles, and therefore does not secrete oil. But the friction ridges of a fingerprint are rows of eccrine glands, sweat pores that release perspiration. The salts from perspiration mix with grease and oil transferred from other parts of the body, particularly the face, and these chemicals are transferred to a surface, leaving a chemical pattern as personal as a signature and as singular as a snowflake.

Tony knelt on Polly's floor and looked for a place to run a test pattern. He needed to test different powders to see which color—green, blue, yellow, or red—performed best on the semi-porous surface. He chose a leg of the bunk bed, close to the floor, which the kidnapper wouldn't have touched, and pressed his thumb against it, leaving a test print. Then he applied green fluorescent powder and swept the blue light over the test pattern. His thumbprint did not appear. Next, he reached for a reddish powder made of moss spores and lycopodium powder. The commercial name was Redwop—"powder" spelled backward. He applied another test pattern and swept the blue light over the wood.

Under the beam, through the orange goggles, his thumbprint turned Day-Glo orange. *Yes!*

He turned on the light source. Using an extra-fine ostrich feather brush and a very light touch, he methodically dusted the bed frame, working slowly from left to right. Fingerprints missed by the conventional dusting began to emerge, forty-eight in all. Each one had to be photographed, lifted with tape, preserved on a fingerprint card, and recorded in a fingerprint log. The work was tedious and meticulous. Maxwell loved it. He didn't think about the fact that he was making history. This was the first time the new technology had been used at an FBI crime scene.

The sixth print, on the upper bunk, overlapped a circular plastic cap that covered the bolt that secured the wooden frame. This would be a challenge. Plastic absorbed oils, amino acids, and salt at a different rate than wood. The same dusting could yield a good print on wood but nothing on plastic. Because of the location of the plastic disc, around shoulder-height, he didn't have the luxury of running a test pattern there. Could he make it visible on both surfaces with the same Redwop powder? Moments like this made him tense. He might have said a prayer.

With a steady hand and a delicate touch, he feathered on the Redwop powder, hoping that if the fingerprints belonged to a child, the procedure wouldn't obliterate them. Then he turned off the lights and scanned the juncture with the ALS tuned to 400 nanometers.

"Oh my!" he exhaled into the dark.

There it was—glowing like campfire embers. It appeared to be a partial palm print. Right hand. Larger than a child's. The luminescent pattern overlapped the plastic disc and the wood. Maxwell was elated to see the ridges and troughs crisply defined on both surfaces.

He flipped on the lights and set up a medium-format Mamiya camera on a tripod a few inches from the bed. Over the camera lens he put an orange filter the same hue as his goggles. Then he turned off the lights and opened the shutter for a time-lapse exposure that would capture the ridge-detail pattern glowing under the light. He always—always—took photographs before lifting a print, as the process of taping and lifting could easily smear or destroy it.

Fingerprint tape resembles Scotch tape and comes in the same kind of dispenser. Maxwell didn't have any four-inch tape, so he carefully over-lapped two-inch tape until it covered the entire print. The print was too large for a single three-by-five-inch fingerprint card, so he taped two of them together. Slowly, cautiously, steadily, he peeled back the layers of tape as one unit. In a brief, tense moment, he affixed the tape to the plastic side of the fingerprint card. Under the ALS, through the goggles, he could see the ridge-pattern detail glowing intact on the card. Now he could exhale.

When he turned the lights back on, the luminescent palm print vanished. In his hands he held a blank white card. Flipping it over to the paper side, he drew a detailed sketch of the bed frame and the precise location and position of the print. He numbered the card—A-6—and copied the same information into the fingerprint log. Next to entry A-6, he scribbled one more word:

Bingo.

After finishing his work in Polly's room, Maxwell turned his focus to the back of the house, specifically the back door and the service door that connected the back porch to Eve's kitchen. Maxwell began dusting the door, the door frame, the glass, the walls, and the hallway. The sun had not yet risen.

As he worked, six-year-old Annie approached him with her mother.

"Can Annie help?" he'd later recall Eve saying. "She wants to look for her sister."

Maxwell got down on one knee to speak eye-to-eye with Annie.

"Do you really want to help?" he said softly.

"Yes," she said.

"Okay," he said, handing her a roll of fingerprint tape. "Don't touch anything. And when I need some tape, you can give it to me. We'll collect all the fingerprints we can find."

This was well outside of protocol. But Maxwell knew he would never regret it as much as he would regret denying her offer to help. Moments like this have the power to scar or heal. For a few very poignant minutes, Annie assisted the FBI. Then she tired and went to find her mother. Before the sun rose on her first day without Polly, Eve lit a candle and placed it in the window of the living room facing the street.

It would flicker every night until Polly was found.

chapter eight

DOUBTS

⌒⌒⌒

Saturday, October 2, around 1 a.m.—Petaluma PD

THE SUN WAS HOURS FROM RISING WHEN EDDIE FREYER AND VAIL BELLO TURNED the crime scene over to the Evidence Response Team and moved to the Petaluma Police Department, where Kate and Gillian were being interviewed. The department's small briefing room was already transforming into the command post, a twenty-four-hour hub of activity and the "brain" of the investigation. Someone wallpapered the room with cream-colored butcher paper. Like a giant collective to-do list, it began filling up with handwritten names, phone numbers, and tips. Investigators' names were scribbled next to each lead. After each lead was chased down, it was scratched off the list. This was the classic system for tracking leads in the chaotic first hours of a case.

FBI agent Tom LaFreniere grabbed a red pen and, in tidy handwriting, created a "possibilities flow chart," starting with the only two explanations—Polly *was* kidnapped; Polly *was not* kidnapped—and branching out from there. If she was kidnapped, was it by a stranger or someone she knew? If the kidnapper wasn't a stranger, could he be a family member? If he wasn't a family member, who did Polly know who might take her? If she was not kidnapped, was she a runaway? Had she snuck off with a boyfriend? Could this be a prank?

That last question was troubling the minds of investigators, who found themselves caught between disbelief and denial. It was also emerging as a recurring theme in the interviews with Kate and Gillian, which were still underway as the command center began to mobilize under the same roof.

In the interview room, Gillian was telling Andy Mazzanti of her initial assumption that the kidnapper was part of an elaborate sleepover prank orchestrated by Polly.

"When he came in, he just said for us to lay facedown on the floor and put our hands behind our backs," Gillian said. "I thought it was some kind of joke."

It would be the simplest explanation for a situation that broke logic. But Mazzanti looked at Gillian's wrists and saw they were red and swollen, still marked by deep impressions where the bindings had creased the skin. Had anyone photographed the girls' hands? Mazzanti made a mental note to request it before the evidence disappeared.

"When you said that for part of the time, you thought it might have been a prank," Mazzanti asked Gillian, "is there anybody you thought might have been pulling this prank on you?"

"No," Gillian said. "I just thought maybe it was a friend of Polly's family. Polly likes to act, she likes drama and everything, so I thought that she was just acting."

In another room, Dennis Nowicki was having Kate reenact the scene of the kidnapper's entry, trying to nail down the precise sequence of events.

"I'm going to stick my head in there, okay?" he told Kate, simulating the kidnapper entering Polly's room.

"I'll lie down like I was," Kate replied. She lay on the floor, belly down, hands under her chin.

"Okay," Nowicki said. "When the door opens up, do you see his whole body?"

"No, it's more like this," Kate said, looking up at him. "He opened the door. His face and the knife are what are showing, like this. He says, 'Everybody lie facedown on the floor now or I'll slit your throats.'"

"Okay, and then he comes in?"

"Once he knows that we're lying down and nobody's looking at him. That's when he comes all the way in. But I could see that he had the neon headband and I could see his face."

"How tall was this guy?" Nowicki asked.

"Could you come in the doorway and just let me look at you?" Kate said, sizing up the six-foot-two detective. "About your size. Maybe a little bit shorter."

"So this guy's about my height," Nowicki said. "How much does he weigh? Is he as heavy as I am?"

"I don't think so. I didn't get a very good glimpse of anything but his face, but I don't think he's quite as heavy. I think he might be a little overweight but I'm not sure."

"How old is he?"

"Probably about thirty or forty years old."

"How old am I?" the detective asked.

"Do you promise me you won't take this offensively?" Kate asked.

"I don't care," said Nowicki. He was forty-one.

"Okay. Ah, thirty to forty-five."

"What color were his eyes?"

"I didn't get a good look. I think they were either dark blue or brown."

"Were they wide or closed?"

"I think they were kind of wide. I'm not sure."

"Color of hair?"

"Black. I think it was curly. I didn't have a good chance to look at him. 'Cause like I said, I was on the floor. I could probably identify this guy if I saw him."

"Okay, if we get a guy to make a drawing or put a little sketch together, would you be able to describe him?"

"Yeah, probably. I'll try my best."

They drew a sketch of the room, the doors, the furniture, where the girls were when the stranger came in. They went through the sequence of events again and again: the stranger's entry, the binding and gagging, the taking of Polly. After she'd recounted the story several times, Nowicki switched gears.

"Okay, what I want you to do is now go in reverse order."

This tactic is often used in interrogations to flush out inconsistencies in a lying suspect's story. If someone is telling the truth, it can help shake free some forgotten details missed in the chronological account.

She recalled that when they were counting to one thousand, "the gag slid up onto Gillian's nose, and she thought she couldn't breathe for a while. Then it was okay but we were afraid to get up and fix it for fear that the man would come back and try to hurt one of us because we were up."

When some of the details changed slightly between tellings, Nowicki began to zero in on those inconsistencies and minor logical snags. Kate recounted the order in which the kidnapper bound them: Polly or Gillian first, then Kate. But Kate thought she was the first to be hooded with a pillowcase, maybe because she was talking so much. She didn't think Polly got a hood, though she did believe Polly was gagged.

Nowicki asked how Kate could know this, if she couldn't see through the hood.

"Because..." Kate paused for a moment. "I think... I'm not sure. I think I—it's hard to explain, I don't know. I just don't think that she had a pillowcase over her head. She might have and she might not have. It's not a great answer, but..."

Kate described the man "ransacking the room," hearing things falling on the floor, sensing him pulling objects off shelves. Nowicki inquired about all that noise.

"Wasn't he concerned that Mom was going to wake up?"

Kate paused. "None of this was very loud."

"Well, things are falling on the ground," he said. "Don't you think Mom's going to notice this?"

Kate sighed. "I could—maybe ransacked isn't the right word. Whatever he did, he did it quietly. But you could... since we were close to him while he was sorting and looking you could hear that he was looking through things and every once in a while something light might drop. And then there was the time when something heavy dropped on Polly's back and she said, 'Ouch.'"

"How could she say 'Ouch' if her mouth was gagged?"

Kate sighed again. "She sort of said it in a muffled voice. You could understand us with gags on, but we were for the most part too afraid to say anything for fear the guy would get angry."

Kate sounded so confident. So self-assured. So calm. Maybe a bit too calm.

"Where do you think Polly is?" Nowicki asked her.

Kate exhaled deeply. "If you want the truth...there are two things that I think. Maybe I've been watching a few too many *Unsolved Mysteries* or something, but I'm really afraid that he might have drowned her in the Petaluma River. Or I think that he might have dropped her off several blocks away from town, if he didn't kill her. Then he probably dropped her off at a park. I thought it was maybe the park at her house, but I think that's already been checked. So maybe it's even far away. Maybe he just dropped her off by the bowling alley or something."

At some point during the interview, Kate had mentioned that when Gillian was being bound, "I think she still thought it was a joke at that point."

"Why?" Nowicki asked.

"Gillian and Polly and I and a couple of girls from school had a slumber party and apparently she'd only told Polly that she had planned a prank similar to that, to invite someone over and they would just for a scare like they were robbing the house and just scare everyone."

"Do you think Polly's pulling this prank on you guys now?" Nowicki asked.

"Of course not," Kate said. "Polly would never do anything this serious. She would never worry anybody like this. I know that she wouldn't do that. I have never, ever heard her cry in my life, but as this guy was taking her away I heard her start to whimper and sob a little bit. It really worries me because..."

"Do you think it's possible for one of your friends to have this guy, you know, a friend of the family, come in and do this?"

"Never. I just think that is—no. No."

"Not even possible?"

"I don't think so. I think this is serious." Kate sighed. "I *know* this is serious. I mean, the guy had a knife. He threatened us. He made us lie down on the floor. He cut off our circulation for half an hour."

"Okay, okay."

This wasn't that kind of prank you'd pull at a slumber party, she explained. "You might bring Silly String and get people in their sleep, or put toothpaste on their face or whatever."

So why did she think this was a joke?

"I just figured, oh my god, there is a man in this house trying to steal stuff. Men in Petaluma don't steal stuff. And so I figured it was some sort of joke. Some sort of relation of Polly's playing some weird joke. But it wasn't. And when he took Polly, she didn't come back."

AROUND TWO-THIRTY A.M. Mazzanti concluded his interview with Gillian and allowed her to join Kate while they waited for someone to come and photograph their wrists. Nowicki made his exit, and the girls were left alone together, perhaps unaware of the tape recorder still running.

Kate told Gillian she'd recalled "the neon headband, and he had dark eyes."

"Basically," Gillian said. "And there was some headband, though. You wouldn't think he would want to wear like a neon headband if he was trying to—"

"—stalk." Kate finished the sentence.

"Yeah," Gillian said. Exactly.

"Oh my golly." Kate sighed, fidgeting in a squeaky office chair.

It was cold in the room, and the girls wished they'd turn down the air conditioner.

"Are they trying to freeze us to death?" Gillian said.

"I'm so glad to be with you, though," Kate said.

"Oh, I know," Gillian said. "I could hear you talking."

"You could?"

"Yeah."

"I'm so worried about Polly," Kate said.

"I know. There's got to be a reason why they can't find her."

"I'm going to be so glad when she's back at home..." Kate said. "She's *not* going to die."

"At least I hope not," Gillian said.

"No. That guy didn't seem like a killer, did he?"

"No. But I heard about people who kidnap people and they take them to other states and other countries." Gillian sighed.

"I don't want to hear it," Kate said. "I just want to think happy little thoughts like Lisa Frank's stickers or whatever. Peter Pan and stuff."

"I want to know the moment they find her."

"I know, whether she's dead or alive."

"I hope they call us."

"Oh, god, they have to."

"Oh, I'm sure they will," Gillian said.

Kate spun in the office chair.

"I think you're going to make me barf, Kate," Gillian said. "Please stop turning in circles—I'm really dizzy."

Gillian noted that when they were bound and lying on the floor, Kate at least was on the rug; Gillian had the bare hard floor. They laughed a little.

"That guy—god," Kate said.

"Psychotic," Gillian added.

"Let's just pray that Polly's okay," Kate said. "No, I mean it. Seriously. That she's being strong and..."

"Kate, would you please stop it?" Gillian interrupted. Kate wouldn't stop spinning.

"Well, I feel like I've been—"

"—questioned for five hours." Gillian finished her sentence.

"I can't go to sleep," Kate said. "I just want Polly back."

"My mom doesn't even know about this," Gillian said. "She's asleep right now."

"God," Kate said. "I'm just glad my parents are going to come."

They were silent for a moment. Gillian coughed.

"Unless we have information on him," Kate wondered, "you don't think this guy would go after us, do you?"

"No," Gillian said.

"No. That only happens in movies," Kate said, spinning and spinning.

"Kate, will you please stop it?" Gillian said. "Here, sit in this chair. This one doesn't move."

Kate sighed and switched chairs. "There."

"Now am I right by saying he was holding the knife in his left hand?" Gillian asked.

"Yeah," Kate said. "That's what I got too."

"Now, was it just me or was he holding a bag? With handles?"

"I didn't see a bag," Kate said, "but I heard the rustle of a bag. I know he had one. He brought that silky material stuff for our hands."

"Yeah. I wish we had Polly here."

"Mm-hmm. I wish she could tell us what to think."

The door opened, and a new officer appeared.

"Freeze! Police!" he said. The girls giggled. "I love saying that."

The officer was Ralph Pata, a police sketch artist from San Rafael.

"Well, you lucky guys," he said, "you get to draw with me now!"

WHILE THE GIRLS were interviewed—together—by the police sketch artist, investigators met for a debriefing. The girls' stories lined up, except for a few key details. Kate recalled a neon yellow bandana tied across the kidnapper's forehead. Gillian never mentioned a yellow headband, even though Mazzanti had specifically asked her about headwear. Kate was adamant that she'd heard a slamming door. Gillian didn't remember this sound.

These "minor inconsistencies" would turn into major problems. A bit of doubt would snowball into mistrust and even suspicion.

"This is bullshit," Nowicki said. "It never happened."

"But did you see their wrists?" Mazzanti replied.

Of course he had. But it wasn't outside the realm of possibility that a co-conspirator tied them up. Perhaps the bindings and gags were all part of the ruse. Maybe this was all a prank. Just kids being kids, making up stories.

Nowicki wasn't alone in his doubts. Several investigators thought the story was fishy. Others believed Polly was legitimately missing—with some other logical explanation. Could she be a runaway? Maybe she'd snuck off with a boyfriend, and her friends were covering for her. Perhaps she had been spirited away, but not entirely against her will.

FBI agents who had worked a number of kidnapping cases had never seen a circumstance quite like this. Many of the cops and feds just didn't believe it—or couldn't bring themselves to believe it. They thought they had seen everything. But this? It made no sense.

Detective Larry Pelton felt himself caught in the same currents of skepticism and disbelief. But one piece of physical evidence nagged at him. The electrical cords used to bind the girls had been cut from Polly's Nintendo.

"Kids," Pelton said, "would not cut their own Nintendo cords for a joke."

chapter nine

LEADS

∽

Saturday morning—Polly's House

AS THE SUN ROSE ON SATURDAY MORNING, POLLY'S NEIGHBORS EMERGED TO A buzz of activity and a web of crime scene tape. Since midnight, police officers had been canvassing the neighborhood, doing a "knock and talk" to interview residents. As people began their morning routines, police intercepted dog-walkers and spoke to bystanders drawn to the commotion. Had they noticed anything suspicious? Unfamiliar faces in the neighborhood? What had they seen and heard in the past twenty-four hours? Any of them might, without knowing it, be a witness.

That's how they had found Kamika Milstead, a fifteen-year-old neighbor who lived on Fourth Street, one block from Polly's house, on the opposite side of the street. Around ten-thirty p.m.—ten minutes before the kidnapping—Kamika had seen an unfamiliar man walking back and forth across Polly's street. She described him as white, with brown hair and a mustache. She didn't recall a beard.

Shortly before the encounter, Kamika had noticed a vehicle that circled the block at least five times before parking on the street outside her home. Unconcerned about the car, Kamika had walked past it on her way to a nearby 7-Eleven. On the way back, she saw the car was unoccupied. That's when she saw the man walking back and forth across

Fourth Street, about a block from Polly's house. As she got closer, she felt his eyes watching her.

When an officer spoke with Kamika at eleven-thirty p.m., an hour after the encounter, Kamika recalled the man had been dressed in all black, but couldn't remember any more details. Asked the make and model of the car, Kamika reported a gray or black Toyota Tercel.

That was the information that had been dispatched out on the all-points bulletin at 12:14 a.m.

The next day, the police spoke with Taleah Miller, an eleven-year-old neighbor who lived two doors down from Polly. She didn't play with Polly, but she had seen her riding bikes with Annie on the sidewalk. Taleah had gone to Petaluma Cinemas to watch *The Good Son* with a friend. After the film, her uncle picked them up. After dropping her friend off at home, they drove down Fourth Street and noticed a man standing at the corner of Fourth and F Street, about a block from Polly's house. Taleah recalled the man was dressed in dark clothes and carrying a duffel bag under his left arm. As her uncle parked on the street, Taleah looked at the man through the car window. He slid his right hand over his face, as if he were trying to hide it, but she glimpsed a dark beard with a patch of gray. She found him "kind of scary looking" and after her uncle parked, she waited to get out of the car until the man had passed. Then he disappeared into the shadows.

A block from Polly's house, police knocked and talked with thirteen-year-old Thomas Georges. Four of his buddies had come over after school to play basketball in his driveway and football at Wickersham Park. His parents fixed them hamburgers for dinner and said they could rent a movie at Kozy Video. Around eight-thirty p.m., Thomas was standing in his driveway, waiting for his friends to come out of the house. That's when he noticed a man he'd never seen in the neighborhood. The stranger was smoking a cigarette, carrying a bag in his left hand, and walking toward Polly's house. He recalled the man's dark clothes and particularly his boots, because they fell on the pavement with a heavy sound.

Thomas's friends came out of the house, and they walked to Kozy Video, passing a basketball back and forth. As they passed Polly's house, they noticed the man standing outside it, smoking. He was still there when they returned with a movie. Thomas dropped the basketball, and it rolled toward the man. When he went to retrieve the ball—it was only about ten feet from the guy—Thomas got a pretty good look at him. He was wearing a dark long-sleeved shirt. His hair was "pepper gray," and he had a beard.

⌒⌒⌒

BY MORNING, A composite sketch was already circulating. It showed a dark-haired man with heavily lidded eyes, a full beard, and a yellow bandana tied prominently across his forehead.

Officers were already walking the streets and presenting this face to anyone willing to look. Investigators grabbed a copy to show the young couple who rented the mother-in-law unit behind Polly's house.

Nineteen-year-old Aaron Thomas was the full-time resident of 427½ Fourth Street, a one-room cottage with a tiny kitchen and just

Early flyer with the first composite sketch.
(COURTESY OF GREG JACOBS)

enough room for a recliner and a sofa-bed. His eighteen-year-old girl-friend, Rochelle Antell, often spent the night. The couple knew Polly only in passing. At the time of her abduction, they'd been spending a mellow Friday night watching movies at home with a friend.

Aaron and Rochelle, who went by Chelle (pronounced Shelly), studied the composite sketch. It reminded them of an unfamiliar face they'd seen in the neighborhood the day before Polly disappeared. On Thursday morning, while leaving their place, they'd noticed a white Ford Aerostar van parked near the intersection of F Street and Fourth—catty-corner to Polly's house. Both front windows were open, and they saw the driver: a white male with brown hair and a full beard.

Two hours later, on the way home, Aaron noticed the van was still parked on the corner, the driver still sitting inside. Finding that odd, he made a U-turn, planning to ask the man why he had been there so long. As he swung the car around, the driver noticed him, started the van, and sped off. Aaron wasn't able to get the license plate, and he hadn't seen the man or the minivan since. The driver resembled the composite sketch—sort of—but Aaron and Chelle weren't sure it was the same guy. They hadn't seen his face all that well.

The following night, when Polly was taken, the couple had not seen or heard anything out of the ordinary. They had been watching movies, with the volume turned up. The neighbor's dog—a barker—hadn't even made a sound. They didn't know anything was wrong until the cops flooded into the neighborhood.

However, Aaron recalled that their visitor, who had been sitting by the open door, had noticed something unusual. After learning of the kidnapping, the friend told him he'd seen a man entering Polly's house.

The witness's name was Sean Bush.

⌒⌒⌒

ON THE NIGHT of the kidnapping, Sean Bush, twenty-five, had arrived at 427½ Fourth Street at 7:57 p.m., a time he would later recall specifically because his friends gave him grief for being late. For the past three weeks they'd fallen into a weekend routine: Gather at Aaron and Chelle's on Friday night to hang out or catch a movie, then go out on

Saturday night. This Friday, Sean was running late, and that derailed their plans to go to the movies, so they decided to stay in and rent videos instead.

At around 8:15 p.m.—about the same time Kate McLean's mother dropped her off at Polly's house—Sean and Aaron left to buy drinks and rent movies. Kate's mother, Alice McLean, recalled seeing a man in dark clothing walking past Polly's house as she backed out of the driveway. Sean and Aaron didn't notice him on their way to Eastman Video. After picking out movies, they made a quick stop at a nearby liquor store to buy wine coolers and returned around nine p.m. That's when Aaron noticed that the back door of Polly's service porch was "wide open," though the door between the porch and the kitchen was closed. They settled in for the night as Sean fiddled with the VCR to get the sound in sync with the stereo.

They started the first movie, *Children of the Corn II*, around nine-thirty p.m. Partway through the film, around ten or 10:15 p.m., Sean got up to use the restroom. The porch light was on as he left the cottage, climbed the steps onto Polly's back deck, and entered the service porch, where the bathroom was off to the right. He saw nothing suspicious. After using the bathroom, Sean returned, and they continued watching the movie. When it was over, they didn't bother to rewind the VHS tape before popping in *The Color Purple*.

The front door of the cottage was open, and cool night air drifted in through the door. Through it, Sean had a view of Polly's back door. He lit a cigarette. During the first part of the film, which he'd seen before, Sean glanced outside and saw a man walking through the backyard, toward the back of Polly's house. The man appeared to notice Sean, and immediately turned his face away. Sean wasn't sure if this guy was avoiding his gaze or just looking where he was going, toward the house he was about to enter.

The light outside the cottage was bright, so Sean was able to see the man clearly. He appeared to be wearing dark pants and a tight, short-sleeved knit shirt. No glasses. Sean guessed he was five-foot-eleven. His skin appeared tanned, and his dark hair was long enough to flip up in the back. Sean didn't recall a beard. As the man approached the back door of the house, he seemed to pause, his head dipping slightly, as if he were peering into Polly's kitchen through the window or the glass in the door. Sean saw the man extend his hand, perhaps to grab the doorknob. Then Sean turned back to the movie. It was roughly ten-thirty p.m.

The man's stride was casual, not particularly fast or stealthy. He moved like he'd been there before, like he knew where he was going. Without giving it much thought, Sean assumed the man belonged there. So he didn't mention it to his friends.

Sean used the restroom again after seeing the man enter the house, but he didn't see or hear anything unusual. He'd been drinking, but not much. Maybe half a wine cooler. He recalled that the neighbor's dog—who usually barked at him whenever he walked to the bathroom—had not barked at the man. Sean had grown up with dogs that were reprimanded for barking, so this noise would have caught his attention.

As the night temperature dropped, they shut the cottage door and turned on the heat. They also turned off the porch light.

Five or ten minutes later, the neighbor's dog began barking. A flashlight appeared in the window. When Aaron went to open the door and see what the matter was, a cop yelled at him to close the door and stay in the house.

⌒⌒⌒

Roughly forty-five minutes after police arrived at Polly's house, Sean Bush figured out what was going on and realized that the man he'd observed may not have belonged at the house. He asked Aaron if other people ever used the back door.

"No," Aaron told him. "They normally don't use that entrance."

Sean told his friends about the man, and they agreed that Sean should inform the police. Sean pulled aside an officer and reported what he had seen. He provided a brief written statement and signed it before going home.

On Saturday morning, two FBI agents showed up at the restaurant where Sean worked. They closed the doors, pulled off their jackets, revealing their guns, and told him they wanted to ask him some questions. At a table in the middle of the restaurant—which delayed its opening for the interview—they grilled him for nearly two hours.

Sean repeated the details of what he'd seen, over and over—five times. He found it "very intimidating." The FBI agents did not appear to believe him, and he wondered if he was a suspect.

"[They kept] telling me that it didn't make sense, and that my description did not match the girls' description," he later recalled. "So what was I talking about and who did I see?"

A key detail he could not corroborate was the presence of a yellow bandana.

MEANWHILE, AT THE Petaluma Police Department, Special Agent Eddie Freyer and Sergeant Vail Bello were quarterbacking the tips and leads pouring into the command center. The butcher paper taped to the walls was filling up with names and notions, people to chase down and interview: possible suspects, potential witnesses, and anyone seen in the neighborhood in the days before Polly's disappearance. Tree trimmers. Painters. Taxi drivers. Neighbors. Friends of neighbors. Sean Bush was eighteenth on the list. Aaron Thomas was number twenty.

The command center operated around the clock, a hive of activity that felt chaotic but also had a systematic flow. Tables were pushed to the perimeter, the middle of the room a terminal where bodies moved briskly in every direction, shuttling information. One table, the "strategy table," served as the hotspot for formulating leads. Another table was the place for dispatching leads and recording new information when cops and agents returned from an investigation. Another table was for processing information and tacking it up on boards.

Clerical staff and dispatchers were answering phones, taking messages, and writing notes. Whenever a call came in, the taker would jot notes on a piece of paper, then run it over to the lead prioritization table, where someone else would assess the validity and urgency of the tip before passing it on to the lead dispatch table. Tips determined to be viable leads were assigned to investigative teams that paired an FBI agent with a Petaluma officer. Reports were handwritten or typed, photocopied, then marked with a rubber stamp that indicated the recipient. Paperwork flowed in every direction. Tips were coming in at the rate of more than a hundred per day, and the paper-based lead-tracking system threatened to buckle under this load.

⌒⌒⌒

ONE OF THE tips led two agents to Petaluma's Fairwest Market and Bar. They were looking to interview witnesses about a man who fit the suspect's description: white male in his mid-thirties or mid-forties, six feet tall, around 235 pounds, dark hair to his shoulders. A full beard.

The bartender said this guy, a local, had come into the bar on Friday evening, straight from the airport. Returning home from a trip to New York, he was carrying three cloth gym bags, and he asked the bartender to keep an eye on them. One of the bags contained a length of rope. The bartender asked what the rope was for. The bearded man replied that it was for some personal business he had to take care of that night.

The next evening, around 7:45 p.m., the man returned to the bar. His shoulder-length hair had been cut—above his ears, still long in the back—and his beard was now a goatee. Around 8:25 p.m., a male patron told him he looked like the guy on the kidnapping poster. That's when the man left the bar.

Several sources said the bearded man was known for illegal drug use, unwanted sexual advances toward women, and bringing minors into the bar and attempting to buy them drinks. A female witness said he'd made unwelcome passes at her and had followed her on several occasions. She'd heard him make lewd remarks about young girls. Another female acquaintance said the man had told her he could "get a hold of a kid any time she [sic] wants one."

He worked as a construction roofer, lived in a barn off Bodega Avenue, drove, but didn't own a vehicle and had a suspended license. A female colleague who worked with him at a construction site in Tomales Bay said they were building a few new houses, and she thought they ought to look there for Polly. Several Petaluma police officers drove out to Tomales Bay to search the construction site but didn't find Polly.

A records search revealed a colorful criminal history: vehicle theft, burglary, battery, assault with a deadly weapon, and assault with intent to murder. He'd served time in prison and currently had an outstanding no-bail warrant for his arrest. They arrested him at his home at three-thirty a.m. and took him to Petaluma PD for an interview.

He gave them an alibi for his whereabouts late Friday night, but the agents didn't trust him. At four-thirty a.m., they concluded the interview and turned him over to the cops, who booked him for an outstanding warrant and took him to Sonoma County Jail. As promising as this lead had appeared, it was a dead end.

He wasn't the guy.

ON SATURDAY EVENING, the phone rang at Marc Klaas's home in Sausalito. Marc and his girlfriend, Violet Cheer, had left that morning but had asked Violet's three sisters to stay at their place and answer the phone. Violet's brother-in-law, Hank Mar, had answered a number of calls that day from family, friends, and the media, when the phone rang again around 10:15 p.m.

"Is Marc there?" said a young girl's voice.

"No," Hank said. "Who is calling?"

"This is Polly."

She sounded nervous and upset, but was speaking clearly.

"Polly!" Mar said. "Where are you?"

"San Francisco—no, Daly City."

"Where in Daly City?"

"The Daly Inn. Who is this?"

"This is Hank."

"Where is my dad?"

"He is in Petaluma with your mother."

"Tell my father I'm fine. He hasn't hurt me. He is coming back."

"Be cool, stay calm, stay there, we'll be there."

The line went dead.

Hank, who was married to Violet's sister, had known Polly for five or six years now. He had no doubt this was her voice.

The news made its way quickly to the command center. Freyer's stomach twisted when he heard about the call. *We blew it.* He had ordered a trap-and-trace* on the mother's phone. But he'd forgotten to tap the father's.

Agents mobilized and quickly discovered there was no Daly Inn in Daly City, just south of San Francisco. After searching every other motel in Daly City and every Days Inn from San Francisco to San Jose, they determined the call was a prank.

Meanwhile, Marc Klaas was staying at a motel in Petaluma, waiting for news of his daughter's rescue. No news came. At three a.m., unable to sleep, he slipped on his shoes, left the room, and walked across the street. In the empty parking lot of a grocery store, he fell to his knees in the moonlight and screamed.

---

* This investigative tool works in concert with the telephone company, allowing incoming calls to be traced to the physical location of the initiated call.

chapter ten

THE VOLUNTEERS

∽

Saturday morning—Downtown Petaluma

ALL OVER PETALUMA, PEOPLE AWOKE TO POLLY'S FACE ON THE MORNING NEWS. Television crews and newspaper reporters were already on the story, tipped off by the police scanners they monitored to eavesdrop on radio traffic.

A local businessman and grandfather was driving downtown when the news spilled out of the radio of his Chevy Blazer.

Twelve-year-old girl... kidnapped... knifepoint... from her home... Petaluma.

Her name—Polly—leaped out like a sign. At that moment, he was driving toward a bakery called Polly Ann.

A little voice inside said: *Pay attention to this.*

Bill Rhodes owned PIP printing, a local print shop in the heart of downtown, on the corner of Kentucky Street and Western Avenue. From his car phone, he dialed the Petaluma police and spoke with Sergeant Mike Kerns. Next he called his wife, Sherry. His voice quavered as he told her about Polly.

White-haired, with a disarming smile and charismatic confidence, fifty-one-year-old Bill Rhodes was the kind of man other men called in a crisis. He was a certified emergency medical technician, he had worked as a paramedic and ambulance driver in Wyoming, and he had served as a state adviser in developing emergency response procedures. He was known to donate his time and printing services to all sorts of local causes, from printing Little League tickets to helping put on the annual Children's Home Society fashion show.

On the car phone, Bill and Sherry Rhodes devised a plan. They could print flyers at the print shop, get volunteers to wallpaper the town. They would organize a community search. Immediately, they started recruiting friends.

By the time Sherry met Bill at the print shop later that morning, the Xerox machines were already churning out copies of the flyer released by police and the FBI. It showed a black-and-white photo of "Polley" next to a composite sketch of the suspect, who was described as a "white male adult 30-40 years, dark or dark gray hair, with full beard, wearing dark clothing." Both the sketch and the written description indicated "a yellow bandana around his head."

Soon, a small crowd began to amass at PIP, eager to help. Friends and neighbors grabbed armfuls of flyers to tape on storefront windows and staple to telephone poles. Within hours, every business in town had a copy. Many had three or four.

⌒⌒⌒

MEANWHILE, IN A nearby Sonoma town, a single mother came home from a work trip to find her thirteen-year-old daughter and babysitter staring, aghast, at the news on TV.

"Oh my god, mom," her daughter said. "Some little girl got kidnapped in Petaluma!"

Joanne Gardner was a producer and director who had been shooting a music video in LA for Rodney Crowell, a country music singer and songwriter. Her daughter, Jessica, looked a lot like Polly Klaas. Gardner saw that the reporters were interviewing "anyone who would stop walking," and much of what they were saying was speculation or just plain nonsense. Someone needed to handle the press and stanch this flow of conjecture. Gardner loaded her daughter in the car and drove to Petaluma, where they entered the crowd at PIP print shop.

"Can you tell me who's running the show here?" Gardner asked.

Someone waved over Bill Rhodes.

"You've got to get your arms around the press," Gardner told him. "This is a big story, and they're letting idiots talk on the camera."

Rhodes said he didn't know how to do that.

"I can help," Gardner said.

She was introduced to Polly's mother, Eve Nichol, who was distraught but optimistic. She said she expected they would find Polly some time that afternoon, but she'd be grateful if Gardner could manage the press until then.

"Of course," Gardner said. "I'll handle it 'til we find her."

Gardner instructed volunteers to stop speculating on camera and scheduled a proper press conference, during which someone with media training could deliver information grounded in fact. Equipped with a BlackBerry phone and a portable computer (laptops were not yet widespread), she parked herself in a corner and wrote a press release, which she printed on a dot-matrix printer and faxed to the Associated Press.

Days later, sensing the need for backup, she would dial a friend, another media-savvy woman she knew from the music industry.

"Gaynell, a little girl has been kidnapped, and I'm surrounded by people who can't make a sentence. I know you do marketing. I need help."

Gaynell Rogers was the manager for blues musician Roy Rogers, considered one of the finest slide guitarists of his generation. They were married and had a seven-year-old daughter who was also named Jessica. Rogers had been trained in music and film publicity, so she knew how to help a journalist get what they needed for a story. Roy was on the road, touring, and she was at home alone with Jessica. But something about the tone in her friend's voice made her drop everything.

"I'll be there as soon as I can."

Across town, a newspaperman at a turning point in his life was hearing the news from his wife, who'd learned about it at the farmer's market. Jay Silverberg, a tall, thin man with kind dark eyes and a touch of gray in his hair, looked up with a new kind of curiosity. He was no longer in the news business. Just three weeks earlier, he had retired from his post as editor-in-chief of the *Marin Independent Journal*, a daily paper in Novato with a circulation of 43,000. He had decided to start a new business, a small public relations firm that specialized in crisis management. The company was still an idea taking shape in his mind. But his skills were already sharp.

Silverberg walked into PIP printing. "I'm looking for your media person."

Someone led him to Joanne Gardner.

"Jay Silverberg," he said, extending his hand. "How can I help?"

Gardner shook his hand, smiled, and handed him a stack of phone slips.

"Sit down," she said. "Take these."

Silverberg flipped through the phone slips, recognizing the names of local reporters. This was his first time on the other side of the news. He nodded and started dialing.

⌒⌒⌒

SATURDAY NIGHT, BILL RHODES attended a local fundraiser that drummed up $60,000 for Petaluma kids with cancer. In front of the full house, he called for help, asking for volunteers to pass out flyers and join the search.

"I care," he later told a TV news crew, voice cracking. "I've got grand-kids that age. I can help."

On Sunday morning, Mayor Patty Hilligoss and City Councilwoman Carole Barlas were among the scores of Petalumans who answered the call. A queue formed along Kentucky Street, where a volunteer dis-patched 140 search teams to different parts of town. In groups of three or four, they walked through alleys, along the Petaluma River, scour-ing the woods and the fields, parting bushes, splashing through creeks, and looking for "anything suspicious." Some searchers rode horses and mountain bikes into the ochre hills and oak-studded valleys. Petaluma PD set guidelines: Don't touch anything that might be evidence; if you see the subject, don't make contact; and call police immediately if you happen to find anything.

Many of the groups included children and teenagers. One of them was twelve-year-old Trisha Stretch, a seventh-grade classmate who had sat next to Polly in history class on the day she disappeared. With her mother, Becky Sutherland, Trisha searched the woods around Western and Webster. They found places that looked to be inhabited by people without homes, but they didn't find Polly. "That was tough," said Sutherland, who thought it was time to contact *America's Most Wanted.*

Meanwhile, in the print shop, Rhodes divided a map of Petaluma into seventeen different areas and assigned groups to plaster each one with flyers. "We even had kids on bicycles coming here asking to help," Rhodes told the *Petaluma Argus-Courier.* "We just gave them a handful of flyers and told them to put them up in an area where they didn't see any."

Bio Bottoms, the mail-order children's clothing company where Eve worked, donated $5,000 in reward money and challenged other local businesses to do the same. Colleagues delivered home-cooked meals to Eve and Annie. One coworker carried her five-and-a-half-month-old daughter as she and her husband walked Lichau Creek, hoping to find Polly. Like Eve, they remained fiercely hopeful. "I think he went in there and got what he wanted," said Bio Bottoms owner Anita Dimondstein. "I expect he will return her and we will see her soon."

By some counts, 1,000 friends and neighbors came out to help. Ruth VanDerBeets of the San Jose–based Vanished Children's Alliance told the *Oakland Tribune* that it was one of the biggest shows of support she's ever seen. By Sunday afternoon, they had printed and posted 100,000 flyers throughout the Bay Area. Sports fans took them to Candlestick Park and slipped them under windshield wipers at the San Francisco 49ers game. Stacks were passed to truckers and Greyhound bus drivers, who broadened their circulation.

As Sunday wound down, 150 people held a vigil by the lake at Lucchesi Park. "It was an impromptu community gathering to show support for Polly and her family," organizer Joan Cooper said. "We want to create some positive energy and send out our love to Polly and her parents."

Another hundred people gathered in prayer at the Petaluma Community Center. One of them, Sharon North, had a thirteen-year-old daughter who was friends with Polly. "I've got a son who slept in a family room last night with the lights on," North told a reporter. "He is six feet tall and one hundred ninety-five pounds, but this is pretty scary."

She said she believed the prayer circle would help. "I have a feeling she would know people are thinking about her."

Candlelight vigils and prayer circles had begun popping up across the region, the emotion rippling outward. Children painted homemade signs—"We love you, Polly!"—and people of all ages pinned on purple ribbons, Polly's favorite color.

"When something happens to any of the kids, the whole community comes out," said Petaluma resident Ruthellen Gerke as she searched the bushes along Petaluma Creek, a sliver of waterway between the highway and the railroad tracks.

⌒⌒

AS FRIENDS AND neighbors and absolute strangers rallied around them, Polly's family oscillated between grief and gratitude. The love and support were overwhelming. So were the fear and uncertainty.

"We're really touched by their efforts," said Polly's stepfather, Allan Nichol. "Everybody's holding up and we're all hopeful."

"We always feared for her because she's so pretty," said Joe Klaas, her grandfather, who drove up from Carmel with his wife, Betty Jane, to accompany Marc to the police station to deliver a set of Polly's fingerprints, taken at a safety fair.

"I expect to come out of a bad dream," said Polly's aunt, Marianna Klaas Ford. "You think you're okay and then you fall apart again. Just when you think people are horrible, you realize people are mostly good and want to do something good to help you. We're so helpless. You try to stay busy but you're exhausted. And you keep thinking about how scared your child is, wherever she is . . . It's a family's worst nightmare."

"She's a beautiful child with a marvelous personality," said Polly's father, Marc. "She's outgoing, funny, bright, smart, and resourceful—"

"—and she is going to grow up to be a beautiful woman," interjected Marc's sister. "She is going to grow up to be a beautiful woman."

One of Polly's best friends, Annette Schott, had been invited to the slumber party but didn't go. "She wouldn't be laughing now, but she was always laughing," Annette said.

Not even forty-eight hours had passed since Kate McLean had

found herself bound and gagged on Polly's bedroom floor. Yet here she was, among the searchers combing the fields between Highway 101 and the Petaluma River.

"You just hold your breath," Kate told a reporter as she searched. "You wait, and you pray."

AT SOME POINT on Saturday, a pager went off in Washington, DC, alerting the staff of *America's Most Wanted* to the news of Polly's abduction. The prime-time TV show featured reenactments of heinous crimes, imploring its national audience to help catch the criminals by phoning in tips on a toll-free hotline. Its host was John Walsh, the father of a kidnapped and murdered child and the founder of the National Center for Missing and Exploited Children (NCMEC), the nation's largest clearinghouse for missing kids. *America's Most Wanted* had caught an average of one criminal per show since its debut in 1988.

The show's missing child coordinator, a young woman named Michelle Hord,* went everywhere with her little sky pager, which alerted her as soon as an abduction was reported by local authorities or the NCMEC. Her first order of business—regardless of the hour—was to send a public service announcement to all Fox affiliates. Next, she'd get herself and a film crew to the scene of the abduction. They landed in Petaluma the very next day.

Hord was only twenty-three at the time, not yet a mother, but something about Polly would linger with her forever. It was a point of pride to be the first national media outlet to break the story. But it was more than a scoop. It was personal. While other reporters were kept at bay by Joanne Gardner's protective PR skills, Hord sat on Polly's couch with Eve, who asked for advice on how to survive the crushing demands of the media. It was a role that other journalists didn't usually have (or get) to play. She took that role very seriously.

---

* Tragically, Michelle Hord would one day be the grieving mother of a murdered child. In 2017, her then-husband killed their seven-year-old daughter, Gabrielle. Hord, a former producer for *Good Morning America*, shared her story of tragedy and resilience in a memoir called *The Other Side of Yet: Finding Light in the Midst of Darkness*.

"Because we were a show that had John Walsh as our host and, really, our north star, we walked in with people expecting not just a reporter but a counselor and a connection to the NCMEC," Hord recalled decades later. "There were all these other roles and expectations, and [access] to law enforcement and the family that 48 *Hours* and 60 *Minutes* and other folks on the lawn weren't getting."

Hord had visited many communities to respond to an abduction. Some towns came out in full force to help search. Others seemed to be more concerned about how the crime made their community look to the rest of the world.

Hord and her crew filmed Polly's segment on Sunday, on a quiet dock by the Petaluma River, where they interviewed Marc and Eve, Kate and Gillian. The episode would be edited quickly and ready to air on Tuesday.

⌒⌒⌒

AFTER RETURNING FROM the taping, Kate was interviewed—again— by the FBI. She and Gillian had been interviewed over and over, so many times, by so many people. They might be young, but they were smart enough to realize many of the people thought they were lying.

But Kate had requested this interview. During the *America's Most Wanted* taping, a new theory had occurred to her: Maybe the kidnapper was hired to take Polly. When asked why she suspected this, she said it was because the kidnapper had been gentle and because of what he had told them. He said he didn't want to hurt them. He only wanted money.

Close your eyes, the agents told her. *Visualize where Polly might be.*

She closed her eyes and saw a warehouse. Maybe in Daly City, just south of San Francisco. She had been over at a friend's house earlier, and her friend's mother had visualized Polly on a road by Helen Putnam Park.

Kate lamented the number of people who had learned that she was a witness. Her brother had told the soccer team, and she was still mad at him about it. She was also surprised at Petaluma's outpouring of concern. And all the attention.

"It's kinda got out of hand, huh?" the agent asked.

"Yeah," Kate said.

How would Polly feel about all of this?

"She'd be as shocked as everyone else," Kate said.

Kate said she had not heard from Polly. If Polly were to contact anyone, she thought it would be her best friend, Annette Schott.

This was all so stressful.

"Picture this," she told the agent. "You go out the bedroom door to get your sleeping bag and there's a man standing there with a butcher knife—a kitchen knife—who tells you to lie on the floor, facedown, or I'll slit your throat."

At this point, it was still believed that the kidnapper had entered the house through a window. Where did Kate believe he entered?

"He had to come in through the window," Kate said. "It was the only thing that was open."

Did she think Polly was safe? Yes. She didn't think the stranger intended to hurt her. He was just doing it for the money.

Did she think the man had anyone helping him?

"No," she said. "I think he went solo."

chapter eleven

SEVENTY-TWO HOURS

∽

Monday, October 4—Petaluma

At a press conference on Monday, Eve Nichol stepped before a crowd of reporters and TV cameras, articulate but visibly trembling. "This child is the light of our lives," she said. "If we could get her back safely, it's just the best possible thing that could happen." Her voice was soft and warm, but strained. "I sense she is okay. Her friends have been feeling her energy. We're optimistic."

The cops and feds were less so. "We have no motives, no demands, no ransoms, no suspects," said FBI spokesman Rick Smith. One-third of the Petaluma police force had been assigned to the case, along with thirty-five FBI agents. They had received more than a thousand tips and had investigated more than 150 leads. None had unearthed a suspect. "It's not great that we haven't heard anything yet," Smith said.

The odds were grim. Mark Mershon, the FBI Assistant Special Agent in Charge (ASAC), had worked a number of kidnapping cases and thought about the "rule of thirds" that applies specifically to stranger abductions. One-third of the victims are recovered alive. One-third are found dead. One-third simply disappear. Agent Tom LaFreniere had also worked a number of kidnappings and was hoping for a ransom call. "In all the kidnappings I've done, I think I've had two ransom calls," he said later. "The rest of them were dead." Most victims who were found alive were located during the first seventy-two hours, Petaluma Sergeant Mike Kerns told the press, noting that this window was rapidly shrinking.

Some clues were emerging. There were no signs of forced entry. Some investigators surmised the kidnapper had entered through a window or unlocked door. Kate and Gillian were fairly sure the front door had been locked, but a window had been open. Sean Bush had seen a man walk into the back door. The girls maintained that the back door was locked, but Polly's mother wasn't so sure. She wondered if Polly had left it unlocked when she put the vacuum cleaner back on the service porch.

A bloodhound was sent from Contra Costa, but the dog lost Polly's scent outside her home. That suggested the kidnapper fled in a car. Locals had noticed an unfamiliar vehicle cruising through the neighborhood on Friday, a gray Honda Civic or Accord with primer paint on the driver's door and left front fender. The car had not been located yet, but a couple of weeks back in Cotati, a town about five miles away, a man was reported for approaching young girls while wearing makeup and a blond wig. He had been driving a gray car.

"It's baffling because of the lack of direction," said Sergeant Mike Kerns. They had so many leads, but they spidered out instead of converging on a common path.

There were several theories circulating, based on the circumstances of the crime. The first was that Polly had been targeted. The kidnapper may have seen her before, walking to Starnes Market for ice cream or Kozy Video to rent movies. This theory was supported by tips that claimed that a man resembling the police sketch had been seen in Wickersham Park, catty-corner to Polly's house, in the days before the abduction. Another theory proposed a crime of opportunity by a burglar who encountered the girls in the act of breaking in and spontaneously decided to kidnap Polly. A third scenario involved a professional hired to steal a little girl. Maybe Polly in particular.

"Did someone hire him to take her? Did he steal her for himself?" said Sergeant Kerns. "It's all speculation. We haven't been able to focus on one motive or one scenario because we don't know. We just don't know."

Eve seemed to believe the second theory, that a burglar, finding nothing better to steal, took Polly. He had asked, "Where are the valuables?" before spiriting her off. "If he gets to know her, he could never hurt her," Eve said, "because she's such a radiant, beautiful child."

Marc disagreed. "I, on the other hand, feel that he came into this house looking intentionally for the little girl who lives in this house. He made a strong point of making sure who she was. It doesn't make any sense to me."

Everyone was puzzled by the kidnapper's question: "Which one of you lives here?" Why would he ask that? The girls had been playing with makeup. Maybe that's why he didn't recognize her. He said there were too many people there. Had he been casing the house?

"My gut feeling is that this kidnapping was not random," Marc said. "She knows this is not a wonderful world for small children... I've always tried to teach her how to handle herself with strangers and keep a cool head. If there is a way out of this, she'll find it. She's a bright girl."

Eve's face was taut with worry, but her voice projected hope. "Polly, we feel your light and energy. We know you are okay. And if you're the man who has Polly, please just take really good care of her and give us a call. She's very special to us."

Polly's little sister, Annie, also had something to say to reporters. At a press conference, she announced in a tiny voice that she had seen the man in the drawing "at the store." She was talking about Starnes Market, where Polly and Gillian had gone to buy ice cream on the evening of the abduction. The owner of Starnes Market later said he believed that Annie was referring to a homeless man who frequented Wickersham Park. The man looked a bit like the composite sketch, the shop owner conceded, but he said the man was an alcoholic, and he didn't believe him to be capable of such a crime.

As Polly's family spoke to the press, some reporters recognized a white-haired, bespectacled man in the room. It was David Collins, the father of Kevin Collins, one of the most prominent kidnapping victims in the Bay Area. Collins had come to Petaluma to support Marc and Eve as soon as he'd heard the news. No one could understand this hell they were in like someone who had gone through it.

Kevin Collins, a seventy-pound fourth grader, had been missing for nine years now. He was last seen on February 10, 1984, as he waited for the bus after basketball practice in San Francisco's Haight-Ashbury District. San Francisco police searched around the clock with hundreds of volunteers who circulated 100,000 posters nationwide. A $10,000 reward was offered for his return. *Newsweek* featured ten-year-old Kevin on the cover for a March 1984 story called "Stolen Children," his haunting eyes hovering above an equally haunting caption: *This child could be yours.*

Kevin's freckle-faced image became a national icon for missing kids. His gap-toothed smile was one of the first to appear on milk cartons featuring missing children, a tradition started by a dairy farmer who envisioned an unorthodox way to spread the word nationwide. The appearance of "Missing" posters and milk carton kids became a cultural motif of the era. A poster with Kevin's face appeared in two 1984 movies: *The Terminator* and *A Nightmare on Elm Street*. He was never found.

When Kevin vanished in 1984, *Newsweek* reported that 1.8 million children a year were going missing, but didn't cite the source of the statistic, further adding to the general confusion and panic about how common abductions actually were. There was no uniform set of criteria for defining who counted as a "missing child," and sociologists such as Joel Best at the University of Delaware have written extensively on the statistical inconsistencies of what came to be known as "the missing child movement." The number of true stranger abductions are particularly poorly quantified, with estimates ranging from 6,000 to 50,000 cases. "Only a few cases are solved," *Newsweek* noted. "Even fewer stranger-abducted children are recovered alive."

Nine years later, the kidnapping data was sharper and a bit more hopeful. Of the cases reported to NCMEC in 1993, there were seventy-three nonfamily abductions in which a child was missing for more than twenty-four hours and fifteen nonfamily abductions in which the child was recovered more than fifty miles from the location of their abduction.

Kevin's disappearance inspired a heroic volume of police work and public support. Two thousand people who lived along Kevin's bus route home were questioned, and tips poured in. Investigators found themselves drowning in false leads. The case had gone cold.

As with many parents of kidnapped children who are killed or never found, Kevin's parents, David and Ann Deasy Collins, coped with their loss by helping others. In 1984, they created the Kevin Collins Foundation to support the families of other missing kids. David, who was a nursing student and truck driver when his son disappeared, became the only paid employee on staff. The work came with meaning, but also great pain. In 1986, two years after its founding, Kevin's mother left the foundation. She and David eventually divorced. But David continued the work, and over the previous nine years he had helped 203 families going through the horror he knew. "I will keep helping parents," David Collins said, "because I know what it's like."

David Collins drove to Petaluma as soon as he heard the news about Polly. Empathetic and realistic, he had a calm and guiding presence that Marc Klaas seemed to lean on.

"Right now, he's in information overload," Collins said. "He's scared and he's trying to process everything. He needs to get some rest. He needs to slow down and let this sink in."

"I'm trying to stay as close to Dave as I can," Marc said. "I think he is the only one here who knows how I feel."

Collins was also a sobering reminder of what could happen. "I'm the realization of the long term," he said later. "I'm the grim reaper. They're hugging me all the time, but I know what they're feeling. They [believe] they can make a difference. But with me, they can't kid themselves."

By MONDAY, PIP printing was too small to contain the one hundred volunteers answering calls, stuffing envelopes, and accepting donations ranging from food to fax machines. With help from the Kevin Collins Foundation and San Jose–based Vanished Children's Alliance, the search center was moved to a larger headquarters in an abandoned storefront at 136 Kentucky Street that would, years later, become Copperfield's Books.

The volunteer effort had a name—the Polly Klaas Search Center—

and was operating increasingly like a nonprofit organization. Donations were initially routed through Petaluma Junior High, but soon the Polly Hannah Klaas Foundation Fund was set up at Great Western Bank to accept donations, which were pouring in.

The new center buzzed with the frenetic urgency of a political campaign, and some said it "had the look of an established war room." Phones rang incessantly as tips and leads were called in to two hotlines: 1-800-587-HELP and 1-800-21POLLY. The doors opened at nine a.m. every morning, and the center stayed elbow-to-elbow crowded until the doors closed at nine p.m.

The media gravitated to the volunteers. In the absence of useful leads or a viable suspect, the volunteers offered a powerful human interest story, a portrait of a community galvanized by a crisis. The volunteers showed hope manifesting in action.

"I've got twenty from a junior college, I have the carpenter's local in here with their wives," Joanne Gardner told the Associated Press. "I have grandparents, I have bikers, I have doctors."

As a music video director, Gardner was a skilled and nuanced storyteller. She knew how to use details and imagery to conjure emotion. On a grander scale, she understood the symbiotic relationship between the volunteers, the media, and the investigation. The volunteers would capture the media's interest. The media coverage would keep volunteers engaged. Both would generate tips that could advance the investigation.

Her first press release, written the day she walked into PIP printing, had generated an Associated Press story that was syndicated by local newspapers from Kansas to West Virginia, North Dakota to Pennsylvania. "This wasn't a faceless, nameless crime," Gardner told the AP. "This wasn't somebody that was in a phone booth in North Hollywood late at night. This was a girl who was very safe at home playing with two girlfriends. Somebody came into the safety of her house and took her. That's what galvanized everybody."

Gardner wanted readers and viewers across the country to see Polly not as a statistic, but as a child who reminded everyone of a daughter, a niece, a grandchild, or a cousin. She wanted everyone to look at Polly's face and think: That could be *my* kid. She became a press release machine, generating a fresh angle every day. She would walk through the volunteer center and think, *What can we give them today?*

One of the volunteers answering phones was Jenni Thompson, a twenty-two-year-old college student living in Rohnert Park, about ten miles north of Petaluma. When she saw Polly's face on the news, Jenni leaned in, her face inches from the TV, drawn by emotions she couldn't explain—"like I needed to be close." A senior at Sonoma State, Jenni was majoring in English and hoped to become a junior high teacher, because kids Polly's age were "still fun and at that age where you can influence them and point them in the right direction." She would stare at Polly's face on the flyer, willing the photograph to whisper a clue that might help them find Polly.

Jenni Thompson had grown up in a small agricultural town. She didn't understand how a little girl could just vanish. She felt called to act. *We can find her. We have to. We can bring her home.*

She drove to Petaluma with a friend and signed in at the volunteer desk.

"Do you want to answer the phone?" the volunteer coordinator asked her.

"Sure."

Jenni joined a group of volunteers operating the phone banks. The hotlines were open twelve hours a day, and the phones rang steadily. Working in shifts, they answered calls and scribbled down tips, which were shuttled to the Petaluma PD and assigned to investigative teams.

Less than an hour into her shift, Jenni answered the phone, and a caller asked for Kevin Collins. She held the receiver aside and addressed the bustling room:

"Somebody's asking for Kevin Collins. Is there a Kevin Collins here?"

The room instantly fell silent. David Collins, Kevin's father, just happened to be at the volunteer center. Jenni felt the heat of a hundred stares as she handed him the phone.

The prank call was creepy, and it frightened her. She asked to be taken off the phones, to stuff envelopes instead. She mailed a batch of flyers to her sister, who put them up all over Fresno.

Jenni Thompson was one of thousands of volunteers compelled by

Polly's story. Many of them would be forever changed by the experience. But perhaps no other volunteer would see their future pivot as profoundly. She would go on to join the FBI, find missing children, change laws. Three decades from this moment, Jenni Thompson would reflect on the course of her life and say:

"It was all because of Polly."

chapter twelve

AMERICA'S MOST WANTED

ᶜᵒ

Tuesday, October 5, 9 p.m.—Volunteer Center

TUESDAY EVENING, JUST BEFORE NINE P.M., TWO DOZEN VOLUNTEERS PUT DOWN the phones and flyers and gathered around a small TV. A dramatic opening theme song filled the volunteer center, followed by a nationally famous deep voice.

Good evening from Washington. I'm John Walsh, and this is America's Most Wanted.

America's Most Wanted was the centerpiece of John Walsh's crusade to avenge the kidnapping and murder of his own son. In 1981, six-year-old Adam Walsh disappeared from a Sears store in Hollywood, Florida, while his mother was shopping a few feet away. As John and Revé Walsh searched for Adam, they learned how ill-equipped law enforcement agencies were to find and save missing children: More than 80 percent of the 320 police departments in Florida were unaware that Adam was missing. Two weeks after Adam vanished, as the couple prepared to publicize his disappearance on *Good Morning America*, they got a call from the cops. Adam's severed head had been found in a drainage canal beside the Florida Turnpike.

As a means of moving forward from this devastating loss, Walsh channeled his anger and grief into actions to help missing kids. He

94

lobbied for the 1982 Missing Children Act, which created a nationwide computerized database of missing children and authorized the FBI to get involved immediately in a child abduction. He and Revé created the National Center for Missing and Exploited Children, which strengthened the collaboration between government and law enforcement agencies. Established by Congress in 1984 and funded by the Department of Justice, NCMEC (pronounced "neck-meck") was a resource for parents, law enforcement agencies, and communities, handling cases of missing or exploited kids from birth through age twenty. Today, it remains the biggest national clearinghouse for information on missing children and resources to help bring them home.

On October 10, 1983, *Adam*, the made-for-TV movie about Adam Walsh, debuted on NBC. At the end of the show, the pictures and names of fifty-five kids were displayed to an audience of 40 million, along with a toll-free number. For three days, more than a hundred calls per hour came in. Thirteen of these kids were located and reunited with their families. *Adam* became one of the highest-rated made-for-TV movies ever; it was rebroadcast twice, and each time, more kids were recovered. In 1986, the sequel, *Adam: His Song Continues*, aired, and Walsh subsequently made a documentary that taught parents how to keep their children safe.

Walsh's advocacy work and notoriety led to his selection as the host of *America's Most Wanted*, a half-hour television show that invited the public to help investigators hunt perpetrators of violent crimes. In February 1988, the first episode aired in a handful of major American cities. Within four days, a fugitive on the FBI's Most Wanted list was captured. Walsh became a celebrity, and his show proved that widespread media coverage was a valuable tool to generate leads and help investigators solve crimes. In the five and a half years that had passed since the show's debut, more than 40 percent of the 670 criminals profiled by John Walsh had been caught—an average of one per show. "That beats most police departments' records at catching bad guys," noted the *San Francisco Examiner*. The week before Walsh arrived in Petaluma, the show caught three fugitives in one day—a record. Two were suspected murderers.

Along with *Unsolved Mysteries*, which debuted in 1987, *America's Most*

Wanted was among the first television shows to harness the crime-fighting power of the media. Every Tuesday, Walsh reached an audience of 15 million viewers and generated 3,000 to 4,000 phone calls per show from people offering tips. Some critics denounced the show's dramatic reenactments as sensationalistic and garish. But then, TV news shows also capitalized on the sensationalism of violent crimes. While the news could leave viewers in helpless despair, *America's Most Wanted* empowered its audience members to do something about it. It turned the nation into "one big Crime Watch neighborhood," as the *San Francisco Examiner* put it.

"I figured something out early," Walsh said. "Rather than fighting the media, I joined the media. I became more successful in the media than most people I know. And you know what? I use the media because every week I see the face of a little child who's missing and a desperate set of parents, and I give them much better odds than I ever had at getting my son back."

America's Most Wanted offered two things Walsh knew to be critical: speed and reach. The more time elapsed, the farther a kidnapper could flee with a victim. So the film crew acted quickly, arriving in Petaluma two days after Polly's kidnapping, one day after being notified. The reach of prime-time TV ensured that no matter how far the kidnapper ran, millions of eyes would be watching.

Now, two days after the taping, the show was airing. Tonight's show was a special on missing children, and the centerpiece was a thirteen-minute segment on Polly Klaas. In the volunteer center, where rows of chairs had been set up near a small TV, Marc and Eve sat close, but not together. Eve, wearing slacks and a button-down shirt, sat quietly, holding hands with Annie, wrapped in a blanket and curled up in a chair beside her. In the row of chairs behind them, Marc and his father, Joe Klaas, watched intensely.

On the show, Kate and Gillian, identified only by their first names, spoke publicly for the first time since Polly's abduction. Kate wore a pink T-shirt and hugged a white teddy bear to her chest, bangs swept to one side of her forehead. Gillian wore a white turtleneck under a dark navy sweater, dark brown hair cropped in a chin-length bob.

Standing side by side on a sailboat docked in the Petaluma River, the twelve-year-olds squinted into the sun and carried themselves with a poise that seemed incongruous with their age. Gillian's voice was softer and younger, but her delivery was calm and articulate. Kate's voice had an adamant edge that seemed to dare anyone to question her veracity. Taking turns, they told the story of what happened.

In a brief home video clip featured in the segment, Polly flitted across a community stage in a play, brown eyes shining, chestnut curls bouncing, a lifetime of dreams ahead of her. It was painful to watch, but also hopeful, because it meant Polly's story had gone national.

"I really hope something can come of this," Marc told a local reporter after the show. "It's been in my thoughts that they will show this show and two hours later, we'll have Polly back, or we'll know where Polly is. I just—I've kind of been putting all my cards on this hand."

Investigators were hopeful too. Petaluma detective Andy Mazzanti had flown to Washington, DC, to be a resource for the phone banks. If a caller claimed to be the kidnapper or offered a questionable tip, he had intimate knowledge of the case and could vet the caller's authenticity.

Some worried that all the publicity could endanger a missing child. Neil Hartman, an assistant clinical professor of psychiatry at UCLA, said the impact of the publicity depended largely on the offender's personality. "It could cause one type of person to panic and thus endanger the victim," he told the *San Francisco Examiner*. Debra Glasser, acting director of the Los Angeles Police Department's Behavioral Science Service section said, "It can go either way. If they like media attention, it could cause them not to release the child." Or it could incite them to bring the child back, because that too would cause attention.

Ernie Allen, president of NCMEC, voiced another perspective. "We're making it more difficult to disappear, far more difficult to outrun the data and the images." He noted a case of an eleven-year-old girl who was kidnapped in a small town on the Gulf Coast of Florida and driven to Alabama. When the kidnapper saw the child on TV, he drove her back to Florida. "There's no question that it maximizes the prospect of her recovery," he told the *Examiner*. "I'm not aware of any case where we could point to it as a direct causative effect of a child being harmed."

America's Most Wanted recharged the investigation at a moment when tips had started to dwindle from a hundred to fifty a day. After the show, investigators began receiving 250 to 350 a day. The majority of the callers mentioned watching the show.

"The publicity has had tremendous impact on the investigation," said Petaluma PD spokesman Mike Kerns. "We don't have much information on the suspect, his motive, his intent. And we have no specific information about a possible location or destination. So we can't overlook any information. We are relying on the public to help us."

FBI spokesman Rick Smith agreed. "The more publicity, the better."

⌒⌒⌒

LARRY MAGID, A tech reporter for the *Los Angeles Times*, was driving south on Highway 101 through the heart of Silicon Valley when the news of Polly's abduction came across the radio of his Volvo. He was headed to San Jose to meet with NetCom, a five-year-old company that provided dial-up access to the World Wide Web. But when he heard about the volunteer effort, he felt a strong impulse to bail on his meeting and join the search. He was a seasoned journalist, maybe even a little jaded, but Polly made him think of his own eleven-year-old daughter. Magid considered pulling off at the nearest exit, turning around, and driving north through San Fransisco, across the Golden Gate Bridge, all the way to Petaluma. Then he realized: *I can do that from here.*

In the middle of writing a book called *Cruising Online: Larry Magid's Guide to the New Digital Highways*, he was an early adopter of the technology he covered. He owned the latest modem, which gave him access to "the information superhighway." As a journalist, he had professional relationships with America Online, CompuServe, and Prodigy—three internet service providers that published his syndicated column. He knew how to post on all the electronic bulletin boards. Sure, he could drive a couple hours north and join the volunteers passing out paper flyers. But he possessed the skills and equipment to distribute them online—all the way to China.

Still driving south on the 101, Magid picked up his cell phone and called the volunteer center in Petaluma. Whoever answered the phone was unfamiliar with the term "email," so he was handed off to a volunteer named Gary Judd, an unemployed computer salesman who was tapping his own personal network to get computers donated to the search center. Gary Judd also happened to own a scanner. He scanned a photo of Polly Klaas and the composite sketch and emailed them to Larry Magid. It probably took an hour to transmit over pre-broadband connections, but both files arrived intact. Larry Magid created a digital poster that could be distributed online. This was well before social media and user-generated content, so he had to convince his contacts at AOL, Prodigy, and CompuServe to post the flyer. They did—in a prominent location.

"Once it gets into the bulletin boards, it's like a good virus," Magid said. "It proliferates." While *America's Most Wanted* told Polly's story to a national audience of 15 million Americans, the internet made it global, available to another 15 million people. "What's unprecedented," Magid said, "is that this technology isn't just in the hands of police agencies, but average citizens." It was, as far as he knew, the first time a missing person flyer had been transmitted digitally. As he predicted, it proliferated until 8 million Polly Klaas flyers had been transmitted, printed, and posted around the world.

Like search center volunteer Jenni Thompson, who went on to become one of the nation's leading experts in child abductions, Larry Magid couldn't predict how Polly Klaas would change the course of his life. At COMDEX, a computer industry trade show in Las Vegas, he would be guest chef at a chili cookoff. That's how he would meet Ernie Allen, head of the National Center for Missing and Exploited Children. Magid would become NCMEC's resident expert on internet safety. Working together, Magid and Allen would find new ways of using technology to help missing children and prevent their abduction. They would write a booklet called "Child Safety on the Information Highway." Magid would go on to found SafeKids.com and ConnectSafely.org, two websites dedicated to educating kids and adults about online safety. He would one day work with John Walsh.

༺✦༻

THE DAY AFTER *America's Most Wanted*, Polly's story dominated the entire front page of the *Santa Rosa Press Democrat* and the *Petaluma*

Argus-Courier. But major metro dailies still treated it as a regional story. The *San Francisco Chronicle, San Francisco Examiner,* and *Los Angeles Times* covered the story, but not on the front page.

Publicity not only generated more leads, but also kept the volunteers engaged and energized. More than a thousand volunteers had come out to help so far, and they had distributed more than 1 million flyers. "What we're doing is trying to leapfrog ahead of the abductor," said Bill Rhodes, the PIP printing owner leading the community search. Rhodes had learned, as an ambulance driver, that "safe recovery was determined by the speed of the response."

David Collins echoed that message. "It's important to act fast." When Kevin went missing from the bus stop, hundreds of volunteers tacked posters of his fourth-grade son to telephone poles and storefront windows all over San Francisco. That was in 1981, four years before the debut of *America's Most Wanted.* New tools and methods existed now. Collins had spent years helping families search for their missing children, and he was a realist, but he was also cautiously hopeful.

"There haven't been a lot of children found alive long-term," he said, "though this case isn't long-term yet." He noted that the vast majority of kidnapped kids—even those abducted by strangers—were returned within six days. Today was day six. "The odds are still pretty good that Polly's abductor is going to drop her off or that she's going to get away."

"This is a huge country," he said, standing outside Polly's house on Fourth Street, where the candle still burned in the window. "There are millions and millions of people across the country who have never heard of Polly. Our job is to make as many people aware of her as possible. The plain truth is that there are a lot of issues and a lot of busy people out there.

"To make them interested in Polly, you really have to sell it."

chapter thirteen

THE CELEBRITY

⌒⌒⌒

Tuesday evening, October 5

ONE OF THE 15 MILLION PEOPLE WATCHING *AMERICA'S MOST WANTED* WAS Polly's favorite actress: Winona Ryder. Pale and petite, with smoky eyes and black hair cropped in a boyish pixie, twenty-one-year-old Ryder listened, rapt, as John Walsh described the abduction. At the mention of the town where this crime had taken place, she recoiled, covering her face with her hands.

No, no, no...this can't be happening!

Ryder had been ten years old when she and her family had moved to Petaluma. She had walked its streets and attended its schools. She'd gone to the movies at Petaluma Theater, where her newest film, *The Age of Innocence*, was now on the marquee. That theater had sparked the resurgence of downtown Petaluma.

Watching the clip of Polly flitting across the stage, Ryder felt "a kinship." She had started acting at Polly's age, trying out for school plays and dreaming the same dreams. She was thirteen when she landed her first movie role—as a lovestruck tomboy in the 1986 film *Lucas*—and changed her last name from Horowitz to Ryder. She had survived the usual adolescent horrors: gossipy cliques and math exams and dreaded PE classes. Just like Polly.

Maybe she could help her.

In a hotel lobby in Los Angeles, Ryder called the volunteer center. Someone handed the phone to Joanne Gardner, who would never forget how Ryder was sobbing. They spent the next hour and a half on the phone.

"What can I do?" Ryder asked.

"Come on up," Gardner said. "We could absolutely use you."

Two days later, Ryder came home to Petaluma. Wearing jeans and a purple ribbon pinned onto her plain white T-shirt, she slipped through the back door of the volunteer center. She came alone, without handlers or bodyguards, and stayed at her mother's house. Maybe it was because she was so tiny and understated, or maybe it was the rush to get 200,000 flyers in the mail by day's end, but the volunteers hardly noticed her. Ryder walked through their midst in a rare moment of near invisibility, drinking in the hopeful energy and feeling a swell of pride. This was how it should be.*

"I hope that every child could have this who is in danger," she told a reporter walking next to her. "I'm just a concerned citizen wanting to help."

She was also a famous movie star, which put her in a unique position to help. Ryder called a meeting with Petaluma police and the FBI to offer a $1 million reward for Polly's safe return. Investigators balked at first, saying that $1 million was too much—that kind of money would trigger an avalanche of con artists and false leads. The reward was reduced to $200,000, an amount they hoped would motivate someone who knew something but was reluctant to come forward. Even the kidnapper himself. Polly's family agreed that he could keep the money if he just brought Polly home.

After arriving in Petaluma, Ryder paid a visit to Eve, and the two women spent a couple of hours sitting on the gold living room couch and talking. "She and Polly just seem like they are kindred spirits," remarked Eve, who told Ryder she was Polly's favorite actress. "I melted," Ryder said.

On Friday, she visited Petaluma Junior High and spoke to 500 of Polly's classmates gathered in the campus quad.

---

* Though it often wasn't the case for kidnapped kids who were not white or privileged.

"It's really great to be back here," she told them. "I hate the reason I'm back here."

The students had been painting a forty-five-foot banner that read, "Please send Polly home" and "Please let Polly go! P.J.H.S. ♥ U!!" One seventh-grade classmate dipped a wide brush in purple paint and swabbed it into the shape of a heart, thinking about Polly, wondering why it felt like she'd already been gone so long. "You know, really, I have never prayed," she said. "But I pray to God now."

Ryder joined them in signing the banner before it was raised over Petaluma Boulevard North, the main drag in the heart of downtown.

"I'm here to support all of you," Ryder told Polly's classmates, encouraging them to be hopeful. "She seems really smart. Everything I've heard about her is she's smart, so maybe she can outsmart some people out there."

"Thanks, Winona!" someone yelled. Someone else screamed: "We love you!" A young boy ran up to hug her.

ACROSS TOWN, AT Polly's house, ERT member David Alford arrived to do another evidence sweep and talk again with Eve. Had Polly carried house keys, and if so, had any of them gone missing? Polly used to have a front door key, Eve said, on a keychain attached to a glitter-filled sphere the size of a golf ball. Polly had lost it from her backpack in April or May. She had access to another house key, though, this one on a pink plastic spiral bracelet. That key was still hanging on the coat rack. Did they even have a key to the back door? Eve wasn't sure.

The more she thought about it, the more certain Eve felt that Polly had been in and out of the back door on the afternoon of the kidnapping. Polly had vacuumed her room for the sleepover, and when she put the vacuum cleaner back on the service porch, she had probably forgotten to lock the door between the service porch and the kitchen. On the other hand, that door also might have been unlocked because Annie liked to wander out back to visit Aaron and Chelle in the cottage. No way to be sure.

As requested, Eve hadn't vacuumed the living room or family room since the night of the kidnapping. She wondered if it was all right to do so now. She'd put a new bag in, save the old one, save the new one, save every hair and bit of dust that might turn out to be evidence. Alford told her that would be fine.

He walked slowly through the house, taking in Polly's habitat, looking for evidence that might have been missed and clues about the girl who lived here. In his notebook he jotted down an inventory, which might be of use to the FBI profiler. Even the smallest details could help paint a portrait of the victim, and a profile of the victim could be used inferentially to paint a portrait of the kidnapper.

Alford studied the bookshelf in the family room: *Jane Eyre, A Room with a View, Slouching Towards Bethlehem, I Know Why the Caged Bird Sings. The Diary of Anne Frank.* In Polly's room, children's classics: *Gulliver's Travels. Nancy Drew. Grimm's Fairy Tales. Harriet the Spy.* Eve pulled out three teen horror novels by R. L. Stine, one of Polly's favorite writers. She loved reading and always had books on hold at the Sonoma County Library.

As Alford looked around Polly's room, Annie came in and started talking to him. He asked her if Polly had a secret place in the house, a spot where she liked to hide things. Annie pointed to a large box in the corner of the room they shared, Polly's costume box. She was not allowed to get into it. Alford opened the box and pulled out a pair of high heels, a white dress, and a long, shimmering white wig. It was Polly's "Jackie Frost" costume, Annie explained, a benevolent character that Polly would assume, which Annie found delightfully entertaining. She showed him Polly's collection of troll dolls, with their impish grins and brightly colored shocks of hair. She plucked a book from a shelf and handed it to him: *Daughters of Eve*, by Lois Duncan.

Alford collected that as evidence along with a copy of *Kidnapped!* by Edward Packard—a choose-your-own-adventure book—and an address book marked with Polly's name. By the time he left the house a few minutes after noon, Eve had already gone to attend the press conference with Ryder. Eve's husband, Allan Nichol, had stayed at the house.

As Alford was ready to leave, Allan Nichol approached him to offer a few ideas. From what he knew about the case, Allan believed the kidnapper to be a blue-collar worker, maybe a father who had lost his own twelve-year-old daughter in a custody dispute, getting by on a small income, keeping Polly as if she were his own. He imagined them staying in some old rundown motel converted into a monthly rental.

Allan thought of a guy they should talk to, a man he thought was infatuated with Eve. He appeared at the volunteer center just about every day. He knew Eve's favorite flowers—gardenias—and sent them to her frequently. Allan didn't have any details about how this man might be connected to the crime, but thought he ought to be interviewed. (It would lead to another dead end.)

Alford then visited Marc Klaas's condo in Sausalito, where Polly had her own room. Here too her bookshelf was lined with classic American tales: *Little House on the Prairie, Beauty and the Beast, The Wizard of Oz.* And her favorite book: Louisa May Alcott's *Little Women.* Her videotape collection favored fairy tales with happy endings: *The Little Mermaid, Cinderella, Sleeping Beauty, E.T.,* and *Alf.* She had subscriptions to *World* and *Cricket* magazines. Her small assortment of CDs showed her taste in music ran a little older: Kenny G, Mariah Carey, and the soundtracks to *Last of the Mohicans* and *Sleepless in Seattle.* Alford noted her clothes—dresses in hues of pink and yellow, and a blue-and-white-patterned jumper—and other belongings: a pamphlet of fifty magic tricks, a book on Yosemite trails, a white photo album filled with snapshots of family trips.

Alford took photographs, documenting Polly's surroundings. The only item he collected as evidence was a school paper Polly had written about a trip to Washington, DC.

⌒⌒⌒

By MIDDAY, A flock of reporters and camera crews had amassed outside Petaluma Police Department for the press conference. Wearing barely any makeup, Ryder walked out in a dark long-sleeved crew-neck shirt with a purple ribbon pinned over her heart. Five-foot-four and 103 pounds, she looked startlingly tiny between the two large men in dark suits, Petaluma sergeant Mike Kerns and FBI agent Jim Freeman.

"This happened in the community I was raised in," she told the cameras, saying she felt compelled to help "because of the connection I felt with Polly."

They had scripted her lines beforehand, and she delivered them with that signature waver in her voice, that luminous vulnerability that would make her an emblem of the decade. She embodied the ethos of Generation X—wary of privilege and money and fame—but she also knew these were precisely the tools she could use to keep Polly in the headlines.

"I just felt that a person in my position, if I could help at all, I should," she said. "I feel fortunate I'm in a position to fund this reward."

The media seemed to respect this. They didn't pound her with questions, grill her about policy, or stalk her like paparazzi. She was here with no entourage, no bodyguards, no handlers. She just wanted to help bring Polly home.

"That's my biggest wish right now," she said, "to meet her in person and to hug her."

Orchestrating this moment was Joanne Gardner, the volunteer media coordinator who spoke to Ryder when she first called the Polly Klaas center. Gardner had always been a fan of Ryder's work, but she was astonished by the young actress's grasp of her role in this situation. "She absolutely knew the power of her presence," Gardner said. "She knew what was going to happen and that the news media would show up if she was there. She doesn't like that—she's very private—but she said, *I can do this.*"

As a self-professed overthinker, Ryder worried that people would see her involvement as an attempt to grab favorable headlines and photo ops. But this was clearly something that resonated deeply and personally. As a child, she had been haunted by real-life kidnappings that would cause her to "lie in bed and be scared." Around Polly's age, she asked to have bars put on her windows because a serial killer was rumored to be in northern California. Now, with Polly, she felt a sense of outrage that inspired her to act with conviction, which meant answering phones and searching on foot in addition to offering a reward. This wasn't a "cause" but a moral duty. "When something like this happens to a child," she said, "the whole world should stand still."

As predicted, Ryder's publicity triggered a new surge of media interest, which in turn caused another influx of possible leads from the public. It came at just the right moment, as tips from the airing of *America's*

Most Wanted had started to wane. After Ryder's $200,000 reward made national headlines, the volume of calls and tips threatened to overwhelm the tip lines.

Ryder's influence set into motion one other important connection that would have Polly's image appearing over and over on MTV.

A few months earlier Ryder had broken off her engagement with actor Johnny Depp, who famously had "Winona Forever"* tattooed on his upper arm. Their three-year relationship was over, and Ryder was now dating Dave Pirner, the lead singer of the alternative rock band Soul Asylum, whom she had met at the band's MTV Unplugged concert in the spring.

Pirner had recently written a new song called "Runaway Train." A haunting, acoustic ballad, it was a softer, melancholy departure from the electrified grunge that the band was typically known for. It was a song that "just kind of rolled off my brain," said Pirner, who'd had the melody in his head for years, but wrote the lyrics in one intense sitting. The song had been released in June 1993—just three months before Polly's kidnapping—and it was now in heavy rotation on MTV and radio stations nationwide. It would peak at number five on the Billboard Top 100 and win a Grammy for best rock song.

The lyrics were inspired by Pirner's plunge into clinical depression. But the music video transformed "Runaway Train" into a different cultural phenomenon: a vehicle for locating missing kids and teens. The concept came from music video director Tony Kaye, after he noticed a missing poster. It gave him the idea of using the video to showcase runaways and missing kids, with the hope that the national exposure would help bring them home.

As the opening chords of the song rang out, the video flashed a sobering statistic: *There are over one million lost youth on the streets of America.* Between cuts of the band and the perpetually bed-headed Pirner, the video flashed the faces and names of thirty-six missing kids and teenagers, supplied by the National Center for Missing and Exploited Children. It closed with a 1-800 hotline.

---

* Depp later had it changed to read "Wino Forever."

When his girlfriend landed in Petaluma to get involved in the Polly Klaas search, Pirner made arrangements to add Polly's photo to the "Runaway Train" video, where it would reach a worldwide audience on cable.

The impact of the video surprised almost everyone, including the band. Twenty-one of the thirty-six children featured in the video were ultimately found. "I couldn't believe you could actually transcend the music video and have it cross over into real life," Pirner said. "It was a really cool experience to realize that wow, there is potential for entertainment to have a positive effect on the real world." Different versions of the video—with different missing kids—were aired in the UK and Australia. The videos even located several runaways who didn't want to be found. "You ruined my life," said one girl, who had run off with her boyfriend and was mortified to see her face on MTV.

In 2018, the twenty-fifth anniversary of the "Runaway Train" video, three contemporary musicians got together to do a remake. Jamie N Commons, Skylar Grey, and Gallant teamed up with NCMEC to produce a music video that featured a new generation of missing kids and a modern pop spin on the song. Like the original, the remake began with a statistic: Each year, there are more than 400,000 reports of missing children in the US.

By this time, MTV had been replaced by YouTube as the primary viewing platform for music videos, which could now be seen by a global audience. And new geo-targeting technology made the content hyper-local. When viewed on the Runaway Train 25 website, the set of missing kids flashing across the screen was specific to each viewer's geographic location.

Pirner, now fifty-four, is still the front man for Soul Asylum. He continued to be astonished at the impact this video concept had made in 1993, and was making again, twenty-five years later. "It really surprised me that it was as effective as it was," Dave Pirner told *Billboard*. "Katie Couric was asking me about runaway children. It was just a direction that was very pleasing to me, because the rock videos were just getting more and more shallow, if you will. So I wanted to do something that had an impact in the real world. And it did."

Pirner stayed involved with NCMEC for many years. Ryder sat on the board of the Polly Klaas Foundation and remained close with Polly's family.

PART II

THE INVESTIGATIVE MACHINE

chapter fourteen

THE POLYGRAPHER

IN THE PARKING LOT OF PETALUMA PD, MARC KLAAS SLOUCHED AGAINST HIS car, legs weak, wanting to curl up inside his grief. He'd been called to the station by police, and he was bracing for bad news. Surely they were going to tell him they had found Polly—dead. The faces gathering around him were a blur. Then one of them leaned in and cut through the fog.

"You better get your act together," said Agent Eddie Freyer, his voice stern but not unkind. "This girl needs you to be there for her."

Marc nodded, pulled it together.

Maybe she's still somewhere out there.

Right then and there in the parking lot, the fear and anguish roiling inside him transmuted into something else, something that looked like anger but felt like purpose. He straightened up and walked into the station. He faced the TV cameras and spoke. From that moment on, he would be ready for any interview. He would become a spokesman, not only for Polly, but for other missing kids and crimes against children.

Two days after Polly's abduction, President Bill Clinton had hosted a televised town hall meeting for a statewide audience. Marc had joined via satellite hookup through KRON, a San Francisco station. He had planned to ask the president a question about child welfare, but the clock had run out. So Marc simply had held up a photo of Polly and the composite sketch. California would at least see her face—and his.

Grief and anger—and maybe the unrelenting spotlight too—would forge a new Marc Klaas, a macabre celebrity anointed with a power that he didn't have before. He had been the owner of a rental car franchise in the Fairmont Hotel. That job felt meaningless now, and he would never again go back to it. Finding his daughter, keeping her story alive in the news, making sure no one ever forgot her, became his new full-time job. His identity. His ultimate reason for being.

Marc's presence in the media grew into something people talked about, first in hushed tones, and months later openly. Many people took pity on him, this father who was out of his mind with grief, his every day a living nightmare. Others found it unsettling, the way he seemed to crave the cameras and how the cameras exploited him. More than a few volunteers worried that Marc was feeding off the attention, making the story a bit too much about Marc. Was he trying to make this a career? Was he trying to become the next John Walsh?

After the prank call from someone pretending to be Polly, Eddie Freyer had ordered a trap-trace on Marc's phone in Sausalito. He and everyone else was hoping for a call from Polly, or at least for a ransom call. A ransom call would suggest a motive—and a reason to keep Polly alive. A motive might lead to a suspect. Now, a week into the investigation, they had nothing.

"Unfortunately, there have not been any new breaks at all," Petaluma sergeant Mike Kerns told the press. "We've received no phone calls and no ransom notes."

Tips were pouring in from the hotlines and volunteer searchers. Many believed they had seen a man who matched the police sketch on the flyer. More than a few said they saw Marc Klaas on the news and believed he was involved.

Marc and his father, Joe Klaas, dismissed the rumors. "Usually the father is the prime suspect," Polly's grandfather said. "But this is no custody case." Marc did his best to stay focused on Polly. "I understand people's doubts and fears, but I don't really care what people think," Marc said. "The only thing that concerns me is the return of my daughter and keeping the story alive."

Investigators did not consider Marc a suspect. The situation lacked the many red flags typically associated with a family abduction. There was no pending divorce. No custody issues. Nothing for the father to gain by taking the child from the mother or by making the child disappear. As Marc had said himself, he and Eve had "a lousy marriage and a great divorce." They had joint custody, and he always paid child support. Polly spent two nights a week with her dad, plus holidays and vacations. They talked on the phone almost every night. Everyone who knew Polly said it was clear how much she adored her father.

Still, he would have to be cleared through a polygraph, a process that any father in his position would dread.

⌒⌒⌒

SPECIAL AGENT RON Hilley was considered one of the two best polygraphers in the FBI. A soft-spoken, mild-mannered agent from the East Bay, Hilley had been involved with all the major child abduction cases in the Bay Area in recent years. Hilley had arrived in Petaluma on Saturday and re-interviewed one of the girls. In all the kidnappings he'd worked, he had never encountered a situation like this—an offender brazen enough to walk into a house occupied by a parent and abduct a girl in full view of two witnesses. A polygraph could help verify the facts and ameliorate suspicions that the girls were telling stories.

Hilley had been recruited into the discipline by Francis "Frank" Connolly, a celebrated agent chosen by the FBI and Department of Justice for special polygraph assignments in Europe, Asia, and the US. In 1981, Hilley went to the US Army Military Police School in Anniston, Alabama, for a three-month program used to train Secret Service, ATF, and FBI agents (basically everyone but the CIA). The training began with classes in psychology, physiology, and psychophysiology. Trainees learned how to operate the mechanical instruments that recorded continuous physiological reactions in respiration, electrodermal activity (changes in sweating), and cardiovascular activity—all functions controlled by the autonomic nervous system. It was all mechanical in those days, with little pens that scratched out trails of ink on a scrolling sheet of paper, forming charts that looked like multiple earthquake seismographs.

After his training in Anniston, Hilley practiced the craft on his ten-year-old twin daughters. He'd put a five-dollar bill in a Tupperware container and have the girls hide it somewhere in the house. Then, administering a modified polygraph test using only electrodermal sensors, he would try to pinpoint the location of the container. Using the same logical approach that he might use to question a murderer about where he hid the body, he'd ask them a series of questions that winnowed down the possibilities. *Is it upstairs? Is it in the bathroom? Is it in the bottom kitchen drawer?* If he was unsuccessful, the girls got to keep the money.

They never kept the money.

By 1993, the polygraph had been around for more than seventy years. In 1917, a Harvard lawyer and psychologist named William Moulton Marston published a paper that indicated systolic blood pressure could be used to detect deception. (Marston went on to achieve greater fame as a cartoonist and creator of Wonder Woman, whose primary weapon was the Lasso of Truth.) A few years later, in 1921, a Berkeley, California, police officer named John Larson used Marston's findings to create a machine that measured changes in blood pressure and respiration. Larson's protege, Leonarde Keeler, upgraded the machine with devices that measured pulse and palm sweat. Keeler named it the polygraph, because it charted multiple measurements at once.

A modern polygraph instrument—like the one Ron Hilley used—records the same physiological functions. Two pneumatic tubes are placed around the subject's chest and stomach to detect changes in breathing patterns (decrease in amplitude, slowing respiration rate, and baseline arousal and return). Electrode sensors are attached to two fingertips or the palm to measure electrodermal activity (the skin's electrical conductivity resulting from changes in sweating). A blood pressure cuff is placed around the biceps to collect cardiovascular activity (changes in relative blood pressure, pulse rate, and pulse amplitude).

A formal polygraph session can take two to four hours and includes three phases: a pre-test, in-test data collection, and a post-test. During the pre-test, Hilley meets the examinee, establishes rapport, explains the purpose of the test, describes the instruments and procedure, and has the subject sign a consent form. He discusses the case with the interviewee to establish their background and narrative, then creates the questions for the test. The examinee practices those questions— answering "yes" or "no"—to ensure the questions are understood. In order to pass the test, they must be truthful to *every* question.

During the in-test phase—data collection—the subject sits on a sensor pad to detect movement during the test (which could potentially distort the tracings or disturb the sensor components). The next step is an "acquaintance test," in which the examinee is asked to lie about something trivial, such as a number. The purpose is to make sure the equipment is adjusted and working properly, the examinee is comfortable, and the charts are of sufficient quality to continue. It also gives the person a chance to acclimate to the testing process and ask questions. The test questions are practiced again to ensure the subject is comfortable and certain about their answers. The questions are asked at least three times, with a short break between each asking.

In the post-test phase, the examiner evaluates the polygraph data by numerical scoring and determines whether the result is truthful, deceptive, or inconclusive. If the result is deceptive, the examiner may try to transition into an interrogation.

A confrontational approach might be: "Clearly you're lying" or "You and I both know you stole the money." Hilley preferred a softer approach. "You're not passing, so there's something you're not telling me. If you tell me, we can do a retest and you'll pass." Sometimes it was a matter of tweaking a question for greater specificity. "If I ask you a question, and you have doubts about it, tell me and we'll change the question."

In the early days of the polygraph, reactions were explained as a result of the autonomic nervous system response involved in "fight or flight." For example, if a rattlesnake crosses your path, your autonomic nervous system reacts before you can even think "Rattlesnake!" and prepares you instantly to react. Your adrenaline surges so you're ready to fight or flee. Your eyes dilate so you can see farther. Your blood pressure spikes and your breathing might change, because you need to get more oxygenated blood to your muscles. Your capillaries constrict on the surface of your skin, so if you're cut you won't bleed as much. Your blood supply is rerouted from the digestive system to limbs that need to move. Your fingers sweat, because moisture affords a better grip.

Early theories attributed these reactions to the fear of getting caught. Current theory suggests that reactions to stimuli (questions) on a polygraph test involve cognition, emotion, and behavioral conditioning. It is not known which of these factors causes a specific reaction, but one or a combination are believed to be involved. Cognitive-emotional factors suggest that someone lying would experience greater emotion (such as fear or anxiety, but we can't know for sure which emotion) and more cognitive effort. Behavioral conditioning (memory) involves a person lying about something they remember doing. Overall, a truthful person would experience fewer cognitive and emotional issues. If you were asked, "Did you rob the bank in San Francisco on Tuesday?" and you had, in fact, done exactly that, in the split-second before you could answer, your brain would recall the bank, the planning, the look on the teller's face. The greater the "cognitive load"—the more processing occurring in your racing mind—the more your autonomic nervous system response will betray you.

Experts say the key to precision is the polygraph administrator's ability to formulate the right questions. Good questions are specific and unambiguous.

There were different types of polygraph tests, and each called for specific techniques and questions. One commonly used by the FBI was the Comparison Question Test. It addressed a specific issue or event with two types of questions: *relevant* questions and *comparison* questions. An example of a relevant question might be: Did you rob the bank? Did you rob the bank on Saturday? A comparison question might be: Before this year, did you ever steal anything? Prior to this year, did you ever steal anything from a business? The relevant question is very specific. The comparison question addresses the same issue (stealing) in a much broader way.

Changes in reactions will be greater on the questions of either

truth-telling or deception to the relevant questions, known as differen-
tial salience. A truthful person will give stronger reactions to the comparison questions. A deceptive person will give stronger reactions to the
relevant questions.

The credibility of the polygraph was called into question almost as
soon as it was invented. In 1923, courts ruled that scientific evidence—
including data obtained through a polygraph—could only be admissible
in court if it was "sufficiently established to have gained general acceptance" in the scientific community. In the decades that followed, the scientific community challenged the polygraph's accuracy. Critics argued
that the technology was created and developed by interrogators, not scientists. In a 2003 study, the National Academy of Sciences reviewed
field studies and found that 10 percent of polygraph tests wrongly implicated truth-tellers or failed to detect deception. The study concluded
that polygraphs performed "well above chance, though well below per-
fection," a reliability too low for the standards of science.

Polygraph tests could accelerate an investigation by ruling out possible but unlikely suspects, allowing investigators to focus limited time
and resources on stronger leads. And when a suspect was identified, a
polygraph test often led to a confession. Polygraphers were evaluated on
their confession rates, and Hilley had one of the best.

One of the abilities that made Hilley such a good polygrapher was
empathy. Some investigators used fear and intimidation to force a confession. Others feigned kindness. Hilley asked questions that opened
the door to a real human connection. He almost always started his pre-
test conversations by asking about family. And then he listened. Often,
that information was the key to figuring out what a subject really cared
about—what meant even more to the person than getting away with the
crime.

Once, before polygraphing a suspect in an embezzlement case,
he asked if the subject had any kids. The man's eyes grew wide as he
gushed, "I had a son this year!" After the man failed the polygraph test,
Hilley asked him, "If your son were sitting in your lap right now, could
you put your arms around him and say you didn't take that money?"
That's when the man confessed. And then he thanked the polygrapher

as if Hilley had done him a favor. In another case, he was interviewing a man who was accused of stabbing a man to death. "If you could do your life over," Hilley asked him, "what would you do differently?" The man started to tear up a bit. "I have only one regret in my life," he said. "And that's my mother. Every time I got out of prison, I promised her I'd never do it again. And I always did." That moment of humility cracked open the door to a criminal confession. The man got two things off his chest.

"You know you've done a good job," Hilley said, "when they fail the test and confess—and then they give you a hug."

To Hilley, polygraphy was not about operating an instrument that spat out results. It was a tool that helped encourage people to tell the truth.

"It's about finding out the truth and clearing people who didn't do it."

A WEEK INTO the investigation, everyone in Polly's family was questioned at length, and all agreed to a polygraph test. A second polygrapher named Ron Homer—the other specialist considered the best in the Bureau—was brought in to help. Eve and Allan Nichol were tested and cleared. But when Marc Klaas came in for his examination on Thursday morning, polygrapher Ron Hilley took one look at him and shook his head. Marc was dead-eyed and doing the zombie shuffle, barely able to lift his feet from the ground. He was clutching the arm of his girlfriend, Violet Cheer. Violet was gently leading him wherever he needed to go.

"Is he sick?" Hilley asked Violet. "Is he on medication?"

In this condition, Marc was untestable—you can't test a subject on heavy medication or drugs or if they're in some sort of psychotic state. A father himself, Hilley imagined the trauma Marc must be feeling. The last thing he wanted to do was to pile on more trauma by asking him if he'd been involved in his daughter's kidnapping. That was Hilley's job, of course, but he could at least delay it until Marc was in better shape.

Eddie Freyer agreed. "Go home, get some rest," he told Marc. "Come back later so we can get you cleared."

When Marc Klaas returned later on that same day, Ron Hilley found him testable, and he passed without any problems. When Ron

Homer polygraphed Eve, he noted some signs of cognitive load. This response was determined to be related to the guilt she'd expressed for taking sleeping pills and being so hard to wake on the night of Polly's abduction. Eve ultimately passed. Allan Nichol and close friends of the family were also tested and cleared.

When asked to test Kate and Gillian, Ron Homer and Ron Hilley felt strong reservations. Neither had ever tested anyone so young, and there wasn't much research supporting the validity of polygraph tests on twelve-year-olds. But they were pressured by investigators fixated on the "minor inconsistencies" between the two girls' accounts. Kate had mentioned seeing a neon yellow bandana around the kidnapper's forehead. Gillian had not. Kate said she heard a screen door slam shut. Gillian had not. And: The screen door on the front porch had remained propped open by two bicycles. It could not have slammed. Investigators wondered if one of the girls was lying. Or not telling the whole truth. They decided to polygraph the girls to verify their stories.*

On October 10, Gillian came to the Santa Rosa PD with her mother. Ron Hilley conducted the polygraph test, in which Gillian confirmed the truthfulness of her prior statements to the FBI. Her story and all the details remained consistent. She recounted the sequence of events leading up to the abduction. She vividly remembered a black duffel bag, about two or three feet long, and a kitchen knife with a brown wooden handle and two metal brads. She did not hear a screen door slam. She did not see a yellow bandana.

Kate, meanwhile, was tested by Ron Homer. Clutching a teddy bear to her chest, she came into the interview room with her father. Homer read the standard consent form, which verified the subject was being polygraphed willingly, not under any coercion. He asked Kate if she understood the meaning of the word "coercion."

"I certainly do," she said. "It means you're not going to force me to do something I don't want to do."

After Kate and her father signed the form, she told her dad he could

---

* Today, the FBI's Child Victim Services program policy states that child victims should not be polygraphed.

leave the room. During the polygraph test, Kate confirmed the details of her prior statements. Like Gillian, she remained consistent on all the details. While Gillian passed her test, Kate's results were deemed "inconclusive." Her charts indicated that some kind of "cognitive load" was occurring. This was a common sign of deception. But it could also occur when the examinee was upset about something else.

After Ron Homer's inconclusive results, Ron Hilley was asked to re-polygraph Kate. It was FBI kidnapping protocol to clear everybody close to Polly. As instructed by his superiors, Hilley pressed her again on the details. Again, her test results were inconclusive.

Case agent Eddie Freyer put more weight on the opinion of the polygrapher than on what the needles said. He asked both Hilley and Homer: "You've got an inconclusive, but what do you really think?" Both said they believed the girls were not lying and that they were not involved in any way with Polly's disappearance.

Investigators deduced an explanation for Kate's test results. The polygraph needles were likely charting the emotional and cognitive conflict she was feeling about the yellow bandana, the slamming door, and the pressure she was feeling. Before the polygraph test, Homer had noticed Kate's behavior: She kept circling the room, clutching her teddy bear, and mumbling something to the effect of *I really messed up this investigation.*

The composite sketch bore a striking resemblance to Detective Dennis Nowicki, the first investigator to interview Kate on the night of Polly's abduction. In boots, he was six-foot-three—the exact height cited on the first flyer—and his grayish beard, deep-set eyes, and dark hair were eerily similar. The resemblance was so apparent that it became an inside joke within the department. *Hey, Dennis, where's your yellow bandana?!*

This was probably not a coincidence. Research in subsequent decades would reveal new information about how trauma affects memory. "Gaps or partial memories are common for anyone who experiences a traumatic situation, whether they're a soldier, a survivor of an accident, or a victim of a sexual assault," wrote Ann Wolbert Burgess, the consultant who worked with profilers John Douglas and Robert Ressler in the FBI's Behavioral Science Unit. "It's how the brain works. With or without the details, the experience never goes away...It's unreasonable to expect someone to have full recall of their trauma."

The first face people see as they're surfacing from unconsciousness or emotional trauma tends to imprint itself on the memory. Often, the first person a victim sees is a police officer. Immediately following her interview with Detective Nowicki, Kate was interviewed by the forensic artist.

Less than forty-eight hours later, on Sunday night, Alice McLean had just put Kate to bed when the phone rang. It was the FBI. They wanted her to bring Kate to the station for yet another interview. Gillian's parents got the same call. The girls were exhausted and emotionally tapped. But they climbed out of bed, got dressed, and came back to help investigators.

Previous interviews had been gentle, if somewhat skeptical. But investigators were desperate to glean any bit of information that the girls might be holding back. Eddie Freyer, Vail Bello, and other experts decided to try a more forceful approach.

Investigators were assigned, some against their will, to "good cop" and "bad cop" roles. The intention was to scare the girls into giving up details they might be withholding. They'd need to "lean on the girls," to push them hard enough that they'd admit this never happened. Detective Dennis Nowicki would interrogate Kate again. FBI profiler Mary Ellen O'Toole would interrogate Gillian.

As instructed, they turned up the heat, framing questions in a way that implied the girls were lying or exaggerating. *If you're lying, that could be a real problem—you could end up in jail.* On top of the threat of juvy, the interviewers poured guilt and shame: *Think about how much pain Polly's parents are in. If you tell us everything, you can make that stop.*

The result: Two weeping twelve-year-old witnesses, and two more highly consistent accounts with absolutely no new details. In all the girls' retellings, the details never changed. There's an adage in law enforcement: *Lies change. Truth always stays the same.*

Five days later, the girls were asked by investigators to reenact the kidnapping in Polly's room, walking through each moment of the crime on videotape.* Two days later, they were asked to take a polygraph test, to press them on the "minor inconsistencies" and make sure they were telling the truth. When Kate's polygraph results were deemed "inconclusive," she was polygraphed again. Kate was told that she had failed, again, to pass the lie-detector test.

This was the final insult. Kate was furious enough with polygrapher Ron Hilley that she wrote him a letter telling him so.

The girls—and their parents—were extremely upset about having their honesty called into question. And rightly so. Each time they retold the truth, they were forced to relive a traumatic moment over and over. They were victims themselves, and yet they'd been treated almost like suspects.

Shortly after Kate's second polygraph, Kate's and Gillian's families decided these girls had been through enough. They told investigators: *We're done.*

---

* More about this later, in Chapter 22.

chapter fifteen

THE FORENSIC ARTIST

Every day in the volunteer center, Joanne Gardner faxed another press release to newsrooms around the country. A press release was the paper equivalent of a cold call, a blast that often got lost in a newsroom's daily slush pile of public relations pitches.

In the second week, around the time Winona Ryder was making news with her $200,000 reward, one of Gardner's faxes landed on the desk of Debbie Alpert, a producer for ABC television. Alpert saw not only a national story but a situation where her personal network might be of use. As she mobilized a film crew for a trip to Petaluma for *The Home Show*, she flipped through her mental Rolodex of experts who could help find Polly.

Her mind instantly flashed on Jeanne Boylan, a thirty-nine-year-old forensic artist from Bend, Oregon. Arrestingly beautiful, with blue eyes and long blond hair, Boylan was a self-taught civilian who had developed a new method of interviewing witnesses to produce a composite sketch. She called it "cognitive interviewing." Alpert had met her about a year ago when Boylan appeared on *The Home Show*.

Though she worked in concert with investigators, Boylan was an independent outsider who pressed against stereotypes and gender bias within the ranks of the law enforcement agencies she worked to assist. When she entered a command center, heads turned and doubters doubted. After her work was done—on cases ranging from the Unabomber to Susan Smith*—she departed trailing a wake of fans, many of whom were the very same cops and agents who doubted her at the beginning.

In hundreds of cases, Boylan had drawn uncannily accurate portraits of crime suspects, piecing together their faces from fraught and fragmented bits of memories teased out of the minds of crime victims and eyewitnesses.

She was known for a unique combination of empathy and artistry, building trust with victims and families by immersing herself in their lives for weeks. The emotional bonds that formed unlocked facts and details that were often repressed deep in the subconscious mind.

Yes, there was an existing sketch. But Kate and Gillian had repeatedly told investigators it wasn't right. And so far, despite the circulation of 3 million flyers emblazoned with that face, no lookalike suspect had emerged, even after ten days and 3,200 leads.

Boylan had seen Polly's story on the news. Who hadn't? She was haunted by Eve's face, those sunken eyes, the "creases that ran to her earlobes, as if tear tracks had already marked her permanently." It felt as if Eve were leaning through the television screen, begging her to help. Boylan had noted the original police composite sketch of the kidnapper with the yellow bandana. It was a good drawing—very good. *Thank God*, she'd thought. *At least there were witnesses who had seen the kidnapper's face.* Then she had turned back to folding laundry. But when Kate and Gillian came on to tell their story, their twelve-year-old voices tugged at her. She couldn't look away.

---

* In October 1994, Susan Smith reported that her two young sons had been kidnapped by a Black man who carjacked her vehicle and drove away with her boys inside. After a nationwide search and investigation, Smith confessed to letting her car roll into a lake with three-year-old Michael and fourteen-month-old Alexander strapped in their car seats. She was convicted of two counts of murder and sentenced to life in prison; she will be eligible for parole in November 2024.

The Forensic Artist | 125

THE ABC NEWS crew picked Boylan up at the San Francisco airport. On the hour-long drive north to Petaluma, field producer Gordon Recht briefed her. The network would cover her airfare in exchange for the right to be the first to show her drawing on the air.

When the van pulled into Petaluma, the streets were thrumming with media trucks, their dish antennas aimed at satellites orbiting invisibly above. Boylan and the crew walked into the volunteer center, where she was impressed by the hive of organized action and optimistic energy. The flyer was everwhere: Polly's dimpled smile, next to the composite sketch of the abductor. Boylan studied the sketch more closely. *It's excellent,* she thought. *But it also looks like it could be anyone.* There was something generic about the face, which lacked any stand-out feature aside from the yellow bandana. Could she improve on it? She wasn't sure.

Something in the written description, however, felt "off." The kidnapper's height: six-foot-three. In the hundreds of cases she'd worked, she couldn't recall seeing a height so specific. It bothered her.

"I'll bet he's a shorter man," Boylan told Recht, the field producer. "I think we're going to need to open that up."

"How do you know?" Recht asked.

Boylan didn't know how she knew. She just knew. She imagined the perspective of a twelve-year-old girl sitting on a bedroom floor, looking up at an unknown intruder grasping a knife. How could he not seem like a giant?

Boylan was led through the volunteer center and introduced to a thin-faced woman slumped in a folding chair. The woman looked up, and Boylan recognized those pleading brown eyes: Polly's mother.

"Thank you for coming," Eve said in a voice hoarse with grief, reaching for Boylan's arm. "I've got to know who has her, who took my baby. We have to see his face. The girls say the sketch is wrong. Did they tell you that?"

Kate's and Gillian's parents had told investigators they needed to disengage in order to heal and return to some semblance of normalcy.

Now, reluctant to expose the girls to further stress, but willing to risk it to help find Polly, they agreed to let Boylan meet with the girls.

Boylan was instructed to wait a half hour for an FBI agent who would take her to meet them. An hour and a half later, she wondered if this person would ever arrive. Then a hush came over the room, and the volunteers parted to make way for two men in dark suits, white shirts, and ties. One of them was ASAC Mark Mershon. His California tan and good looks reminded Boylan of an LA news anchor, "though his clothes and manner said 'agent' all the way." He gestured for Boylan to follow him.

"We need to have a meeting."

The other agent blocked the camera crew from joining them. Boylan followed Mershon away from the crowd, down a staircase into the empty basement, where he spoke in a curt and lowered voice.

"For reasons we are unable to disclose," he said, "you will not be interviewing the girls."

"Excuse me?" Boylan said, confused. "Do you mean—"

"For reasons we are *unable* to disclose," he repeated, louder now, "you will *not* be interviewing the girls. We apologize for the inconvenience. Thank you for coming."

Bewildered, Boylan climbed the stairs and delivered the news to Recht and the crew. They climbed in the van and drove to Polly's house to let Eve know. As they pulled up, Boylan noticed the candle burning in the bay window. When Eve heard that Boylan was being sent home, she put her head in her hands and wept.

"No," she pleaded. "You *have* to stay!"

A white car pulled up to the house, and four men in suits emerged and ran to the windows and doors. They said nothing, but Boylan took it as her cue to depart. She and the news crew returned to the Petaluma PD, where an officer pulled her aside for a reprimand. "If you attempt to interview the girls, you will be arrested for obstruction of justice."

She flew back to Oregon. At home, the light on her answering machine was blinking. She hit play.

"Miss Boylan, this is Agent Mark Mershon of the FBI. We would like you to interview the two eyewitnesses in the Polly Klaas case."

An old message? No.

"Would you please get on the first available flight and return to Petaluma?" he said, perhaps a bit sheepishly. "Thank you. And, oh, by the way, we apologize for the inconvenience."

She later learned there had been a mistake. A few days before her arrival in Petaluma, a reporter had scaled a wall to reach the home of one of the young eyewitnesses to get an interview. In an effort to protect the girls, Polly's family, and the integrity of the case, the feds had issued a blanket warning to the press about talking to the eyewitnesses. When Boylan had showed up with a camera crew, a Petaluma officer thought she was a reporter. That explained the "obstruction of justice" threat.

Boylan drove back to the airport.

IN PETALUMA, BOYLAN walked into a briefing room, filled with mostly male cops and feds, dressed in her standard work uniform: a boxy, double-breasted beige Donna Karan business suit that obscured her curves and turned her into "a stunt double for a cardboard box." She listened intently as investigators voiced their doubts about the girls' accounts, based on the inconsistencies between their recollections. Some wondered if Polly had run off with an older boyfriend. Maybe Kate and Gillian were trying to cover for her.

"Do you have ways in your interviews to detect if these girls are lying?" Mershon asked Boylan.

"I do," Boylan said. But she didn't think that inconsistencies were evidence of untruthfulness. In fact, it would be more unusual for them to remember the event exactly the same. "The differences should actually have served to authenticate each girl's story, which would in turn have validated and more firmly implanted the images and details in their memories for later needs," she explained. "Instead, they'd been doubted, a good first step toward damaging their memories and...destroying the evidence."

Boylan had learned this through sixteen years of interviewing crime victims, many of them traumatized by the experience they were being asked to recount. They were extremely useful lessons learned on a career path that was decidedly different from that of the typical forensic artist.

Boylan had been raised in a small mountain town in Colorado, the third of six siblings in a hardworking Irish Catholic family. The homecoming queen of Montrose High, she had never been more than sixty miles from home when she boarded a Greyhound bus the day after high school graduation and ended up in Kansas City, Missouri. She spent a few years hitchhiking across the country, taking college courses here and there whenever she could save enough money. She eventually settled in Portland.

In 1977, to earn money for college tuition, Boylan began working for a sheriff's office in Oregon in a pilot program that employed civilians as criminal investigative assistants. She conducted follow-up interviews with victims and witnesses in the "Person's Crimes" division, which included cases of rape, assault, robbery, and murder. Boylan was a natural listener, and as victims described what had happened to them, she learned facts and details that the law enforcement officers had missed. She also picked up on frequent discrepancies between composite drawings and the descriptions she heard from the victims.

"The only consistency was the inconsistency between what I was hearing the victims telling me and what I'd later see in the sketches," she observed. "Then I began seeing patterns emerge in interviews. Time lapses after a crime seemed to affect how people remembered things. Witnesses would have one account the night of the event, and another one five or ten days later."

She wondered why.

"Their memories could be swayed by something so simple as the way a question was formed or the tone of voice used," she noted. "I could ask a question in two ways and get two different answers. If trauma was involved, recall became like putty."

Boylan noticed how susceptible a witness's mind could be to the power of suggestion. If she used specific words in her attempt to elicit a description, a witness would often latch on to the very first words that came out of her mouth. If she showed them photos or pictures, their verbal descriptions of the assailant would shift to mirror these images. "I could find nothing in police training about emotion or perception relating to suspect descriptions," she wrote. "Yet there had to be reasons."

As she began exploring these questions, she was reprimanded for straying outside of her lane. "Jeanne," her bosses told her, "either stay within the rules or be fired."

They could dictate what she did on the job, but not on her own time. After hours, she let the victims talk as much as they needed. As she listened, she noticed some interesting patterns. At first, their description of what happened almost seemed to obscure the details, "like a bandage over a wound," as she put it, "skewed by shock, emotion, and confusion." The longer she listened, the more details she saw emerge in their memory.

She also noticed that the words that witnesses tended to use were those conveying emotions and sensory perceptions. Confused. Terrified. Nervous. Mean. They didn't tend to use concrete terms such as "square jaw" or "closely spaced eyes." "It seemed not to be about what they *saw*," as she put it. "It was what they *felt* that formed their vocabulary."

Trying to cross this gap, she began doodling, attempting to sketch what the witnesses were trying to describe. It wasn't well received. When the year-long criminal investigative assistant program ended in 1979, she moved on.

After spending a few months traveling around Europe, she returned to Portland, enrolled in night school, and sought a job at the Portland Police Bureau. "I asked for permission—free rein—to focus solely and unencumbered on the complex dynamics of eyewitness memory by re-interviewing high-trauma case victims."

Boylan sought training programs that could teach her how to elicit accurate images from highly traumatized minds, then assemble those often fragmented details into a realistic portrait of an assailant. The only courses she could find were five-day "sketchfests" that awarded every paying participant a certificate of completion.

Seeking peers, she called police agencies everywhere, but she couldn't find anyone doing what she wanted to learn. She then turned to academia, where she found a mentor in Dr. Elizabeth Loftus, a University of Washington psychology professor who was leading a scholarly study of eyewitnesses' recall. Loftus was often vilified for her role as an expert witness, hired by defense attorneys to discredit eyewitness testimony. But her research validated what Boylan was observing in her own work: that "memory is not static, that ideas can be implanted, recall skewed, and images overridden if an eyewitness is exposed to suggestion in any form."

Boylan studied the academic findings and put them into practice. For years, she applied them to thousands of cases, refining her interviewing methods and developing her own unique methodology* for producing composite sketches. "Unlike a departmental police artist, I didn't use the 'pick a nose' system of facial catalogs or spend time doing courtroom sketches, crime-scene drawings, or portraits of retiring police chiefs."

Reporters began to pick up on her "nonconformity," and soon stories about Boylan and her work began appearing in national newspapers and magazines. Years later, Debbie Alpert called her to Petaluma and got her involved in Polly's case.

---

* Years later, Boylan would attempt to train others in her methodology, but no one could quite produce the same results.

chapter sixteen

THE PROFILER

While Jeanne Boylan was beginning to produce an image of the kidnapper's face, an FBI criminal profiler was developing a psychological sketch.

Mary Ellen O'Toole was a rising star in the Bureau's Behavioral Science Unit. Working as a field profile coordinator based in San Francisco, she was embedded in various cases involving unknown subjects—UNSUBs—and providing investigative support. She served as a liaison between field agents and FBI profilers at Quantico.

Quietly intense, with unflinching blue eyes and shoulder-length blond hair, O'Toole had a gift for listening and getting others to open up. Deep curiosity about people was her most defining character trait and also a well-deployed tactical skill: She always left the room knowing more about others than they would ever know about her. In a field without many women, she was well respected as an expert on serial killers and other violent offenders, on her way to becoming the FBI's leading expert on psychopathy and other anti-social personality disorders. Her voice was soft and her manner gentle, but she could cuss like a convict if needed—another professional skill—and among her mostly male colleagues she spoke and acted with gravity.

O'Toole had always been fascinated by criminal minds and aberrant human behavior. How do criminals think? What goes through their minds before, during, and after the act of a crime? Why do they do what they do? She loved unraveling the intricacies of human behavior as it devolved into violence. The child of an FBI agent and a secretary who took shorthand for J. Edgar Hoover, she had wondered, even as a grade school kid, what murderers were thinking in the moment they watched a life flicker out.

Before joining the FBI, O'Toole was a criminal investigator for the San Francisco district attorney's office. Working in the Career Criminal Program, she had the opportunity to interview violent offenders.

O'Toole joined the FBI in 1981—the year Polly Klaas was born. As a new agent, she flew to Quantico several times to take in-service courses on subjects including sex crimes, serial murders, hostage negotiation, and crimes against children. Because of her interests, the Bureau assigned her to cases of violent crime—serial killers, kidnappings, mass murders—instead of white-collar crimes like fraud or money laundering. She had participated in the hunt for the Zodiac Killer, the Green River Killer, and several other serial murderers.

The new discipline of criminal profiling had emerged in response to an increase in murders and sexual assaults during the 1960s and 1970s. An FBI agent named Howard Teten had developed a theory about criminal profiling. "By about 1960, I had developed a hypothesis that you'd be able to determine the kind of person you were looking for by what you could see at the crime scene." He reviewed unusual homicides and, based on the details, developed a description of the UNSUB. When a suspect was arrested, he compared his profile to the perpetrator and evaluated the similarities.

In 1970, Teten developed his first criminal profile for a murder case in which a woman was stabbed to death in her home. Teten evaluated the evidence and the circumstances of her death and surmised that the killer was an adolescent boy who lived nearby. A knock-and-talk in the victim's neighborhood turned up such a suspect. When confronted, the boy immediately confessed. Teten was right on.

Teten teamed up with Patrick Mullany, an expert in abnormal psychology, to create a criminal psychology program at the FBI academy, a forty-hour course that taught behavioral analysis to agents as an investigative tool.

Teten and Mullany led the creation of the FBI's Behavioral Science Unit (BSU) in 1974 to investigate the rising number of homicide and rape cases and to hunt down serial killers including the Zodiac Killer, the Son of Sam, and the Hillside Strangler. One of their students at the FBI academy was a young agent named John Douglas. To better understand the minds of serial killers, Douglas conducted a research study with FBI agent Robert Ressler and Ann Wolbert Burgess, a Boston College professor and researcher who became one of the only non-agents working in the BSU in the seventies as a consultant.

Douglas and Ressler visited prisons to interview thirty-six of the most notorious violent offenders of the time, among them Ted Bundy, Charles Manson, John Wayne Gacy, Ed Kemper, and Richard Speck. To ensure their criminal personality study would yield useful data, Burgess created a research methodology and structure for their prison interviews. Their work became the basis for the BSU and the Netflix show *Mindhunter*.

WHEN MARY ELLEN O'TOOLE officially joined their ranks in 1995, the BSU had been renamed the Investigative Support Unit (ISU). Shortly thereafter, it would be changed again to Behavioral Analysis Unit (BAU), a name that persists today. Now, in addition to her role as a field profile coordinator, O'Toole was teaching FBI courses on Coast Guard Island, an artificial island between Oakland and Alameda used for tactical training. Her courses included criminal profiling, crimes against children, psychopathic offenders, serial murder, sex crimes, and child abduction.

In her role as a field profile coordinator, O'Toole assisted local law enforcement in various capacities. She developed offender profiles for UNSUBs in unsolved cases. She helped conduct interviews or briefed investigators on the best interviewing strategy for a particular offender. She often played a key role in developing investigative strategies. Working a full caseload sent her all over northern California, from the Oregon border to just south of Carmel.

She worked closely with polygrapher Ron Hilley on everything from kidnappings to hostage negotiation. They had teamed up on many child abductions in the Bay Area, called out to the command post during the earliest hours of a case. They stayed close at hand, briefed daily on the latest details, so when a polygraph test was needed, they had up-to-the-minute information with which to write clear and relevant questions.

O'Toole and Hilley had driven to Petaluma together on the night of the kidnapping. Well after midnight, they re-interviewed Kate and Gillian simultaneously and separately. They found the girls bright, articulate, tired, and scared. Like many others in the early hours, O'Toole initially found their story almost unbelievable. Of all the kidnappings she had worked, this pattern of behavior was one she had never seen before. Most of the other kidnapped children were outside, walking to the bus, playing in the front yard, riding their bike to a nearby store.

Her biggest initial question: *Was Polly targeted? Or a victim of opportunity?*

One of the most telling clues was the location of the crime: inside a stranger's house—with a parent at home—in the middle of a quiet neighborhood, on a busy Friday night. The kidnapper didn't attempt to conceal his identity with a face mask or wear gloves to avoid leaving fingerprints. He committed the abduction in full view of two wide-eyed witnesses, who could see his face and hear his voice. This was a high-risk crime by a highly motivated offender. Bringing a bag with precut bindings was evidence that this wasn't unplanned or impulsive. All of which suggested the kidnapper had targeted Polly.

O'Toole strongly believed the offender knew the neighborhood and was familiar with Polly and her home. From the rental unit behind the house, Sean Bush had witnessed a man casually walk through the yard and enter the back door of the house, moving with body language so comfortable that Bush assumed he belonged there. That could mean the kidnapper had been in Polly's house before. If not, the ease with which he entered and exited suggested the abduction was planned.

The kidnapper's behavior in Polly's room—calm and collected—said a lot about him. To be so comfortable while committing a brazen, high-risk crime in a stranger's home suggested two things. First: This probably wasn't his first time in such a situation, so he would likely have priors—burglary or breaking and entering. Maybe even kidnapping or assault. Second: He doesn't respond to stressful situations like most people do. He might be the type of criminal who strived to engage in high-risk behaviors because they excited him. One of the traits of psychopathy is a proclivity for thrill-seeking actions, for crimes that involve otherwise inexplicable high-risk behavior.

Kate and Gillian hadn't smelled booze on his breath or the skunky scent of marijuana. He hadn't slurred his speech. He didn't appear to be drunk or high or having a psychotic episode. Based on his behavior, he seemed to know what he was doing. The language he used with the girls was even more revealing. He had asked them, "Who lives here?" which suggested he was looking for Polly in particular. He had asked, "Where are the valuables?" That could mean he was here for a burglary, but O'Toole strongly believed it was likely a diversionary tactic to keep the girls calm. When Polly told him she had thirty dollars hidden in her jewelry box, he didn't try to find it. "I won't touch you," he had told the girls, and promised once they had counted to one thousand, Polly would be back.

His language and behavior had been effective in preventing the girls from freaking out and screaming. The girls had said, again and again, they didn't believe he was there to hurt them. When they had complained about the ligatures being too tight, he had apologized and loosened them. Was that evidence of empathy? Or calculated manipulation? His statement, "I'm just doing this for the money," was curious to O'Toole, who suspected his primary motive was sexual. But crimes like this can have multiple motives, so she kept an open mind.

One other very interesting thing the kidnapper said in Polly's room: "There shouldn't be so many people." That suggested he knew exactly how many people lived in that house, and possibly their age range. That indicated he had been engaged in some sort of prior surveillance. He might be a service worker—a cable guy, painter, appliance repairman, or delivery man—with a valid reason to be in the neighborhood, or even in the house. That role, and the uniform that came with it, would help him fly under the radar of a watchful neighborhood. He'd be able to hide in plain sight, come and go without raising concern.

Based on this information, O'Toole recommended another neighborhood canvass. In the primary round of knock-and-talks, there was no questionnaire, so agents and cops were all asking different questions. That made it hard to compare and contrast the answers, to analyze responses for patterns and common clues.

To standardize the information being gathered, O'Toole developed a three-page questionnaire. It required investigators to record physical characteristics of the person being questioned—height, weight, build, complexion, eye color, hair color, scars or tattoos—as well as the number and age of the occupants living in that person's residence, and how long each had lived there. The collective result of these questions was a real-time census of Polly's neighborhood and its dynamics. A portrait of a community began to emerge.

The neighborhood questionnaire included questions specific to Polly:

> Have you heard about Polly Klaas?
>
> What have you heard about what happened to her?
>
> Have you been contacted by the police or have you furnished any information to the police concerning Polly?
>
> Have you volunteered in any of the efforts to locate Polly?
>
> Were you in the neighborhood on October 1, 1993?
>
> Who else was here?
>
> What, if anything do you recall from that evening?

The most generative questions were open-ended, inviting more than a yes-or-no answer. They were needed to elicit details that a potential witness might not necessarily consider relevant. O'Toole wanted to know the typical neighborhood dynamics, and what "normal" components were missing that night. If the UPS driver usually came by at five o'clock, did he fail to show up that evening? If painters or an electrician happened to be working on a nearby house, what did they look like? Those workers might be suspects. Or they might be witnesses who saw the offender without realizing it. When a child goes missing in a neighborhood, someone always sees something. But they don't always immediately grasp the significance of what they saw.

Officers read part of the questionnaire like a script:

> We believe that the person who is responsible for Polly's abduction
> may have been in the area before. They could have lived, worked,
> or visited the neighborhood. Because the offender may have been
> here for purely legitimate reasons, he may not have stood out in
> your mind. Please keep in mind that the man (men) responsible for
> Polly's abduction would not necessarily appear strange, threatening,
> or "weird" to you if you would have had some type of interaction
> with them.

An offender who makes a lot of "noise" before or after the crime will likely stand out in a neighborhood like Polly's, a quiet street where residents would have noticed any unusual or threatening behavior. So far, investigators had no reports of strange or menacing lurkers. This meant the offender was probably a normal-looking guy who didn't draw too much attention to himself.

Embedded in the questionnaire was a bit of a criminal profile:

> We believe the offender has reasonably good interpersonal skills,
> does not use an unusual amount of profanity, is generally calm and
> patient, and is comfortable in the neighborhood, would not neces-
> sarily stand out for any reason, somewhat of a loner, and following
> the abduction would have indicated concern or worry over what
> happened to Polly.

The kidnapper was able to engage with Kate and Gillian and have a conversation without appearing too dangerous to them. That meant he probably had strong interpersonal skills. He hadn't used an excessive amount of profanity. A foul-mouthed stranger casing the neighborhood likely would have stood out to other people around him. There were no reports of this.

They hadn't ruled out the possibility that the kidnapper lived in Polly's neighborhood or personally knew her family. If so, he might find opportunities to inquire about Polly's abduction, expressing concern in order to monitor the cops and agents and keep tabs on what they knew. Some perpetrators were known to insert themselves in the investigation, embedding themselves so deeply they were able to hide in plain sight.

Such cases were chilling. After kidnapping and murdering twelve-year-old Jonelle Matthews in Greeley, Colorado, in 1984, Steven Pankey monitored news coverage of the case obsessively and repeatedly asked to speak with detectives, claiming knowledge of the crime. When he was convicted in 2022, thirty-eight years after the crime, the trial was based largely on the decades of incriminating statements he made to law enforcement officers and his (now former) spouse.

chapter seventeen

THE COMPOSITE

AFTER FLYING BACK FROM OREGON, FORENSIC ARTIST JEANNE BOYLAN ARRIVED at the police station ready to get to work. But first, Kate McLean's parents wanted to speak with her privately.

"Our daughter does not lie," Kate's father began, grasping his wife's hand.

She had been through two polygraph tests and several intense interviews. Kate was a good kid, and this was traumatic, having her honesty repeatedly called into question. To protect her, Kate's parents had told investigators, "We're done." Why should they continue to help a team that just kept treating these girls with suspicion?

Boylan felt the girls and their parents had every right to feel defensive. Investigators had not just doubted the girls. Case agent Eddie Freyer and Petaluma sergeant Vail Bello had instructed certain interviewers to "lean on them," crossing the boundary between interviewing and interrogation. It was the typical approach when dealing with a suspect believed to be lying. But it was also, as they were learning, a sure way to alienate the twelve-year-old girls and possibly lose two key witnesses if this ever came before a jury.

Kate was not shy about making her feelings known. In addition to

Kate McLean with the "No Hugs" sign.
(COURTESY OF JEANNE BOYLAN)

writing an angry letter to polygrapher Ron Hilley, she had constructed a hand-drawn sign made of two index cards stapled to a Popsicle stick. Her sign declared: *I'm fine, Please don't ask!* She had written the word "HUGS" inside a circle with a slash.

Boylan explained to Kate's parents how her approach would be different from what Kate had endured. "I'm not here to doubt her or bombard her with confusing photographs, in effect telling her what she saw," Boylan said. "I'm not here to grill her or to judge her or compare her words to anyone else's. I just want to hear what she has to say."

"But they are saying Kate's lying," Kate's mother said. "Now she's trying to tell them that the image is wrong, and they're casting doubt even on that. We are not going to put her through this again!"

"Let me explain what's happened here," Boylan said. "An image that is taken into memory under a traumatic circumstance is fragile. With exposure to as few as a dozen photographs, that image will start to distort and diffuse." Since Polly's disappearance, Kate had been shown a number of suspect photographs and an array of facial features. "It's no wonder there's a mix-up here. It's nothing she's done."

Boylan worried this would diminish the chances of eliciting an accurate image from Kate's memory. If this case should ever go to trial and the outcome hinged on eyewitness recall—in the absence of other tangible evidence—"any defense attorney with the most basic knowledge of eyewitness contamination could blast these little girls' testimony right off the witness stand." She would write that in a future memoir. But she didn't say that now.

"Kate's confusion isn't about what she *saw*," Boylan told Kate's parents. "The problems began in the way she was *asked* about it. I want to try to recover the image—the *actual* image she saw—this time by fully listening to her words. I promise you that I won't disregard or dismantle her memory by suggesting to her that I know more than she does."

Kate's parents agreed to let Boylan interview her. Boylan recommended they do so at their home, on Kate's turf, a safe place unafflicted by the emotional trauma associated with the kidnapping and subsequent interviews. She would present herself as Kate's guest, not an authority figure.

Boylan rode to Kate's house in the ABC news van, stopping at a gas station to change out of her beige business suit into blue jeans, a sweatshirt, and Nikes. She didn't want to dress like an authority figure, since it was the authorities who had earned Kate's mistrust.

At the house, Kate's mother led Boylan through a hallway where Kate had been permitted to write and draw on the walls since she was little. "Look at this," Alice McLean said, nodding at the faces, symbols, and sayings. Studying the mural, Boylan could see how visually inclined Kate was, and it provided insights into the girl's young mind.

"Kate's 'drawing wall' was a valuable clue to how she thought," Boylan wrote some years later. "It gave me a translation guide with which to structure my questions so that we'd be speaking in the same language. I'd be better able not just to speak with her but to *hear* her answers if I used the same frames of reference that she used to relate to her own world."

Kate's mother ushered Boylan to the dining room, where Kate was sitting at the table, hunched over, eyes downcast, sitting on her hands. Boylan's heart ached when she saw Kate's handmade sign—*I'm fine, please don't ask!*

She began her work as she always did, by chatting about topics unrelated to the crime. "Engaging her in conversation was easy," Boylan recalled. "She had a near-genius-level IQ, and conversing with her was like talking to a contemporary over a second glass of wine. World issues were well in her scope."

Kate slowly opened up, confessing her anger at investigators.

"Every time I tell them something, they tell me I'm lying!"

Boylan's technique, which she called cognitive interviewing, was very different from the standard approach. Based on the idea that recognition is easier than recall, many police sketch artists asked witnesses to flip through books of noses, eyes, chins, and other facial features, from which they could assemble the face of their assailant. Some cops referred to this as "the Mr. Potato Head method."

Boylan's approach began with getting the subject talking about topics that would make them feel safe and at ease. She'd often look around the room for a photo or book, a natural conversation starter. The objective was to help witnesses relax, allowing the interviewer to gently probe into the traumatic memories encoded in the memory. Here lay the challenge: The more trauma and emotion involved in the event, the more likely the subject had encoded the details, but the harder it could be to access them. The same phenomenon causes test anxiety—when you can't remember information you're certain you know due to the heightened stress of the situation that demands you recall it. By minimizing the stress of the interview, Boylan could maximize the accuracy of the details recalled.

Once the interviewee was talking comfortably about "safe" topics, Boylan would interject a single question every twenty minutes or so. She always phrased the question in the present tense, to "anchor [the subject] emotionally in the safety of the current moment, and to distance her from the emotions connected to her memory of the event." For example, in trying to conjure the shape of a nose: "Would you create a shape that's longer than wide or the same length as width?"

In order to minimize anxiety, she avoided direct mention of the suspect or the crime, referring instead to "shapes and textures in the context of an inanimate form, such as a pliable substance like clay, and how she might tape that clay into the form of a face." She avoided leading questions.

With every question, Boylan carefully modulated the inflection of her voice. Ending a question with an upswing could emphasize a particular word or create a question bias. "A simple uplifted tone will be more 'attractive' than one uttered in a base tone," Boylan often explained, "and a crime victim, suffering from the depression that results from trauma, subconsciously seeks any form of relief."

She also knew how a change in eye contact could be suggestive, so she made sure to hold a subject's gaze throughout the entire question. Or she avoided it entirely. "Every nuance mattered," Boylan said years later.

At first, Kate balked at these intermittent questions. Whenever Boylan interjected one, she'd stiffen and resist.

"I don't know. I didn't see."

Boylan made sure not to react with concern, guiding the conversation back toward safe ground. She'd try again in fifteen or twenty minutes, casually slipping in a relevant question. During these interviews, she typically kept the drawing board on her lap. "By keeping the board low and unobtrusive, nearly out of sight, the sketching takes a distant second place to the unrelated conversation taking place," Boylan explained.

After talking with Kate for an hour and a half, Boylan pulled the board from her lap and placed it on the dining room table. It was blank.

"Kate, you know what?" she whispered, leaning in. "If I were you, and I'd been through half the shit you've been through...and if I had that image in my mind...I wouldn't tell *anyone*."

"Yeah!" Kate said, her brown eyes wide. "Because every time I tell them something, they tell me I'm lying!"

Validation was the turning point, the common ground they'd needed to reach. Kate needed someone to believe her, because what she had been through was real. After this breakthrough, the details began to surface. The face emerged, as Boylan would later describe it, "like black-and-white film gently being rocked in a developing tray."

After three hours of working quietly with Kate, Boylan completed a composite drawing very different from the one in circulation. She held it in her hands as she walked down the front steps, escorted by Kate, and out to the news van. The TV crew had dozed off while waiting, so they didn't have cameras rolling when Kate wrapped her arms around Jeanne Boylan to say goodbye.

⌒⌒⌒

AT THE POLICE station, Boylan met Petaluma captain Pat Parks, who looked to her like "a Ron Howard look-alike with freckles, invisible blond eyelashes, and a heart on his sleeve." Partnered with ASAC Mark Mershon, Parks was the co-incident commander for the case.

"Any success?" Parks asked.

"I think so," she said. "But I'm not prepared to show anything until I talk with the second girl and decide which sketch I'll go with."

Boylan always—always—interviewed witnesses separately. In joint interviews, one personality tended to dominate, and that could undermine the memory or the confidence of the other. Moreover, an image or overheard phrase recalled by one mind could seep into another mind, inadvertently contaminating the "evidence." Because the girls had been interviewed jointly by the first forensic artist, Boylan worried it might be too late to prevent such cross-contamination. Nonetheless, she was hopeful, because their memories were still fresh. At least once she was asked to produce a composite seven years after the crime. (She was successful.)

She would avoid "homogenizing" the descriptions of different witnesses, keeping each individual's memory intact on the drawing board. "Each witness's recall must be regarded as a single entity." Based on how she felt about the interviews—which memory she felt was most "intact," Boylan would choose the one that would be released to the media and the public. "My credibility was built on my own set of rules."

Boylan's interview with Gillian was to take place at an "undisclosed location"—protected from the lurking media—in a calm, quiet setting away from home, where her brother and dog might distract her. To avoid being followed by the press, Boylan ducked into an unmarked police car and hunkered on the floorboard of the passenger seat while Captain Pat Parks drove her past the camera crews swarming outside the PD.

"You can get up now," he said, laughing, as he turned onto Petaluma Boulevard.

Then he looked in his rear mirror and saw a blue media van.

"Fasten your seat belt," he said. "We're being followed."

Parks pressed on the gas, careened around corners, circled a pizza parlor, and wove through neighborhoods to lose their tail. They pulled up to a traffic light and saw the blue van across the intersection headed the opposite way. As soon as the light turned green, Parks sped off. Once he was confident he'd lost them, Parks pulled into the community center, where Gillian and her mother were waiting in a quiet room with a long table, pale blue carpet, and window blinds closed. A good, calm setting.

But Gillian was not calm.

"Look, mom, my fish flop!" she cried, floundering on the blue carpet. She ducked under the conference table and asked if someone would time her as she crawled underneath it, end to end. Goofy and childlike, she was quite the opposite of serious Kate.

Boylan had worked with many traumatized people, and she had seen how anxiety and emotion could manifest in many different ways. Hysterical laughter at a murder scene. Unexpected calmness in the wake of something horrific. Hyperactive silliness. Boylan saw the release of emotion as a promising sign, because she believed that whatever form it took, it would help them "reach the needed image."

As Boylan began her process, they were interrupted by a knock on the door. It was her ABC producer, Gordon, looking frustrated and maybe even a bit forlorn.

"Why did you run?" he said.

His blue van was parked outside. Union rules had required a shift change, and a fresh camera crew arrived in a different vehicle—the one they thought had been tailing them, that Captain Parks had successfully dropped. Now they would be waiting outside, again, for the opportunity to run the first image of the new composite. That moment was hours away.

Boylan turned to Gillian, who by now had settled down. Boylan usually sent family members away, preferring to work alone so she could build a one-on-one connection without distractions or interference from overpowering parents. But after observing Gillian with her mother, Diane—she could sense the bond and the trust between them—she decided to break her own precedent.

She began as she always did, chatting with Gillian about neutral matters and interjecting a question every twenty to thirty minutes. The questions had to be open-ended to avoid leading the witness with suggestive language. Any descriptive word had to be counterbalanced with a word on the other end of the spectrum. Narrow or wide. Light or dark.

Based on where she was sitting when the kidnapper entered the room, Gillian should have had a better vantage point to see his face. But after two hours of trying to retrieve this face from her memory, Boylan was staring at another blank page. When Gillian's mother asked for a break, Boylan was secretly relieved. She needed one herself.

It was getting late, and Jeanne felt the pressure building. In fourteen hours, her sketch would be shown on national TV. She laid her head down on her arms, shoulders aching, fighting tears. She had a last resort, one she rarely used and never took lightly. She prayed.

Dear God, I don't ask for much. But Polly is still out there somewhere, and Gillian is our last hope for finding her alive. The face of the kidnapper went through her eyes, through those pupils. She was there. Please, I need you. Help me find the image. Take my arm, take my hand, just use me. If this little girl has ever had a serious thought, please let her have one now. Help me reveal that face through the end of the pencil. I am asking you. No, I am begging you.

She dried the tears with her sleeve and waited for Gillian and her mother to return. After a half hour, they came back. Boylan noticed instantly that something felt different. Gillian was calm, still, and centered. Fine details came into focus: Hooded eyelids. An extra-wide nose bridge. Thick eyebrows that wrapped around the sockets of black, sunken eyes. A creased forehead. A full lower lip. Coarse, wavy hair. A salt-and-pepper beard. A distinct face emerged from Gillian's memory.

Boylan's pencil flew over the drawing board and soon she was staring into the dark eyes of a singular face. *We have him,* she thought. Or did they? It was time for Gillian to view the sketch.

The reveal had to happen in a certain way: a single image, life-sized, flashed briefly to avoid overwriting the actual image encoded in Gillian's mind. "Every precaution has to be taken to protect the memory," she said. "There are no second chances to recode it—the suspect is not likely to come back." Any discrepancies would be immediately and instinctively evident, and Boylan would fine-tune the drawing accordingly.

Boylan wrapped her fingers around the drawing board on her lap and took a deep breath. When Gillian was ready, she flashed the face before her.

"Yep, that's him exactly," Gillian said. "Okay, Mom, can we go home?"

It was a little too certain, a little too fast. Boylan cringed, wanting real critical feedback. But Gillian was satisfied, so Boylan didn't push her. After Gillian and her mother left, Boylan put her head down on the conference table, grateful and exhausted. It was two-thirty a.m.

Agent Mark Mershon walked in and looked at the drawing, shaking his head in astonishment.

"*How*—do you do this?" he asked.

"You know," she said, shaking her head back at him, "I thought you'd never ask."

The next morning, Boylan pulled on her boxy suit and pinned a purple ribbon on the lapel. Her ABC crew would air their exclusive at seven a.m., and then an hour later, the drawing would be presented to the rest of the media.

At the press conference, Boylan and FBI ASAC Mark Mershon stepped in front of a wall of cameras and a bank of microphones so thick it threatened to collapse the table. *Please,* she said under her breath, *let this be right.*

When Mershon flipped the drawing around to reveal the new composite, the room erupted with shouts and flashbulbs. One question rose above the din.

"Ms. Boylan! What about the headband?"

She felt the hot flush of panic—*How had she forgotten this salient detail?* Then a calm overcame her. The answer was simple.

"There was no headband," she said.

Her job was not to "improve" the original composite, but to draw what each witness recalled. Neither one of them had mentioned a headband.

⌒⌒⌒

NEUROSCIENCE WOULD SUGGEST possible explanations for the headband. "Memory is not a videotape," explains Dr. David Diamond, a professor at the University of South Florida and a scientist who studies the effects of trauma on memory formation and loss. "Memory is the brain's ability to create a *representation* of an experience. It's almost like an optical illusion. What you perceive is not necessarily what's out there in the world."

Memories—and particularly stressful memories—can be highly inaccurate. One of the reasons is the brain's evolutionary instinct to focus on the details causing the stress. If you'd had a gun pointed at your face, you might not be able to remember whether or not the perpetrator had a mustache, because you were focused on the gun. But chances are you'd remember that gun with exquisite, indelible detail. This phenomenon, called "weapon focus," has been discussed by neuroscientists for many years, and it suggests why Kate and Gillian had exact and consistent descriptions of the knife in the kidnapper's left hand, down to the metal rivets in the wooden handle.

Kate's and Gillian's recollection of the most critical details—what the kidnapper did and said in Polly's room—were extremely consistent between their accounts and throughout many subsequent interviews. That's likely due to a phenomenon in which the brain processes events as if a camera had taken an indelible picture. The result—a "flashbulb memory"—is encoded during moments of heightened emotion, as though a flashbulb had frozen the moment in time. Unlike other memories, the details of a flashbulb memory don't tend to degrade in the future. As one researcher famously put it, "an impression may be so exciting emotionally as almost to leave a scar upon the cerebral tissues." A heightened degree of emotionality, however, also decreases the brain's ability to process a wide range of cues. Which explains why the girls remembered the knife so clearly, but were less certain about the kidnapper's shoes.

A traumatic memory—a flashbulb memory of a horrific event—tends to have gaps. In a horrific or potentially life-threatening situation, the hippocampus (the part of the brain that plays a major role in processing conscious fact-based memories) is activated along with the amygdala (which is necessary for processing emotions like fear and anxiety). Together, the hippocampus and amygdala create the flashbulb memory for the moment of the greatest stress or trauma. The amygdala then calls on the other components of the limbic system to engage in the fight, flight, or freeze response. As a result, trauma survivors often find that certain moments of extreme fear result in "intrusive memories" and "stuck points" after the traumatic event is over. Stuck points refer to negative beliefs that anchor survivors of trauma in a negative emotional state that may lead to acute stress disorder or post-traumatic stress disorder.

When people who have experienced trauma find themselves experiencing flashbulb memories over and over, the intrusive memories can begin to impose on the activities of daily life. In turn, the memories may latch onto the negative belief system of certain stuck points, which further augment the flashbulb memory in a vicious cycle. The memory of certain aspects of a trauma shine that much brighter, but they may also cast shadows on the other details the brain deemed less important for survival in the moment the trauma occurred. This explains why a traumatized victim might be able to describe sensory impressions—the sound of breaking glass in a car accident, the feeling of a rapist's hand on your mouth—but not the make of the oncoming car or the clothing of the rapist.

Memories encoded after the traumatic event, when the brain shifts back into a more normal state of processing, are more malleable, susceptible to corruption by information that comes in after the traumatic experience. This might explain why the first composite sketch resembled Petaluma detective Dennis Nowicki, who interviewed Kate. Perhaps because his interviewing style was a bit more interrogatory, Kate may have encoded it under stress. And that stress may have caused what neuroscientist David Diamond calls a "double weapon focus" phenomenon. The trauma of the kidnapping and the trauma of the interview were two threats that bled together in her memory.

So what about the yellow bandana? Diamond supposes there may have been something yellow in the room that Kate happened to lay eyes upon during the stressful event of the kidnapping. Maybe it was some object. Maybe the light through the pillowcase-hood had a yellow hue. That color could have infused itself into her memory of the kidnapper's face, which she only saw very briefly before being forced to lie facedown on the floor. If there was something yellow in the room, and Kate saw it before or during the stressful incident, the two memories could have merged.*

Boylan believed the reason for the yellow headband could be even simpler. The first forensic artist had shown the girls a booklet of facial features and headwear. Deep creases across the kidnapper's forehead may have somehow morphed into a bandana. It showed how vulnerable memories are to the power of suggestion. (And even though the bandana had been removed from Boylan's forensic sketch, it would surface again in the investigation.)

Boylan also insisted that the kidnapper's physical description be changed. His height—previously noted as an unusually specific six-foot-three—was changed to a broader range: between five-foot-ten and six-foot-three. She impressed upon the investigative team her theory that the girls' vantage point, sitting on the floor, would have made a threatening intruder appear much larger than he really was. Boylan told the press that both girls had given a full description of the suspect, but one had a clearer vision. She wouldn't say which one.

"There's personality in it, with real eyes and real features," Marc Klaas said after viewing the sketch. "It chilled me to the bone."

Said Eve, with a gentle irony: "He looks nice."

---

* In one crime scene photograph of Polly's room, a bright yellow umbrella is hanging from the top bunk. From where Kate was lying on the floor, it seems plausible that her gaze passed over it when she looked up at the kidnapper entering the room. Diamond did not see this photograph or know about the umbrella when he offered his possible explanation for the yellow bandana.

Jeanne Boylan and ASAC Mark Mershon unveil the new composite sketch at a press conference.

(COURTESY OF JEANNE BOYLAN)

chapter eighteen

VICTIMOLOGY

EARLY IN THE CASE, FBI LEADERSHIP PRESSED MARY ELLEN O'TOOLE TO PROFILE Polly's abductor. In the phase of an investigation before a key suspect comes into focus, a profile can be a valuable lens through which to evaluate other evidence and a filter for quickly winnowing down a large field of possible suspects. It could help investigators prioritize leads and focus their time and resources in specific directions.

There wasn't enough information yet to produce a formal written profile. That involved analyzing criminal elements such as the modus operandi (method of committing the crime) and "signature" (the idiosyncratic crime-scene details and patterns a particular offender leaves behind).

Kidnappings are unlike other investigations. There's no body to analyze, no murder weapon to trace, and often no clear motive. Stranger abductions in particular are notorious for a paucity of evidence. They can begin with a seemingly friendly encounter and present no signs of struggle.

In the absence of sufficient information for a profile, there was another valuable tool: victimology. A comprehensive analysis of the victim, victimology analyzes everything in the victim's lifestyle—personality, wardrobe, hobbies, habits, fears, emotional age, and much more. It also considers a victim's particular risk level: Based on their lifestyle habits and practices, is the victim at high or low risk for becoming the victim of a violent crime?

By creating a psychological profile of the victim, the profiler can infer what kind of predator would pursue this kind of prey. In addition to the victim's physical and psychological makeup, the profiler considers any possible connection to the perpetrator, the timing of the attack, and what might have made that particular victim more vulnerable in that moment. If a victim was targeted, victimology can help deduce why.

"These are the pieces of victimology that will shed light on the offender's motive," writes criminologist Ann Wolbert Burgess in *A Killer by Design*, her memoir about her foundational work in the Behavioral Science Unit. "And by analyzing both the victim and the motive, as well as all the other files you've collected on the crime, you'll start to narrow in on the defining characteristics of the offender. You'll reduce the pool of suspects to the smallest possible list. You'll chip away at the rogue's gallery of options until you're left with the one choice that's clear and obvious. Because, ultimately, that's what victimology does—it holds a mirror to the perpetrator of the crime."

O'Toole studied Polly's drawings posted on the refrigerator, looked through Polly's closet, noted the books and toys in her room. She read her school papers and her diary, collected and logged into evidence. She needed to see the world through Polly's eyes.

On Saturday, October 16, O'Toole sat down with Eve for an interview that lasted several hours. They spoke at the Petaluma PD, where O'Toole recorded the conversation.

"I think the best place to start is to just have you describe Polly—her appearance, her personality, her character," O'Toole began. "Let's take it in blocks of years. Looking at, say, the first three years. What kind of a little girl was she?"

"She was a gorgeous baby," Eve began. "She looked like a little china doll..."

Polly talked early, walked late, and was very strong-willed, especially when fighting bedtime. Her teachers described her as "very bright." She was three years old when Eve and Marc divorced, a sad and traumatic experience because Polly adored her father. But she never had to go more than five or six days without seeing him.

When Polly was four, Eve married Allan Nichol, an architect with three kids from a previous marriage. After being an only child for six years, Polly suddenly had a brother and two sisters, the youngest of whom was a girl named Jessica, the same age as Polly. Eve described Polly and Jessie as "soul mates" and said Polly always referred to her siblings as "my brother and sisters," never using the word "step." A few years later, Eve and Allan had Annie. The sisters loved and annoyed each other.

Like Eve, Polly was an introvert. She liked to laugh and play with friends, but at the end of a very social day, she'd need to recharge in her room alone. She cried easily and was slow to warm up to people she didn't know, even good friends of her parents. True strangers made her "physically and emotionally uncomfortable," Eve said.

O'Toole wondered whether Polly might have had a prior encounter with the kidnapper in the park or on the street. How would she react?

"If somebody approached Polly and was really friendly..." O'Toole began.

"No," Eve said. "No."

Polly was "extremely mistrustful" of strangers, frightened of the homeless people loitering around the library in Santa Rosa. On a recent family outing to San Francisco, they had sailed across the bay on the ferry from Sausalito and rode the cable car up the city's incredible hills. But the homeless people scared her, and she said she didn't want to go back to the city again. Eve believed that it wasn't pity her daughter felt. It was fear.

O'Toole asked more questions, trying to understand the root of that fear. Eve said she thought it was an innate personality trait, but also that Polly's father had instilled in her a sense of caution.

O'Toole asked about her taste in movies. Polly had loved *Jurassic Park*, *Sleepless in Seattle*, and *In the Line of Fire*. She loved comedies, thrillers, even some scary movies. *Indiana Jones*, *Innerspace*, and *Dave*. She looked up to Winona Ryder and Meg Ryan. She had wanted to see

The Bodyguard, but her mother had said no, because the movie was rated R. When Eve suggested going to see *Free Willy* with Annie, Polly had flatly refused.

"Forget it," she said. "I'm not gonna see a movie about a whale."

Polly wasn't a big risk taker, but she had just been on a roller coaster for the first time that summer, and she had just started diving into the pool. "I think she enjoyed the aspect that she was finding that she was capable of pushing herself a little bit further," Eve told O'Toole.

She was interested in astronomy—her dad had purchased a telescope—and for three years she talked about becoming an astronaut. Despite her interest in the stars, she didn't like to go outside at night. Even on nights when the moon shone big and full, her mother would have to coax her outside to see it.

"Polly, come outside and look!"

"I don't have shoes on."

"Come out anyway."

Polly wasn't particularly fond of the outdoors, and it was a struggle to get her to go on a hike with Allan, an avid hiker and naturalist. Maybe it was Allan's track record of tricking the girls into eight-mile hikes. Or maybe it just wasn't her thing. As Eve put it, "It's like her grandma said: 'These feet were meant for expensive boots, not for walking.'" She would rather stay home and play Super Nintendo, practice the clarinet, or read.

"What does she read?" O'Toole asked. "I know we've got her books."

She would find an author she liked and read everything they had written. She preferred Eve go to the library and pick books out for her. Eve had offered to drop her off at the library for an hour or two, then pick her up later, but Polly refused. "I don't know the kids there. They make me uncomfortable. They look at me."

In sixth grade, there was a group of girls that devolved into cliques and started doing cruel things to one another. It turned into something like *Lord of the Flies*. They would spy on one another and snitch. Lots of drama. Kids coming home in tears. This went on for about six weeks. Polly claimed innocence, but some teachers said she may have been a ringleader. One of the teachers said Polly had treated her, at times, in a nasty and defiant way.

She could be sassy to her mother. She could be "willful, stubborn . . . she could be very nasty. It doesn't sound like the same little angel I've been describing, but particularly if she doesn't get her way, she can be mean." Eve noted her sarcastic, black-humor streak.

"Do you have any tapes that came out of that tape recorder they took?" Eve asked. "There's probably a lot of stuff on there. She recorded herself all the time."

O'Toole said there wasn't anything of value as a lead on the tape.

"I'm kind of interested in her interaction with you in particular."

"If I said something she didn't like, she would half-seriously, half-playfully say, 'Shut up, Mom.' Which to some people is quite shocking. But we had a relationship where we understood each other and so we could sort of fling insults. She was really good at flinging insults back and forth."

She was not a morning person, "not a happy camper when she wakes up in the morning," Eve said. "I was looking forward to the time she started drinking coffee, hoping that would help."

"Why—and this is really important—if you can put a time frame on it, at what point did she start being cynical and kind of caustic?"

"It's been a while. I'd say maybe three, four years."

Eve had adapted her parenting style, and that had helped.

"Sometimes people don't even try the easiest thing to try, and that's just to kill someone with kindness. That's basically what I did. Even when [she] was behaving badly, I would, like, sit on her lap or hug her and kiss her, and she would go 'MOM!' But she was instantly out of that mood because she was so tickled by the fact that not only was I not getting mad at her, but instead I was being affectionate to her. And she responded profoundly to that."

Their relationship had improved considerably over the last few months.

"I just didn't want to lose touch with her," Eve said. "'Cause this is the time when you can really lose the bond with your kid, and this is my little girl, and I really wanted to keep her. She's a really sensitive kid, and she really, really loves me a lot."

"How did she show you affection?"

She loved the opportunity to hug, and she would sometimes come up to Eve and wrap her arms around her. She always kissed her mother good night (but never in the morning). She didn't like sleeping alone, and found it a real treat to snuggle in bed with her mom. At her grandparents' house, she preferred sleeping on a futon in their bedroom rather than in a guest room.

Marc and Violet had bought a two-bedroom condo so Polly could have her own room, which was something she really wanted until she realized she'd have to sleep alone.

O'Toole asked if Polly had any hiding places where she kept things. Eve said she didn't think so. Polly had a diary and wrote in it for a few months—the FBI had taken that too. But Annie found it and drew in it, and Polly was terribly upset and eventually gave it up. Polly and her best friend, Annette Schott, sometimes wrote to each other in code. The FBI had collected one such letter, written in childlike hieroglyphics used in place of letters. Special Agent Larry Taylor had cracked the code.

Eve said that sleepovers with multiple friends were common among Polly's friends, but at her house she was usually only up to host one friend at a time. So inviting both Kate and Gillian was a rare and special event.

"I think that's why she was so excited, because she thought she would have a hard time convincing me to have a second over, and I agreed to it readily, which is my new campaign to be a terrific mom and not give her any flack if she did her end."

Though O'Toole didn't have enough information yet to develop a written profile, she had identified certain behavioral characteristics of the kidnapper based on Kate's and Gillian's descriptions of his behavior.

"He's gonna look normal. Probably has at least some type of a job. Could have seen Polly or one of the girls ten minutes before. Or felt comfortable in your house because of previous contact years before. But we're not looking for somebody who is going to be real scary-looking.

"This person, I'm telling ya, did not just come off of 101. If he did, where the heck did he start looking? If he was a stranger to the area. And Petaluma is as nice a town as you're ever gonna want to get. So we've got to take a look at the neighborhood, your house, and Polly. Why, why, why? And as we narrow that down, I think we stand a heck of a lot better chance resolving this. So please don't take my questions personally."

"I would just . . . Rather than beating around the bush, I would prefer that you just sort of ask me directly, what is it you wanna try and get at," Eve said. "And I'll rack my brain to think of any possible connection."

"But I don't want you to have to do that because that information you may not know 'cause we don't know."

"Um-hmm."

"But what you've said so far has been real helpful because we've come up with scenarios and situations that give a lot more insights into Polly."

"Good."

"And I don't want you to walk away after all you've been [through] and think the FBI still has doubts."

"Uh-huh."

"The worst thing is to try to understand the motivation here," O'Toole said. "I think once we understand that, it's gonna be a lot better."

They talked about Polly's teachers. Eve thought about a music teacher Polly had in fifth grade. A stocky man in his forties, no wife or kids. Salt-and-pepper hair. A beard. Sweatshirts and jeans. He primarily taught private lessons to children, working one-on-one in his studio. After two months of lessons, Polly refused to go back.

"Don't make me go again," she said. "I don't like him."

Eve cancelled.

Mary Ellen paused the tape to relay the name of this music teacher to agent Larry Taylor, then came back to resume the interview.

"Was it typical of Polly to say, 'Mom, that's it, I don't wanna go back. I don't want anything more to do with this person'? Is that in keeping with her suspicious kind of . . . so it may be, probably nothing?"

"She's had numerous music lessons. This is the first time she ever reacted this way to a music teacher."

She thought for a moment. "And there was a recital he was gonna do and she wouldn't go to it. One of her friends said that he called her name and she wasn't there."

"That's a pretty strong feeling for her to have."

"Mm-hmm . . ."

"Do you think there was something there that he, maybe, tried something with her?"

"I don't know. I don't know. And I don't know why I forgot about it 'til now."

"We'll check it out."

"But, you know what, he does have these heavy glasses," Eve said, thinking about the man in the composite. "Now of course, he could have been wearing contacts, but you would think she would recognize him. Unless he looked so different without his glasses on. I mean, you would really think she'd know him."

"Um-hmm."

"Unless she just didn't. He said, 'Who lives here?' So it's probably not him, for Christ's sake. I'm just turning into a paranoid."

"Well, we definitely need to check it out."

"If you see him, you will be startled at how similar he looks to this picture."

"We all wish we could reach in there and make you feel better, but you wouldn't let us do it anyway, because you're not gonna feel better until she's home."

"I know as much as you do and it's been two weeks."

"Yeah," O'Toole said. "I don't know that I could hold up as well as you are."

Eve sighed. "It's hard."

"I know it is," said O'Toole.

"Would they be able to let me know about this guy?"

"That's what I'm hoping for. I told them that you wanted to know as soon as possible."

"Okay. 'Cause they haven't been telling me anything, really. I figured they'd just tell me what I need to know. But this particular one, I'd really like to know."

"I will ask them when we leave," O'Toole said. "You know, it does seem like you're not getting a lot of information."

"That's all right," Eve said. "I trust you all implicitly. And the other issue about more information is, because of all this media, it would be nice, without endangering anything, to be able to give them something. Because the first thing they all say is, 'Any more leads?'"

O'Toole recommended they discuss it with Mike Kerns, the

Petaluma sergeant handling the media. It was important for them to be in sync since Eve would continue to be interviewed.

"*People* magazine's coming out Monday with a big story," Eve said. "They have millions of readers. I hope to God Joanne [Gardner] got them the new composite. It was questionable whether she could get it in, because their deadline was past. But she was gonna try."

"Good."

"They just keep saying, 'Can you give me anything?' They really want to keep coming back."

"They're a great asset because they really get the word out too. But it's very likely that whoever's responsible [for the kidnapping] is monitoring this investigation, through what you're saying. So you do have to be aware and I don't think that's a good idea to say that to the media, although they all know that too. So I would certainly suggest that as angry as you feel, you don't want to use any red-flag terms."

"In fact," Eve said, "I made them take 'at knife-point' off the poster."

"Good for you. What made you do that?"

"Because it's what, fifteen years more, if there's a weapon? I don't want this guy to feel any more desperate than he does. I want this guy to feel like, just let her go, everything's gonna be fine. We just want our little girl back. I made this big thing out of saying all victims are victims, and whoever did this must have been hurt at some time. Every time Marc starts, you know, I just want to kick him."

"That's really, really an excellent observation."

"And I try to put energy out to him, like that. You know, light. And just, it's okay. It's okay to let her go."

"'Cause you have to imagine this person is very stressed out right now," O'Toole said. "What do I do, what do I do? How do I get out of this situation?"

"But hopefully he realizes that by not hurting her he's gonna be far better off than if he does."

"You bet. And it sounds like Polly is not gonna create lots of problems for him."

"No," Eve said. "No. No. But she's probably gonna cry an awful lot. That might make someone angry. I just don't know."

"It's hard to say what anybody would do under the circumstances. She may read the writing on the wall very well and know what you can and can't do."

"But when she's frightened, she cries," Eve said. "Very much so."

"I think that she's a strong little girl, though."

O'Toole asked about Polly's relationship with boys. Was there any romance?

Eve said that Polly was friends with some boys, but she had never had a boyfriend. Once, at a school dance, she had danced with a boy. He was a classmate, a little chubby, bookish, with braces. He would turn around in his seat and smile at Polly whenever he finished his work. This boy had called Polly on the phone many times, to the great consternation of her father. But Eve said he was smart and had "a sweetness about him."

Polly had started asking her mom hypothetical questions about hanging out with boys. "If my friends and I wanted to go to the movies, like in a group, and let's say there were a boy or two, would you let us do that?" So far, that was still hypothetical.

"Has anybody that you've come into contact with shown an unusual interest? Or been monitoring the investigation? Or [been] overly reassuring, saying everything's gonna turn out okay?"

"No," Eve said. "Everyone's been saying [we] don't know how you can hold it together, I'd be going absolutely berserk. Nobody's been reassuring me. Some of my close friends think they can feel her energy, and they think she's okay. But those are close friends."

"What is the strangest part of this scenario to you, as you've heard it?"

"The fact that he would come in with people home all over, to me, is just beyond belief. And the fact that he didn't know I was there. His reaction was he was so startled and so angry—I heard the girls go over it a few times, not only right after it happened but when they did this reenactment. I'm sure you've seen the tapes. It was quite obvious to them that he was *sure* there was no adult there. And to me that says this wasn't a planned thing at all."

O'Toole asked if Eve had any scenarios she had considered.

"At first I thought he had just taken her to cover himself when he found out there was an adult there. That it was a hit-and-run type of thing. And then when I found out he brought stuff to tie someone up, and he didn't bring enough to tie all these kids up . . . It's just so weird! It doesn't make sense to me. I mean, if he wanted to just get Polly, there would have been so many more ways he could've done it that would have been far less risk to him."

"Mm-hmm."

"It just doesn't make sense," Eve said. "It's like this guy came from the moon. If you wanted to kidnap a kid, you'd come when the mother isn't there. If you were gonna tie up two other kids for whatever reason, you would tie them up in such a way that they're not gonna get loose quick. Or see you."

"And cover your face up."

They had been talking for more than three hours. Before wrapping up the interview around 6:05 p.m., O'Toole gave Eve the opportunity to ask questions.

"I do have one question," Eve said. "Is there a lot more to be known than I know?"

"As far as . . . ?"

"Where she is."

O'Toole understood why Eve would feel this way. Every day was a maelstrom of activity—in the command center, in the searches of fields and woods, in the hundreds of calls to the tip lines. What more there was to know involved a mind-bending flow of information. Some of it looked promising, at least at first, but the vast majority turned out to be completely unrelated. Cases like this were an emotional roller coaster of hot leads and dead ends. A tip comes in, looks like a viable lead, and you chase it down—spending minutes or months—until it filters out into nothing. It didn't make sense to expose Eve to that soul-crushing cycle of hope and despair any more than she already was.

"No," O'Toole said. "Believe me, they're not withholding any information that you need to know."

"I didn't think so."

chapter nineteen

RAPID START

By the time Mary Ellen O'Toole was interviewing Eve, a new flyer had been circulating for two days. It featured Boylan's lifelike portrait, a different photo of Polly, and the attention-grabbing promise of a $200,000 reward. The response was immediate and overwhelming: 800 calls a day. Additional phone lines were installed at the command center to handle the volume of incoming tips.

Three million flyers with the old composite sketch had already been distributed nationwide, at a cost of $90,000. Now volunteers sought to raise another $100,000 to dispatch the new one. Almost immediately, fifteen fundraisers were planned for the coming week. The new flyer was plastered on toll booths and airport sliding doors and truck stop bulletin boards in every state.

The first *New York Times* story about Polly's abduction appeared on Friday, October 15, the day after Boylan released her sketch. It focused on the community response in Petaluma, where most volunteers were parents who "[could] no longer pretend things are normal in what they believed to be a safe community." The crime had seeped into the collective conscience of the town, and everyone was haunted by the details. "I can't sleep at night," a local music teacher said. "No one can."

New flyer with Jeanne Boylan's sketch.
(COURTESY OF JEANNE BOYLAN AND GREG JACOBS)

AS EXPECTED, MORE publicity generated more calls, and more calls produced more tips, and investigators had to quickly triage to determine which of those tips were viable leads. In the command center, the butcher paper filled with handwritten track leads had long since been ripped down. The old-school analog system had been replaced by a system called Rapid Start.

Less than a year in existence, Rapid Start was the FBI's new electronic lead-tracking system, created to manage cases with thousands of leads and rivers of incoming data. A proprietary system created by the FBI, its central mechanism was a software program that enabled the rapid ingestion of leads, so they could be stored, organized, prioritized, and searched. Instant access to key information could speed up the process of obtaining warrants, accelerating an investigation.

The creator of Rapid Start, an agent named Phil Buvia, conceived and developed the case management tool in the fall of 1992. The idea surfaced during a mail bombing case in Birmingham, Alabama—a

"Bureau Special"* code-named VANCEBOM. As the squad supervisor, Agent Buvia was told he could have all the resources he needed, including one hundred of the best handpicked agents from across the country. But leads were pouring in faster than they could be assigned. The ability to quickly capture the data and develop leads was inadequate. Without a tool to manage the information, all those agents would be sitting on their thumbs.

Even when better technology existed, security concerns stymied its adoption by the FBI. The massive bureau operated under a "stovepipe" system at that time, which made it impossible to share sensitive case information in real time between divisions. The VANCEBOM case was managed out of the Atlanta division and supported by the Birmingham division—160 miles away. Information developed each day in Birmingham had to be copied to a computer disc and flown to Atlanta by Bureau plane, which would fly back to Birmingham hours later with a similar disc from Atlanta. This cycle repeated every twenty-four hours.

Even in the early 2000s, when the internet was commercially available, the FBI would strictly use an intranet to guard against outside hackers. No one in the Bureau was allowed to surf the web or send an email—not even to the Justice Department. As Buvia recalled, "You could not hook a modem to any FBI computer in the world—period."

All Bureau Specials have an "After Action," a post-mortem critique to identify what could have been done better. In the mail-bombing case, Buvia realized they had amassed information far more quickly than they could store and retrieve it. They needed some software product—something that could be used in a classified setting—that would help them manage the reams of data that accumulated in a big case. Buvia wrote a memo to FBI headquarters criticizing the Information Management Division for not providing a tool for managing leads that needed

---

* "Bureau Special" is an FBI insider term for a case that summons agents with appropriate specialized skills and disciplines needed to address complex investigations requiring niche expertise.

to be assigned, tracked, and shared between multiple agencies and locations.

In typical Bureau fashion, he was "promoted" to FBI headquarters and put in charge of developing such a tool. "For brick agents, that's like a demotion," Buvia said. At headquarters he oversaw hundreds of direct reports, and he wasn't relieved of his day job. The development of Rapid Start—which didn't even have a name yet—was "collateral duty"—a side project without funding or staffing.

Rapid Start was still a prototype when it was put to the test in the Brown's Chicken Massacre, a 1993 mass murder in which seven employees of a family-owned chicken restaurant were brutally murdered and shoved inside two walk-in freezers in Palatine, Illinois, a suburb thirty-five miles northwest of Chicago. The Palatine chief of police reached out to the FBI for assistance, and Buvia was offered up.

Buvia's superiors asked him what he needed. "I need six people and six laptops," he replied. "And I need them for however long the FBI authorizes us to be there." He also asked for the authority to report to the chief of police instead of the FBI, breaking precedent in a move that earned trust and rapport with local authorities.

In Palatine, he told the investigative team: "We have to enter every scrap of paper, every lead, into this system." They worked night and day, ingesting every tip and clue, and soon they were approaching the limits of their data storage capacity. Rapid Start became integral to the massive* manhunt, which coordinated the efforts of one hundred investigators. As the usefulness of the new technology was proven in this very complex case, Buvia pushed to expand the system and make it more sophisticated.

The need for Rapid Start grew exponentially. Buvia was called to assist with the Rodney King retrial in LA. While he was in LA, he was called to respond to the Waco massacre in Texas. While he was in Waco, the first World Trade Center bombing occurred, and he was sent

---

* Fourteen years after the massacre, the case was solved with technology that didn't exist at the time of the crime: DNA tests conducted on a partially eaten chicken dinner retrieved from the trash and frozen to preserve the DNA. In 2007, investigators linked saliva DNA on the chicken with saliva samples taken from the suspects.

to New York. He found himself running three Rapid Start teams simultaneously, all of them working eighteen hours a day, seven days a week.

When the Unabomber sent a mail bomb to a professor in Tiburon, California, in 1993, the FBI made the UNABOM* case a "Bureau Special" and assigned a team to the San Francisco office. Buvia and four of his people provided on-site information management support to the investigative team.

That's where Phil Buvia was when he got the call about Polly Klaas.

BUVIA AND THE Rapid Start team arrived in Petaluma fifteen hours after Polly's abduction. After receiving the request on that first Saturday, Buvia decided it was too urgent to wait for formal approval on Monday. He'd have to back-brief his bosses.

They loaded the Rapid Start program on laptops in the command center and did the initial data capture while training agents on the Polly Klaas team. Buvia and his team had to return to their UNABOM duties on Monday morning, but they would support their colleagues remotely.

Special agents Gary Joseph and Steve Donohue were chosen to oversee Rapid Start for the Polly Klaas case. Both senior agents, they had the experience and judgment necessary to review and evaluate leads in real time, assign each one a priority, and delegate action. Leads were assigned to one of twelve investigative teams, which paired an FBI agent with a Petaluma detective. Each team chased down a handful of leads at a time and returned with handwritten reports, which were then entered into Rapid Start. At the end of each day, the system printed a summary for Eddie Freyer to review.

By the two-week mark, more than 3,200 tips had been called in to the command center. Three weeks in, investigators had received more

---

*"UNABOM" was the FBI's internal code name—a mashup of "university" and "airline" (Ted Kaczynski's targets) and "bombing." The media later coined the "Unabomber" moniker. As in the Polly Klaas case, the media would play an essential role in solving the case: In 1995, FBI Director Louis Freeh and Attorney General Janet Reno allowed the *New York Times*, the *Washington Post*, and *Penthouse* magazine to publish the Unabomber's manifesto. Ted Kaczynski's sister-in-law read it, recognized the ideas, and convinced her husband to turn his brother in.

than 5,000 tips and chased about 700 leads. Numerous suspects had been identified and either were eliminated or were still under investigation. They still did not have a prime suspect.

The *Chicago Tribune* called Rapid Start* teams "the Untouchables of information management." Freyer nicknamed his team "the mushroom heads." Because Joseph and Donohue spent so much time indoors, bathed in the blue light of their computer screens, mushrooms were bound to start growing on their heads.

ONE OF THE priority leads came from a series of handwritten letters mailed to the *San Francisco Chronicle* and the Drug Enforcement Agency. Scrawled on three-ring notebook paper in childlike handwriting, riddled with misspellings and grammar errors, the letters were signed by someone named "Rhonda" who identified herself as "a truk driver and a drug runner."

Rhonda claimed to be involved with the "#1 trannsport drug ring in the U.S." for the distribution of cocaine. She also claimed to know the whereabouts of Polly and other missing children.

"I no tak Polley," Rhonda wrote. "I no whare she be today."

She was willing to provide information about Polly Klaas as well as inside tips that could help bring down the drug ring. Rhonda said that her husband had been killed and the FBI and DEA were responsible. She believed they wanted her dead as well, so she wanted out of the drug ring, which she said was responsible for a number of kidnappings—including Polly's.

"DEA—FBI play gams I no tel whare Polley Klaas be. Plan gams

---

* Rapid Start was used in the November 18, 1993, kidnapping of Angie Housman, nine, and the December 1, 1993, abduction of Cassidy Senter, ten. Investigators feared a child serial killer after both girls' bodies were found (separately) nine days after they disappeared in St. Louis. That was ruled out in February 1994 when Cassidy's killer, a fast-food worker who lived in her neighborhood, was charged and ruled out as a suspect in Angie's death. Twenty-six years later, in 2019, police found Angie's killer: Earl Webster Cox, a convicted pedophile who ran a child pornography ring. They found him using (previously undetected) DNA on Angie's underwear, matching it with a DNA profile in a national crime database.

Polley hert bad—mabe be ded. Chek on nams—Jaycee Lee Dugard, Amanda "Nikky" Cambell, Scott Christian Echols—all be in sam as manny mor—som liv—som hert bad—manny sel bodie—nott pretty—mothers no lik this—not sam boy or girl."

In order to give up more information, Rhonda had a condition: She wanted out of the drug ring, and wanted the FBI and DEA to "git the man I want," a man named David Cox, who could be contacted via a handheld amateur radio—more commonly called a "ham radio." She warned there would be consequences if she wasn't taken seriously.

"This girl—1 chans. Up to you know. Many others allso—girls boys. You play gams I donnt. I no tak Polley but no whare she is. She git hert if you play gams. Liv or ded your move."

Investigators acted immediately and identified Rhonda Sue Garland, a former FBI informant who reported on drug matters and whose husband had been killed.

The man Rhonda wanted to implicate—David Connell Cox—had been interviewed by the FBI in 1992 after he was found to be "the source of telephonic threats concerning the abduction of children." That same year, an anonymous ham radio transmission had relayed an almost identical message—that four children had been kidnapped in Texas, California, and Arizona and were being held hostage, and that more children would be taken if the DEA did not cease operations in those states. Cox was found to be in possession of ham radio equipment. He had also been convicted of phoning in bomb threats in Dallas, and child molestation in Los Angeles. He was five-foot-eleven, age fifty-one, with brown hair and a graying brown beard. His eyes were blue.

A teletype from the FBI director was dispatched to FBI offices in nine major cities where there had been kidnappings. Marked "immediate"—the highest priority—the teletype noted "Cox's similarities to the composite of Klaas' abductor."

About a week later, the FBI found him in Sacramento, living at a transitional center for people with disabilities. He said he had been diagnosed as an incomplete paraquad, with only partial use of his limbs. On the night of Polly's abduction, he was at home—just ask his caretaker. (They did. The alibi stood.) At face value, he would seem to be off the hook. But deeper digging revealed that Cox was being investigated for welfare fraud and fraudulently receiving disability benefits. He had made false reports in the past.

Cox said he did know a woman named Rhonda who drove a refrigerated truck between California and Florida with her husband, who went by the CB handle "Arkansas Hillbilly." Investigators had been to her last known address, but she had moved on. Asked about her whereabouts, Cox said, "If it's the Rhonda I know, you'll never find her."

Attempts to find Rhonda led to dead ends. But David Cox would remain under investigation by the FBI's Violent Crime Apprehension Program (ViCAP), which helps different law enforcement agencies coordinate efforts to investigate violent serial offenders. He would be arrested on November 19, 1993, three days after *America's Most Wanted* featured the unsolved murder of a teenage girl whose body was found near Pendleton, Oregon, in 1981. Information received after the show would identify Cox as the murderer.

◠◠◠

TWO DAYS AFTER Boylan's sketch was released, one of Polly's neighbors saw it and had a flashback. Daryl Stone, who lived on Fifth Street a couple of blocks from Polly, recalled walking his dog around five p.m. on the evening of Polly's abduction. They were cruising along their normal route—along F Street, across Petaluma Boulevard, down Second Street, up G Street, and back across Petaluma Boulevard, past Starnes Market and Wickersham Park.

Just a few hours before Polly was kidnapped, he noticed a car in the neighborhood. It was a silver Honda Civic station wagon—the same car that his daughter drove—and he briefly wondered if she was coming for a surprise visit. But it wasn't his daughter's car. The driver's side front fender was discolored—possibly gold or red—like a replacement part from a wrecking yard. It was heading slowly south on Fourth Street, as if the driver were hunting for an address. The man behind the wheel looked to be in his forties.

That face rang a bell. Stone remembered seeing this man in the neighborhood about a week before, sitting on a bench in Wickersham

Park. Stone was getting ready for a fly-fishing trip, and he was planning to take his fly rod to the park to practice casting in the open green space. But when he saw the man and another person sitting on a park bench and drinking from a paper bag, he decided not to come back. He had seen the same man at Walnut Park, a few blocks between Polly's house and downtown. Again, the man had been drinking.

The day after he saw the man in Wickersham Park, Daryl Stone heard the news about Polly. But he wouldn't make the connection until two weeks later, right after he saw Jeanne Boylan's sketch. That face reminded him of the man from the park, and that's what prompted him to call the police and offer a witness statement.

Stone's call was logged into Rapid Start as lead number 652. When Dennis Nowicki and Agent Charles Pardee interviewed him on November 5, they asked Stone for a physical description of the driver. Stone recalled a bearded man with curly salt-and-pepper hair.

In later interviews, Stone would recall a sweatshirt with cut-off sleeves, exposing arms that were heavily tattooed.

And also a yellow bandana.

chapter twenty

THE ERT TEAM

A WEEK AFTER POLLY'S ABDUCTION, ON OCTOBER 8, AN ANONYMOUS CALLER phoned to say he knew of Polly's whereabouts and wanted the reward. The call was traced to Vallejo, about an hour south of Petaluma in the East Bay. Investigators raced to the source of the call: a phone booth.

ERT members Tony Maxwell and Frank Doyle came prepared to fingerprint the phone, buttons, phone booth glass, and all the coins inside. They wanted to use a hypersensitive chemical method to capture prints on the coins, but the process required specific temperature conditions that they couldn't control in the field. They tried to pry open the coin box so they could take the change to the lab. No luck.

"Frank," Maxwell said, "let's just take the whole booth."

They called in the local fire department. A hook and ladder truck arrived with heavy-duty tools, and the fire crew sawed the phone booth off at the base. Maxwell and Doyle wrapped everything in plastic and transported it to the FBI office in San Francisco, where the ERT had a small lab-like room in the basement.

A locksmith opened the coin box and carefully removed the change. They'd use cyanoacrylate fuming—a technique most people called "Supergluing"—to chemically harden the fingerprints onto any surface.

that was susceptible to smudging.* It could adhere the print to the object so it could never be erased.

Maxwell and Doyle laid the coins at the bottom of an empty fish tank—the very first piece of equipment purchased for the ERT. Next to the tank, they poured a tube of Superglue onto a heating plate and raised the temperature to seventy-two degrees. Once the Superglue began to fume, they put it inside the fish tank, added a glass of water to the tank to raise the humidity, and covered the tank. Soon a white frost began to form on the coins. That's when they knew it was ready.

The white frost was a thin film of cyanoacrylate that "locked" the fingerprints onto the coins so they couldn't be damaged by the dusting. ERT colleague and fingerprint specialist Mike Stapleton then used fluorescent powder and the ALS. He was able to lift several prints.

The fingerprints were never matched with a suspect, so the lead turned into a very expensive red herring—the phone booth owner sent a $2,000 bill, which the FBI paid—that didn't advance the case. However, it was a milestone for the ERT. To their knowledge, this was the first time Supergluing had ever been used to successfully lift prints from coins. And this was just one of many investigative "firsts" documented in Polly's case—which ultimately served as a proving ground for the FBI's brand-new Evidence Response Team program.

THE ERT CONCEPT emerged during security planning for the 1984 Summer Olympics in Los Angeles. The FBI plays a role in risk assessment and security for Olympic events held on US soil, and an increase in terrorist attacks over the previous decade underscored the need for counterterrorism measures and capabilities for crisis response.

A temporary ERT was formed to respond to any emergencies that should arise at the LA Olympics. After the event, the team disbanded, but the concept persisted. Three years later, a California plane crash got

---

* Years later, Maxwell used Supergluing to lift fingerprints from the body of a murder victim.

forensic experts in the San Francisco FBI field office thinking about the need to form their own ERT.

On December 7, 1987, a plane crashed near the town of Cayucos, California, hitting the ground with such force that the plane disintegrated. All forty-three people aboard Pacific Southwest Airlines flight 1771 were killed. Five people, including two pilots, were believed to have been shot by a disgruntled airline employee. On board as a passenger, he took over the plane, causing it to nose-dive and crash in a cattle field on its route from LA to San Francisco.

The disgruntled employee was David Burke. The day before the crash, he had gone to his boss, Ray Thomson, to settle a past grievance, explaining that he wouldn't be able to take care of his family without consideration of his request. Thomson declined his request. Burke knew his boss was scheduled to fly from LA to San Francisco the following day, and he bought a ticket to board that flight. Burke smuggled a Smith & Wesson Magnum .44 onto the plane.

Among the millions of pieces of evidence recovered from the crime scene was an air sickness bag inscribed with a handwritten note, an airline seat with two bullet holes, and a gun with six spent cartridges. A fragment of a finger was still stuck in the trigger guard. That finger yielded a print that led to a positive identification of the disgruntled employee. The message written on the air sickness bag revealed his motive.

Hi Ray. I think it's sort of ironical that we ended up like this. I asked for leniency for my family. Remember? Well, I got none and you'll get none.

Tony Maxwell, who was working on the San Francisco bomb squad, had honeymooned near the crash site, so he knew it was barely two minutes of flight time from crashing in his division and becoming his responsibility. The San Francisco division—his territory—wouldn't have had the resources, personnel, and budget, to be able to respond. The LA division was able to dispatch some of the members of the disbanded Olympic ERT to process the massive crime scene. The San Francisco division didn't have those resources.

Plane crashes were complicated places to gather evidence, not only because of their massive size, but also because of overlapping jurisdiction. The National Transportation Safety Board (NTSB) sent aircraft experts to the crash site to gather evidence of a mechanical failure. The FBI sent agents trained in collecting evidence of a crime. An FBI agent and NTSB officer would walk the site together, each recognizing the value of different types of evidence—body parts, jewelry, personal effects, as well as parts of the airplane.

Only later, once the evidence was examined and the cause of the crash was determined, would one agency take the lead. If the plane had been hijacked, the FBI would take over. If the crash was caused by a mechanical failure, the NTSB would call the shots.

In San Francisco, Maxwell worked on the bomb squad with Doyle, a brilliant evidence technician who would one day become the explosives expert on a TV show called *Mythbusters*. Both enjoyed their work— collecting evidence after a bomb blast—but in their spare time they had started acquiring other forensic skills, like fingerprinting and crime scene sketching. They discussed the sobering reality that their division would not have been prepared to respond to the PSA plane crash. They started kicking around the idea of forming a permanent ERT.

In those days, the FBI was known for a heavily top-down culture. If an idea didn't come from headquarters, it was a challenge to get support. Maxwell and Doyle encountered pushback from every direction. Headquarters was disinclined to allocate the funds. Fellow agents didn't understand why the system should be changed. The FBI lab forbade the use of chemical tests in the field. And its latent prints section felt that tools such as fluorescent powder and ALS should be used only in the controlled environment of the lab, not at a crime scene in the field.

Complicating things further, the methods of the bomb squad were different from the meticulous procedures of CSI teams because of the nature of the evidence and the crime scene. The two very different roles and subcultures often clashed. At a bomb site, bits of evidence landed randomly. But at crime scenes, the placement and patterns were presumed to have logical significance, and documenting that order was integral to reconstructing a crime.

Meanwhile, their colleague, David Alford, was encountering similar needs. Prior to joining the FBI, Alford had worked at the Kentucky Police State Crime Lab, where he became an expert in serology, blood spatter analysis, and hair and fibers. His employer sent him to the FBI lab for training in serology, and he learned how to examine body fluids: blood, semen, urine, vaginal fluid, fecal matter, and saliva. By the time he joined the FBI in 1984, he was among the most experienced forensic experts in the Bureau.

In 1990, Alford was called out with a team to investigate a murder on a fishing trawler just off Half Moon Bay. The boat had left the dock with three crew members on board, but only two came back alive. The third was found dead in the engine compartment. Since the crime took place in the Pacific Ocean—offshore—it fell under federal jurisdiction. The FBI sent its San Francisco–based violent crime squad, which over-saw crimes on government reservations, fugitives, and crimes on the high seas.

At the time, the FBI typically relied on local police departments or crime labs to come out on request and assist with major crime scene investigations. It was an informal arrangement based on good will: Most of those local departments received a great deal of free training—on everything from crime lab techniques to interviewing—from the FBI, so they were expected to help the feds in return. This time, no agency was available to respond. The feds would have to do it themselves.

Alford drove to Half Moon Bay with the other members of the vio-lent crime squad and their supervisor, Gerald L. Mack. After stepping aboard the floating crime scene and sizing up the situation, Alford real-ized they didn't even have the most basic supplies for bagging and tag-ging. So he drove to a local grocery store and bought a stack of brown paper grocery bags. Back at the boat, he noticed the bags were printed with propaganda advocating the legalization of marijuana. Alford chuck-led as he packaged crime scene evidence and imagined eyebrows raising in the lab when someone saw the writing on the bag.

This incident made it painfully clear how ill-prepared the FBI was to process crime scenes without outside help. Mack, the supervisory special agent in charge of the responding squad, vowed never again to be put in that position. Mack wrote the famous memo that led to the 1990 creation of the San Francisco ERT. Maxwell and Doyle would also be credited for developing the concept and pushing for its approval. Doyle,

Maxwell, and Alford became three of the thirteen original members of the FBI's first ERT.

The Polly Klaas kidnapping was their first major case.*

◦◠◠◦

WHILE MAXWELL, DOYLE, and Stapleton were processing the phone booth where the call about Polly had been made, David Alford was making the first of three trips to hand-carry evidence to the FBI lab in DC.

Booked on a commercial flight, Alford was transporting more than one hundred pieces of evidence. The majority of his haul was evidence collected from Polly's house. These specimens included electrostatic dust lifts, vacuum sweepings, brushes containing Polly's locks, head hair samples from family and friends, cords from the Super Nintendo, bedding from Polly's top bunk, crime scene photos, latent prints, and the blue area rug from Polly's floor, where the girls had been playing.

At Washington International, Alford hailed a cab to the J. Edgar Hoover Building, a seven-story, 2.8-million-square-foot Brutalist complex that housed 7,000 feds on two square blocks of Pennsylvania Avenue. Designed in the 1960s, the inward-facing concrete fortress had all the charm of a 1970s computer server mated with a Rubik's Cube. The physical embodiment of the word "bureau," it was declared "the ugliest building in DC" by architectural critics and described by the FBI itself as a building that "retained the idea of a central core of files."

Alford walked up the stone steps, flashed his credentials at a security guard, and proceeded through the turnstile. He took the elevator to the third floor. The Hoover Building was vast, and it was easy to get lost in its maze of endless beige hallways and side corridors. Even though he had been to headquarters a number of times, he had to stop and ask directions to the Trace Evidence Unit.†

---

* The ERT program was authorized by FBI director Louis Freeh on October 1, 1996—the three-year anniversary of Polly's abduction. Soon every FBI field office in the nation had its own ERT. Today there are around 1,000 ERT members nationwide, and each of the FBI's fifty-six field offices has its own team.

† This unit has had several names throughout its history, including the Microscopic Analysis Unit and the Hair and Fibers Unit.

To get there, Alford navigated hallways decorated with black-and-white portraits of FBI directors, passed gun exhibits and galleries of mug shots from the FBI's "Most Wanted" list. An escalator delivered him to the FBI lab.*

The lab was the only part of the Hoover Building open to the public. Every day, docents led public tours of the lab, where visitors could peer through glass walls at evidence technicians and examiners doing their jobs. On the other side of the glass, the work environment could feel oddly zoo-like, but lab workers learned how to tune out the parade of curious faces. The glass walls were thick enough to block out the sound of tour guides exclaiming, "The examiners you see are working on *real cases!*"

The Scientific Analysis Section of the FBI's Laboratory Division included multiple units: DNA, Serology, Firearms/Toolmarks, Hair and Fibers, Materials Analysis, Chemistry and Toxicology, Questioned Documents, and the Graphics Unit. The Trace Evidence Unit focused on evidence too small to be seen by the naked eye. As one technician put it, "If you have to use a microscope to look at something, we're probably going to get it."

At this point in time, all lab examiners were required to be FBI agents, though they could be assisted by civilian evidence technicians. The examiners were expected to adhere to the standard FBI dress code: sport coat, white shirt, understated tie for men; business casual for women. Once they arrived in the lab, they could exchange the sport coat for a white laboratory coat, the tie still peeking out from the collar.

Tall and good-looking, with a serious face and impeccable manners, Hair and Fibers examiner Chris Allen was a former dentist who had joined the FBI in 1987. One day he opened his fridge in Virginia and noticed Polly's face on a milk carton. That's when he knew this case was big.

In a crime lab, hairs and fibers from unknown sources are known as "question samples" ("Q samples" in lab speak). They're compared to "known samples" ("K samples"), such as fibers from carpets, couches,

---

* The FBI lab was moved to Quantico a decade later.

rugs, and other sources at a crime scene. Other known samples include hairs plucked from the heads of people who had a legitimate reason to be there.

Alford and Tony Maxwell's use of the electrostatic dust print lifters had yielded a number of tiny fibers that were challenging to identify. Between the vacuuming of the rug and the electrostatic lifts, there could be thousands or even tens of thousands of fibers collected in a mishmash. Polly's vacuuming of her room that day had certainly decreased the volume of unrelated fibers, and that made the job of sorting through the rest a little bit easier.

Allen donned colored goggles that accentuated the infinitesimal fibers in the blue-toned light of the ALS. This made some fibers glow like white cotton under a blacklight. Using tweezers, Allen transferred a number of similar fibers to a microscope slide to prepare them for the painstaking process of analysis. He arranged them in tidy patterns and loops, securing them in the center of the slide with a dollop of xylene, a mounting fluid. He blotted off the excess fluid and added drops of Permount to affix the paper-thin cover slide he then pressed onto the specimen.

Scrutinizing these fibers under a microscope, Allen needed to figure out their source. He believed they likely came from the carpet inside of an automobile. Determining the exact material and source of specific carpet fiber is no small feat. The ERT had gathered particulates from a number of items and surfaces. Any one lift or sweep could yield thousands of fibers to analyze, with no promise of finding anything useful to investigators. Each type of unknown fiber had to be mounted and viewed under a microscope.

Seeing the need for a collection of known samples, Allen's supervisor, unit chief Doug Deedrick, was in the process of creating the FBI's automotive carpet fiber database. It would be a clearinghouse of fiber samples of home, industrial, and automotive carpets. The problem was, the carpets were constantly changing. With so many makes and models of cars released each year, keeping up with the latest automotive fibers was a Sisyphean task. Isolating and pinpointing fiber types often came down to the lab examiner's experience and expertise. While crime scene investigators were increasingly being recognized with a touch of glory, the creative thinking and investigative insights that occurred in the lab often went unsung.

The other thing about hair and fiber analysis was that it often took months to connect the dots, so it required patience as well as meticulous attention to detail. After Allen determined the source of the fibers was likely an automobile carpet, he compared them with fiber samples obtained from vehicles owned by Polly's family and friends. After eliminating these known vehicles as the source, he set these unknown carpet fiber samples aside for future use. They might have value down the road, if and when more evidence was found.

David Alford, who had hand-carried the evidence from Sonoma, had done similar work on hair and fibers in the Kentucky State Police Crime Lab. Now he considered the improbable journey these fibers must have made if they had indeed come from the kidnapper's car. They would have affixed themselves to the kidnapper's shoe, clung to his sole as he walked across asphalt, dirt, and grass, only to detach, silently and invisibly, at just the right moment, as he stood on the bedroom floor. Hours later, compelled by static electricity, they would have to rise and cling to the Mylar film, then travel thousands of miles to DC. Wherever they came from, these fibers were now providing silent testimony on the stage of an FBI microscope. Alford had been doing forensic work for years, but the improbable possibilities never failed to amaze him.

While examining the white bindings, Allen had discovered a fiber that looked unlike the rest. He had also set this aside to compare against future samples. This tiny fiber would turn out to be critical.

The other crucial piece of evidence had come from the blue floral area rug where the girls had been sitting and playing. Allen had discovered it by vacuuming the rug that Polly had so diligently vacuumed herself on the afternoon of the sleepover. Two human hairs. One of them, dark brown in color, was only about a centimeter long. Under the microscope, Allen saw it had a four-millimeter root sheath—an infinitesimal bit of skin from the scalp. When a hair that is actively growing is pulled or yanked out, it retains a bit of the follicle, with small amounts of tissue. The presence of a root sheath indicated that the hair hadn't been naturally shed. It had been "forcibly removed." Evidence of a struggle. The tiny bit of tissue also contained a small amount of DNA. There's DNA in a hair shaft, but not much, so tissue is advantageous.

As valuable as the hair and carpet fibers might turn out to be, they couldn't flush out a suspect. Like fingerprints, Q samples are not useful until you have a suspect and a search warrant to obtain hairs from his head and body and fibers from his clothes, home, and automobile.

These tiny bits of evidence would sit unchallenged for fifty-two days.

chapter twenty-one

THE SWAT TEAM

∽◠∾

October 17, 1993

ON THE SECOND SUNDAY AFTER POLLY'S DISAPPEARANCE, THE *SAN FRANCISCO Examiner* published a message for Polly and her kidnapper, written by Marc and Eve:

> *Whoever you are, wherever you are, please return Polly to her family. She belongs here. We miss Polly so much. We miss the twinkle in her eye and her sweet humor. We long to see her beautiful smile and hear her beautiful voice. Darling, if you can read this, please know that your mommy and daddy love you so much and we will continue to search for you until we can hold you safely in our loving arms again.*

Later that day, a ransom call came into the Petaluma police command center. The man claimed to know the whereabouts of Polly and demanded $10,000 for her safe return.

The amount triggered red flags. Why would he ask for ten grand when the reward for Polly's safe return—guaranteed to even the kidnapper himself—was $200,000?

Later that day, the man called twice more. His third call was traced to 470 Lakeville Circle, a condominium complex in Petaluma. He phoned again four times on Monday, providing ransom instructions: He wanted the money dropped off around five p.m. at a bus stop on Fretis Road and Lakeville Highway. After he had collected the money, Polly would be delivered safely to Casa Grande High School in Petaluma.

Despite strong suspicions about the dubious amount of the ransom demand, the FBI assembled a team of eight agents and orchestrated the drop. One agent would place the ransom package, wrapped in a white plastic trash bag, under a bench at the bus stop, then leave the vicinity. Three mobile surveillance units—agents working in teams of two— would be watching from different concealed positions surrounding the bus stop. When the UNSUB appeared to collect the money, they would converge upon him and make the arrest.

This was the job of the Special Operations Group (SOG), a team of FBI agents who support various cases as a surveillance asset. Not to be confused with the Special Surveillance Group (SSG), a counter-intelligence team of full-time specialists who aren't sworn agents but are considered the best surveillance assets in the world, the SOG consists largely of agents who operate in undercover situations but don't make a career of it. They are furnished with an identity and the documents to support it. Wherever they're working, they dress and groom themselves to blend in with locals. Operating out of covert locations, they drive private or commercial vehicles and may appear to be plumbers, landscapers, or soccer moms. You may see them, but you'd never notice them.

SOG teams conduct two types of surveillance: mobile and stationary. Mobile involves a combination of aircraft and vehicles, often working in concert to avoid detection. Stationary may involve renting a house, as in the UNABOM case, when agents rented a house near the Unabomber's cabin and posed as neighbors. The SOG also installs trap-traces on phone lines and plants bugs in unexpected locations—at least once in a graveyard where a subject was believed to visit and speak to his victim's tombstone. (They called him "Tombstone Timmy.")

Now, approaching the hour of the five p.m. ransom drop, three mobile surveillance units took their positions around the drop site, a three-sided bus stop structure on Fretis Road Circle. Concealed or disguised, they watched everyone who came near the bus stop. At four p.m., a tall, thin man appeared walking east, dressed in a dark jacket, dark pants, and a baseball cap. He kept walking. Ten minutes later, a white man riding a bicycle stopped briefly at the bus stop. He went on his way.

Around 4:24 p.m., when the coast was clear, an agent walked casually to the bus stop and slid the white garbage bag underneath a bench, then left the area. The SOG units waited and watched. Ten minutes passed. Twenty minutes. Thirty. An hour later, no one had come. At 5:24 p.m., agents retrieved the package and the surveillance operation ended.

Plan B was already unfolding. Anticipating the likelihood of a no-show, investigators had prepared an affidavit for a search warrant on the condo where the ransom calls had originated. Search warrants typically take a few days, but can be expedited in the case of imminent danger, and the chance that Polly was still alive supported that. At 4:45 p.m., as agents were surveilling the drop site, a federal judge across town was signing the search warrant. Within an hour, outside a brown condominium, the SWAT team was staging.

❧

BY THE EARLY 1990s, SWAT teams were still a relatively new phenomenon in the FBI. The concept of Special Weapons Assault Teams (later renamed Special Weapons and Tactics) had originated in police departments across the country in the late 1960s as a response to sniping incidents against police officers and civilians. After the 1965 Watts riots in Los Angeles, the LAPD had formed the nation's first so-called SWAT team. Other cities followed.

On September 5, 1972, ten days into the Summer Olympics in Munich, Germany, eight terrorists dressed in track suits snuck into the Olympic Village at four a.m. Armed with Kalashnikovs and duffel bags filled with grenades, they were members of Black September, a militant group affiliated with the Palestinian Liberation Army. The commandos slipped into an athlete housing complex, where they killed two members of Israel's Olympic team and took nine others hostage, demanding the release of 234 Palestinian prisoners in Israel and two leaders of a West German terrorist group.

The West German police attempted to ambush the terrorists and rescue the hostages. But they didn't have trained snipers or an organized tactical response. Their botched rescue attempt ended twenty hours later with seventeen people dead: all eleven Israeli athletes, five of the eight hostage-takers, and one West German policeman. The hostage crisis hijacked international media coverage of the Olympics, making this incident the first major terrorist attack broadcast live to a worldwide audience. By some estimates, 900 million people watched it unfold on TV.

It was a wake-up call for the world and for anyone working in law enforcement. At the time of the 1972 Munich massacre, the FBI had no formal SWAT teams. The concept was under development at Quantico, but it wasn't formalized until after the Wounded Knee occupation of 1973. The seventy-one-day standoff began when 200 armed activists seized the town of Wounded Knee, on South Dakota's Pine Ridge Reservation, to protest corruption in tribal leadership and mistreatment by the US government. The occupation escalated into a standoff where the FBI faced armed opponents who were not traditional "bad guys" but protesting citizens.

Wounded Knee, following so closely on the heels of the Munich Olympics, compelled the FBI to find a better way to respond. "The lack of organization not only of the SWAT teams but also the lack of qualified command personnel was a serious problem that continually played out in major incidents around the country in following years," former agent James Botting wrote in *Bullets, Bombs, and Fast Talk*.

As with the evolution of the ERT, the impetus arose during security planning for the 1984 Summer Olympics in Los Angeles. Responsible for preventing and responding to domestic terrorist attacks, the FBI needed to plan for—and guard against—another Munich massacre.

Counterterrorism security concerns for the 1984 LA Olympics accelerated the FBI's SWAT program. In the event of a terrorism strike, the FBI would take the leading role over local police in responding, deploying its own SWAT team as well as the Delta "Blue Light" Team, a multiservice tactical team that some described as "the United States' answer to British Special Air Service and the West German GSG9."

Since then, the FBI had expanded its program to include regional SWAT teams that could mobilize highly trained members from different states to respond immediately to a crisis. The effectiveness of a SWAT team was predicated on speed, the element of surprise, and the ability to outnumber and overwhelm subjects. Most surrendered without a fight.

The San Francisco SWAT team combined agents who worked in different areas and on assignments ranging from bank robberies to counterterrorism. They trained together twice a month and kept a go-bag handy for rapid deployments. They received no extra pay for this collateral duty, but most did it because the work was exciting and, when not terrifying, fun. It also tended to form bonds of trust and lifelong friendships. Which was the reason that Eddie Freyer had called SWAT colleague Tom LaFreniere to come with him on the night of Polly's kidnapping, even though LaFreniere worked in another investigative program within the San Francisco Division. LaFreniere would come to assist with the Polly Klaas case on nights and weekends, after his regular duties.

⌒⌒⌒

As the SWAT team leader, LaFreniere was in charge of writing the operations order for each mission. This one would deploy a joint SWAT team with members from Petaluma PD and the FBI. Hoping to find Polly, they would enter the condo where the ransom calls had originated. The two-bedroom unit was the residence of a twenty-year-old certified nursing assistant named Sophia Simms, who lived with her fiancé and two other roommates.

After photographing the condo, the SWAT team entered the residence. Moving in pairs, they flowed through the condo in a precise sequence orchestrated in advance: six agents and cops in the living room, two or three in each bedroom, one in the bathroom.

The two men and two women inside the condo were handcuffed and taken down to the police station for questioning. Then the agents and cops searched the condo. They collected a personal journal located in a bedroom and three *San Francisco Examiner* papers dated October 15, 16, and 17—the dates immediately following the release of Boylan's sketch. LaFreniere photographed the interior of the condo, and they were out by 7:45 p.m.

At the police station, the primary suspect was identified: James Heard, a twenty-year-old nursing assistant at a convalescent hospital. Simms was his fiancée.

In his first interview with detective Larry Pelton, Heard denied making the ransom calls. Pelton played him an audio recording. The voice on the tape—that wasn't his, Heard said. He had nothing to do with this nonsense.

Then they brought in polygrapher Ron Hilley.

Heard again denied making the ransom calls. Then, under the influence of the polygraph test, his story began to change. Heard admitted he'd made the calls, but only because he was threatened with death if he refused. He described two white men walking into his home, pointing a long-barrel revolver at his head, and forcing him to make the calls, telling him every word to say. The intruders purportedly drove him to a pay phone near a deli by Casa Grande High School. Again, they dialed the command center number and told him what to say. He made a third call from the pay phone, after which the men pushed him away and departed. He walked two miles home. One of the men had called him later and asked him if he'd told anyone about the calls. He replied that he had not. "Keep it that way," the man supposedly said, "or I'm going to shoot you."

Hilley and his polygraph gently nudged him toward the truth.

Heard then admitted that he had lied. He'd made the calls "because I needed the money." He said he owed $10,000 in gambling debts, $2,000 to a local acquaintance, and $7,000 to a guy in New York. He didn't recall how many calls he had made—maybe four or five. The recording of the ransom calls—yes, that was his voice. The polygrapher brought the detectives back into the room, and they asked Heard to repeat his admissions and provide a written statement.

Heard was taken into custody and charged with two felonies: attempted extortion and posing as a kidnapper. He would be prosecuted by the Sonoma County DA and sentenced, in 1994, to six months in jail after pleading guilty.

A FEW WEEKS later, an FBI informant called in with a tip that Polly was being held captive in a remote cabin somewhere in Mendocino. LaFreniere mobilized the SWAT team, this time for a covert night operation.

Instead of wearing their "all-blacks"—the standard SWAT uniform—they dressed in camouflage and face paint. LaFreniere was a skilled night navigator able to read the terrain and find his way with a topographical map and compass. But it was a moonless night, too dark to see the ridges and draws, so he had to resort to a compass vector and dead reckoning.

The terrain was treacherous in the dark. They waded through a hip-deep creek, fought their way through blackberry bushes, and descended slopes so steep that one SWAT team member lost purchase and tumbled into a ravine. The bottom of the ravine didn't have enough light for night-vision goggles to function. They had to switch to infrared.

Belly-crawling up a slope so steep they had to use climbing techniques, the SWAT team crested a ridge and spotted the cabin.

The cabin was empty.

chapter twenty-two

TROUBLE WITHIN

༼ ༽

Mid-October

THREE WEEKS INTO THE SEARCH, INCOMING LEADS HAD SLOWED TO A MANAGE-
able pace. Most Petaluma officers returned to their regular assignments,
and the FBI reduced the number of agents working full-time on the
case. The joint investigation was winnowed down to a core team: twelve
Petaluma officers and twelve FBI agents. The team was led by Eddie
Freyer and Vail Bello and supervised by Mark Mershon and Pat Parks.

While the feds had a massive budget, the City of Petaluma was
burning through limited cash reserves. In just the first two weeks, police
had logged more than 2,200 hours of overtime—a full year of one officer's time. The $100,000 cost was four times more than the department
reserved for overtime in any given month. But Petaluma was willing to
spend every penny of the city's $337,000 reserve fund if that's what it
took. "We have to find Polly," said city manager John Scharer. "As long
as there are active leads, we have to let the police work."

Those officers had not taken a day off since the kidnapping. The
biggest cost was human, and it wasn't limited to the investigators. Those
officers were coming home—when they even came home at all—to
exhausted spouses and family relationships strained by their ongoing
absence.

A new city order in mid-October mandated every Petaluma officer on the investigative team to take at least one day off every two weeks. The timing of the order lined up with a longstanding hunting trip that several buddies on the force had planned and paid for months ago. All were members of the investigations unit: Captain Dave Long, Sergeant Vail Bello, and Detectives Gene Wallace and Danny Fish, a duo nicknamed "The A Team" for their speed in chasing down leads.

The trip became the topic of a big group discussion: Should they cancel it? Police chief Dennis DeWitt decided they should go. There was enough of a lull in leads that others could cover for them. The break could be beneficial, for the investigation as well as the individuals. A few days in the wild would help the guys decompress, recharge, and return with clear-minded perspective. If there was a break in the case and they were needed, the chief could call the local sheriffs and have them drive out to the hunting camp.

Off the grid in Colorado, they tried not to think about the case. But not even bourbon and bullshitting around a campfire could drive it out of their minds. They cut the trip short and came home early, without spotting a single deer or elk. What they did see, on the drive through Colorado and Nevada, were gas stations and truck stops displaying Polly's smile on missing-person posters.

On their first morning back, Bello walked into the command center and assumed his duties. But everyone was acting oddly.

"Hey, man," Freyer said. "What are you doing?"

"Just trying to get back up to snuff."

"You talk to anyone yet?"

"What do you mean?"

"Let's go to breakfast."

At a local diner, Freyer broke the news. There had been some changes in leadership while Bello was away.

"Nobody told you?" Freyer said.

"No, man," Bello said.

"Dude," Freyer said, "you're out."

The chief had taken Bello off the case. He'd been replaced by Mike

Meese, a rival. Bello felt his face grow hot and his hands beginning to shake.

"Why'd you go?" Freyer said.

"What do you mean?" Bello said. "We all talked about it!"

"Yeah, but why'd you go?"

Bello would probably ask himself that question every day for the rest of his life. Back at the command center, he stormed down the hall into the office of his supervisor, Dave Long, who had been with him on the hunting trip and came back to the same surprise.

"What the fuck is going on around here?" Bello said loudly.

Long lowered his head and raised his palms in silence. What could he say?

"Am I out?" Bello said.

"Vail, I just . . ." Long's face said the rest.

"You know what?" Bello yelled, shaking with rage. "Fuck this place! Fuck you! Fuck everybody! I quit. If I'm out, then I'm fucking out."

He slammed his badge on Long's desk and drove home.

Ironically, Bello himself had predicted this. Weeks before, as the investigation had begun to take on a life of its own, Bello had thought to himself: *We're gonna lose people because of this case.*

He never thought he would be the first one.

EVERY LAW ENFORCEMENT agency in the world has its share of rivalries, petty jealousies, and interpersonal conflicts. In the crucible of a major case, these pre-existing issues tend to catalyze and combust.

Well before the kidnapping, Petaluma PD had two factions. The camps were defined by the two captains: Pat Parks and Dave Long. They reported to Chief Dennis DeWitt and led the two primary units within the department: patrol and investigations.

Most officers fell into one of the "camps," and not necessarily the one where they fell on the org chart. Andy Mazzanti felt caught in the middle. He liked and respected both Parks and Long, and he had a long history with both of them. He saw them both as great leaders, though their personalities, strengths, and leadership styles were very different.

Mazzanti had met Dave Long as a teenager on the wrong side of the law. Attending a Merle Haggard concert at the Petaluma fair, Mazzanti and his friends drank a little too much and ended up in a massive brawl. When a sergeant tried to subdue him with a night stick, Mazzanti used his "Mongo" size and linebacker skills to shrug him off. Eventually he and a dozen others involved in the melee were handcuffed, arrested, and booked. He rode to jail in the back of Long's patrol car. As they sobered up in the cell, he and his buddies raked Dixie cups across the bars and sang every prison song they could think of, yelling, "Let us out, screws!" Long chuckled at their antics but eventually made them knock it off. They saw Long again in court, where the charges were dropped.

When Mazzanti was a little older, he did a ride-along shift with Long—an opportunity available to any interested citizen. The ride-along included a 115-mile-per-hour car chase to catch a fugitive who had been involved in a stabbing. The half-hour chase ended in an apple orchard, where a young and wide-eyed Mazzanti watched, from the safety of the patrol car, as Long and other officers chased the suspect on foot and cuffed him under the apple trees.

Mazzanti signed up for the police academy the very next Monday.

Long was confident, compassionate, and stoic. He endured hardship without complaining, valued structure, and honored the chain of command. He was an implementer who could take a directive and make it happen. He had a quieter leadership style but didn't hesitate to speak up for what he believed.

Mazzanti had also met Pat Parks during his teenage years, when he and his friends, "occasionally involved in mischief," got to know the freckled, red-headed young officer who had a good rapport with youth from all walks of life. The teenagers teased him—*Hey, Howdy Doody!*—though he really looked more like Steve Bolander, Ron Howard's character in the film *American Graffiti*. High-energy and outgoing, he had a strong sense of integrity but also a good sense of humor.

When Mazzanti joined the force, he got to know Parks as a leader who was intuitive, kind, creative, and willing to think outside of the box.

Parks was sensitive and empathetic, not afraid to shed tears or show real emotion. Some of the tough-guy personalities on the force dismissed it as softness, but those very traits enabled him to build a strong rapport with witnesses and victims. Of everyone on the investigative team, he was closest with Polly's family.

Parks once had to investigate Mazzanti for an internal affairs situation. An arrestee who was booked and detained overnight claimed his confiscated wallet had been returned with $100 missing. (It turned out to be a clerical error on the property receipt.) Mazzanti asserted he had not stolen the money. Parks said he believed him, but wanted him to submit to hypnosis. Mazzanti did some research and refused, citing reasons related to his faith. After questioning Mazzanti about how his faith factored into the decision, Parks agreed to go to church with him one Sunday. That was the day he became a Christian. Years later, he would officiate Mazzanti's wedding. Decades later, he would retire from law enforcement and become the pastor of Bodega Bay Church.

Mazzanti liked and respected both captains. As a detective, he reported to Long, who oversaw investigations. Parks was in charge of patrol. Parks and Long didn't always see eye to eye, and each of their camps contained officers who felt loyal to one captain but reported to the other. Mazzanti tried to stay neutral, but he could see the rift widening under the pressure of the investigation. Personalities were clashing at every level. Petaluma chief Dennis DeWitt was kind and magnanimous, if not particularly decisive, and many of the petty jealousies festered where they might have been squelched.

If the dynamics inside the investigation had been anything like they are in the movies, the friction would have come from a pissing match between police and the FBI. The Bureau had a reputation, not entirely undeserved, for coming in and taking over. While that may have happened in other cases, this one was an exception that would be held up as an example of how a joint investigation can and should work. The cops and feds worked collaboratively in pairs of equal rank, and many of those teams would evolve into lifelong friendships. This was true for Sergeant Bello and Case Agent Freyer. On the leadership front, the same bonds were forming between Captain Parks and ASAC Mark Mershon.

Much of the tension inside the investigation existed not *between* the two agencies, but rather *within* them—between levels on the chain of command. Many of these cops and agents exemplified the type-A personality: driven, competitive, impatient, and motivated to achieve. They were all competent, but they didn't always agree on what should be done and how—which is actually beneficial for an investigation, because it means more avenues are explored, and theories are vetted more thoroughly.

There were many heroes and zero villains (other than the kidnapper), and everyone did the best they could with what they had. That's the one thing they would always agree on. But the conflicts inside the investigation ultimately turned into bad blood that would persist for decades, and wounds that would never quite heal. These same problems yielded insights and lessons that would prove useful in the future, rippling out through debriefings and classes. These lessons, passed on, would save lives.

༒

To UNDERSTAND THESE insights, it helps to rewind to the beginning and understand the chain of command.

On the night of the kidnapping, Dave Long, the captain in charge of investigations, was off duty and briefly off the grid on a weekend camping trip. In his absence, it was protocol for the patrol captain to step into his role. Pat Parks was notified of the kidnapping that night, and he was told that the incident commander—Vail Bello, who reported to Long—had everything under control. The FBI was on its way, and Petaluma PD was mobilized. So Parks came in early Saturday morning and assumed the supervisory role.

When Long returned a day or two later, protocol called for the baton to be passed from Parks (patrol) to Long (investigations), and that's precisely what happened. However, so much had occurred in those blistering forty-eight hours that Parks had amassed a considerable amount of investigative knowledge, and Long was in the position of having to get up to speed. It made sense for Parks to stay involved, so he did. His skills and knowledge served the investigation well, but some colleagues would complain whenever they felt Parks was going "out of his lane."

Nearly three decades later, Long would reflect and wonder if he should have swapped roles with Parks, for the sake of "the continuity of the investigation."

Much of the conflict inside the investigation regarded the handling of Kate and Gillian. Child and Adolescent Forensic Interviewers (CAFIs) did not yet exist, and investigators with interviewing and interrogation skills didn't have any training in or knowledge of how to handle child witnesses. So they treated them like miniature adults. As a result, Kate and Gillian were, as Freyer put it, "roughed up," with negative psychological consequences—not only for the girls, but for certain investigators and also for the morale of the team.

Detective Dennis Nowicki, the bearded, six-foot-three bear of a cop who resembled the first composite sketch, had interviewed Kate on the night of the kidnapping, while Mazzanti interviewed Gillian. Nowicki came out of the interview feeling highly doubtful, but he later changed his mind.

Five days later, when the girls were subjected to a late-night interrogation, Nowicki was forced to re-interview Kate—this time, in the "bad cop" role.

"I don't want to do this," he said. His initial skepticism had faded, and now he believed the girls were telling the truth—and had been all along. He had the chops to lean on a bad guy, but these were twelve-year-old girls. He had a two-year-old daughter himself, and a son around Polly's age. But someone had to do the job. Freyer and Bello decided it would be Nowicki.

The things said to those girls in that room would, three years later, inspire district attorney Greg Jacobs to pick up the phone and call the girls to tell them how shocked and sorry he was at how they had been treated. In hindsight, everyone would agree: That was a huge mistake.

Five days after the "bad cop" interview, the investigative team developed another approach to elicit more details from Kate and Gillian. They'd have the girls reenact the crime—on videotape—in Polly's room.

At the time, it seemed like a good idea. Perhaps the act of physically recreating the crime, instead of just talking about it, would jog free some repressed or forgotten detail. The videotape could be a tool for bringing other investigators up to speed on what had happened. It was an opportunity to repair rapport with the girls. The investigative team was in agreement about what to do, but not who should do it.

Bello wanted to send in Nowicki, to let him rebuild the trust he had lost when he had to play "bad cop." Nowicki was hurting. He felt guilty for having made the girls cry and resentful for having been put in a villainous role. And since Nowicki had already interviewed Kate twice, it made sense for the continuity of the investigation.

On the other hand, Pat Parks, the captain in charge of patrol, had a good rapport with Polly's family. He was gentle, empathetic, and physically less imposing. His calm presence might be more likely to comfort and encourage the girls. He was the key liaison with Polly's family and had earned Eve's trust. Since the reenactment would take place at her house, maybe Parks should do it.

"Vail, this is your case," said Chief DeWitt. "What do you think?"

"I don't know who should do it," said Bello, who was rankled by the idea of a supervisor stepping into a practitioner's role. "But I know who shouldn't do it, and that's Captain Parks."

Parks was taken aback.

"These girls are already pissed at us," Vail said. "If you say one thing that makes them think we don't believe them, we've lost them forever."

The discussion grew heated. DeWitt made the call: Parks would do it.

Bello's Irish temper went nuclear.

"Dude," Parks told Bello later in the hallway. "Sometimes you've got more balls than brains."

Kate and Gillian and their families agreed to the reenactment. Parks guided the girls through each moment and detail of the crime. Exactly where and how they were sitting on the rug when the kidnapper came through the door. How they were bound and hooded and made to lie down. How they worked free from the bindings. Eve found it painful to watch, but agreed "it had to be done." The reenactment was filmed with a camcorder, and a few hours later it was shown to the whole investigative team, so they could see the inside of the home and hear the witnesses firsthand. No new information emerged, but the girls seemed back on board.

More damaging was the choice to subject the girls to the polygraph—a developmentally inappropriate method of interviewing young witnesses, as research would soon reveal. That would leave the deepest scars. It would also yield useful lessons.

Weeks later, after the girls had been rehabilitated by the empathetic nurturing of forensic artist Jeanne Boylan, FBI case agent Eddie Freyer realized how demoralizing the interviews had been and how close they had come to losing the girls as cooperating witnesses. He felt they deserved a sincere apology.

Freyer hadn't taken a day off since the beginning of the case, arriving at the command center every day for a seven a.m. team briefing and getting home after his kids had gone to bed. Invisible to the press, he worked behind the scenes, making decisions and calling in resources like the wizard of some ever-expanding Oz. In a rare moment of down time, he slipped away to visit Kate and Gillian.

Bearing a stuffed animal and a dozen roses for each, he apologized on behalf of himself, the FBI, and the entire investigative team.

LATER, THEY WOULD all wonder.

Parks would wonder if the reenactment was a huge mistake. Had it re-traumatized the girls?

Long would wonder if he should have immediately swapped units with Parks for the duration of the investigation. Would it have reduced internal drama and helped the continuity of the case?

Bello would wonder why he was really taken off the case. Should he have cancelled the hunting trip? Was it because he had lost his temper in the chief's office?

Freyer would wonder: What didn't they think of? What else could they have done?

Such questions have a way of fermenting, consciously and subconsciously, and haunting the mind for decades. Anger, resentment, and regret form a cocktail so caustic that it slowly corrodes its container. This is among the great costs of this work.

Bello rejoined the force after cooling off, and though he was no longer Freyer's partner, he would still provide moral support as a friend and professional support as a detective and a SWAT team member. But being replaced still ate at him. One day months later, Bello's wife found him banging about in the bathroom, wrenching open drawers and slamming cabinet doors.

"What's wrong?" Tonia said.

"I can't find the contact lens solution."

"Well I'll go get some," she said. "What is wrong with you?"

"What's *wrong* with me? I don't know if I want to be married anymore!"

He felt like he was spinning down a deep tunnel, reaching out to grab hold of the sides, but the sides were too smooth and the tailspin too fast. He couldn't grab on to anything. He didn't have any control.

After a three-week separation, Bello met with a counselor who helped a lot of cops. She validated his anger and acknowledged he was still processing the emotions. And, like all good therapists do, she led him gently to his own epiphany. Three decades later, he would recite it and feel chills.

"I took control of the one thing I could," Bello said. "And I tried to screw it up—because I *could*."

"You think?" the counselor asked.

"I'd better go call my wife."

⌒⌒⌒

NEARLY A MONTH into the investigation, morale was low. In a morning briefing, ASAC Mark Mershon read the room and made an announcement.

"It's been enough time," he said. "We all suspect Polly is dead."

The room was silent.

"That's really discouraging, and I know it's tough to get motivated."

He gave voice to the thing that everyone feared but no one wanted to admit.

"Whoever did this is going to do it again. If you're not of a mind that we're truly looking to save Polly," he said, "believe we're looking to save the next little girl."

chapter twenty-three

THE FOUNDATION

∽

Early November

WHILE COPS AND AGENTS STRUGGLED WITH INTERNAL CONFLICTS INVISIBLE TO those on the outside, volunteers frustrated with the apparent lack of progress added new external pressure. Bill Rhodes, president of the newly formed Polly Klaas Foundation, began blasting lead investigators in the press. A month in, they had still had no prime suspect, and Petaluma PD had appointed a new lead investigator—who had never worked a kidnapping.

Mike Meese, Eddie Freyer's new partner, was not even a detective in the investigations unit of Petaluma PD. He was an administrative sergeant in charge of new officer training and background checks. Prior to joining Petaluma PD in 1981—part of the same police academy class as Andy Mazzanti—Meese had worked as a military policeman. This was not his first major investigation, but it was his first child abduction case.

"We want a Joe Montana, not a goddamned greenhorn out of training camp!" Rhodes spouted off in the press. "This is not on-the-job training."

The volunteer effort was still going strong—so strong, in fact, that the shops on Kentucky Street were complaining that the volunteer center was monopolizing downtown parking and hurting their business. The volunteers started looking for a newer, bigger headquarters.

In just weeks, the volunteers had evolved from a group of envelope-stuffing citizens to a formal operation. On October 23, they formed the Polly Klaas Foundation, an official legal entity that could operate more like a small business. Marc, Eve, and Winona Ryder would serve on the eleven-member board of directors, along with Joanne Gardner and other key leaders of the volunteer effort. The foundation named a president: Bill Rhodes, the white-haired community leader whose small business, PIP printing, had served as the first volunteer rallying point.

"At first it was crisis management," said Rhodes. "Now we're becoming a formal organization."

Joanne Gardner and Gaynell Rogers were not only managing the media but planning a blockbuster fundraising event in late October. Flipping through their personal Rolodexes, they booked celebrities and solicited autographed items. Hosted at the Luther Burbank Center, a performing arts venue in Santa Rosa, their four-hour show would bring together all sorts of performers: Robin Williams. Musician Charlie Musselwhite. Paul Kantner, from Jefferson Starship. Even Polly's junior high band had a place on the set list. Legendary Woodstock emcee Wavy Gravy would host the evening.

Gardner also had a secret project that she hoped would steal the show: a music video featuring Polly. After gathering photographs and home videos from Marc and Eve, Gardner set up a makeshift film studio in her father's garage. Spreading the photographs over the floor, she chose images that would evoke emotion and nostalgia: Polly as a baby, Polly dressing up on Halloween, blowing out birthday candles, unwrapping gifts under a Christmas tree. The video ended with Polly speaking into the camera during a game at a friend's birthday party.

She edited everything into a short but powerful music video, set to Polly's favorite song: "Somewhere Out There." Linda Ronstadt and James Ingram had sung the Grammy-winning ballad on the soundtrack to *An American Tail*, the 1986 animated film that came out when Polly was five. Gardner chose the song because it was Polly's favorite, but the lyrics were chillingly apt:

Somewhere out there, beneath the pale moonlight
Someone's thinking of me and loving me tonight

Gardner planned to kick off the event with the video. Knowing it would be an emotional moment, she limited press access to a few hand-picked media outlets. They would be allowed to film the video and the first few minutes of Robin Williams and Wavy Gravy, but then they had to leave. The video would keep the spotlight on Polly—not the celebrities.

"I needed everyone to feel that this wasn't just some kid—this was *our* kid," Gardner recalled years later. "I needed to connect with the people who weren't connecting. I didn't want anyone to look the other way."

On October 25, more than 700 guests arrived at the Luther Burbank Center for the celebrity auction. Robin Williams made them roar with his impression of President Bill Clinton. The Petaluma Junior High band played Beethoven's "Ode to Joy" and "Love Will Keep Us Together," and Paul Kantner from Jefferson Starship sat with them, wearing a "Polly-flower" T-shirt printed with Polly's face and a purple rose. The band left an empty seat in the clarinet section, where Polly should have been. Wavy Gravy auctioned off a harmonica signed by Huey Lewis, CDs and tapes donated by Jerry Garcia, and many bottles of wine. When a baseball signed by Willie Mays stalled out in the bidding war, Robin Williams grabbed it, signed it, and spiked the price to $1,750.

Polly, of course, stole the show. When Gardner played her music video, the room swelled with emotion. No one could look away, and many could hardly see through the tears. Marc sobbed next to his girlfriend and his sister. The upwelling of emotion opened hearts and checkbooks. The one-night event and auction raised more than $30,000 for Polly's search.

By early November, volunteer coffers were up to $317,000. But the assets had become a liability. The money was still being administered by the Petaluma Junior High PTA, whose nonprofit status served to keep the funds tax-free. Now the PTA wanted out. All checks drawn on the account had to be signed by the PTA president or another board member, which was not only a hassle but an increasing source of interpersonal conflict. In an emotional meeting on November 3, PTA members said the search had become "a media circus" and played a tape of TV news broadcasts showing Marc Klaas and Bill Rhodes criticizing the PTA president for not turning over the money to hire a private investigator.

Citing "liability concerns and personality conflicts," the PTA announced its desire to offload the account by distributing the funds to Polly's parents to disburse however they wished. But Polly's parents did not want the money (or the controversy), and legal advisers said that wasn't an option.

It was clear that volunteers needed to establish a nonprofit organization as quickly as possible. That process usually required months of waiting for IRS approval. Gardner and Rogers solved the problem—again—with their personal network. A political connection stepped in to fast-track the application. Within ten days, quite possibly a record, the Polly Klaas Foundation was a new 501(c)(3).

Now that the foundation had plenty of funds (and a legal place to put them), it needed ways to spend the money to effectively bring Polly home. Leaders wanted to reach beyond distributing flyers and invest in the actual search.

They had already accepted free training from Rick Benningfield, a missing persons expert who offered to fly in from Texas to help train the volunteers in professional search procedures. Benningfield was the executive director of the Heidi Search Center, a San Antonio–based organization named in honor of Heidi Seeman, an eleven-year-old girl who was abducted and found murdered in August 1990.* His organization had worked on fourteen child abductions, and in at least three of those cases—including Heidi Seeman's—a leader in the search for the missing person turned into a suspect. Benningfield urged the Polly Klaas

---

* When Heidi Seeman disappeared from her neighborhood in San Antonio in 1990, more than 8,000 volunteers searched for three weeks, covering an area of 1,200 miles. Her body was later found sixty miles from home, in Wimberley. The Heidi Search Center went on to help the families of more than 4,000 missing people with search assistance, resources, and emotional support, before shutting its doors in 2018, citing funding issues and high property taxes. Heidi's case is still unsolved.

Foundation to run background checks on key members of the volunteer effort. "Believe it or not, that is the normal course for an abductor," he said. "They like to be a part of the search. That's part of the thrill."

Bill Rhodes vehemently rejected the suggestion. He said it was a waste of time and might run off some volunteers.

Meanwhile, the foundation's board of directors voted to spend $5,000 to retain a private investigator to search for Polly on behalf of the family and the nonprofit. As October rolled into November, the foundation hired Hal Lipset, a seventy-four-year-old private detective from San Francisco. Regarded by some as "the dean of California private investigators," Lipset was to oversee an aggressive in-house investigation on behalf of the volunteers. He would re-examine evidence and follow new leads—including tips from psychics,* which the cops and feds refused to entertain.

"The search team felt we needed a new perspective," Marc told a reporter. "It was decided that this was a good way to go. He's had a lot of successes in his career. He has wisdom, knowledge, and the contacts, and so we just thought we'd expand our horizons a little bit and see if he can bring Polly home to us."

Lipset told the press he believed that the kidnapper had been hired to abduct Polly—a theory that investigators had long since ruled out. He was careful not to be too critical of the investigative team, which controlled access to evidence and inside information he needed.

"They put a tremendous amount of hard work and effort in this," he told the press. "However, there are no suspects, and we don't have Polly."

Lipset asked the FBI and police to give him access to all the internal case files. Both agencies flatly refused. Captain Dave Long said they would meet with Lipset and brief him, but they were legally prohibited from sharing documents generated by the joint investigation. Granting any outsider access to sensitive information could compromise the investigation.

---

* On October 16, Joe Klaas asked a psychic to assist with the search. The psychic listed sites that should be searched and said Jeanne Boylan's sketch was not right, claiming the actual kidnapper was not as stocky and didn't have dark hair. The FBI had a policy of not following psychic leads.

At the same time, Petaluma PD desperately needed funds and resources to sustain it. The overtime cost was draining the budget reserves, and the investigative team had been reduced from the original twenty-four to twelve, and was now cut down to ten. The FBI was expected to keep five agents in place for at least a few more weeks. Beyond that, nobody knew for sure. Police chief Dennis DeWitt told the *Petaluma Argus-Courier* that he hoped the volunteer center would consider donating $100,000 to allow the department to hire two more officers.

Taking that cue, the Polly Klaas Foundation offered $50,000 to the Petaluma PD to hire an investigator "with experience in solving child abductions." "We understand this investigation has taxed the resources of Petaluma," Gardner said. "The last thing we want is to have the effort slowed because of lack of funds." Marc Klaas told reporters if law officials didn't accept the offer "we'll blast them" in the media. "Maybe if we hire more police officials or detectives to help on this case we can accelerate this thing."

The FBI and Petaluma PD discussed the offer, but made the joint decision to decline. "It is in the best interests of the investigation to maintain continuity in the investigation," said Captain Dave Long. The City of Petaluma also deliberated over whether the money could be used to replenish its overtime funds or hire additional officers. City officials ultimately decided against it, to avoid setting a dangerous precedent they couldn't commit to in future cases.* However, they *could* accept the foundation's offer of providing five volunteers every day to assist the police by answering phones and searching areas specifically identified by authorities.

༺༻

BY NOVEMBER, MARC KLAAS was fighting despair.

"I feel impotent at this point," he said. "Absolutely impotent."

He leaned on a metal folding chair in his office at the Polly Klaas

---

* The FBI eventually picked up the tab and paid for the overtime of their local law-enforcement partners.

Foundation, where he spent most of his waking hours, and some of his nights as well. "We've done absolutely everything everybody's ever asked us to do," Marc told a reporter. "Yet we still don't have a clue where Polly is."

Marc had done everything in his power, and yet he still felt powerless. The act that most seemed to comfort him was talking to the press. Polly was now his purpose and his platform, and he used it to advocate for laws and systemic changes that might make the world a safer place for kids.

His heart and his objectives were surely in the right place. But friends and strangers alike were increasingly put off by Marc and his father's engagement with the media. Whenever Marc went on camera, he didn't seem to employ a filter. Joanne Gardner found herself constantly having to put out little fires caused by his public remarks and indiscretion.

"We needed to keep the search and the story alive by talking about Polly, not by highlighting whatever slights Marc wanted to relate at any given time," Gardner said years later. "The limelight was new to Marc, and from my perspective, he found it intoxicating."

Gardner did her best to keep Marc engaged appropriately with the media, and he was more than game to do it. In November, they flew to New York together to make the rounds on the talk-show circuit. *Geraldo. Donahue. Larry King Live.* (Gardner decided to turn down *Oprah*, whose producers wanted an exclusive. That didn't seem appropriate since Polly was still missing.)

Gardner was one of many who expressed concern that Marc was angling to become "the next John Walsh." This was evident to the leaders at the Polly Klaas Foundation, including his fellow board members; to distant acquaintances in the community; and to producers at *America's Most Wanted*. It was even apparent to John Walsh himself. One day, backstage at a national TV show, Gardner watched Marc conversing with Walsh. As she recalled years later, Walsh turned to Marc with a firm but compassionate look.

"You don't want to be me," Walsh said, putting a gentle hand on his arm. "Trust me. This isn't fun."

No one could have said it with more authority. But any effect it might have had was short-lived.

Polly's parents were proof that grief and trauma manifest in distinct and singular ways, and everyone copes uniquely. For two people who shared a child and had once shared a life, their response to a common experience—what everyone aptly called "a parent's worst nightmare"—could not have been more different.

While Marc responded with anger and action, Eve remained contemplative and willfully optimistic. Marc became more visible and voluble, in the press and in the community. Eve withdrew from the media and retreated to her home, waiting by the phone she hoped would ring with a call from Polly. Marc, a self-declared atheist, projected rage and blame at external targets. Eve, a follower of the spiritual teacher Baba Ram Dass, cultivated inner strength through her faith in the trans-formative power of love.

Five weeks after Polly went missing, Eve clung to her faith and to a chocolate brown poodle named Ozzie, a gift from a Fresno breeder who thought Eve ought to have a watchdog. The candle still burned in her window. Hope still burned in her heart.

Whenever Eve spoke about Polly's return, she always said "when"—not "if." Any time she caught herself starting to describe the situation as a "tragedy," she would stop herself from uttering the word and replace it with "crisis."

She had racked her brain to retrace her steps, reliving every moment she could remember in the past several years in which she might have encountered someone who decided to take Polly.

"I try to figure out any possible time or place or situation where she could have been seen by someone," she said. "The more I think back, the more things I come up with. They all seem extremely remote. But then again, the chances of this happening also seem remote."

She had gone through her datebook time and again, scouring the schedule of bygone days, wondering which seemingly trivial detail might yield a meaningful lead. Luckily, she wrote everything down. There was so much she couldn't remember. She'd looked closely at all social ties to see if someone had vanished or receded.

"No one from our circle of family and friends is missing from the picture. Everyone I've ever known in life, including people from grade school, relatives and distant cousins, have been here," she said. "It's absolutely overwhelming. It's like every day is a reunion."

Eve had not returned to her job at Bio Bottoms, the children's clothing catalog company, but her employer was still paying her salary, holding her job for whenever she felt ready to come back.

"It's likely my career path is going to change," she said, though she wasn't sure exactly how. Maybe she'd work with the Polly Klaas Foundation on educational programs to safeguard and nurture kids. Something in her heart must have told her that Polly's kidnapper hadn't had a good childhood. "As a result of child abuse and neglect, kids grow up to be adults that do things like this."

It was Eve's hope that someday, somehow, others would be helped through her misfortune. She believed that Polly would be pleased by this possibility.

"I think if Polly were here with us, she would be very excited about that," Eve said. "She would want to know this nightmare resulted in something good happening."

chapter twenty-four

THE INSIDER

∽

November 16

ON SATURDAY, NOVEMBER 13, JUST EIGHT DAYS AFTER BECOMING AN OFFICIAL nonprofit, the Polly Klaas Foundation moved into its headquarters. The move was marked with a formal procession: Leading the way in a red 1957 vintage car, Marc Klaas drove Eve Nichol, Violet Cheer, and Polly's twelve-year-old stepsister, Jessica, across town. Followed by a string of cars festooned with purple-and-white streamers, they left the old command post on Kentucky Street in the rearview mirror and arrived together at the new center: a 6,000-square-foot office complex on Petaluma Boulevard North. It had an ample parking lot and an optimal location—right across from the Petaluma police station and the *Petaluma Argus-Courier.*

The following Tuesday, the new center was christened with a special appearance by Oakland A's pitchers Dennis Eckersley and Ron Darling, who autographed T-shirts for fans—and a troll doll for Polly—while their wives stuffed envelopes with flyers. "We never go with our husbands," said Nancy Eckersley, "but in this case we could be of some help." Both mothers, they found themselves moved by the same force that powered every volunteer: empathy. As Toni Darling put it, "I just think, there go I but for the grace of God."

Fans of Darling and "the Eck" heard about the fundraiser on the radio and drove from all over the Bay Area to stand in line to meet them and buy a twenty-dollar T-shirt. In just a couple of hours, the pitchers signed 300 shirts printed with the names of eight missing children, raising at least $6,000 for four missing children's organizations. When everyone thanked them for promoting a good cause, Darling redirected the praise to the volunteers. "We're only here for a couple of hours, but they are working night and day," he said. "They are the real heroes."

They were, and the whole town saw them that way. That same day, foundation president Bill Rhodes was featured in a profile on the front page of the *Petaluma Argus-Courier*. "At the helm again," the headline proclaimed above a photo of the white-haired, avuncular hometown hero working the phones on a twelve-hour shift.

In the viral volunteerism that had spread through Petaluma, Bill Rhodes was patient zero. His PIP print shop had been the first rallying point, and Rhodes had led the charge. "On his very own, he got three hundred thousand flyers out that first day, and he hasn't slowed down," Marc Klaas said. "Bill was instrumental in how quickly the effort got going."

To those who knew him, this was no surprise. A longtime public servant, Rhodes had a way of rising to the top of any group he joined. "He's a natural leader," said his wife, Sherry.

The *Argus-Courier* described him as the "consummate family man," who cuddled grandchildren, painted Easter eggs, and never missed a birthday party. "He derives his greatest joys from the simplest activities: bouncing his grandchildren on his knee, catching them as they jump from a stool into his sturdy embrace, or wrapping his arms around them as they slumber in his lap." Sherry proudly pointed to a photo of Rhodes holding an infant in each arm. "This is the real Bill Rhodes."

Rhodes was so well regarded in Petaluma that he was awarded the town's coveted "Good Egg Award" in 1989. He founded the Petaluma River Festival, volunteered with the Children's Home Society fashion show fundraiser, and served as a longtime master of ceremonies for the Miss Petaluma pageant. He was, quite literally, a model citizen—immortalized in bronze as half of the wrist-wrestling statue[*] on Petaluma Boulevard North.

Ever since he heard about Polly's kidnapping on the radio during his drive to the Polly Ann bakery, Rhodes had devoted himself to the search. He'd had the charisma to politely hijack a Saturday-night cancer fundraiser to solicit volunteers to search and pass out flyers on that first Sunday. Hundreds answered his call for help, even the mayor.

"And like the pied piper," the *Argus-Courier* story said, "his charisma never fails to draw followers to his cause."

⌒⌒⌒

Two days after the Oakland A's event and the glowing profile of Bill Rhodes, the foundation seemed to be humming along. Jay Silverberg, the former *Marin Independent Journal* newspaper editor helping manage the media with Joanne Gardner, was proud of what they were doing.

The Polly Klaas Foundation was running like a first-rate operation. Silverberg and his wife had found themselves so deeply engrossed in the search that it now seemed "like part of our DNA." After stepping down as editor, he was planning to launch his own PR company specializing in crisis management. But he was enjoying the volunteer work and wanted to continue. His skills were put to good use here, and something about this cause, this group, provided a great sense of purpose. Silverberg agreed to serve on the board of directors, perhaps for years to come.

That Thursday, November 18, he was away from the center, doing PR for a golf event, when his cell phone rang with a call from Joanne Gardner. Over the past seven weeks, he had worked closely with Gardner and Gaynell Rogers, two profoundly capable women who seemed to solve any problem with levelheaded creativity. So he was surprised when he answered the call and heard something resembling panic in Gardner's voice.

"Jay!" she yell-whispered. "I need you here—now!"

---

[*] Every October, Petaluma hosts the World Wrist Wrestling Championship, and Rhodes was the Lightweight World Champion Wrist Wrestler in 1973 and 1996. He served as the model for half of the statue—the anonymous opponent of Bill Soberanes, who started the tradition in a Petaluma bar in 1953.

He dropped everything and rushed to the center, where a new crisis had metastasized in the very heart of the foundation. Or rather, the head: Bill Rhodes, their leader and president, had been accused of molesting a nine-year-old girl more than twenty years ago.

That girl was now a thirty-two-year-old woman. Identified only as "Victoria Anne," she claimed in a civil lawsuit that Rhodes had sexually molested her between 1970 and 1971. She said she repressed the trauma for decades. But when she served as a juror on a child sexual abuse case, the experience had dislodged memories of her own abuse as a child. Over the course of six months, she alleged, a neighbor and friend of the family had lured her to a secluded area near her home and repeatedly molested her.

Never mind the fact that the media was going to have a field day; could Rhodes be Polly's abductor—hiding all this time in plain view? Hadn't Rick Benningfield, the missing person expert from Texas, told them to background-check key volunteers precisely for this reason? He had. And that recommendation had been flatly rejected—by Bill Rhodes.

Rhodes had called the allegations "ridiculous" and "bizarre."

It turns out that the Petaluma PD had known about Victoria Anne and Bill Rhodes.

A year earlier, in November 1992, Victoria Anne had contacted the Petaluma police to report the past sexual abuse and request they investigate Rhodes. They told her the criminal statute of limitations had long expired, so they couldn't open an investigation. But she could still pursue a civil complaint against her abuser. She contacted an attorney in February 1993 and began the long process, which required mental health examinations and other procedures. They prepared the suit and planned to file it in October 1993.

That's when Polly Klaas disappeared.

When Rhodes became a prominent leader of the volunteer effort, Victoria and her lawyer didn't want to make a move that could possibly hurt the search for Polly. So they held off. By November they decided they had waited long enough. They filed the complaint—three days after Rhodes's hometown-hero profile in the *Petaluma Argus-Courier*.

At the volunteer center, Joanne Gardner and Jay Silverberg sent everyone home, locked the doors, and posted a handwritten sign: *Sorry—We are closed for the rest of the day. We will be open Sat 9:00. Please come back. We are looking for Polly.*

It was time for Silverberg to test his crisis management skills. They didn't yet know if the allegations were true, so they had to do some very careful damage control. He and Gardner drafted a press release and a statement on behalf of the foundation: "We are deeply shocked and disturbed by the news of these allegations. We are not in a position to judge or defend Mr. Rhodes regarding his past."

The media, rabid from seven weeks of waiting for the emergence of a prime suspect, was poised to pounce. The police, the foundation, and Rhodes himself—they were all going to be eaten alive.

Especially when the media started digging further into Rhodes's past.

<hr />

INSIDE THE INVESTIGATION, the cops and feds knew a lot more than they could let on.

Because they knew about Rhodes's background (thanks in part to Victoria Anne) they had questioned him as a possible suspect before ruling him out. They also knew about other sex crime allegations in his past. But they couldn't share that with the media, or even Polly's parents, because releasing his criminal background information would be illegal.

Investigators had cleared Rhodes as a suspect very early on. He had an alibi—he was at the movies with his wife—on the night Polly was kidnapped. They also found no tie between Rhodes and Polly.

But now, under increased scrutiny from the public and the press, investigators needed to dig a bit deeper. The FBI dispatched a surveillance team to keep an eye on Rhodes and ordered a full investigation of his background. He needed to pass a polygraph.

Ron Hilley polygraphed Rhodes and found the results "inconclusive."

On the morning of October 24, Andy Mazzanti and Agent Scott Smith drove to Rhodes's house to formally interview him. Rhodes admitted fondling the breast of his stepdaughter when she was ten. He would sneak out of the house in the morning to stand outside her window and watch her while she dressed.

The investigation of his background revealed more sex crimes and allegations. Between 1960 and 1970, Rhodes was arrested three times for lewd acts and exposing himself. In 1967, he was convicted of masturbating in front of young girls. That same year, he was charged with molesting four girls at an elementary school—at knifepoint.

The details of that case gave investigators reasons to worry. The four victims, girls between the ages of eight and thirteen, told detectives they had been playing in the schoolyard when a man pretending to be a teacher offered them a quarter to come into his classroom and help him stack some books. Inside, he grabbed the youngest girl and held a knife to her throat, threatening to cut it if the others didn't take off their clothes. The girls did what he said. They were blindfolded with tape, fondled, and heard what sounded like the click of a camera shutter. The man told them to count to 200 before getting dressed. That's when he fled.

Rhodes, twenty-five, was tried and acquitted of those charges. But the similarities to Polly's case—blindfolding, making them count, using a knife as a controlling weapon—were disturbingly similar.

"Have you ever fantasized about tying up young children or kidnapping them for the purpose of sexual assault?" Mazzanti asked Rhodes, point-blank.

He said no, explaining that his fantasies were more voyeuristic, with a victim unaware of being watched.

Rhodes agreed to a second polygraph examination by Ron Hilley. This time, after pressing Rhodes further, Hilley attributed the inconclusive results to guilt related to his previous sex crimes.

Some investigators eventually came to believe that his efforts to find Polly were genuine, possibly a form of atonement for his past.

⌒⌒⌒

BY THE TIME Rhodes was once again ruled out as a suspect, the damage was done. The bad press, internal outrage, and embarrassment of having a child molester heading the volunteer effort eroded the stability of the Polly Klaas Foundation and the investigation.

Rhodes resigned from the foundation immediately, and the ten-member board of directors scrambled to appoint a new president. They named Gary French, a recently laid-off computer systems salesman who was on the board and had been there since the beginning. He had worked with tech journalist Larry Magid to distribute Polly's posters through the World Wide Web.

While Rhodes took his family on "a long holiday" out of town and essentially disappeared, volunteer leaders tried to collect themselves and refocus on the search for Polly. Gardner and Silverberg were pleased to see sixty people show up the next day.

chapter twenty-five

THE SUSPECT

ᴄᴀᴄ

Late November

Invisibly to anyone outside the case—especially the press—Eddie Freyer and Mike Meese had been zeroing in on a suspect since the middle of October. He wasn't yet a "prime suspect" (or in FBI terms, "a subject"*) but he was the closest thing they had. His looks, his priors, his modus operandi—every bit of evidence fit the composite, profile, and timeline.

The suspect emerged on their radar ten days after Polly's abduction. About thirty miles from Petaluma, he was caught breaking into the home of a brown-eyed twelve-year-old girl named Tiffany. She was at home with her single mother, who heard a noise and called 911. Vallejo officers responded at 10:50 p.m., just in time to spot a dark-haired, bearded man running away with a gym bag. They sprinted after him as he ran to a Volkswagen Beetle and sped off into the night. The car chase through the neighborhood lasted less than a mile before the man leaped out of his vehicle and ran, still clutching the gym bag.

The officers chased him on foot and caught him. When they unzipped his bag and looked inside, they found a ski mask, duct tape, a

---

* Police generally refer to suspected offenders as "suspects." But in FBI culture, individuals are called "subjects" when they become the clear focus of the investigation.

stun gun, a jar of Vaseline filled with hairs, a Lifestyles condom, rubber gloves, nylon pantyhose in several hues, a large rubber dildo with a condom on it, and a knife with a wooden handle.

They had a name for this: a "rape kit."

The perpetrator's name was Xavier Garcia Garcia. A forty-three-year-old man from Vallejo, he had brown hair that fell to his collar, a full beard, a creased forehead, olive skin, thick brows, and heavily lidded eyes. He also had a long rap sheet. He quickly emerged as a suspect in the Polly Klaas case, and within the investigation he would come to be known as "Garcia Garcia."

Garcia Garcia had a history of sexual offenses that began in 1966, at age sixteen, and continued "with regularity" well into middle age. His prior arrests included rape, assault with intent to commit rape, attempted rape, assault with a deadly weapon, kidnapping, and burglary. He also preyed on children, with convictions ranging from annoying or molesting a child to lewd and lascivious conduct with a child and failing to register as a sex offender.

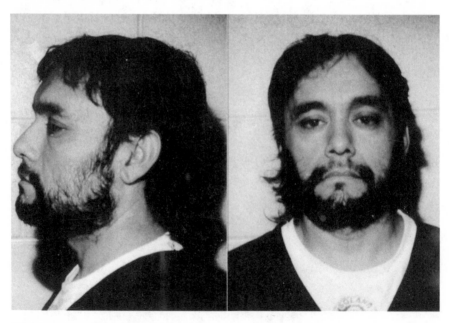

Wrong suspect Xavier Garcia Garcia.
(COURTESY OF GREG JACOBS)

In 1974, he was arrested for molesting a twelve-year-old girl in a department store. Posing as a security guard, he told her he needed to see if she had stolen anything. He led her to a secluded spot in the store, made her undress, attempted intercourse, and demanded oral sex. Once she was dressed again, she broke free and ran for help.

In 1977, he used a pillowcase and a knife to assault a twenty-five-year-old woman in Sebastopol, a town near Petaluma. The use of a knife as a "controlling instrument" was consistent with the behavior of Polly's kidnapper. A year later in the same town, he assaulted a twenty-seven-year-old woman, again with a knife and a pillowcase.

In 1991, Garcia was arrested again for molesting another young girl, also in a department store.

⌒⌒⌒

ON NOVEMBER 6, ERT member Frank Doyle drove to Fairfield to visit Garcia in the Solano County Jail, where he was detained in anticipation of charges for his attempted burglary of Tiffany's house. In the jail's medical facility, Doyle served a federal search warrant for Garcia's head and body hair. With the assistance of a registered nurse, he took samples by plucking and combing.

On November 12, seven FBI agents executed another search warrant on Garcia's former apartment in Vallejo, where his roommate still resided. In his bedroom, draped over a TV antenna, they found a yellow headband. It was a sweatband, not a bandana. They bagged and tagged it along with other potential evidence: a wad of duct tape, an open condom wrapper, yellow rubber gloves, a used condom with suspected semen inside, and an open tube of K-Y lubricant.

In the master bedroom, they found a khaki drawstring bag containing two black whips, seven clothespins, two restraints, a length of white rope, handcuffs, and a wooden paddle. From the kitchen counter they gathered two wood-handled knives with metal rivets. They peeled linoleum from the kitchen floor, wall board from the living room, fabric from the sofa, and carpet from the bedroom—known samples that could be set aside and compared to potential question samples. They pulled wet hair from the bathtub drain, and took the vacuum bag from the Kenmore Power Center vacuum cleaner in the hallway closet.

In the side yard, they found brown nylon pantyhose, potentially used as a mask. Later searches turned up a black hooded sweatshirt and black faded jeans that lined up with witness accounts of what Polly's kidnapper was wearing.

Neighborhood witnesses recalled seeing a Volkswagen Beetle in front of Polly's house on the night she went missing. In two separate searches, the ERT processed Garcia Garcia's orange 1972 Volkswagen Beetle, which had gray primer on the left rear fender. On October 19, they peeled silver duct tape from the driver's seat, collected eyeglass cases and a pirated audio cassette tape of music by Janet Jackson. They found a comb, barrettes, hair ties, and a blue-and-white hair clip with black stars. Offenders often keep such items as souvenirs, exciting reminders of past attacks.

On November 12, they went even deeper. An FBI mechanic dismantled parts of the vehicle that might reveal bits of trace evidence: the valve covers, air filter, light fixtures, tires, gas tank, door panels, and seat cushions. He peeled back the roof lining and the carpet on the floor pan. The ERT bagged a button trapped under the floor lining, a foil gum wrapper found under a seat, and hair stuck to a panel by the floorboard. They collected debris from the interior surfaces, paint samples from the exterior, and the liner of the trunk, all with the potential to yield DNA or trace evidence.

During the three-hour search, they noticed stains that looked like they might be blood: on the interior of the front trunk hood, on the lower side of a headlight, and on the seam of the gas cap door. David Alford tested them using the phenolphthalein test, a preliminary chemical test that can detect the presence of blood. All tested negative.

The ERT went on to process a red Volkswagen that had previously been owned by Garcia. They took the floor mats, miscellaneous debris, tapings from the seats, floor, and other interior surfaces, and the carpet mat over the front floorboard center hump, again, with the hope of finding DNA or other evidence that might be a match for evidence collected previously—or at some point in the future.

ON NOVEMBER 8, detective Andy Mazzanti and FBI agent Gordon McNeil went to interview Garcia's ex-wife at her home in Camino Alto. Lori (not her real name) said they had met through a friend at a McDonald's in Napa in the fall of 1988. She was working at Mervyns, and one day Garcia came into the department store to ask her out to dinner. She said yes, and he took her to Bob's Big Boy.

At first, Garcia was quite charming, she said. Before they had sex, he was tender and sweet, and he seemed like a really kind person. They went dancing and liked to watch movies—he loved *Die Hard* and the Godfather series, and watched *Silence of the Lambs* over and over. On Thanksgiving and other holidays, he joined her at family gatherings in Glen Ellen and Kenwood. They liked going to the beach at Bodega or Tomales Bay, stopping to pick up a picnic lunch along the way. Sometimes they went to Goat Rock State Park. They spent an occasional weekend in Sacramento, where his cousin lived. She said they never visited Petaluma.

But when they grew intimate, she learned that "regular" sex bored Garcia. He would talk dirty while making love, and he liked to call himself "Daddy." During "straight sex" he often had difficulty maintaining an erection and sometimes feigned orgasm. When she found his videotapes with "strange sex scenes," he "acted like a little kid who had been caught." He never raped her, but he liked to cover her mouth and take her from behind. Some investigators interpreted this as an indication of his fantasizing about sex with an abductee.

Sometimes he would see a teenage girl and tell Lori, "She's real hot—I could go for that..." She chalked it up to the hubris of a middle-aged man yearning for his glory years. Then she remembered a trip to Kmart when he told her they were going to do something he had "done before with friends." They had wandered around the store until he picked out a brown-haired girl between the ages of eleven and thirteen. They trailed her around the store and followed her out to the parking lot, where they watched her get in a car with her parents. They followed the car home, where the young girl saw them and smiled. Garcia remarked how fun it would be to "get to know" this girl and have sex with her.

And then there were his gym bags. He always had a gym bag—usually in his car—and he seemed rather protective of it. He would swap out bags from time to time, ditching one and picking out another from Goodwill. Whenever he said he was going to the gym, he'd be gone for two or three hours.

WITHIN THE INVESTIGATION, there was "mixed interest" in Garcia Garcia. He was the closest thing they'd found to a prime suspect. A few felt certain: *This is our guy!* Others believed he was unrelated due to the absence of a link to Petaluma.

Many facts supported the potential that Garcia Garcia could be the kidnapper. His modus operandi involved pillowcases, knives, and gags. Garcia carried a gym bag filled with means to bind his victims' hands. He engaged in high-risk behavior, choosing victims in public locations or entering occupied homes. He preyed on little girls.

After he was caught breaking into Tiffany's home, Garcia admitted that he had intended to rape her. Tiffany had brown eyes and long chestnut hair, and agents noted she looked "very much like Polly in appearance." He appeared to have had his eye on her for some time. Two years earlier, he had posed as a security guard in a Safeway grocery store, where he tried—unsuccessfully—to escort Tiffany out of the store to molest her.

Eve Nichol had received a number of phone calls with hang-ups, and those stopped after Garcia was arrested on October 11. That didn't seem like a coincidence.

FBI profiler Mary Ellen O'Toole was coordinating a detailed review of the case with the Behavioral Science Unit at Quantico. Agents involved in the investigation worked with Quantico to review the crime scene, victimology assessments, and the background of Garcia Garcia. O'Toole said he appeared to be "acting out" his fantasies, and based on the interview with his ex-wife, those fantasies included abduction. His behavior fit the profile of a "power reassurance rapist."

On the other hand, the barrettes and hair ties found in Garcia's car were shown to Eve with no information about their provenance. She was asked to look at them and determine whether they might have belonged to Polly. She felt certain they did not.

Eddie Freyer was feeling pressure from a number of colleagues and superiors to focus on Garcia Garcia. His partner, Mike Meese, felt strongly that this was their guy. But Freyer couldn't find anything that could tie him to Petaluma. Four investigators were rigorously searching for a connection. Without this essential link, this might not be the right guy. Freyer's gut said this could very well be a red herring.

And yet.

A review of unsolved rape and assault cases in Vallejo turned up two more assaults attributable to Garcia, both of them occurring on Friday nights between 10:30 and 11:20 p.m.—around the same time Polly was abducted.

He had no alibi for the night of October 1. The FBI interviewed Garcia's roommate, who was home that evening but said that Garcia was out, and he had no idea where. Colleagues and friends could not vouch for his whereabouts. Through his lawyer, Garcia refused to be interviewed about the night that Polly was kidnapped.

On October 28, investigators showed a photograph of Garcia Garcia to Sean Bush, who had been watching movies in the cottage behind Polly's house on the night of the abduction. Bush studied the photo. He wasn't sure, but he thought it *could* be the same person he saw go into the back door of Polly's house when he looked up from *Children of the Corn 2.* "Sure as hell looks like the guy walking up the back porch," Bush said. "Same hair, same build, same size."

Taleah Miller, the twelve-year-old neighborhood witness who saw an unfamiliar man walking toward Polly's house when her uncle drove her home from the movies around 10:20 p.m., described the man as a white male with dark, collar-length hair. She recalled a small duffel bag under his left arm. When he raised his right hand to cover his face, she noticed a watch on that wrist. When Garcia Garcia was arrested eleven days later, he was carrying a small gym bag and wearing a watch—on his right wrist.

But when Taleah Miller was taken to the Solano County Jail to view an in-person lineup on November 12, she did not pick anyone out of the mix. When asked about Garcia, she thought he was too short. Another lineup with Kate and Gillian was scheduled for a couple weeks later.

In an effort to focus on Garcia Garcia—or finally rule him out—investigators were reviewing his credit card activity, inspecting his telephone records, interviewing his associates, looking up unsolved rape and assault cases in surrounding cities, and conducting a neighborhood canvass with a photo of the suspect's face and also his VW bug. They were acquiring security camera videotapes from neighborhood stores, scanning the grainy footage for anyone resembling a photograph of Garcia or the sketch by Jeanne Boylan. They were contacting retail stores to see if anyone had recently posed as a security guard. They paid a visit to Better Buy Foods, where Garcia worked, to see if he was given gloves or knives for his job, which involved stocking vegetables.

Meanwhile, he was just one of thirty to forty look-alike suspects under investigation. Anyone with facial hair was getting a side-eye in Petaluma. One bearded individual told agents he'd been pulled over fourteen times.

By Thanksgiving, the family, volunteers, and media were beyond tired of waiting for a suspect. Investigators couldn't tell them otherwise without compromising the investigation. Besides, the media and the volunteers were still focused on the Bill Rhodes situation, which had left everybody shaken.

Eddie Freyer was starting to buckle under all the compounding forces. An unsolved case. Public scrutiny. The media's savage appetite. Disappointment and flagging confidence from volunteers and Polly's family. And most of all, the fact that somewhere out there, a little girl was still missing.

Polly was either alive and scared—or not.

So this is what a nervous breakdown feels like, Freyer thought. *Welcome to a robe and slippers.*

PART III

THE TURNING POINT

chapter twenty-six

PYTHIAN ROAD

◠◠◠

Saturday, November 27, 1993, 4:30 p.m.—
Pythian Road, Sonoma County

ON THE SATURDAY AFTER THANKSGIVING—FIFTY-EIGHT DAYS AFTER TWO DEPUTIES removed a midnight trespasser from her road—Dana Jaffe laced up her shoes to hike around her wooded hills in Sonoma. She had recently hired a team of woodcutters to thin the deadwood on the 192-acre property, just up the hill from St. Francis Winery. When she'd noticed them cutting live trees, she'd made them stop, and now she needed to survey the damage. She had invited a friend to come out to the house for dinner and a hike.

By the time they set out into the woods, dusk was falling fast. They meandered along an overgrown fire road in the direction of Hood Mountain Regional Park, which bordered Jaffe's property to the north. While surveying the slash left by the woodcutters, they noticed an oil can and a couple of empty oil bottles the crew had used for their chainsaws. They plucked this litter from the leaves and carried it as they walked.

As the light faded, the oaks and madrone that towered above them made it challenging to navigate. Jaffe's friend grew disoriented and worried they were lost.

"Well, let me show you a little trick here," Jaffe told her. "Let me show you how you can find the road."

Jaffe picked a direction and guided them in a straight path, explaining that they would eventually pop out on her driveway or one of the roads that encircled her land. The terrain was steep and uneven, and they had to scramble over downed trees and bushwhack through thick undergrowth, trying to avoid the patches of poison oak. They began moving faster, aware of the failing light. As they rounded the thick trunk of an oak and ducked under a low-hanging branch, a tangle of red cloth on the ground caught Jaffe's eye.

"Gee," Jaffe said. "What have we got here?"

She walked over for a closer look. Scattered in the dead leaves was a collection of suspicious items. A pair of red child-sized tights, the legs tied into a knot. An adult-sized black sweatshirt, turned inside out. A strip of white silky cloth, knotted in several places.

Jaffe picked up the knotted white cloth and put it to her nose. It smelled clean, like laundry detergent. Her friend picked up the sweatshirt and turned it right-side out. The clothing seemed fairly fresh, unbleached by the sun and not muddy or moldy from rain. Jaffe wondered how long it had been there. Protected by the thick tree canopy, it might have been there for days or even weeks.

Jaffe had grown up on the streets of San Francisco after running away at age twelve. She had developed the ability to read people and identify signs of danger. She read this situation as the scene of an assault. She and her friend replaced the items just as they'd found them, except the sweatshirt was right-side out. After poking around in the bushes to make sure they hadn't missed anything, they decided to get back to the house immediately and notify the police. Jaffe took the oil can she had been carrying and placed it on the ground as a marker to help them relocate this spot in the woods.

As they hiked out through the gathering darkness, an image flashed through Jaffe's mind: the dimpled grin of Polly Klaas. Having watched the relentless news coverage over the past two months, Jaffe wondered if these items could be related to Polly's kidnapping. Her friend was thinking the very same thing. They discussed it, but both found it "outside the realm of possibility."

When they got back to the house, they decided this situation didn't warrant calling 911, so they opened the phone book and looked up the number for the Sonoma County Sheriff's Office. It was after business hours, and Jaffe got a recording. She decided to call in the morning. Jaffe cooked dinner as planned and tried to enjoy the evening.

THE NEXT MORNING, on Sunday, November 28, Jaffe woke early to a phone call from her boss at John Ash & Co., the wine country restaurant where she worked as a sous chef. A colleague had called in sick, so Jaffe was needed to come in early. She told her boss about what she had found in the woods the previous evening, and her boss suggested calling the sheriff's office again before coming in.

The nearest sheriff's substation was several miles down two-lane Highway 12, between the tiny wine country towns of Kenwood and Glen Ellen. She called several times but kept getting a recording. It was around eight-thirty a.m. Maybe no one was there yet. She looked out the window and saw it had started to rain. She decided she wasn't going to work until she got a live voice on the other end of the line.

Finally, a woman answered. Jaffe told her she had "found some things on my property that were disturbing." She explained that she had been called in to work and was worried about the items getting wet in the rain. Should she go out and pick them up? Leave them be? The woman told Jaffe to stand by, that someone would call her right back.

Five or ten minutes later, Jaffe got a call from Deputy Sheriff Mike McManus, who said he would come out immediately. He arrived at Jaffe's house around fifteen minutes later, at 9:33 a.m. Jaffe climbed into his patrol car and guided him down the steep driveway to a place where they could hike in from the road. It was just uphill from the gate.

As soon as they rounded a bend in the driveway, Jaffe spotted the oil can she had left in the woods as a marker. They parked, walked across a small ditch on the hill side of the driveway, and climbed a steep embankment toward the oak tree with the low-hanging branch. Jaffe felt the pull of the hill against her calves, acutely aware of the pitch.

She led McManus to the objects, which lay about thirty yards from her driveway—closer to the road than she'd realized in the fading light of dusk. Standing over them, looking back down the hill toward the road, Jaffe figured they were only a few hundred feet from the ditch where the trespasser's car had been stuck. Through the bushes and the undergrowth, she could see the very spot. She tried to remember the timing. That had been, what…two months ago? Right about the time of Polly's kidnapping.

Jaffe told the deputy everything she remembered about that night. The pay phone call from her babysitter, Shannon Lynch, warning her about the scary guy stuck on her driveway. Dressing quickly and leaving the house with Kelila. Passing the car—a white hatchback—stuck in the ditch. Wondering where the trespasser was. Coming back with the two deputies to find the man leaning on his car, not trying to get out. How he said he was "sightseeing"—in the middle of the night? How she noticed, the next day, some money missing from the house. She recalled leaving twenty dollars on the dresser for the babysitter and Kelila, in case they wanted to go to the movies. It wasn't there the next day. She'd had a strong suspicion that the man had gone into her house after she and Kelila had left to drive into town and call 911.

In the flat light of the drizzly morning, Jaffe noticed a few things she had not seen the evening before. Glancing down at her feet, she caught the flicker of something reflective. At first she thought it was Saran wrap. She picked it up and identified two strips of "strapping tape"—transparent packing tape reinforced with threads. She called out to Deputy McManus that she'd found something that looked like bindings.

McManus, scanning the ground nearby, spotted a condom—unrolled—about an arm's length left of the clothing. A torn condom wrapper lay close to the sweatshirt. To the right of the clothing was a blue book of matches, a plastic six-pack holder, and an empty beer bottle that looked as if it had been there much longer than everything else. The strapping tape was about two feet below the sweatshirt. All of the objects appeared to be clustered in a three-foot radius.

McManus studied the scene with growing concern. The ground was covered with duff—decaying vegetation from the trees and bushes—and it appeared disturbed, exposing a bare patch of soil below. A sign of a possible struggle. Or of something dragged through the woods.

The black sweatshirt was a men's size large, BVD brand. It appeared to have some holes in one sleeve. The white cloth was silky and smudged with stains that looked like they might be makeup. It was tied into three or four knots. The red tights, too small for a twelve-year-old girl, were knotted at the knees.

Jaffe told McManus that she and her friend had handled the sweatshirt and the white cloth, but they hadn't touched the red tights. She had to get to the restaurant, but he could stay as long as he needed. After driving Jaffe back to her house, McManus returned to the woods to figure out what to do. This didn't look like flotsam and jetsam. This had to be a crime scene.

Crime scene investigation protocol calls for photographing evidence exactly as it is found, identifying and marking everything with numbered placards before anything is touched or moved. Each object is gathered individually, handled with gloves, placed in a plastic evidence bag, tagged with source information, and transported back to the station to be logged by an evidence custodian. Usually this procedure is performed by a team of forensic technicians.

But the rain was coming down heavier now, and by the time a forensic team arrived, the items would be soaked. Even though they'd likely been out there for months, he worried about the rain potentially damaging trace evidence. McManus decided to gather the sweatshirt, tights, white cloth, blue matchbook, six-pack rings, and empty beer bottle, placing them in a cardboard box in the trunk of his patrol car. He locked the trunk and went back to do a sweep for anything he might have missed. He found nothing else. He left the condom and wrapper on the ground, in part because he didn't have any gloves, and also as a way of marking the spot for when he came back with other investigators.

When McManus returned to the Sonoma Valley substation, everything in the box was damp, so he spread paper towels across a desk and an office chair, then carefully laid each item out, hoping that drying at room temperature would preserve any trace evidence. He snapped a photograph as the cloth soaked through the paper towels.

At 11:24 a.m. he checked the computer daily log and called up the dispatch incident report for the trespassing call that Dana Jaffe had described. It identified the responding deputies as Mike Rankin and Tom Howard, recorded the license plate of the white hatchback, and revealed the trespasser's name.

Richard Allen Davis.

A record check on Davis revealed an "extensive criminal history" that included a 288APC, 207PC, and 220PC: Kidnapping. Committing a "lewd or lascivious act" with a minor under age fourteen. Assault with intent to commit a sex crime. His rap sheet was eight pages long.

McManus picked up the phone and dialed the Petaluma PD.

PETALUMA DETECTIVE LARRY PELTON was writing case-related paperwork when Sergeant Mike Meese asked him to meet McManus and take a look at what the deputy had found in the woods.

As one of the first detectives to lay eyes on Polly's room after her abduction, Pelton was very familiar with the evidence that had been found there. Now, driving to the Sonoma sheriff's substation in Glen Ellen, he thought about all the times he'd been asked to examine clothing found by investigators and volunteers. In two months of searching for clues, he had seen no clothing he thought was related to the kidnapping.

His gut said this time would be different, because the facts were finally starting to align. The location was secluded, on private property—less than an hour from Polly's house. Exactly where the two sheriff's deputies had contacted the trespasser—about an hour and a half after Polly disappeared. The trespasser's behavior and story had triggered their suspicions.

By the time Pelton arrived at the substation around 12:45 p.m., the wet clothing had soaked through the paper towels. Pelton's eyes immediately landed on item number three, the knotted strip of cloth. Everything about it was familiar. The off-white color and silky texture of the material, like that of a woman's nylon slip. The way the knots were tied.

The jagged edges, hastily cut or torn. It was smudged with a pinkish substance he believed was probably makeup. The girls had been playing with makeup.

Pelton's gut stirred with instinct and emotion. This was it. The first break in the case. The first real step toward finding Polly. But he fought a sick feeling in his stomach when he thought about how the deputies encountered the trespasser.

Alone.

❦

EDDIE FREYER AND MIKE MEESE got to Pythian Road as soon as they could, arriving well after dark. They parked on Dana Jaffe's driveway and walked up the steep embankment. Mist shrouded the mountain and a light rain fell. At the spot where Jaffe had stumbled upon the suspicious items, they met Pelton, Bello, and McManus, who had replaced the evidence in paper bags and brought it back to the crime scene.

Freyer and Meese shared a glance. *This is it.*

For the first time in fifty-nine days, they had a subject.

chapter twenty-seven

THE SUBJECT

⌒⌒⌒

Sunday, November 28, 1993, dusk—Pythian Road

FLASHBULBS POPPED AND WHINED IN THE DARKENING WOODS OFF PYTHIAN Road, illuminating the falling rain. ERT members Tony Maxwell and Frank Doyle were photographing the soggy crime scene. The black sweatshirt, red tights, and white ligatures had been gathered by Deputy McManus that morning, so all that remained were the condom and its wrapper. McManus handed over the evidence—and the crime scene—to Eddie Freyer and Mike Meese around four-thirty p.m. After photographing the dripping trees and the fallen leaves disturbed on the ground where the evidence had been lying, Maxwell and Doyle bagged and tagged the evidence for an overnight trip to the FBI lab.

At the FBI office in Santa Rosa, ERT member David Alford was packing for a red-eye flight to hand-deliver another batch of evidence to Chris Allen in the FBI lab. Most of the items—whips, duct tape, a kitchen knife, and a yellow headband—were related to Garcia Garcia, the bearded suspect who had been caught breaking into the home of twelve-year-old Tiffany. Until yesterday, Garcia Garcia had been, if not yet a prime suspect, the closest thing they had.

On his drive from Santa Rosa to the San Francisco airport, Alford swung by Pythian Road. Around five-thirty p.m. he turned in to the parking lot of Los Guilicos, the criminal justice training complex, which had become the command center for the Pythian search. Case agent Eddie Freyer and Sergeant Mike Meese gave him the latest evidence, still damp from the morning rain. It was placed in new luggage, secured with locks. Tony Maxwell packed up his camera gear, grabbed an overnight bag, and joined Alford.

At the airport, they realized their luggage would exceed the carry-on limit. They identified themselves as FBI and requested permission to place the bags of evidence in the seat between them to maintain chain of custody. But the flight was full, so that wasn't possible. The airline crew allowed Alford to walk on the tarmac and personally load the evidence in the cargo hold of the plane—last bags in. He sealed the cargo door with crime scene tape. On the other end, he would unpeel the tape and carefully unload the bags of evidence.

AS THE EVIDENCE began its 3,000-mile journey to Washington, Detective Andy Mazzanti drove to the police station at ten-thirty p.m. to begin a "full workup" on Richard Allen Davis, a parolee with an outstanding warrant for a recent DUI and a failure to check in with his parole officer. The FBI had officially named him a "subject" in the kidnapping of Polly Klaas.

Before attempting to contact Davis, who went by Rick, they needed to know everything about him: his priors, where he had lived, what kind of jobs he'd had, how neighbors and coworkers felt about him, what kind of cigarettes he smoked. Who was this guy? How did he operate? What kind of life did he lead? Where was his family?

Mazzanti hoped to find answers on the paper trail of records from police departments, jail bookings, state parole boards, DA's offices, hospitals—any agency that had ever had contact with the subject. A full workup was, as colleague Vail Bello put it, the investigative equivalent of "crawling up his ass with a microscope."

Mazzanti started with Davis's record of arrests and prosecutions—his rap sheet—a permanent record stored in the National Criminal Information Center database. Reading this eight-page litany of prior arrests, detentions, convictions, charges, and probation violations, Maz-zanti saw the biography of a career criminal.

⌒⌒⌒

RICHARD ALLEN DAVIS, thirty-nine, had spent most of his adult life behind bars, incarcerated for fourteen of the past twenty years. He had been paroled on June 27, 1993, from the California Men's Colony, a state prison in San Luis Obispo, where he had served half of a sixteen-year sentence for kidnap, robbery, first-degree burglary, and assault with great bodily force.

His first detention was in 1973, at the age of nineteen, for disor-derly conduct—public drunkenness—and resisting a public officer. Two months later, at age twenty: burglary and contributing to the delinquency of a minor. Six months after that: car theft, sentenced to six months in the county jail, followed by three years' probation.

In 1974, five weeks into probation, Davis was caught breaking into South San Francisco High School. At the age of twenty-one, he was given his first prison sentence: six months to fifteen years. This broad range was an example of the indeterminate sentences that convicts in California, and much of the country, received under the penal system in 1974, which gave parole boards discretion to decide when inmates could be released.

At the time of his first conviction, the system was about to change. There was a movement that argued parole boards had too much arbitrary power, which could result in wild inconsistency in the way sentences were applied. Conservatives, on the other hand, pointed to inmates who were let out before serving their full sentences, only to reoffend. Both sides converged in 1977 with a system change to determinate sentenc-ing, in which a specific sentence would be given for a specific crime, diminishing the authority of the parole board. But this change had not yet gone into effect at the time of Davis's first prison stay. Factoring in his age and the nonviolent nature of his crimes, his parole board released him after he had served a year.

Seven weeks after his release, on September 24, 1976, the twenty-two-year-old Davis lurked at dusk outside a BART station in Hayward, a Bay Area suburb. He watched a twenty-six-year-old legal secretary named Frances Mays step off the commuter train and cross the parking lot. As Mays unlocked the door of her light blue Volkswagen Beetle, she felt a knifepoint press at her back. Davis shoved her into the passenger seat, grabbed the keys, and drove away, telling her he had just gotten out of prison, was being followed, and only needed to get away. When Mays began to cry hysterically, he told her to shut up and hit her over the head with his fist. He then drove to a secluded area, stopped the car, exposed himself, and said, "I'm going to count to three—you know what I want you to do." Mays grabbed the knife, slicing her hand on the blade, unlocked the car with her other hand, threw open the door, and ran. She flagged down a passing car, which happened to be driven by an off-duty California Highway Patrol officer, who drew his gun and arrested Davis.

While in jail for the abduction of Frances Mays, Davis faked a suicide attempt so that he would be transferred to Napa State Hospital, a psychiatric institution where he could more easily escape. While incarcerated, he had learned the facility had no fence or security, so he knew he could simply walk away. And he did, kicking off a five-day spree.

On December 17, 1976—the day after his escape—Davis broke into the home of Marjorie Mitchell, a thirty-two-year-old nurse and single mother who lived with her daughter in Napa. He had brought with him a tube sock filled with bars of soap, but found a better weapon in the house. Mitchell woke up in her bed to searing pain and the realization that she was being struck repeatedly in the head with a fireplace poker. Her thirteen-year-old daughter, sleeping in a nearby room, awoke to her mother's screams and blood-streaked face. Davis, who later said such crimes released tension and gave him "a glow," went away thinking: *We both got something out of this.* Such utter lack of empathy and an egocentric mindset are hallmarks of a psychopathic mind. It would take twelve hours in the hospital and thirty sutures to close Marjorie Mitchell's physical wounds. The psychological damage would never quite heal.

Next, Davis burglarized the Napa County Animal Shelter, stealing a shotgun. Around midnight on December 20, 1976, he lurked in a parking lot outside the Pancake House, a restaurant and bar in Napa. He watched twenty-something Hazel Frost come out of the bar, where she'd joined some friends for a couple of drinks after a Christmas party. Still dressed up from the party, Frost walked through the darkened parking lot and got into her Cadillac convertible.

As soon as she slipped the keys into the ignition, Davis jumped into the passenger seat, pressed the stolen shotgun into her neck, and told her to drive to Santa Rosa. Frost saw him pull a roll of gauze or tape from his pocket and assumed he would use it to tie her up. As the car came to a stop in the darkness behind the bar, Davis told Frost to turn off the lights. Seizing the opportunity, she threw the car in park, yanked open the door, and rolled onto the ground, grabbing the pistol she kept hidden under the driver's seat. As Davis ran, she fired six shots at his fleeing back. "Well," she muttered as he disappeared, "[you'd] better just get on out of here." Instead of heading home or to the nearest police station, she drove to a friend's bar and ordered another drink. "A double."

The very next day, on December 21, a bank clerk named Josephine Kreiger came home to find her La Honda house had been burglarized. A window was broken, drawers were ransacked, and cigarette butts were all over the place. Kreiger and her boyfriend surveyed the damage—jewelry, clothing, and a coin collection were missing—then called the cops. A San Mateo sheriff's deputy arrived within minutes. Searching the grounds, he found Davis hiding under a bush near a fence, concealed except for his hands and the barrel of a shotgun. He was arrested and taken into custody, ending his five-day crime spree.

Davis was convicted of kidnapping Frances Mays. It was still a year before the sentencing system changed, and so he was given an indeterminate sentence of one to twenty-five years. The parole board exercised its discretion and let him out after five.

Two years later, in 1985, Davis went back to prison for the kidnapping and armed robbery of a woman named Selina Varich, a crime he committed with a girlfriend-accomplice. (More on this in a minute.)

By now the sentencing laws had changed. The 1977 law had put determinate sentencing into effect and gave inmates the chance to shave up to one-third of their sentences off for good behavior. Six years later, in 1983, an attempt to alleviate prison overcrowding changed the law again, and well-behaved inmates could potentially cut their sentences in half.

When Davis was convicted of kidnapping Selina Varich in 1985, he was sent to prison for sixteen years—the maximum sentence at that time. He got out after eight. The parole board of California Men's Colony authorized Davis's release on June 27, 1993. They described him as a "model parolee."

He walked free three months and four days before the disappearance of Polly Klaas.

DETECTIVE MAZZANTI WORKED the phones late into the night, calling every law enforcement agency listed on Davis's rap sheet. He wanted everything in the files—booking sheets, mug shots, police reports, records of any and all contact.

There was one particular item he needed more than anything: a palm print. The fingerprints found in Polly's room were all accounted for. They had been matched with elimination prints taken from Polly's family and friends, and therefore ruled out as related to the kidnapping.

All but one.

It was the palm print found on the upper rail of Polly's wooden bunk bed—one of the forty-eight latent prints Tony Maxwell lifted in the dark with Redwop powder and the alternate light source. Something about it had made him gasp and scribble the word "Bingo" next to entry A-6 in the fingerprint log. David Alford had hand-delivered it to the FBI lab on October 5. There it sat for two months, of little use without a suspect.

Now that they had a suspect, investigators needed his palm print. They already had a set of inked prints from Davis, but it didn't include his palm. Whenever an offender was arrested and taken to jail, fingerprinting was part of the booking procedure, but they usually rolled only the fingers. Palm prints were less common, typically reserved for more serious felonies—bank robberies, kidnappings, violent crimes—at the discretion of investigators.

Mazzanti called the California Department of Corrections and Rehabilitation, Napa State Hospital, the California Highway Patrol, and a number of police departments that had booked Davis at some point. None of them had palm prints.

Around midnight, Mazzanti called the Stanislaus County Sheriff's Office in Modesto, California, where Davis's rap sheet noted he had been charged with robbery. That was back in the spring of 1985, when Davis and his twenty-four-year-old girlfriend, Susan Edwards, had teamed up on a series of robberies. Davis did the robbing and Edwards drove the getaway car. Most of their targets were mom-and-pop businesses. In Modesto: a Yogurt Cup shop, a Happy Steak restaurant—places that yielded little more than a handful of petty cash.

As Mazzanti made those late-night calls, he saw the opportunity to retrieve a palm print rapidly shrinking. He was working his way down the list of kidnappings, robberies, and assaults, yet not one of those case files contained what the FBI refers to as "major case prints"—a set with the palms, full fingers, and sides of each palm.

The offense that would ultimately yield the palm print was a broken taillight.

<hr />

ON THE MORNING of Saturday March 9, 1985, Davis walked into Delta National Bank in Modesto, a target Sue Edwards had chosen and cased. Wearing a black-and-gray Pendleton shirt, but no mask, he approached the teller window, where two female tellers were tallying the night-deposit bag and counting quarters.

One teller saw a handgun in his right hand.

"Give me all that money," he demanded. "The hundreds, tens, and all that money."

The gun, square-muzzled and black, looked to her like a toy—*was that a seam in the molded plastic?*—so she thought it was maybe a joke. But no sense taking chances.

"Here," she said, pushing the sack of quarters toward Davis. "Take the whole bag."

"You're stupid," he said. "Give me all that money."

She opened the cash drawer and reached for stack after stack of bills. Twenties, tens, fives, and ones. She flung it all on the counter in front of him.

"I'm no fool," Davis snarled, grabbing at the cash. A few bills fluttered to the floor. He pointed the gun—which was in fact a BB gun resembling a .45 caliber pistol—at another teller and made her empty her drawer too. Along with the cash, she handed him a stack of bait money attached to a clip that would trigger an alarm. By the time they responded, Davis had already run out of the bank with the money—$2,850—and leaped into the getaway car beside Edwards. The couple celebrated with a trip to Disneyland.

Later that month, in March, Davis and Edwards were caught, arrested, and charged with robbery and false imprisonment for the three crimes in Modesto. Davis willingly took the fall to save Edwards from going to prison.

It was one of the only acts in his life that suggested something like love.

∽᠊᠊᠊᠊᠊᠊᠊᠊᠊

THE 1985 MODESTO robberies, it turns out, were the grand finale of a crime spree that consummated their three-year romance.

They had gotten together not long after Davis got out of prison in 1982 for kidnapping Frances Mays. Sue Edwards was twenty-one then, the mother of two young boys, and a wife in an unstable marriage. With bleached-blond hair and an income from dealing crank, she was described by her own lawyer as "what you call a 'motorcycle mama.'" Soon Edwards's kids were living with their father, and Davis and Edwards were living a Bonnie and Clyde existence.

One of their first joint ventures was the kidnapping that eventually sent him to jail and spoiled their love affair: the kidnapping of Selina Varich, an acquaintance and the ex-girlfriend of Edwards's sister.

On the morning of November 30, 1984, Davis and Edwards forced their way into Varich's Redwood City apartment and threatened to kill her, along with her father and daughter, if she didn't give them $6,000. When the terrified Varich tried to run away, Davis pulled her back inside and pistol-whipped her in the head several times, gashing her scalp and splattering blood. They made her shower to wash the blood out of her hair, then drove her to the bank and forced her to withdraw the money and hand it over. Varich, who needed five sutures to close her head wound, later described Davis as "evil, with scary eyes and gloating expressions."

After escaping with the money, Davis and Edwards decided they had better get out of San Mateo, where Selina Varich could identify them. Between December 1984 and 1985, they drifted from town to town in California, Oregon, and Washington, supporting themselves by selling drugs and stealing.

They alit briefly in Kennewick, Washington, where they conducted a series of robberies, scoring $129 from a Red Steer restaurant, $200 from a Giant T drug store, $350 from Nob Hill Market, a mom-and-pop grocery store, and $1,134 from a pie shop called Frontier Pies. Their biggest heist was $4,193 from Frontier Federal Savings and Loan on December 20, 1984. Davis gave all of the money to Edwards, who controlled their spending.

They might never have been caught had they not returned to Modesto, where a broken taillight triggered their downfall. A week or two after their Modesto robberies in the first weeks of March 1985, it appeared they had gotten away with it all. Then on March 21, 1985, a cop noticed a defective taillight on their pickup truck and pulled them over. The records check flagged outstanding warrants for their brutal attack on Selina Varich.

Davis was arrested, booked, and convicted for kidnapping and armed robbery. This was the point when changing sentencing laws happened to work in his favor. Under the forthcoming three-strikes law—which would give repeat offenders life in prison after their third felony—this would have been his third strike. But three strikes, proposed and hotly debated, had not yet been signed into law. Under the previous indeterminate sentencing system, Davis also might have received a life sentence—with the possibility of early parole. But under the determinate sentencing system in effect at the time of the Varich crime, the prescribed terms for each of his crimes did not add up to life. He was given the maximum sentence a judge could give under the new law: sixteen years. Life in prison was not an option.

On August 8, 1986, Davis was locked up in San Luis Obispo's California Men's Colony, the state's biggest prison. He shared a roof with 3,500 inmates, nearly one-third of whom were serving life sentences.

Davis and Edwards made a deal. Davis would take the fall for the robberies to keep Edwards out of prison. In return, Edwards would put money in his prison account and remain loyal to him during his sentence. She did neither.

Edwards broke her promises and (if he had one) his heart. First she got involved with Floyd Baily, an inmate at a different prison. Then, in August 1988, she married a man named Mike Mrava. (She was still separated—though not divorced—from the father of her children.) This new husband was murdered three months later by her jealous inmate-boyfriend, who by then was out on parole. An insurance company awarded her a $200,000 settlement for the death of her husband. (The second one.)

Davis craved revenge.

In November 1989, while incarcerated in the San Luis Obispo prison, Davis requested to speak with an FBI agent. He waived his Miranda rights and told the agent about the bank robbery and four armed robberies he had committed in Kennewick, Washington—"aided and assisted by his girlfriend, Susan Brinkley." (Brinkley was her maiden name and one of her many aliases: Edwards, Valentine, Brinkley, Mrava.)

Ratting out Edwards was an act of vengeance that came with a cost: implicating himself in crimes for which he had not been caught, and probably never would have been, had he not confessed. As a career criminal, perhaps he figured that because he was already in prison, they wouldn't bother charging and prosecuting him for the Kennewick robberies.

However, they could still come back to haunt him in ways he never imagined. If Davis should ever go to trial for future crimes—say, kidnapping and murder—the unprosecuted Kennewick crimes could come up in the penalty phase, used to support the weight of evidence of his habitual penchant for violence. This kind of recurrent violence might help sway a jury deliberating between a life sentence and the death penalty.

As he ratted out his ex-girlfriend, Davis told the FBI what Edwards shared on a prison visit in January 1989. He claimed she confessed to planning the murder of Mike Mrava—her second husband—and subsequently receiving the $200,000 insurance settlement for his death. But she was still legally married to Mike Edwards, a fact that a probate attorney told her she ought to keep to herself, since it made her ineligible for the settlement.

Davis told the FBI agent he thought the insurance company should give him a monetary reward for providing this information. He suggested $23,000 would be a fair amount. (He didn't get the money.)

As for Susan Edwards/Mrava/Valentine/Brinkley, the cops were closing in. During the investigation of the murder of her husband, Mike Mrava, police discovered she had never been legally divorced from her first husband. She was convicted of bigamy, grand theft, and perjury, and sentenced to six years in prison. She was still in prison when Davis was paroled in June 1993.

⌒⌒⌒

Detective Andy Mazzanti didn't know any of this on the night he searched for a palm print. He didn't know he'd hit the jackpot when he called the Stanislaus County Sheriff's Office to ask for records. It was late, and most folks had gone home for the night, so he left a message requesting files. The details would unfold in the documents that later streamed in page by page.

Mazzanti left the police department several hours after midnight and went home with a heavy heart. He had just learned that his eighty-nine-year-old grandfather had died of cancer.

Hours later, on the morning of Monday, November 29, forty-three pages of records from Stanislaus County scrolled out of the fax machine in the Petaluma command center. They included a set of "major case prints"—ten fingers, both palms, and the blade of each hand. The prints were dated March 22, 1985—when Davis was stopped for a broken taillight and arrested on a warrant for crimes he thought he'd gotten away with.

Detective Andy Mazzanti wasn't there to grab the fax. He was out for two days on bereavement leave to attend Poppy's funeral. He would not know—for twenty-nine years—that he was the one who found the inked palm print.

chapter twenty-eight

THE LAB

༺༒༻

Monday, November 29, 1993—Washington, DC

AROUND THE TIME DETECTIVE ANDY MAZZANTI WAS CHASING DOWN A PALM print, ERT member David Alford was nodding off on a red-eye flight arcing toward Washington, DC. Dressed in a dark suit, he got off the plane with bags of evidence from Pythian Road and Polly's house. Foregoing a hotel room and a hot shower, he went straight to FBI headquarters.

Nearly seven weeks had passed since Alford had made his first trip to the lab to transport the first batch of evidence. Hair and fibers examiner Chris Allen had been through all of it, so he was as anxious to see the new evidence as Alford was to deliver it.

Before anything was handled in a physical exam, they photographed it in the bright light of the lab, positioning a ruler-like "scale" next to each item. Then they began with the white cloth ligatures found in the woods near Pythian Road. Alford watched intently as Allen untied the bindings and unfurled the cloth. They noted the jagged edges, where the fabric had been hastily cut. Next to them, Allen spread the bindings that had been used to tie Kate and Gillian's wrists, bagged and tagged in Polly's bedroom on the night of October 1.

It didn't take a microscope to see that the color, texture, and weave of the cloth found at Pythian appeared identical to the cloth from Polly's room. The silky material was made of nylon, consistent with the type of fabric used in a ladies' slip or nightgown.

Allen arranged the nylon bindings from both crime scenes on a lab table, smoothing out the wrinkles. Slowly, meticulously, he slid them around, rearranging them. Their jagged edges aligned perfectly, like pieces of a jigsaw puzzle.

It was a perfect physical match.

Microscopic analysis later confirmed what Allen and Alford could see with the naked eye: The bindings from Polly's room and those from Pythian had been cut from the same piece of cloth. Adrenaline surged as this pivotal revelation came into sharp focus. Two crime scenes had been linked by physical evidence. Eyewitnesses might misremember. Physical evidence holds far more than memory; it speaks the inescapable truth.

David Alford called Eddie Freyer to deliver the good news.

In the Petaluma command center, Freyer called everyone to attention, and the commotion paused. He flicked a glossy black-and-white

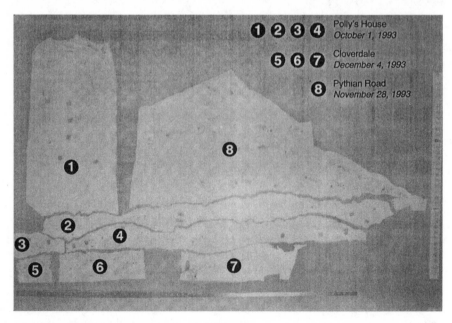

Matching ligatures line up in the FBI lab.
(Courtesy of Greg Jacobs)

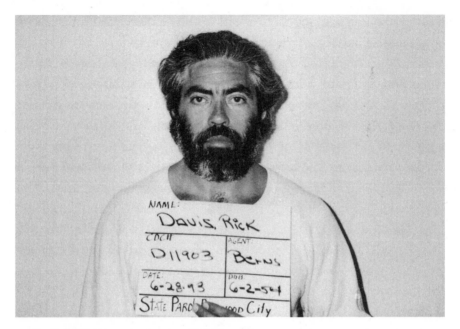

Richard Allen Davis on the day of his parole.
(COURTESY OF GREG JACOBS)

photograph onto a table. The mug shot spun in a circle, the image a hazy blur. As the picture slowed and eventually stopped, a face came into focus.

It was the face of Richard Allen Davis: Jeanne Boylan's sketch come to life. A collective gasp filled the room.

AFTER MATCHING THE white ligatures, Alford and Allen turned their attention to the other fabric found in the woods near Pythian Road. The process began in the "scraping room," where they spread a large, clean sheet of pale butcher paper over a large examination table. Above it, on an adjustable metal rack, they hung the red tights and black sweatshirt. Using a metal spatula, they carefully scraped each garment, dislodging hairs, fibers, and particles. Infinitesimal specks of trace evidence rained down upon the paper—dust, soil, hairs, and fibers. They carefully transferred the flecks of material into a small clear plastic "pill box" and sorted the contents, separating hairs from fibers, then pubic hairs from head hairs, marking each "question sample" for identification. Next he needed "known" samples from Richard Allen Davis.

Back in Petaluma, Freyer was dispatching agents to get them. Obtaining hair and fiber samples from a subject required a lot of paperwork and procedure: an affidavit for search warrants to process the subject's residence, another for his vehicle, and another for his person—to get samples of hair and blood. So many warrants were needed that Freyer had assigned an agent to the task full-time. Brian Guy was so skilled at writing the affidavits his colleagues called him "The Golden Pen."

As soon as the warrants were signed, the ERT moved quickly. In Mendocino, Frank Doyle escorted Davis from the jail to a nearby hospital, where a nurse collected specimens of head, facial, and pubic hairs—they needed thirty of each.

The nurse assured Doyle that she had done this many times, so he didn't micromanage. After the procedure, he sent several envelopes of samples to the FBI lab. But as soon as Allen received the samples, Doyle received bad news: The samples were "no good."

The nurse, it turned out, had *clipped* the hairs—instead of plucking. This was a problem. Plucked hairs came out with the root sheath, a tiny bit of tissue that could be used for DNA testing as well as for comparison to the "forcibly removed" hair found in Polly's blue rug. Doyle returned to Mendocino to oversee the plucking.

Davis was not happy about this. He was about to be even less so.

When it came to pubic hair samples, suspects are typically given a choice: Pluck it yourself, or let an expert do the job. In this case, the corrections officers did not wish to remove the handcuffs from Richard Allen Davis. Doyle would have to do it.

But first, they needed a blood sample. Davis's heavily tattooed arms made it hard to find a vein, so the phlebotomist applied a warm compress to make the veins swell and rise. When it was time for plucking, Davis grew agitated and started to complain. A stout deputy reminded him that this was a court order. Doyle donned rubber gloves, bent down, and did the job.

It wasn't the best day at work. But it also wasn't the worst.

In the lab, Allen had already compared question samples of hairs found in Polly's room to known samples taken from Polly's hairbrush, family, and friends. He had done the same thing with fibers from the carpets in her house and from vehicles belonging to friends and family.

In this tedious procedure, Allen slid the question sample onto one stage of a comparison microscope, and the known sample on the other. An optical bridge allowed him to view them side by side, magnified somewhere between forty and four hundred times their normal size. He compared the structure of each hair, examining fifteen different characteristics and jotting down notes.

Hair and fibers experts liked to compare the anatomy of a hair to the structure of a number two pencil. The yellow paint is the cuticle; the wood is the cortex; and the lead is the medulla. Each of these components can vary a great deal: the thickness of the cuticle wall, the pattern of pigmentation that varies from dark to light, ovoid bodies in the cortex.

If you were to slice a hair shaft like a loaf of bread, the shape of that slice would vary in a way that speaks to its origin. Facial hair is triangular. Pubic and head hair can be round or oval or flat, depending on multiple factors, including a person's race.* Asian hair is very round and tends to be straight. European hair tends to be oval, and often curly. African hair is flatter and folds back and forth like a ribbon. The exterior of a hair is covered with "cuticles" that look like fish scales under a microscope. These scales vary in size, texture (smooth or flaky), and placement.

The thing about hairs is, you can never say—with absolute certainty—that two hairs came from the same person. You can only say that they "exhibit similar color and microscopic characteristics" and it's possible they "could have originated from a common source." These visual characteristics are hard to quantify. As a result, hair analysis is fraught with a degree of subjectivity and has come under heavy scrutiny.†

---

* In the 1990s, the terms "Caucasian," "Mongoloid," and "Negroid" were used by scientists to describe the racial origin of a hair. These terms are now considered outdated.
† In 2002, the FBI conducted DNA tests and found that hair and fibers examiners found false hair matches in more than 11 percent of examinations. Beginning in 2012, the FBI and Department of Justice conducted a massive investigation of forensic work by the FBI laboratory's hair and fibers unit, scrutinizing trial testimony by the unit's experts in the 1980s–1990s. The investigation found that the FBI lab's hair and fibers examiners provided flawed forensic testimony in 95 percent of trials reviewed. This case was not one of them.

Fibers are a different story. Because they vary so greatly in origin and appearance, fibers can have many more characteristics than hairs. Fibers fall into one of two categories: natural and manmade. Natural fibers include cotton, wool, linen, and silk, and their appearance varies widely. For example, you could study thirty different types of cotton and see individualized evidence in the natural twists and turns of the fiber that would suggest where each type of cotton was grown. Manmade fibers—like nylon, rayon, Lycra, and polypropylene—tend to be more uniform.

Then there's the treatment of the fiber—how it is dyed or woven. For example, some types of cotton absorb dye evenly, while others absorb dye only on the edges or in the middle. Because different fibers have a vast number of sources, their color can be so unique that it's possible to make a chemical match between samples. For instance, nylon carpet fibers could be made of nylon 6 or nylon 66. It's possible to run tests to confirm the type of nylon. Color can be compared by mass spectrometry and chromatography.

Chris Allen would log countless hours at the microscope, meticulously comparing the fibers. But first he flew to Petaluma to assist the ERT in processing the white Ford Pinto.

$\sim$

EXAMINING THE CONDOM was the job of Thomas Lynch. To help lab examiners identify the brand and provenance—there were between 120 and 140 condom manufacturers on the market—the FBI lab had a "condom library" of specimens. To create this resource, someone had visited a New York store called Condom Mania and procured sixty different condoms that represented what was on the US market.

Examining the condom involved various lab tests. To determine if the condom would return to the same size and shape after use, Lynch filled it with hot water "like you were going to make a water balloon." He then dipped it in three liters of acetone, a solvent that would "extract or solubilize or plasticize other chemicals found in the condom as well as dilute spermicide or other lubricants." He took one-fifth of a drop of the solution in a small cup, dried it, and inserted it into a mass spectrometer, an instrument used to detect known chemical substances. All he found was a reaction to iodine, which indicated little more than the possible presence of an oily fingerprint. He later learned that the latent fingerprint department had treated the condom with chemicals and sprays to try to develop latent prints, but came up empty-handed.

Next, he looked for semen. The best way to determine the presence of semen was to look under a microscope for sperm. If you look at a sample and see sperm, it's definitely semen. But if a man has had a vasectomy, the absence of sperm does not mean that it's not semen. Unlike hairs and fibers, sperm is pretty straightforward to identify. The head has a classic appearance. The tail may or may not still be present, depending on the age of the specimen and the extent of its exposure to the elements. The longer a sample has been exposed in nature, the more likely that bacteria will have eaten away the tail.

No semen was detected on the condom. No DNA was found on the condom, either. This was no surprise. The three enemies of DNA are heat, sunlight, and moisture. Ultraviolet light from the sun can destroy DNA in a day, or even within minutes, in direct sun. The condom had lain for two months on the hillside, exposed to sun, rain, and bacteria in the soil.

As EVIDENCE UPDATES streamed in from the lab, Eddie Freyer contacted the district attorney's office to get a prosecutor involved. The district attorney, Gene Tunney, Jr., was the son of world heavyweight champion boxer Gene Tunney, known for defending his title against Jack Dempsey in one of the most famous boxing matches in history.

Tunney Jr. called in Assistant District Attorney Greg Jacobs, a high-strung, fastidious prosecutor who had grown up enamored with Sherlock Holmes and Perry Mason. A trial lawyer with an impressive batting average, he was highly intelligent but never pretentious. Juries found him down-to-earth and relatable. He was also a father of two girls. One of them had attended the same elementary school as Polly.

Jacobs stepped into the DA's office, where Tunney gave him the news. "There's been a break in the Polly Klaas case."

At forty-eight, Jacobs was a twenty-year veteran who had already prosecuted two death penalty cases. He knew what this meant. He gulped, pulled out a fountain pen, and started taking notes.

chapter twenty-nine

SWAT RAID

༺༒༻

Tuesday, November 30, 1993, 10 a.m.

ON THE MORNING OF THE SWAT RAID, SERGEANT MIKE KERNS WALKED OUT of Petaluma PD in uniform to conduct a press conference. Dozens of reporters were waiting with notebooks in hand, and crews from twenty TV stations were setting up their cameras and testing their satellite feeds. Trucks with giant antennas were clustered around the station.

After two months of hearing "no solid leads," the media were rabid for new information. Anything more concrete. The atmosphere vibrated with expectation.

Whenever Kerns set up for a press conference, he usually stood facing south, with the police station behind him. This morning, though, he flipped things around, so the press had their backs to the station. With their lenses trained on Kerns, they might not notice the caravan of police cars and FBI vehicles pulling out of the station behind them, heading north for a SWAT raid. If the press caught on and gave chase, the operation would be compromised.

In the day or so following the discovery of the suspicious items on Dana Jaffe's property, the FBI Special Operations Group had tracked Davis to the Coyote Valley Rancheria, a small reservation eighty-five miles north of Petaluma, just north of the town of Ukiah. He was staying at the home of his sister and brother-in-law, Darlene and Richard Schwarm, who lived with their young children—two girls and two boys—in a rental house on the reservation. The Schwarms were not members of the Pomo tribe, and they were living there illegally, as their lease had not been approved by the tribal council. The tribe considered them squatters and had been trying to evict them for two years.

A surveillance team had eyes on the Schwarm house through the night, while search warrants were written and signed. Davis's October 19 DUI provided the basis for an arrest warrant. An arrest of any kind was an automatic violation of parole, and his subsequent failure to appear in court for the DUI arrest was another violation. He had also failed to check in with his parole officer.

The plan was straightforward: A SWAT team would enter the house with the element of surprise, swiftly arrest Davis for the parole violation, and take him into custody. Once he was safely detained in jail, they'd question him about the kidnapping. Tom LaFreniere, who had led the raid on the apartment of James Heard, the fake kidnapper who'd demanded ransom, would be the SWAT team leader in charge of orchestrating this next big mission.

<hr/>

AFTER PULLING OUT of Petaluma PD, the caravan of SWAT team members made the eighty-mile drive north on the 101 to the Mendocino sheriff's office, a fifteen-minute drive from the location of the raid. They needed a place to stage and practice the raid out of sight of the media.

More than thirty people gathered for the briefing by Tom LaFreniere, who would be directing the operation from a mobile command center parked nearby. Today's mission would deploy three SWAT teams: two ten-member assault teams from the FBI, and one from Petaluma PD. Two snipers would provide cover. The men—all SWAT members were male at this time—had to work like clockwork to accomplish the objective: arrest Richard Allen Davis and bring him into custody.

LaFreniere went over the operations order, a detailed written plan that outlined every tick and tock of the tactical mission. It began with intel about the house, anything that could provide an idea of the floor

Aerial view of the Schwarms' house after SWAT raid.
(COURTESY OF TONY MAXWELL)

plan. In the era before Google Earth, LaFreniere could look at an aerial photograph of a house and study "the stacks"—the position of chimneys and vents on the roof—to deduce the location of bathrooms, kitchens, and fireplaces. In this case, the Special Operations Group had floor plan details from someone who'd been inside the house, a tribal officer or a sheriff's deputy.

The sequence would begin as snipers stationed themselves covertly in the woods, watching the house through their long-range scopes and providing cover. SWAT vehicles would deliver the assault teams to "phase line yellow"—out of sight of the house, but just around the corner. They would stage there, waiting for an all-clear from the snipers. Once the snipers relayed the all-clear, they would advance to "phase line green"—the final staging area before the breach point—and they'd fall into "the stack," a predetermined entry order. LaFreniere would give the final command: "Execute. Execute. Execute." The team leaders would use hand and voice signals to direct the team from there.

Each person had a specific assignment: their entry order in "the stack," a specific room or area to clear, and in some cases a particular role. They had a choreographed pattern in which they would flow through the house and clear each room. They rehearsed this choreography in the parking lot, where the floor plan was outlined in yellow tape on the asphalt. They practiced unloading from the vehicles that would deliver them close to the target, then ran through the sequence several times. The group's movements were as fluid as a murmuration of starlings.

The plan almost always changed, of course, as soon as they entered the target and encountered the unexpected, which is why each SWAT team trained together at least twice a month. They practiced hostage-rescue scenarios in booby-trapped "shooting houses" staged with all sorts of variables and elements of surprise. It trained them to react quickly and operate under pressure in chaotic and potentially deadly situations. Hours of weapons practice made them the sharpest shooters in their agency. But the training and teamwork ensured they almost never had to shoot. Many SWAT team members—including Eddie Freyer—would retire after decades without ever firing their weapon in the line of duty.

A member of the FBI Bravo assault team, Joe Davidson, was excited about his assignment: cuffing Davis as he made the arrest. Instead of an MP5 rifle, he would carry a pistol, which he could quickly holster, freeing his hands to manipulate the handcuffs. In the event he had to wrestle a bit with Davis, he didn't want to tussle with a long gun slung over his shoulder.

Davidson and his team were dressed in "all blacks"—the typical SWAT team uniform, everything black from boots to tactical helmet, faces hidden behind balaclavas. Part of the SWAT team magic was their ability to overwhelm, scaring criminals into giving up without a fight. Davidson pulled on a Kevlar vest, but opted out of the metal body armor. It could stop a rifle round, but it was also heavy and cumbersome. He wanted to be light and agile, prepared for hand-to-hand combat. The only skin showing was surrounding his eyes—he felt more confident shooting without goggles—and his hands. Sometimes he wore gloves, but he shot with even greater precision when he could feel the trigger against his skin.

The number-one entry guy, Phil Sena, would train the muzzle of his assault rifle directly at the door as everyone else fell into their place in the stack. Davidson was behind him. Depending on the situation, they would do a "knock and announce"—*BAM-BAM-BAM!* "FBI!"—or, if they heard signs of violence or evidence being destroyed on the other side of the door, the search warrant gave them discretion to bust it down. That was the job of the breacher, who would heave the battering ram and step aside.

The SWAT team would flow through the house with arresting speed, usually in a crisscross pattern or a series of button-hooks. They would tell everyone to get down on the floor and put their hands behind their heads. Briefed on the number and names of people expected to be present, they'd do a head count and figure out right away if someone was hiding.

Once the movement stilled, the people in the house were immobilized, and all known threats were disabled, Joe Davidson would complete the mission. He would slap the cuffs on Davis and say, "You're under arrest."

⌒⌒⌒

THE MOBILE COMMAND post was parked just up the road from the house and out of sight. Roughly the size of a large U-Haul moving truck, it was painted black on the outside and rigged on the inside with radios, whiteboards, and benches that doubled as storage lockers for guns and other gear. On the benches rested a table where the incident commander could spread out maps, photographs, and documents.

Working with tribal authorities, a number of local agencies secured a perimeter around the reservation, establishing roadblocks to prevent civilian vehicles from entering during the mission. A young deputy from the Mendocino County Sheriff's Office was stationed at the entrance, where he was instructed to stop cars and politely explain the wait. Rusty Noe had missed the morning briefing at the sheriff's office, so he didn't have any details about the operation. But that didn't usually matter to deputies stationed on the outer perimeter.

At three-thirty p.m., the operation began. The roadblock closed. The snipers were in position, the assault teams loaded in a small convoy. Tom LaFreniere was in the command post. The leaders of the investigative team were stationed around the corner from the house. Each pair of federal-local partners was working in sync. Case agent Eddie Freyer and Sergeant Mike Meese. ASAC Mark Mershon and Captain Pat Parks. FBI kidnapping expert Larry Taylor and Supervising Special Agent Lillian Zilius were also present. The ERT members were waiting in the wings, ready to fan out as soon as the house was cleared and safe.

LaFreniere raised the radio to his lips.

"Okay, snipers. What do you see?"

"All clear."

"Execute. Execute. Execute."

The convoy snaked through the empty streets of the reservation, stopping just out of sight of the house. Men in black spilled out and began flowing into formation, moving swiftly toward the house. No one recalls if they knocked or breached.

On the other side of the door was a confusing state of clutter. The people present in the house raised their hands and did not resist. The men in black flowed through the house, infiltrating every room and closet, poking at piles of clothes and unmade beds to make sure there wasn't a person hiding beneath.

Outside the house, the Petaluma SWAT team fanned out through the yard, which was filled with rusty cars in various states of decay. Matt Stapleton's* assignment was to clear a shed, a doghouse, and any other small outbuildings. He cleared them quickly. Then he heard a radio transmission from Bruce Burroughs, the leader of team Bravo, the FBI team in the house.

"He's not here!"

Every member of the operation collectively had the same thought. *WHAT?!*

In the yard, Stapleton felt a surge of adrenaline and shock. Had he missed him? After returning to the outbuildings, and finding them still empty, he scanned the surroundings for a possible escape route. The yard was fenced.

Inside the house, the assault team members lowered their weapons.

---

* Not to be confused with Mike Stapleton, the ERT fingerprint specialist.

Around the corner, all heads swiveled toward Eddie Freyer.

Where is he? How could he have slipped past surveillance?

The tension crested like a wave, and the radio crackled with an update from the outer perimeter. It was the voice of the FBI radio tech, who was stationed at the roadblock near the entrance of the reservation.

"Hey, I think your guy is waiting in line here."

Mike Meese, Pat Parks, and Mark Mershon leaped into the nearest vehicle and peeled out.

⌒⌒⌒

AT THE ROADBLOCK, the redheaded deputy from Mendocino, Rusty Noe, was standing beside a gray van, chatting casually through the driver's-side window with a man he presumed to be a regular civilian. The driver had black-and-gray hair to his shoulders, dark eyes, and a mustache. No beard.

Noe politely explained the reason for the traffic stop. The driver seemed rather curious about what was going on. Noe said it was a law enforcement procedure, but he didn't have any details. Which was true. Having missed the morning briefing, he didn't know anything about the nature of the raid—or the suspect.

Just then, a car came tearing in from the reservation and squealed to a stop. Two feds and a cop emerged. The redheaded deputy stepped back as the trio approached the van. Captain Parks drew his gun but kept it at his hip, pointed down.

Mershon was a half step behind him. "Are you Richard Allen Davis?"

"Yeah." He stared straight ahead, eyes blank. He kept both hands on the wheel.

Parks, still pointing his gun at the ground, opened the van door.

"Keep your hands where I can see them," Mershon said. He looked in the back of the van and saw two or three nieces and nephews.

Davis got out of the van and raised his hands.

Meese reached for his handcuffs.

"You're under arrest."

chapter thirty

THE FIRST INTERVIEW

⌒

Tuesday, November 30, 4:17 p.m.—Mendocino County Jail

RICHARD ALLEN DAVIS WAS TRANSPORTED TO THE MENDOCINO COUNTY JAIL BY Rusty Noe, the thirty-seven-year-old redheaded deputy, who was rather upset. That morning, he'd been having coffee with colleagues when a lieutenant called with an urgent message to report to the sheriff's office for a multi-agency briefing. As they arrived, three SWAT teams were pulling into the station to stage. Then a Crown Victoria rolled up—a "fed sled," as Noe put it—and a bunch of agents emerged. Someone said the vehicles needed to be guarded in the parking lot during the briefing. That sounded like the easy job, so Noe volunteered.

Now that a handcuffed suspect was riding in the back of his patrol car, Noe wished he'd been in that briefing. He was annoyed that his colleagues had let him stand there, just a few steps from a presumably dangerous man, talking to the suspect as if he was just some harmless civilian.

When the cops and fed swooped in and read the guy his rights, they declared he was being arrested for a drunk-driving warrant. Noe found himself as puzzled as the man in cuffs. A SWAT team raid for a DUI? It didn't make any sense.

Only after the man was in custody did Rusty Noe learn the whole story. After delivering Davis to the Mendocino jail, he would never see him again.

⌒⌒⌒

THE INTERVIEW ROOM at Mendocino was barely big enough for a table and two chairs. The fluorescent lights cast a greenish pall, like the sky before a tornado. A video camera hummed in one corner, near the ceiling.

This was a big moment for investigators, who had spent two months hunting him down. They had vetted 60,000 tips and investigated 12,000 leads. Now, at last, they would face him.

"Sit down. Have a seat," said Mike Meese. He introduced the two men who would be asking some questions.

"Larry Taylor," he said to the burly FBI agent from Texas, "this is Rick Davis." Then he nodded at the Petaluma detective who had processed Polly's room. "This is Larry Pelton."

There had been some discussion that morning about who should conduct this interview. It was the start of a relationship that could go sideways at any moment. Press him too hard, and Davis could invoke his Miranda rights, which would bring all questioning to a halt. Approach him too gently, and they risked wasting time. Polly was somewhere out there. If she was alive, every minute mattered.

The investigative team had decided to send the two Larrys. Larry Taylor was an FBI expert on kidnappings, and he had worked a number of child abduction cases in the Bay Area. Detective Larry Pelton had experience interviewing homicide suspects and solving whodunnit murder cases.

Pelton had the most intimate knowledge of the case and had been present at several of the crime scenes. He'd take the lead. He hadn't taken any formal interview and interrogation classes, so he wasn't trained to interpret body language, eye movements, shifts in voice tone, or other indications of deception. But years of experience had sharpened his instincts and honed his approach: get a story—true or false—that you can later verify or disprove. "The more a suspect talks, the better chance you have of getting pieces of the truth and discovering lies."

That morning at Petaluma PD, as the SWAT team was slipping away during the press conference, Pelton and Taylor met with FBI profiler Mary Ellen O'Toole. They wanted her opinion on the best approach to use when talking to Davis. Based on Davis's personality and past criminal behavior—his violent crimes and propensity for lying—O'Toole advised a confrontational approach.

Pelton knew that could be risky. An up-front accusation can make a suspect clam up and invoke his Miranda rights. But if you get a story—even one filled with lies—at least you have something to work with. There's always some truth mixed in with the lies. And even the lies can be useful.

Following his gut, Pelton started with a softer approach.

"You know you've been arrested on a parole violation," Pelton told Davis. "It's kind of obvious we want to talk to you about something else also."

"What's this concerning?" Davis said.

"It's concerning a number of different things," Pelton said. "We can go into that. I'm sure you know your rights."

"For what, though?" Davis said. "All I did was violate parole. Got a DUI."

Agent Taylor interjected in his Texan drawl. Before they went any further, he said, "You have to be advised of your rights."

"I never been interrogated like this before," Davis said.

Pelton put fresh batteries in the tape recorder and read Davis his Miranda rights. Taylor passed him a consent form, a legal agreement to waive them. Davis signed it.

"Understanding this," Pelton said, "do you wish to talk to us?"

"Well, I just have one question."

"Okay."

"What's all this pertain to?"

"You know," Pelton said, "you had a beard. You look kind of like the composite."

Davis laughed.

"That's what we want to talk to you about—the Polly Klaas kidnapping."

"Yeah, it ain't me," Davis said. "It ain't even my type [of] criminal behavior. I've helped kill people like that."

The quick reply told Pelton that Davis knew exactly what this pertained to. And the comment that this wasn't his "type of criminal behavior" was telling. The only type of criminal behavior publicized in the media was a kidnapping. He'd kidnapped before. The comment suggested that Davis knew something much worse had happened to Polly.

"Do you remember where you were on October first?" Pelton said. "That's a Friday night."

"Yeah. I was on a pass."

His response came a little too quickly. Most people can't remember what they did last Tuesday. Never mind two months ago. That meant he'd been thinking about this particular date—and he had a story ready.

Davis said he was living at Turning Point, a halfway house in San Mateo.

"Did you hear about the kidnapping?" Pelton asked.

"Yeah," Davis said. "I'm sure everybody heard about it."

"Do you remember when you heard about the kidnapping?"

"Saturday. I think it was the following day. I think it was later on that day. I was watching the news or something."

"Where had you been on the pass?"

"Went to go see some people that I knew, living toward Napa. Dude I used to deal weed with a long time ago. I ended up getting stuck on some people's property, and the sheriffs had to pull me out of a ditch."

Pelton didn't let on that he knew about the Pythian Road incident.

"You were coming back from this guy's house, or you were going?"

On a weekend pass from Turning Point, he said he'd left San Mateo a little before dark on the Friday of Polly's abduction. Six or seven o'clock. That was a fact that Pelton could check with the Turning Point logbook.* He could also calculate the distance and drive time to Petaluma: fifty-eight miles. About an hour and a half without traffic.

---

* Eddie Freyer recalled that when they later checked the logbook at Turning Point, the entry for Richard Allen Davis on this date appeared to be missing. They sent the logbook to the FBI lab, which removed a layer of Wite-Out that an employee had used to obscure the entry.

Pelton asked how he got to Pythian Road. Davis said he drove up Highway 101, through San Francisco, across the Golden Gate Bridge. Then he drove toward Napa, through some little town. Couldn't recall the name of it.

"I got to the town where they lived, and I hit the side roads but couldn't find it. Backed out of two places, went into town and bought a six-pack of beer, drank a few, went back up trying to find the right road."

"What's the name of the friend you were going to see?"

"I can't say that."

"You don't want to tell us?"

"No."

He knew better than to give up names. The cops would then track them down.

"Where did you go after you got unstuck?"

"Back home. Back to San Mateo."

"Then sometime after that you heard about the kidnapping," Pelton said. "What did you think about it?"

"Someone's a sick fuck."

"What kind of person would do that?"

"Sick fuck. I've done enough time, I done sixteen years in prison." Davis laughed. "I've met enough sick motherfuckers."

"When you got back to Turning Point did you see anybody who can vouch for what time you were there?"

"Yeah, a lot of people."

He couldn't recall any of their names.

They asked about his family. He said he was close to his sister Darlene, six years younger. His dad had died while Davis was in prison. He had other siblings and a mother. "I've got nothing to do with them."

"Where do they live?"

"I don't give a fuck."

"You don't know?"

"I don't care."

"They don't care about you at all, you mean."

"Doesn't matter either way. I don't give a fuck. It doesn't matter what they think."

Pelton wanted more details about Friday, October 1. Where did he exit the 101? Where did he buy the beer? At a liquor store, yes, but which one? He couldn't remember the name.

"Did you charge things so we can verify your story?"

"Charge?"

"Or do you pay cash?"

"I just got out of prison in June. How the fuck am I going to get a credit card unless I steal it?"

"Then you paid cash," Pelton said. "That's all I'm asking."

"Yeah," Davis snorted.

Pelton noticed inconsistency in the level of detail Davis claimed to remember. Some details about the night of the kidnapping were quite clear—backing out of two places, going into town and buying a six-pack of beer—but not where he bought that beer. That was a fact they could verify, if not with a credit card record then maybe with surveillance videos.

Pelton looked for a way to establish some logical link to Petaluma.

"Do you have any friends in Petaluma?"

"All my friends are in prison."

"Do you know anybody in Petaluma?"

"My mother."

"Your mother lives in Petaluma?"

"But I ain't got no contact with her."

"What's her name?"

"Not from me, you ain't gonna get it. I got nothing to do with the bitch. When she divorced my father in '62 she never had contact with us again."

"When did you shave off your beard? Your parole officer showed us a picture and you had a beard."

"Shaved about three weeks ago. A month ago, three weeks, two weeks."

"I'm sure you saw a picture of the suspect on the Polly Klaas kidnapping. What did you think? Did you look similar?"

"Not me. A few people at the program said something. Dude named Brad made some statement towards me. Doesn't matter what he said. Fuck him up. I just shined it off."

"Something about you look like—"

"Yeah, yeah, yeah, yeah. He's the only one that's ever said anything."

"Uh-huh," Pelton said.

"Any reason why you could think anybody may say you were in Petaluma?"

"They say I was in Petaluma?"

"They thought they saw you in Petaluma that night."

"I wasn't in Petaluma. You can check with the sheriffs. They're the ones that pulled me out of that ditch."

"Was there anybody else with you that night?"

"No. They searched the car. Because they said it was marijuana country."

"Do you know what time that was?"

"Between ten, eleven...somewhere around there."

"Do you have a watch?"

"No, I don't like watches. They remind me of handcuffs. I can't wear a watch."

They had his rap sheet, knew he had been charged with kidnapping, robbery, assault. He started to get agitated when they pressed him on his whereabouts.

"I mean you want every fucking movement."

"We got to make sure you weren't involved."

"I know in here I wasn't involved."

"Okay."

"I told you before, I helped kill dudes like that."

"You what?"

"I told you before I helped kill dudes like that in the joint. I helped fuck up a lot of people."

"You're saying because of kidnapping a little girl, you mean?"

"Yeah, it's a sick fucking crime, rape, whatever you want to call it. I think it's a coward's crime, you know."

They hadn't said anything about rape.*

---

* Also, no mention of rape had ever appeared in the press. When the suspect volunteers details that only the offender could know, that's a red flag.

Special Agent Larry Taylor stepped in, looming, losing his patience. His Texas drawl had an edge now.

"I think really it's time we started talking a little straight," Taylor said. "I'm just gonna start from square one, and if I'm wrong you correct me."

"Yeah."

"You didn't have a pass on October first."

"Yeah, I did."

"No, you didn't," Taylor said. "I got a copy of your files."

"Thought I did."

"And you didn't tell the deputies that you arrived looking for a friend. You told the deputies you were out sightseeing."

"No..."

"I got the report right here."

"I don't remember telling them that."

"Well, they didn't conjure that up."

"Well, I'm saying I didn't remember telling them that."

"Okay," Agent Taylor said. It was time to tip his hand, show Davis a bit of what they knew so he'd realize they could catch him in a lie. "I just want to lay a few things out and then we can go from there. The lady coming down the hill saw you in the dark sweatshirt. And when the deputies got there you were wearing a buttoned-down striped shirt."

"Yeah," Davis said. "Yellow and white."

Detective Pelton jumped in. "What did you do with the sweatshirt?"

"I didn't have...unless that's...that's it...the charcoal-colored one that I got. It's the only dark sweatshirt I got."

"That's all you got now, maybe," Pelton said. "What did you have then?"

"That's all I had."

"What happens when you drink?" Taylor asked.

"What happens when I drink?"

"Uh-huh. What happens to you when you drink?"

"Get a lightweight buzz."

"I mean your personality," Taylor said. "You go from Mr. Nice Guy, go over and lay in the car and go to sleep? Become a fighter? What do you do?"

"No, I wouldn't fight," Davis said. "Only fight if I drink whiskey or something like that. Drink beer, whatever, just kick back."

Detective Pelton asked, "Do you ever black out?"

"Long time ago," Davis said. "That's when I stopped drinking whiskey."

"Do you know if you ever blacked out the last couple months?"

"I didn't drink no whiskey. I told myself that when I got out."

"So you wouldn't black out on beer or anything like that if you got bombed?"

"No. I'd probably have to drink a whole lot of beer to black out."

"Well, I don't know," Pelton said. "Some people are different—do something they normally wouldn't do."

"I haven't blacked out yet drinking beer."

"What about getting so drunk you'd end up doing something you wouldn't normally do?"

"Not even."

Agent Taylor leaned in to make a point. "You telling me, then, anything you did . . . you would have been aware of it?"

"Hell yeah," Davis said.

This was important. A statement against which future statements could be called out as inconsistent.

"Well," Taylor said. "What I'm telling you is, we think you took Polly Klaas. And you know, I'm not sitting here telling you that simply because I think I [can] just go around telling you that. I've got reasons because of what we've found. And we are talking about physical evidence."

Pelton added, "Trace evidence. You heard about trace evidence? Little minute hairs and fibers."

"Uh-huh," Davis said.

"I tell you," Taylor said, "at this point I'm not asking you whether you did it. We're comfortable that you did it. The only thing I care about is *why*. I just want you to tell me why."

"I can't."

"Why?" Pelton repeated.

"I ain't done nothing to be answering no why."

"You have a child," Pelton said.

"Not that I know of," Davis said. "Maybe I've been told I have one, but I've never seen him."

"Little boy...or a girl?"

"They're twelve years old now," Davis said.

"A boy or a girl?"

"Yeah."

"I understand you weren't close," Pelton said. "I guess because you were in prison a lot. Did you have some kind of relationship with them earlier?"

"Never saw 'em."

"Never even saw 'em," Pelton said. "Okay."

"Mother married someone who wanted a legitimate name. I wasn't willing to do that. Saw my father go through all of his divorces. Fuck all that."

"Your sister, how many kids do they have?"

"Four."

"You pretty close to them? Do you love them?"

"Oh yeah."

"They're good kids?"

"Uh, well..."

"They're kids," Pelton said. "But your sister loves them, right?"

"Uh-huh."

"And your brother-in-law loves them."

"Sure do."

"How do you think they'd feel if one of them was missing?"

"Real bad."

"Real bad," Pelton said. "They'd want to know what happened one way or another, right?"

"Yeah."

"They'd probably feel really sick not knowing what's happening to them, right? And not knowing why somebody did something to them."

"Why ya asking me why?" Davis said. "I couldn't—"

"Because we told you why," Pelton said.

"Well then book me and let's get a lawyer and let's go for it man, you know?"

"We're just trying to talk to you," Pelton said.

"Book me," Davis said, "and let's shit or get off the pot. Let's go for it."

"So is that what you want to do?" Pelton said. "Or do you want to talk and try to tell us what's going on?"

"You were asking a lot [of] these different questions in the beginning," Davis said. "I don't mind telling you [you] ask a lot of stupid questions."

"We do," Pelton said.

"Now it's getting to the point, you tell me, oh, you know I did it. You want to know why. You got a little evidence. You guys feel that much that I did do it, hey, then let's shit or get off the pot."

Agent Taylor stepped in. "It's going to happen."

"Well, let's go for it," Davis said. "That's the end. The end."

"You don't want to talk no more," Pelton said.

"Get real," Davis said. "You think I should?"

"That's up to you," Pelton said.

"Fuck."

"Like I said," Agent Taylor said, "what we want to know is why?"

Pelton said, "'Cause this is our opportunity to get it from you."

"I can't tell you something I don't know."

"So we can tell the parents why," Pelton said. "That's why we're asking you this stuff."

"I can't answer that question," Davis said. "Get real. I ain't done it. How can I answer it?"

"What," Pelton said. "You know nothing about it?"

"Hell no," Davis said. "I didn't kidnap that little fucking broad, man. Get real."

That line would come back to haunt him.

"You talked about rape and things like that. We never mentioned anything about that. We mentioned kidnapping of Polly Klaas. Nobody said anything about sexual assault of a little girl."

"I just told you I didn't snatch the little girl."

"I know," Pelton said. "But earlier you said those people are sick."

"Yeah."

"The rapists," Pelton said.

"Rapists, child molesters, they got ex-cops in there and, you know, ex-CHPs," Davis said. "I've done enough time I've seen a lot of sick motherfuckers, you know what I mean?"

"I'll give you this much," Agent Taylor said. "From reading your reports, I don't know you from Adam, I would say you're right. That's the reason I'm asking about the alcohol. Because in reading the report, it doesn't seem that you would do something like that unless [there was] something taking you completely out of your personality."

"You know ... there ain't no way whatever you're saying that I might have gotten so drunk," Davis said. "If I was so drunk when the cops pulled me out of that ditch, why didn't they take me to jail?"

"Right," Pelton said. "I don't know. I don't know."

"Well."

"Before that, or later than that, we don't know."

"Well," Davis said. "I told you I ain't got no watch. I just know a round figure. But as far as these questions are going, get me a lawyer and let's get on down the road."

"So you want a lawyer," Pelton said. "You don't want to talk anymore?"

"Hey, it's over and done now," Davis said. "Like I say, shit or get off the pot. Let's go."

By asking for a lawyer and asking to end the interview, Davis had invoked his Miranda rights. The cops and feds could not legally ask him any more questions about the crime. He was handcuffed and taken back to his cell in the Mendocino jail. The sheriff moved him to a medical isolation unit, where the lights stayed on twenty-four hours and Davis could be monitored.

Suicide watch.

chapter thirty-one

THE PALM PRINT

⌒⌒⌒

December 1, 1993

THE LATENT PALM PRINT FROM POLLY'S BUNK BED HAD BEEN SITTING IN THE FBI lab for two months, useless without a suspect and his palm. It was one of the forty-eight latent prints missed in the initial dusting, found with Tony Maxwell's Redwop powder and alternate light source. In the fingerprint log, it was entry A-6, the one next to which he'd scribbled the word *Bingo*.

It was a "question print"—as opposed to a "known print" belonging to the victim or some other individual with reason to be in her room. The Q samples, as they were called in the lab, were quickly matched with K samples from Polly and her family and friends and eliminated as evidence.

All but one: this palm print.

It was too big to belong to a child. And its location was suggestive: pressed into one of the wooden slats supporting the upper rail of the bunk bed, as if some adult had momentarily leaned against it for balance. As specimens go, it wasn't the cleanest—only a partial impression of a palm, its whorls and ridge lines smudged in spots or interrupted by gaps between the wooden frame and two cylindrical dowels that held it together. Viewed out of context, the print might appear more like a Rorschach test than part of a human hand.

The latent palm print lifted with Redwop powder and ALS.
(COURTESY OF TONY MAXWELL)

Some police agencies had fingerprint experts, but the FBI had a strict policy of not accepting any evidence that had been processed by another agency. So the latent print—along with any other evidence that needed examination by the FBI lab—would have been logged into evidence by the Petaluma PD but sent directly to the FBI lab.

This palm print was now in the hands of Michael J. Smith, a fingerprint specialist in the Latent Fingerprint Section of the FBI laboratory in Washington, DC. It had been hand-delivered on November 8 by ERT member David Alford, who flew in from San Francisco with the first batch of evidence collected from Polly's house.

An automated fingerprint identification system was under development, but it wouldn't be operational until 1999. The FBI's Integrated Automated Fingerprint Identification System (IAFIS, pronounced I-AY-fis) would become the world's largest digital collection of fingerprint images and criminal histories. It would include footprints, palm prints, photographs, and other biometric data from not only criminals who had been booked and arrested but also law-abiding citizens finger-printed for employment, security, or other reasons.

Until then, it was the job of people like Michael J. Smith to visu-ally compare inked and latent prints—from fingers, palms, feet, and even lips—hoping to find a match among the 200 million or so recorded imprints in the FBI's National Crime Information Center (NCIC) in West Virginia. Before IAFIS, it was up to investigators on a given case to identify a list of candidates to consider as possible suspects. Once they had suspects, finding their fingerprints required cold-calling every agency that might have them in some file cabinet. That's what Detec-tive Andy Mazzanti had to do during his full workup on Richard Allen Davis. Those fingerprints were then sent to a trained specialist like Smith. If there were no fingerprint records to be found for a candidate, that person was located and asked to come in to have their fingerprints and palm prints rolled. If this person refused, a court order or subpoena would compel cooperation.

Becoming qualified to examine latent prints required years of train-ing and experience. For Smith it began with thirteen weeks of classroom instruction, then a month of on-the-job training in which he practiced the classification, identification, and filing of fingerprint cards. After seven years in that role, Smith was offered the opportunity to take the latent print section examination, a two-day test that qualified him for another six months of highly supervised classroom training, plus six more months of on-the-job training in developing and identifying latent prints. Now in his eighteenth year at the lab, Smith trained police officers and forensic technicians throughout the country in the science of fingerprints. He was often called in to testify as an expert witness in trials, and he had an articulate way of teaching juries about the science of fingerprints.

"Present on the palmar side of your hands and finger and soles of the feet are raised portions of skin," he would explain to a jury. "These raised portions of skin [are] called friction ridges. They have tiny, little openings called pores which exhibit perspiration." When you touch your face or your hair, or handle other materials, the friction ridges pick up oils, sweat, and dirt. Then, when you touch an object, those substances are transferred to its surface. "A latent print is normally invisible," Smith said, "and will require some method of development, such as lasers, fingerprint powders, or chemicals to make it visible."

By contrast, an inked print was created by applying a thin film of black printer's ink to the friction ridges and transferring it onto a fingerprint card.

When Davis was pulled over in Modesto for a broken taillight on March 21, 1985, he was arrested on a warrant for the kidnapping of Selina Varich and booked in the Stanislaus County Jail. The fingerprint card was dated March 22, 1985, which probably meant he was booked after midnight. Kidnapping was a serious offense, so they had rolled his palms as well as his digits. Those prints had been tucked in a file for eight years, until Andy Mazzanti's late-night call on November 28, 1993.

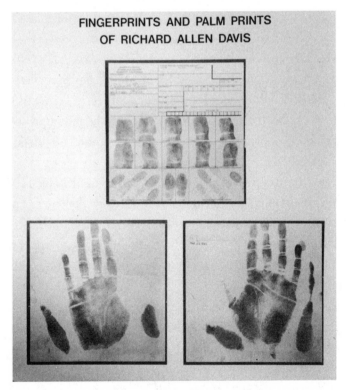

FINGERPRINTS AND PALM PRINTS
OF RICHARD ALLEN DAVIS

The inked prints Andy Mazzanti obtained from Stanislaus County Sheriff's Office, compared with the latent palm print to establish a positive ID of Richard Allen Davis.

(COURTESY OF TONY MAXWELL)

After the palm print from Stanislaus County was spat out of the fax in Petaluma on November 29, someone must have grabbed it and quickly dispatched it to the FBI lab in DC. It isn't clear how the palm print was transmitted or transported—no one involved in the investigation can remember this detail after nearly three decades. It's questionable whether a fax of a fax would have been crisp enough for a conclusive lab comparison.

The next day, on November 30, an FBI agent quickly contacted the Stanislaus County Sheriff's Office to request the original inked prints. How those arrived at the FBI lab is also a mystery. FedEx wasn't commonly used at the time by the Bureau for transporting sensitive documents, so for expedited shipping, an agent would often drive to the nearest airport and hand-deliver a package to a commercial pilot, who would sign off on the chain of custody. When the flight landed, there would be another FBI agent waiting at the gate to receive the package. This may have been how the records traveled, one rung above first class.

However it got there, the inked palm print from Stanislaus County arrived in the FBI lab on Wednesday, December 1. This was a critical moment in the case. If the inked print matched the latent print found on Polly's bunk bed, it would be the first piece of physical evidence linking Davis to Polly's bedroom.

To begin the examination, Smith had the latent print from Polly's bunk bed photographed. Because it was lifted with fluorescent powder—which produced an image of light ridge lines on a dark background—Smith had the image reversed, so the ridge lines would appear dark on light, like an inked print. Using a four-power magnifier he compared the two images side-by-side.

He was looking for "points of identity," places where the raised ridge lines merged and divided. This arrangement is unique to every human in the world. In establishing a match, Smith had to consider the number of points of identity in each print, and, as he described it, "the similarity of these ridges and the unit relationship of these characteristics to each other." Imagining the prints as two topographical maps, would the peaks and valleys, rivers and ridge lines be positioned in the same places?

How many points of identity are required to conclude a match?

No set number is required by law. "The smallest number I ever heard was about seven," said Mike Stapleton, a member of the San Francisco ERT who worked on Polly's case and went on to become a fingerprint instructor for the FBI and other agencies. When testifying in court, an expert witness—someone like Smith—is allowed to provide an opinion, based on their educational background, training, and experience. (Other witnesses typically are not permitted to provide opinions in court testimony.) "Until approximately 1942, the FBI followed the Edmond Locard standard that finding a minimum of twelve characteristics established identity," Stapleton said. In 1993, however, the Locard standard was no longer followed. "Our experts—through time, practice, and experience—determined that identity could be established in fewer than twelve characteristics."

In his comparison of the latent print lifted from Polly's bed and the inked print taken from Davis in 1985, Smith found eleven points of identity. More inked palm prints would be taken from Davis in custody, but for now, this was sufficient to confidently conclude that Richard Allen Davis had been present in the bedroom of Polly Klaas.

On December 1, 1993, the FBI announced the news internally.

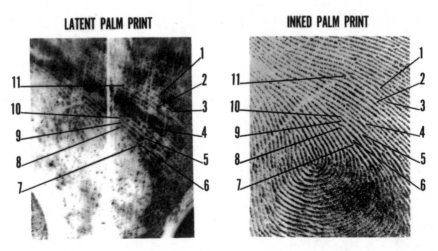

Fingerprint analysis showing eleven points of identity found by FBI examiner Michael J. Smith.

(COURTESY OF TONY MAXWELL)

Three time zones and nearly 3,000 miles away in Petaluma, ASAC Mark Mershon was pulling into the parking lot of the command center when someone told him to call the FBI lab. That's when he learned the good news.

"You mean the latent is a match with Davis!?" Mershon exclaimed.

"Actually, Mark, we use the term 'match' for comparing physical evidence," Smith clarified. The fabric from the ligatures, for instance, was a match. "For fingerprints, we use the term 'ident' when there is a positive identification."

Eddie Freyer was in the Mendocino command center when he got the call.

"Eddie, it's close," Smith said, "but I can get enough identifying points."

"What do you mean?"

"I'm calling it," Smith said. "It's ident."

Freyer felt butterflies in his stomach. The pieces were falling into place. They still didn't have Polly, but they had what they needed to build a solid case against her abductor. Eyewitness testimony. Physical evidence linking two crime scenes. And now, hard proof that Davis had been present in Polly's bedroom. It was now up to the Sonoma County district attorney's office to decide if evidence was sufficient to file charges, transforming Davis from a *suspect* into a *subject*—one significant step closer to an arrest.

Freyer stood up in the command center and cleared his throat.

"Can I have your attention please?"

The command center's state of perpetual motion stilled to a hush.

"I just got confirmation from our laboratory that we've matched the palm print from the bedroom to Davis," Freyer announced. "We can place him in the bedroom."

The room erupted with shouts and cheers as papers flew into the air.

Detective Dennis Nowicki tackled Freyer with a bear hug and squeezed the air out of his lungs.

chapter thirty-two

THE LINEUP

∽

Wednesday, December 1, 1993

ON WEDNESDAY MORNING, KATE MCLEAN'S MOTHER WOKE HER UP EARLY FOR
school. Alice McLean had waited to share the news, to make sure her
daughter got a good night's rest.

"Kate," she said, "it's time for you to go to Ukiah for a lineup with
the guy."

The FBI and police had finally named a prime suspect, a man they
had enough evidence to believe was Polly's abductor. Now they needed
Kate and Gillian to try to pick this man out of a lineup. Kate instantly
felt the worry and pressure set in. What if the kidnapper wasn't one of
the guys in the lineup? What if he was, and she didn't recognize him?
Kate worried that whatever she did could "mess up" the investigation.

Ever since the night she had witnessed her friend abducted by an
intruder, Kate had felt terrified, anxious, and insecure. She had trouble
falling asleep and worried the kidnapper would come after her. Her family installed a burglar alarm to help alleviate her fears. Kate also worried
obsessively that her actions had undermined Polly's safety. It wasn't just
the kidnapping that had inflicted emotional trauma. It was also the way
she'd been treated and doubted and intimidated by the FBI.

Thrust into the heart of the investigation, a crucible with life-or-death stakes, Kate and Gillian had endured a series of experiences that would one day serve as a case study of how *not* to handle child witnesses. They had been put through two polygraph tests, a videotaped reenactment staged and filmed at the crime scene, and at least four interviews that had increasingly come to feel more like interrogations.

Investigators' initial skepticism had been amplified by the "minor inconsistencies"—that godforsaken bandana and the sound of a door that could not have slammed shut. When polygrapher Ron Hilley had pressed Kate on these details, it felt like an attack on her integrity—like being called a liar. Then, when Jeanne Boylan's sketch featured no yellow bandana, it deflated her self-confidence and eroded her faith in her memory. Kate—mature, intelligent Kate—had started to doubt herself.

The brutal interrogation forty-eight hours after the kidnapping left the deepest scars. As Kate remembered it—a memory she had been conditioned by now to question (but one that was in fact accurate)—she'd been dragged out of bed late one night and brought in by the FBI for yet another round of questioning. Kate had come out of that "bad cop" interview crying hysterically. She fell into her mother's arms and sobbed, "I don't even know what I know anymore."

This mishandling of the young witnesses was one of the biggest mistakes of the case. It inflicted trauma on top of trauma. The girls were not just witnesses to their best friend being victimized. They were victims themselves. The investigators would one day try to make up for it by honoring them with a special award for courage, but to the girls it would feel hollow. Being courageous is a choice. The girls had not been given that choice. What other option did they have?

Kate had always been exceptional in her verbal ability and her powers of observation. But this "harrowing" experience with the FBI obliterated her confidence. "It was a real earth-shaking experience with her," her mother told Andy Mazzanti. "It shook her to the roots of her being, to be questioned in such a way." The damage would last a lifetime and could never be undone.

ON THE MORNING of the lineup, Kate was already feeling "stressed out" by the time she got to school. To her dismay, news about the lineup had already made its way through the halls of Petaluma Junior High. Kate and Gillian found themselves assaulted with questions from peers and well-meaning but discomfiting attention from teachers.

After surviving a few stares in homeroom class and a second-period meeting to coordinate yearbook pages dedicated to Polly, Kate was picked up at school by her mother. She was pretty wound up, a feeling she described as "hyper." They went to an appointment with Kate's therapist, who reassured and encouraged her, trying to alleviate the pressure she felt by explaining that Kate was just one small part of a large investigation. The outcome wasn't resting on her shoulders. After therapy, Kate felt a bit better. They drove home to meet Sergeant Vail Bello and an FBI agent, who would chauffeur them to the lineup.

Kate and her mother rode to Ukiah in the back seat of a boxy white Chevy Caprice. After a quick stop at the 7-Eleven to buy a round of Slurpees, Bello and the agent explained how the lineup process would go. They encouraged Kate not to pressure herself to identify an individual if she didn't feel certain she recognized the kidnapper in the lineup. They explained that even if she couldn't make a positive ID, they still had enough to get the guy who had taken Polly.

Pulling into the parking lot of Mendocino County Jail, they encountered the mob of media already clustered around the building. As they got out of the car, Kate found herself surrounded by camera lenses and microphones shoved in her face. It made her feel "like a celebrity," but also taken aback. One reporter yelled a question. They were so aggressive! Kate coolly replied, "No comment."

They entered the jail and made their way down several dark hallways to the viewing room. Someone explained the two-way mirror and let Kate stand on the other side, in the room where the men would line up. She could only see her reflection. Kate understood that she wouldn't be visible, but it was still "creepy" and she felt "a little scared" about what she was going to see.

Larry Pelton read her the lineup instructions:

"Because a police officer is showing you a group of subjects, this should not influence your judgment in any way. The person who committed this crime may or may not be in the group of subjects you are viewing. You are in no way obligated to identify anyone. Study each subject carefully before making any comments. Consider that hair styles change and persons can alter their identity by growing or shaving facial hair."

"I don't know why we're doing this," Kate said, "because the subject won't be there."

After she returned to the darkened viewing room, six men in orange prison uniforms walked into the brightly lit room on the other side of the glass. Each of them held a number. The men were instructed to turn to the left, turn to the right, face forward, walk to the back of the room, turn, and walk toward the mirror. One by one, they were instructed to say certain phrases:

"Don't scream or I'll slit your throats."

"Is anyone else in the house?"

"Who lives here?"

"You're supposed to be alone."

"Show me where the valuables are."

"Lie down, put your hands behind you."

"Count to a thousand."

Kate leaned into the glass, studying the figures intensely. Investigators warned her to scoot back a bit, so the men couldn't see her silhouette. She backed away, eyes moving from one face to the next. No face stood out as instantly recognizable. Some of them had a mustache, but no one had a salt-and-pepper beard.

Kate asked if the men could read the phrases again. As number one began talking, Kate lay facedown on the floor of the viewing room and put her hands behind her back. She stayed in this position as number two and number three spoke. When she heard the voice of number four, Kate raised her head and looked at him. Then she put her nose back to the floor and listened to the rest.

Kate ruled out two of the subjects—a redhead, and a white-haired man who was a good bit shorter than the rest. But the others—she just wasn't sure. Kate identified four men as "possibles," but didn't single one out. Numbers two, three, four, and six sort of sounded and looked like the guy. She told investigators she was sorry that she couldn't be more specific.

After the lineup, as Kate waited in the back seat of the Chevy Caprice, a photographer snapped a photo of her haunted face peering out through the car's rear windshield. On the eighty-mile drive home, Vail Bello stopped at 7-Eleven to treat Kate to another Slurpee, a "humongous" one, as a reward. But she chewed her fingernails all the way back to Petaluma.

⌒⌒⌒

OVER THE COURSE of six hours, investigators presented the lineup to ten different witnesses. Most of them were unable to make a positive identification.

When Gillian viewed the lineup, the subjects read the same remarks they recited for Kate. Gillian said she couldn't identify anyone, though the hair on number six looked familiar. (Number six was an FBI agent asked to stand in to complete a lineup of six white males of similar age and build.)

Sean Bush said number four looked very close to the man he saw walking up to Polly's back door. He had the same wiry hair—lighter on top, darker on the bottom—and same skin tone, neck size, weight, and eyes. But he wasn't certain enough to call it a positive ID.

Kamika Milstead didn't recognize the man she'd seen walking on Polly's block shortly before the abduction. "I don't think any of them were the guy," she said, noting "major differences." In her statement, she wrote: "Number four looks familiar, but I don't think he's the one." Taleah Miller, who had noticed a scary-looking guy with a bag while getting out of the car with her uncle, said she didn't see this man in the lineup.

Thomas Georges, the middle-school neighbor who spotted the suspect along with his friends, thought it could possibly be number two. "He is about the right height and weight," he wrote, "but I am not positive that it is him. He also walked like the guy I saw." His friend, Ben Morrison, selected number four and number six. "It is hard to tell," he wrote, "because the person that I saw was standing far away and it was dark." Another friend, Paul Kingsbury, selected number four, whose posture looked familiar. The other friend, David Ciabattari, said he didn't recognize any of them.

The only witness who was able to make a positive ID was Daryl Stone, the neighbor who had been walking his dog on a nearby street when he saw the suspect. "Number four closely resembles a man I saw the afternoon of the incident," he wrote in his statement. "Profile very similar. Hair color very close. I'm sure it's the person I saw."

THAT NIGHT, AT home in Petaluma, Kate and her mother were watching the news when a photo of Richard Allen Davis flashed up on the screen. In this mug shot, he had a full salt-and-pepper beard, with a particular dark patch that really "set it off." Kate flashed back instantly to the lineup. Was this the number five guy? Or number four?

"Did he look that evil?" Kate's mother asked her.

Kate turned her face away.

On the news, Jeanne Boylan's sketch filled the TV screen. Then, through some sleight of video editing, the drawing melted into the photo of Richard Allen Davis.

Maybe it was the power of suggestion, seeing the sketch morph into the face, but Kate was almost positive it was the face she had seen for a split-second in Polly's room. But she was not *quite* certain enough to tell that to the police. She had learned to second-guess herself, and the thought of coming forward and telling investigators made her nervous. "I was worried that I wasn't right," Kate would say, days later. "And then I would get in trouble or something. Or, I would mess up the case."

The following night, around midnight, she cried herself to sleep.

Two days after the lineup, on Friday, December 3, Detective Andy Mazzanti went to Kate's house an hour or so before noon. Mazzanti was the giant Italian who had interviewed Gillian on the night of the kidnapping. He was the cop his colleagues called "Mongo" because of his size and monobrow, and the detective who still didn't know that he had been the one to locate the matching inked palm print.

They sat down in the living room, and Andy turned on the tape recorder. Kate's mother, Alice, said she wanted to stay in the room this time. "I just got really sick of being out of it," she said. "You guys are doing a wonderful, fantastic job. But I just wanna be here." Mazzanti agreed, as long as Kate was allowed to speak for herself.

Mazzanti asked her to recount everything she remembered about Wednesday. When they reached the moment of viewing the lineup, he asked Kate what was going on in her head.

"I don't want to push it," she said. "I don't want to mess anything up."

He asked where that pressure was coming from. Friends? The media? Parents? The police and the FBI?

That's when she let it all spill out.

"In the first couple of weeks of the case I was pretty confident in myself. And then I flunked several polygraph tests and I still couldn't understand why, because I wasn't sure of myself enough to know what I had done wrong even. Or whether or not I had exaggerated. I still don't know. It just . . . you don't have enough confidence after a while, you know? After flunking polygraph tests or being so unsure of yourself to the point where you can't even tell you were honest or dishonest. I have pretty much got that straightened out, but I still don't think I'll feel quite confident with this case as I did in the first place."

To make matters worse, the media had found her phone number. One day Kate answered a call from a reporter who needled for information in a way that Kate felt was rather "slimy." Several newspapers had printed erroneously that Kate and Gillian had viewed the lineup and made a positive identification.

"No, no," Kate told the reporter on the phone. "Where did the papers get the information that we positively identified the man?"

"Oh," the reporter said, "so are you saying that you *didn't* positively identify him?"

"I'm not saying that," Kate replied. "And I'm not saying anything else. I'm saying where did you get the information? Because I don't think the police would release it."

That's when her mother grabbed the phone and "had a cow."

Kate told Mazzanti she had come to mistrust the press and worried that they were going to undermine the investigation.

"They say, 'We want Polly to be okay. We're experienced in this field. I've dealt with several kidnappings.' But how does that make you experienced? Does that mean you understand? Does that mean you even care about the kidnapped victims? Or is it just your papers you care about? Or your TV show?"

Mazzanti pulled out six photographs of the men who'd appeared in the lineup.

"The person who committed the kidnapping may or may not be in these pictures, okay? You are in no way obligated to identify anybody."

"Even if I just said, 'I don't know,' you wouldn't care?" Kate asked.

"Right," Mazzanti said. "If that's the truth and that's what you feel, that's what we want you to say."

"Absolutely," she said. "Cool."

"Study each of the photographs carefully before making any comments. Consider that the photographs could be old or new, that hair styles change, and that the persons could alter their [appearance] by growing or—"

"By shaving facial hair," she said.

"So I'm gonna show you six in here. I want you to go ahead and take a look at them." He paused. "And what I want you to concentrate on is that split second that you saw him the night of the kidnapping and not so much on what you saw since then."

Kate studied the row of photographs laid out before her.

"No...Don't know...Don't know...Don't know...Don't know..."

"So number one is definitely out?"

"Yeah."

"And six is definitely out?"

"Yeah, and number five is out also."

"So number two, three, or four is a possibility."

"I think number four probably the most. When I saw him in those pictures from the media, you could still see, like, brown highlights in his beard."

She pointed to suspect number four. Now her voice was certain.

"This is Mr. Davis."

chapter thirty-three

SYSTEM FAILURES

༲

December 2

ON THE MORNING OF THURSDAY, DECEMBER 2, THE MEDIA—AND THE WORLD—
got its first live glimpse of the new prime suspect. At eleven-thirty a.m.,
Richard Allen Davis was brought from the Mendocino jail to the Mount
Sanhedrin Municipal Court to attend his arraignment on drunk driving
and subsequent failure to appear in court.

"Here he comes!" echoed through the corridor as Davis walked
toward a courtroom jammed with cameras and reporters. He was
dressed in a jail-issue orange jumpsuit and a red T-shirt. Several days of
whisker growth hinted at the salt-and-pepper beard that he had shaved
into a mustache. With shackled wrists and ankles, he was escorted by
the sheriff and three deputies to a seat in the small jury box, where he
calmly looked around.

Davis pleaded guilty to the charge of drunken driving. Judge Henry
Nelson sentenced him to thirty days in jail, with a credit for three days
served. Within minutes, he was escorted back to his cell in the Mendocino jail.

Back in Petaluma, there was talk of forming a "lynch mob" to greet
him if he was ever moved to the jail in Polly's hometown.

⌒⌒⌒

THE ARRAIGNMENT REVEALED that Davis had been in contact with law enforcement—twice—since Polly's disappearance.

The first time, one hour and twenty-eight minutes after Polly's abduction, was the thirty-eight-minute encounter with the two Sonoma County deputies as they responded to Dana Jaffe's call about a trespasser on her property off Pythian Road.

The second occasion was a very brief stay at the Mendocino County Jail after he was arrested for a DUI on October 19. It was eighteen days after Polly's abduction, the day after James Heard was arrested for impersonating a kidnapper and attempting to extort a $10,000 reward. Davis was driving up to Ukiah to visit his sister and brother-in-law when California Highway Patrol officer Robert McIntosh noticed a white Pinto weaving at seventy-five miles per hour in a fifty-five-mile-an-hour zone on Highway 101 near Ukiah. Richard Allen Davis was behind the wheel. He still had shoulder-length gray hair, but he had shaved his salt-and-pepper beard into a mustache, so he didn't look quite as much like Jeanne Boylan's heavily circulated sketch.

Davis said he had been trying to catch up with a car ahead, in which he'd noticed a female driver. He wanted to see "if she was hot." The CHP officer took his license and called it in to dispatch for a records check. The dispatcher checked the computer and radioed back: no outstanding warrants.

The officer smelled alcohol on his breath, so he conducted a field sobriety test. Asking Davis to follow his finger with his eyes, the officer noticed a lateral nystagmus—an eye bounce—which was a sign of intoxication. He then asked Davis to recite the alphabet, another simple field sobriety test. Davis forgot the "S" and the "V." A subsequent breathalyzer test registered a blood alcohol content of .12 (above the .08 legal limit).

Officer McIntosh arrested Davis for a DUI and booked him into the Mendocino County Jail, where he was searched and his car was impounded. He stayed in the drunk tank for just a few hours before sobering up and being released.

While an arrest for any crime is a violation of parole, the warrant wasn't triggered until Davis's parole agent learned about it. That was another failure of the system.

⌒⌒⌒

FOUR MONTHS EARLIER, on June 28—the day after Davis was released from California Men's Colony—he was assigned to his parole agent, Thomas Berns. Berns's job was to check in with Davis twice a month, supervise where he lived and worked, and keep track of any contact he had with police and how he handled himself in the community.

For their first meeting, Berns met Davis at a hotel where he was staying and helped him set up an interview at Turning Point, a halfway house. After the interview, Davis was accepted for a residency of 90 to 120 days.

On July 7, Davis informed Berns that he'd gotten a job at a sheet metal company. They touched base three times in August. All seemed to be going well. But on August 9, Laureen Lundin, an employee at Turning Point, called Berns to report her concerns about Davis "holding court in the street" and bragging about "shootouts, robberies, and getting high for days." Berns, knowing Davis's background and penchant for crime sprees, didn't seem too concerned. Lundin later testified that Berns told her, "If Mr. Davis did something, he would not do it here and he would do it all in one day."

On September 23, Berns gave Davis a three-day travel pass to leave his fifty-mile boundary and visit his sister and brother-in-law. Davis rode a Greyhound bus to Ukiah and drove back in the Pinto, which he bought from his brother-in-law for $200—70 percent of his savings. Berns did not make sure that Davis returned from Ukiah on time after his three-day pass.

There was no contact between Davis and Berns until October 12, when Berns did a collateral check with Lundin at Turning Point. It was during that ninety-day gap that Polly Klaas disappeared.

On November 2, Davis received permission to visit the Schwarms again in Ukiah. But he failed to return as planned on November 15.

THOUGH INVESTIGATORS HAD announced Davis as the prime suspect in the kidnapping, he had not yet been charged with anything—other than the DUI. He was still awaiting a hearing for parole violation.

But as the media dug into his criminal history and printed a litany of his priors, readers and viewers were shocked and angry.

"This guy's been in prison more times than I've brushed my teeth," said a man in Petaluma. "The police should have been more concerned."

Naturally, Marc Klaas was outraged too.

"We've had enough of this!" Marc told the press. "We've had enough of this as a country. We need to make changes. It's time to protect our children. It has to happen, because if it doesn't happen we're dead as a society."

Tom Howard and Mike Rankin, the two Sonoma deputies who had encountered Davis on Pythian Road, were called in by investigators and asked to write supplemental reports. Not knowing all of the details and legal limitations, the public and the media began to excoriate them.

"Sightseeing on a Friday night in the middle of winter?" said the general manager of a lumber company. "That's a little suspicious."

"If he is the guy and they had him an hour later, it's really pathetic our system can't deal with that," said a Petaluma mother interviewed by a reporter as she carried her groceries to the car.

EVERYONE IN PETALUMA was reeling from the emotional concussion. "I would say that this is probably the most emotional up-and-down day," said Gary Judd, a board member of the Polly Klaas Foundation. He and others had learned, a little past midnight on Wednesday morning, that investigators had identified a prime suspect. Judd couldn't go back to sleep that night, thinking about what was to come, bracing for "the onslaught."

The news of a prime suspect—at last—recharged their hope. Joanne Gardner and other volunteers remained "very optimistic." She noticed the careful statements police were making to protect the investigation and inferred that they were working under the assumption that Polly was still alive.

The Bill Rhodes debacle had left the volunteers shaken and bewildered to think that a sex offender had been their leader. As Gardner put it: "There was a collective sigh of relief that it was not someone we knew."

When a TV station reported that human remains had been discovered, the hope and relief evaporated and plunged the volunteers into despair. When it turned out to be a rumor, their spirits rebounded, but the optimism was guarded. They had weathered many a rumor du jour over the past two months, and it was emotionally exhausting.

"I know I'm supposed to think happy thoughts," said an eleven-year-old classmate of Polly's. "But somehow, y'know, I feel she just might be dead."

Eve had gone into seclusion, and Joanne Gardner was shielding her from the media. Marc honored his promise to the FBI not to speak to the press about any details of the investigation, but he praised the efforts of both authorities and volunteers, who "pulled a needle out of a haystack."

Marc hadn't slept since the day Davis was arrested, and he wore his anguish visibly. He thought about the timeline, the eighty-eight minutes between Polly's 10:40 p.m. abduction and the deputies' 12:08 a.m. arrival at Pythian Road. He couldn't see how it was possible for Davis to have kidnapped her, driven thirty miles, taken her into the woods, and killed her—in an hour and twenty-eight minutes. He suggested she had been taken and then handed over to others.

"I don't know if she's with people or with angels," Marc said. "I don't know whether my daughter is alive or dead."

chapter thirty-four

THE WILD CARD

༺◌༻

December 4, 1993

IN MORNING PAPERS ACROSS THE BAY AREA, HEADLINES ANNOUNCED THE BIG break in the case. The front page of the *Santa Rosa Press Democrat* summed it up in four words and six syllables:

PRINT LINKS DAVIS, POLLY

Richard Allen Davis had no way of knowing this. He was being held in isolation in Mendocino County Jail, cut off from TV news and other sources of outside information. Technically, he was just serving a thirty-day sentence for drunken driving. A DUI—or any crime—was a violation of parole. Now he was awaiting a hearing for three possible parole violations—failing to report to his parole officer, his October 19 DUI, and his subsequent failure to appear in court for the DUI.

Around nine-thirty a.m., an unexpected visitor showed up at Mendocino County Jail and asked if he could visit Davis. The shift lieutenant called Eddie Freyer.

"We have a visitor here who wants to see Davis," the jailer told him.

"Who is he?"

"He says he's a friend."

It seemed risky. Could this friend tip Davis off in a way that could further jeopardize Polly's safety? Could it compromise the integrity of the case? Maybe they could intercept this guy first and ask him some questions. Once they knew the reasons for his visit, they could make a better decision about whether to allow it. On the other hand, intercepting the friend could have legal ramifications. If investigators spoke with him first, that could make the friend an "accessory" to the investigation, which could cause legal problems later. Freyer asked if there were any rules that prohibited a prisoner in isolation from receiving visitors.

"No," the lieutenant said.

"Okay, then. Let them meet," Freyer said. "We'll talk to him after the meeting."*

THE FRIEND, MARVIN WHITE, was a former employer of Davis. He ran a sheet metal company that hired ex-convicts to help them transition from prison back into society. They'd met in the early 1980s, when Davis did sheet metal work for White in Redwood City. They had crossed paths again in 1984, this time as peers, both employed by Prime Metals, where Davis worked as a specialized brake operator. That job required close-tolerance work with a paper-thin margin of error. Davis made a few mistakes and ruined a number of parts, so his bosses demoted him and lowered his pay. Davis, despondent, wanted to quit.

"I can't take this," he told White.

White offered to help him get back on track. "Don't throw in the towel," White told him. "We can work through it."

Davis quit anyway, after four weeks on the job.

White hadn't seen Davis since. And then, just a few days ago, a mutual acquaintance called White and told him to turn on the Channel 4

---

* This was a key tactical decision. If they had intercepted White before his meeting with Davis and had any kind of conversation, it could have raised the issue of White becoming "an agent of law enforcement." That could have complicated the issue of the admissibility (in court) of anything said by Davis. Because White acted of his own volition, any conversation between the two men under the circumstances would be admissible in a trial.

news. White flipped on the TV in time to see the mug shot of his erstwhile colleague, and he was shocked to learn the latest development in the case: The FBI had found Davis's palm print in the bedroom of Polly Klaas. The wheels of his mind started spinning. Could he help bring Polly home? He decided to pay Davis a visit.

On the morning of Saturday, December 1, White woke early, around five-thirty or six a.m., and called Mendocino County Jail to see if Davis was allowed to receive any visitors. White was told that yes, it was possible, but only during visiting hours. That window of time—and the three-and-a-half-hour drive to Ukiah—didn't give him much time to decide. He jumped in the car and headed north. He was lucky it was a Saturday, so he'd miss the rush-hour traffic famous in Silicon Valley and San Francisco.

White arrived in Mendocino around nine-thirty a.m. In the visiting room, he spoke face-to-face with Davis for about half an hour. At some point, he leaned close, pointed an index finger at his opposite palm, and mouthed the words: "They found a palm print."

Davis shrugged and nodded in acknowledgment but said nothing.

WHILE MARVIN WHITE was in the visiting room with Davis, Agent Larry Taylor and Sergeant Mike Meese were coincidentally en route to the jail. When they arrived around ten a.m., they were surprised to learn that Davis had already had a visitor. They hadn't been in touch with Eddie Freyer.

They were there to roll a fresh set of prints from Davis. Even though the latent palm print match had been confirmed and was already making headlines, they needed a newer, cleaner set.

A corrections officer opened the cell door, handcuffed Davis, and brought him into the fingerprint room, where Meese and Taylor were waiting. Davis was agitated over having to move between cells, and he complained about the accommodations. The sheriff had him on suicide watch in a medical isolation cell, which had a bed, a toilet, and a little slot in the door where food was passed through. The lights stayed on twenty-four hours.

Davis brightened when he recognized one of the corrections officers, who had been a guard at a prison where he was previously incarcerated. "It was sort of like a class reunion," Taylor would later recall. "Like old lodge brothers coming together."

Corrections Deputy Troy Furman pressed each of Davis's fingers into a pad of black ink, then rolled them carefully, one by one, on a white paper fingerprint card. Next, he rolled both palms. If Davis had been harboring doubts about the veracity of White's message, this moment must have wiped those doubts away.

When the process was done, Furman brought Davis into the hall. Meese asked if he could speak to Davis for a second. "Sure," Furman said, and stepped into another room, leaving Meese and Davis in the hallway.

"All you're looking at is a kidnapping right now," Meese said.

"I don't know what the fuck you're talking about," Davis replied.

Meese shrugged. It didn't matter. They had all the physical evidence they needed to make the case, with or without a statement. But if Polly was still alive, he ought to consider telling them. As long as she stayed alive, the charge would be kidnapping—not murder. Meese patted his pockets, looking for a business card. He couldn't find one.

"I'm gonna leave my name and number with those guys," Meese told Davis, nodding at the deputies. "And if you ever wanna talk about it, give me a call."

MEESE LEFT THE jail and drove toward Pythian, where a massive two-day search was underway. He was nearly there when his pager beeped with a message to call the Mendocino jail. He pulled over at Los Guilicos Training Center and slipped a quarter into the lobby pay phone.

The deputy who answered the phone said Davis had asked to speak with him. Meese heard the phone being handed off, then recognized the voice.

"I want to talk to you," Davis said. "There are two things I want, though."

He wanted two packs of Camels to smoke while he talked. He also wanted "PC"—protective custody—and to be transferred to "a bigger jail."

Those arrangements could be made.

"I fucked up big time," Davis told Meese.

"How big?"

"Big, big time."

Was Polly still alive?

"No," he said.

Was she located where they were searching?

"Where's that?"

Near the spot where he'd gotten his Pinto stuck.

"No," Davis said. "She's not there."

Where was she?

"I'll tell you when you get up here to talk to me."

Davis asked about the possibility of pleading "life without."

Meese asked him what he meant by that.

"Life in prison, no parole."

Meese told him that wasn't his call to make. Meese had no say in the charges, and he couldn't make any deals. That would all be up to the Sonoma County district attorney, but Meese could call him and ask what was possible. Did Davis still want to talk?

"I fucked up big time, big time," he said. "I'll talk to you when you get here."

EDDIE FREYER WAS driving north on the 101, halfway to Ukiah, when his cell phone rang. "Get some tapes for recording and get down to Petaluma," someone said. "Davis wants to talk." He pulled off the nearest exit, turned around, and headed back south. His head was already spinning; the investigation now spanned hundreds of square miles in northern California.

At Pythian, 300 trained searchers were combing the woods around Dana Jaffe's house. A number of search dogs—bloodhounds but also cadaver dogs—had their noses to the ground, trying to pick up a scent.

The searchers had unearthed a scattering of bones, but they turned out to be animal bones.

In Petaluma, evidence technicians were processing Davis's white Pinto. The vehicle had been wrapped in blue plastic tarps—to capture any dust, leaves, or trace evidence—before being loaded on a flatbed truck and delivered to Petaluma. Examiners from the FBI lab had flown in from DC to examine the Pinto in the "bike barn," a large warehouse behind Petaluma PD used for processing evidence. Hair and fibers expert Chris Allen vacuumed the car's interior, including the seats and floor pan. ERT member Mike Stapleton used an ALS to scan every surface in the Pinto, hoping to find a fingerprint from Polly. A bloodhound named Sadie sniffed her way through the car.

In Ukiah, ERT members were crawling over every inch of the Schwarms' residence, a small blue one-story rental house with a fenced-in backyard that looked somewhere between a salvage yard and a dump site. That's where they'd found the Pinto parked, partially concealed by brush and rubbish, on the afternoon of the SWAT raid.

David Alford was leading the search there. He had been to advanced body recovery training at Quantico and was considered the resident expert. He was walking a pattern across the property with the cadaver dog handlers. In the spot where the Pinto had been parked, they discovered a packed-down mound of dirt—a sign of a possible burial site. They dug up the mound, but found nothing.

About a quarter-mile from the house—far enough to be out of the line of sight—they found a depression in the earth. Another possible burial site. They contacted the reservation officials to see if anyone knew anything about it. Then they started their painstaking process. Working like archaeologists, they measured the width and depth of the hole so they could record, in three dimensions, anything they found. They dug delicately, with hand tools, filtering the dirt through screens for any small bits of evidence. A hole that might normally have taken fifteen minutes to dig took two hours.

They had been working a little more than an hour when a little boy, maybe twelve or so, rode up on his bike.

"Hey!" the boy said. "What are you doing?"

They told him, more or less.

"That's my dog," the kid said. "I buried him there. He's wrapped in a blue blanket."

The kid seemed guileless. They had no reason not to believe him. But you never know, and so they kept on digging. A bit of blue fabric emerged from the dirt. As promised, it shrouded the bones of a little boy's pet.

IN UKIAH, MEESE AND TAYLOR were expecting Eddie Freyer to join them, maybe interview Davis along with Meese. But wires had been crossed, and Freyer was on his way to Petaluma, where someone had told him to bring audio cassettes. By the time Freyer realized Davis was in Mendocino, he was more than an hour's drive south. Meese called Freyer to ask if they should wait for him to get here.

"No," Freyer said. "Don't give him time to change his mind."

chapter thirty-five

THE CONFESSION

⌒⌒⌒

*Saturday, December 4, 3:30 p.m.—Mendocino County
Sheriff's Department*

LATE SATURDAY AFTERNOON, RICHARD ALLEN DAVIS WAS BROUGHT FROM HIS
cell to the interview room in the Mendocino County Sheriff's Office. It
had just enough room for a table, a chair, and three men. Davis, dressed
in an orange jumpsuit, glanced up at the video camera in the top corner
of the room. Meese and Taylor unshackled him.

"Yeah," Davis said. "I ain't gonna try nothin'."

"I didn't figure," Taylor drawled.

Sergeant Meese took the lead on the interview. Even though this was
his first kidnapping case, Meese had more intimate knowledge of the
details and better rapport with the subject. It had started with the arrest,
which was calmer and more respectful than it might otherwise have been.
When Davis decided he wanted to talk, he'd specifically asked for Meese.

"Want some coffee, Rick?"

"Yeah." He eyed the pack of Camels in Taylor's hand. "Can I have
one of those?"

They were, of course, his favorite smokes. Someone had run out to
get those.

"Help yourself."

"When I first went into Petaluma," Davis began, "I didn't get a pass from my parole officer, 'cause I was gonna try to visit my mother, you know."

Taylor stopped him. They had to re-Mirandize Davis before anything was on the record and therefore usable in court. "Let's go through the formalities first."

"This is Saturday, the fourth of December 1993," Meese said. "Do you take cream or sugar?"

"Black," Davis said.

"Can't vouch for the coffee," Meese said.

"I've had this coffee before. It's hot."

The cigarettes, the coffee—all part of the first phase of interviewing and interrogation: building rapport.

"Okay," Meese said. "Before we—"

"You're going to read me the rights," Davis said. He knew the drill. But first, there was something he desperately needed to know.

"What did the DA say?"

In the hours between Davis's phone call and the interview, Meese had spoken with the Sonoma County district attorney. Davis had asked about the possibility of "life without." The DA gave Meese the green light to offer a life sentence without parole—instead of a potential death penalty—if that's what it would take to get Davis to lead them to Polly's body. This was the single most valuable bargaining chip they had.

Before Meese had a chance to answer, Taylor casually interrupted.

"We got some more forms."

This blip in the conversation—an auspicious redirect—was either lucky timing or an exquisite moment of investigative tact.* It was so subtle that some of the investigators watching the tape later missed it entirely. Distracted by the paperwork, Davis forgot the most important question of his life.

"Before you answer any questions, I have to inform you of your rights. You're aware that we're investigating the kidnap and disappearance of Polly Klaas, okay?"

---

* Larry Taylor, who at eighty-two says his memory isn't what it used to be, can't say for sure if it was deliberate. He says he was always very careful to get the Miranda paperwork done before any talking began, so it may simply have been lucky timing.

Davis nodded, took a drag.

"You have the right to remain silent. Anything you say can and will be used against you in a court of law. You have the right to talk to a lawyer and have one present with you before or during any questioning. And if you cannot afford to hire an attorney, one will be appointed to represent you before any questioning if you wish. Okay?"

"Yes."

"I know you've heard these rights before," Meese said. Then he read them again, one by one. Davis gave verbal consent and initialed each one on a consent form, acknowledging his choice to waive his Miranda rights.

In the world of criminal law, this pivotal moment was exceptionally rare. Once a suspect invokes his Miranda rights—as Davis had at the end of his November 30 interview with Taylor and Detective Larry Pelton—the interrogation must cease. Law enforcement officers can no longer ask any questions about the crime. They can chat about the weather, jail food, the Giants—anything but the crime.

By requesting to speak with Meese, Davis had *voluntarily* re-established communication with investigators. This unlocked an exception to the Miranda law. As long as the subject was reread his rights—and explicitly consented to waive them—the questioning could resume.

Davis stubbed out his cigarette and picked up the pen. After initialing each line, he signed his name on the form. His cursive was large and bubbly, not unlike a twelve-year-old girl's.

Davis slumped against the table shaking his head. His left hand rose to wipe his eyes. They might have been tears of remorse. Or they might have been a physiological release to months of mounting tension.

"Better get some Kleenex," Davis said.

"You seem a little upset," Meese said. His voice was soft and gentle. He leaned over in his chair and reached out to put his hand on Davis's neck, delivering a few pats. Taylor left the room to get a box of tissue.

FBI profiler Mary Ellen O'Toole had recommended confrontation. But Meese read Davis's body language—back of his chair against the wall, shoulders squared to the interviewer. He was showing signs—real or feigned—of something resembling regret. So Meese took a different approach.

"You want to go ahead and tell me what you were upset about?"

"About everything," Davis said, dabbing at his eyes.

"About everything. This been bugging you? Eatin' at you?"

"Yeah." He reached for another smoke.

"Is she alive?" Meese said, leaning close, the dome of his head catching the light. "Can we go get her?"

This is where Meese went off script for a bit. Master interrogators almost always start with open-ended questions. *What happened? What happened next?* Let them tell the whole story, with minimal interruptions. Then, when it's all on the record, go back and make them tell it again, this time with direct and clarifying questions. But based on Davis's phone call, Meese had walked into this interview expecting a confession. It was a gamble, but Meese lobbed the million-dollar question.

"Is she alive?"

Cigarette poised, eyes glued to the table, Davis slowly shook his head. "She's not alive."

Sixty-five days into the search, five minutes and forty-four seconds into the interview, they finally had the answer. The answer nobody wanted.

"Do you know where she is now?"

"Yeah."

"Can you tell me?"

"I'll show you," Davis said, wiping his eyes. "I'll show you."

"It's important to let the family know."

"Yeah."

"Can you tell me about where she is?"

"Alongside the freeway. Just as you leave Cloverdale. Going south."

"Going south back towards Santa Rosa?"

"Off the side of the road. I'll show you guys."

Taylor rose and silently left the room. He relayed the news to Eddie Freyer, setting other wheels into motion.

"She where somebody could walk up and find her?" Meese asked.

"Yeah, surprised nobody did it yet. Or smelled anything. She ain't buried."*

---

* This key piece of information is missing from the official transcript but was heard by the author and verified by Andy Mazzanti in the videotape.

"If I was to go look for her, what would I look for?"

"I'll show you," Davis said, using one cigarette to light the next. "Better off that way."

⌒⌒⌒

EDDIE FREYER WAS back in the Petaluma command center when he got the call. His heart sank. There was no time to process the upwelling of emotions, so he channeled them into action.

He was already overseeing investigations in several different locations: A massive ground search at Pythian Road. A thorough search of the Schwarms' house and forensic excavations on the reservation. An ERT processing of the Pinto at the Petaluma PD.

Now he needed to mobilize a body recovery team and protect another crime scene—without alerting the media. He needed to stage his team near Cloverdale, far enough to keep any tailgating media trucks away, but close enough to swoop in once they knew the precise location. Freyer quickly assembled three dozen investigators: detectives, ERT members, and SWAT team members to guard the perimeter.

⌒⌒⌒

AT PYTHIAN ROAD, three hundred people were combing the woods around Dana Jaffe's house. Despite the dismal odds, they moved with an urgency founded upon the belief that Polly was still alive. The core leaders of the ERT were actively searching for evidence, and Supervising Special Agent Lillian Zilius was standing by to make sure they had what they needed.

David Alford was walking through the woods when he began to hear whispers: *She's not here.* The media were everywhere with directional mics, so they had to be very careful. Knowing this, Zilius passed written notes to the ERT members: *As casually as you can, wrap up what you're doing.* Separately, Alford, Tony Maxwell, and Frank Doyle slipped away, trying not to draw attention to their departure.

The team convened at Chateau Souverain,* a winery in Geyserville.

---

* Now Francis Ford Coppola Winery.

They would stage in the parking lot and wait for Davis to lead them to the body.

⌒⌒

IN MENDOCINO, MEESE AND TAYLOR pulled out a map and pressed Davis to pinpoint the location. He pointed to an exit south of Cloverdale, to a service road that paralleled Highway 101.

"If I was to go look for her, what would I look for?" Meese asked. "Is she right next to the road or did you walk off the road?"

Davis rubbed his head, exhaled smoke, and answered in a monotone. "She's a quarter-mile off the road."

"Did you walk in?"

"No, I drove in," Davis said. "She's off to the side of the road, somewhere in some bushes."

"Is she wrapped in anything?" Meese asked. "Just laying there?"

"Yeah."

"Does she have anything on?"

"Yeah. The clothes she was wearing."

"What kind of clothes was she wearing? Do you remember?"

"White skirt and red top."

"Feel better gettin' that off your chest?"

"No." Davis sighed and briefly met his eye. "I know I'm a piece of shit. You ain't gotta show me no—"

"This is hard, I know," Meese said. "I understand and appreciate you being man enough to own up to what happened."

Validation and empathy are valuable tools. If someone feels heard and understood, they're more inclined to open up. Meese wasn't known among colleagues as particularly empathetic, but he now deployed it with verisimilitude. Then he pivoted and went back on script, asking open-ended questions that invited the bigger story.

"Why don't we back up to October first. Why don't you tell me what happened that night?"

chapter thirty-six

ANATOMY OF A LIE

ॱॱॱ

The Interrogation—an Expert Analysis

THE UNBLINKING EYE OF THE VIDEO CAMERA IN THE TOP CORNER OF THE ROOM recorded one hour and forty-eight minutes of an interview on which lives and futures would pivot. This tape would be referred to as "the confession tape" even though, legally speaking, it was an "admission," not a "confession." A confession—the ultimate evidence of guilt in the eyes of the law—is a statement in which a defendant acknowledges his guilt in every element of the crime. An admission is a statement made by the defendant that can be used against him in court. Both are powerful evidence to bring before a jury.

This confession tape is not only rare, but unusual. Longstanding FBI policy prohibited agents from recording or videotaping interviews. The culture of Hoover's FBI held that an agent's word should be enough to stand up in court. For decades, that was the case. This videotape exists because this was a joint investigation. It was standard practice for police officers to record interviews by audio or video—preferably both, as was the case here.

Decades after the case, case agent Eddie Freyer asked the current district attorney for a copy of the tape to use in his Interview and

Interrogation (I&I) class at the Behavioral Analysis Training Institute (BATI). His request was denied.*

Sergeant Mike Meese, who led the interview, used techniques consistent with BATI's science-based I&I methods.† It has been used as a sort of case study to teach future investigators how to study body language, detect shifts in volume, tone, and pitch, and notice other "deceptive markers" that help distinguish truth from lies.‡

⌒⌒⌒

"WHY DON'T WE back up to October first," Meese said. "Why don't you tell me what happened that night?"§

This is how a good interview begins, with open-ended questions designed to elicit what Meese called "an open narrative." It's also a chance to observe a subject's unique "truth-telling style." Posture, eye contact, phrasing, changes in vocal volume, pitch, and tone establish a behavior baseline against which future statements and behavior are measured. Davis began with his shoulders open and facing Meese. He made intermittent eye contact, delivering detailed answers without much pause to think. In this manner, he laid out his narrative of Polly's kidnapping.

On Friday, October 1, Davis said he got a weekend pass from Turning Point, his halfway house in San Mateo. Because he was planning to visit his mother in Petaluma—to see if she'd help him out—and didn't plan to travel outside his fifty-mile limit, he didn't think he needed a pass from his parole officer, so he didn't ask.

---

* After it was obtained in the reporting for this book, Freyer began using the confession tape to teach interview and interrogation classes for the Behavioral Analysis Training Institute, which has trained more than 33,000 investigators in the art and science of lie detection and eliciting the truth. It's one of four mandatory courses for investigators, along with child abuse, sexual assault, and homicide.

† Mike Meese was deceased before the reporting of this book, and his family and colleagues weren't certain whether he attended BATI or another training program for interview and interrogation techniques.

‡ It's worth noting that there is no behavior unique to lying, and that lying and guilt are two distinct things.

§ As in previous interview chapters, this dialogue is verbatim, other than cuts for length and redundancy and summary of truthful facts.

In the white Pinto he bought from his brother-in-law, he drove to Petaluma, where he parked somewhere downtown. His description of where he parked is rich in specific details, which all turned out to be true.

"There's an old store that was all tore down, some little restaurant-like deal, like a hamburger stand," he said. "Bunch of the homeless people hang out right [by] the bus area and post office and shit."

Davis said he tried to look up his mother's address in the phone book (presumably at a phone booth). When he couldn't find his mother's address, he went to the 7-Eleven (there was one a few blocks from Polly's house) and bought a quart of beer. He took it back to the park around the corner from where he'd parked "by some Dairy Freeze." (There was a Foster's Freeze across the street from Walnut Park.)

"Drunk the quart of beer and I was gonna go back to the 7-Eleven and get another one, and I saw all these homeless people sitting out there. I went over there and one of the dudes asked me if I wanted to buy a joint. I told him I didn't, and I kept on walkin'. Then I changed my mind and came back."

"Mm-hmm," Meese said. His objective in this phase of the interview was to keep the subject talking, to get the whole story on record, with minimal interruption.

"So I bought a joint off the dude, went and got another quart of beer and sat in that park, smoked a joint. It wasn't all-the-way weed—had some other shit in it. I got pretty well toasted off it. Things got kinda fuzzy after that."

Smoking a joint laced with something that clouded his judgment could minimize culpability and set the stage for a future defense. If you're too toasted to know what you're doing, how can you be held accountable? It was also inconsistent with what he told the Larrys.

"I remember sitting there and people walking all around. I got up and, uh...I don't know how I ended up at their house or whatever, you know. But uh...went in and, uh..."

The pauses indicate cognitive processing. He's deciding what to say. Up to this point, the answers came quickly (some too quickly), without his pausing a beat to think.

"What'd you do? What do you remember about going in?"

"Uh . . . just going in through the window."

"Which window did you go in?"

"It was the front window I think. Not sure."

He would maintain, throughout the interview, that he had entered through the front window, repeating this statement several times. But the front bay windows did not open. The windows in the sunroom were painted shut, and the investigators who arrived that night noticed cobwebs outside them, undisturbed.

"So I went in, and I remember hearing all the voices and everything. I guess I went in and told 'em to all lie down or whatever."

"Where were they?"

"They were in the bedroom, I guess. There was three of them in there."

"Okay."

"That's when I started telling them all stuff you had me read off that deal."

He was referring to the lineup, when he and others were asked to read the statements Kate and Gillian had recalled.

"What do you remember?" Meese asked. "Do you remember telling them those things?"

"Not really. I was pretty well toasted. The next thing I remember is driving down the road, I had her in the front seat and got turned off on some road. That's why I ended up where I was."

His description of events this far was rich in specific details. Homeless people in the park. Buying a quart of beer at a 7-Eleven. The post office, hamburger stand, and torn-down store on the street where he parked his Pinto. But as soon as he began to describe the crime, details became scarce or blurry. Suddenly, there was a lot he couldn't recall. He skipped big parts of the narrative—everything between entering the house and driving down the highway with Polly. He couldn't remember major moments of the crime: entering the house, leaving with Polly, getting her into his car. Freyer later pointed out these gaps as clear "deceptive markers." A good interviewer had to notice these gaps and remember to bring them up later.

Meese inquired about Pythian Road. "You ever been there before?"

"No. That's how I got lost up there. I didn't know what else I was going to do when I came to. And then when I finally realized what I had done, she was still alive and everything. Trying to figure out what the fuck I was going to do with that at that point. Just got out of the joint, you know, and snagged this little girl . . . I don't know what all was going on. And the car got stuck. I had her get out of the car and go sit up on the embankment and I tried to get the car out. Couldn't get it out. The lady [babysitter Shannon Lynch] came down—"

"Where was she when the lady came down?"

"She was up sitting on the embankment. And, uh, the lady left and the cops came."

The veracity of this one statement would be debated for decades. Davis claimed that Polly was sitting, alive and unbound, on a nearby embankment during his entire thirty-eight-minute encounter with the two sheriff's deputies. The spot where the black sweatshirt, red tights, white bindings, and condom were found was remarkably close to Jaffe's driveway—around thirty paces. Though fall foliage might have blocked visibility, she would have been within earshot of the gate on the road, where the deputies parked their patrol cars—with headlights on and radios at full volume.

"The cops came? What happened?"

"The cops came, pulled me out, searched the car and everything. Pulled me out, followed me out of town. I waited on the other side of town for about half an hour. Turned around. I was lucky I found . . . guess it wasn't lucky for her."

"Mmm-hmm."

"I pulled in the ditch. Went up, got her, got her back in the car and . . . didn't know where to go at that point or what to do. So I started driving, almost out of gas, had to pull into some gas station to get gas. She wanted to use the bathroom so I went and got the key. Let her go to the bathroom."

That might sound like a small act of kindness. It was also a checkable fact. Meese and Taylor made a mental note to try to find that gas station.

"She got back in the car. I asked the lady at the gas station how to get back to San Francisco or whatever. She told me to follow the road this way to 'Frisco, follow it this way, it'll take you up north.* Went all the way up north and, uh, got up around Cloverdale, I guess."

"Uh-huh."

"And a few times up along the way, a couple sheriff's cars pulled up alongside me, I guess to check the car out. She was sleeping and they buzzed on by."

Sleeping? That seemed highly unlikely.

"And got up there and sat there, trying to figure out what the fuck to do, what to do and she kept—"

"She kept what?" Meese wanted to hear how Polly was behaving after Pythian, where the condom and condom wrapper were found by the inside-out black sweatshirt: evidence of a sexual assault.

"She kept asking me when she was going to be able to go home," Davis said.

"Uh-huh."

"And I told her, in a while. In a while. Let me figure out where I was, what's going on. Said she had to go to the bathroom, so let her out. She went to the bathroom. I was outta the car."

"Mmm-hmm."

"And, uh..." He paused.

"What?" Meese urged him on, not giving him time to think of a story.

"That's when I strangled her. When she was comin' back, back to the car to get in."

"Strangled her?"

"Yeah..."

MEESE NOW TRANSITIONED from open-ended questions to direct questions. The first phase of the interview focused on *what* had happened. Now he aimed to clarify *how* and *when* it happened. A timeline emerged, along with key details.

---

* This doesn't make sense; San Francisco is south. Cloverdale is north.

"What'd you use to strangle her?" Meese asked. (Subtext: What was the murder weapon?)

"Piece of cloth."

"Where's the cloth?" (Where could they find this murder weapon?)

"Still around her neck."

"Where did you get the cloth?"

"I don't know. I got it somewhere, I don't know where I found it. Some kinda yellow material. I don't know where it came from. I don't remember. And, I uh..."

"Whadja do?" Meese said, guiding him back to the narrative. "Whadja do next?"

"Drug her over by the berry bushes, like drug her up in there, laid her down."

His choice of words—*laid her down*—framed the action as almost gentle. By the end of the interview his word choice would change.

"Did you cover her up?"

"Yeah."

"What do you cover her up with?"

"A piece of plywood. From underneath the shed where the car was parked. There was a shed there."

"There was a shed there? Where whose car was parked?"

"Mine. And I drove back to where I was staying in San Mateo."

That was something they could verify by checking the Turning Point logbook, a time-stamped record of residents' comings and goings.

"I didn't know what I'd left. I didn't know if I'd left fingerprints or whatever, you know, and then that morning when I got back and all the details started flashing..."

The details he was now unable to remember?

"I thought, man, somebody's gonna...One guy at the program said, 'Why don't you go get your yellow bandana and put it on?'"

Again, the yellow bandana—that didn't appear to exist.

"And then this other guy made a statement, 'Do you got her out from the trunk?' I told him, 'Yeah...' and made some stupid comment. Mostly I was just sitting there waiting. Figurin' somebody's gonna show up and take me on."

But nobody did. Not after the sketch with the yellow bandana. Not even after the second sketch, his spitting image drawn by Jeanne Boylan. Eight million flyers had been distributed as far away as China. *America's Most Wanted* had shown the sketches in several episodes. Thousands of calls and tips came in from people who thought they had seen that face. But none of them had led to Davis.

"A few people made comments."

"So that was it, huh? Nobody ever showed up?"

"No, nobody. And I shaved. It was a month later when I shaved, and [my] parole officer never said nothin' the whole time I was going to see him."

"Never said a word to ya?"

"No."

"Did that surprise you?"

"Yeah. It was eatin' at me. I used to look at dudes like that in the joint, and here I had done something like that, you know?"

This was an interesting segue—an abrupt pivot from outside perceptions to Davis's interior self-perception, and his guilt for doing "something like that." He had already done time for kidnapping. So his allusion to "something like that" implied something more severe. The way he "used to look at dudes like that in the joint," alluded to the pecking order in prison, where child molesters are judged, harassed, beaten, or killed by fellow inmates.

"You been back to her body since then?"

"No."

"No? Okay. Never?"

"Drove by."

"Did you drive by?"

"Had to on the freeway."

"Going back and forth," Meese said.

Back and forth on Highway 101 between Turning Point in San Mateo and his sister's house in Ukiah. A strategic choice for a body disposal site. If an ERT team were there, they'd be easy to spot. He could keep an eye on the crime scene without having to go there—and lead a potential surveillance team directly to the body.

MEESE WENT ON, using the interrogation tactic of "themes." Themes offer moral justifications for the crime—external pressures, circumstances, or blaming someone else. Themes frame the crime in a way that offers some psychological relief to a guilty person and encourages them to unburden themselves by admitting or confessing at least some part of their role in the crime.

"I know this is a difficult time, and I heard you say it yourself—I don't have to try to make you feel better, you're a piece of shit. Whether you are or not, it's up for somebody else to judge."

Here, Meese projected a neutral stance—*I'm not here to judge you*—and acknowledged Davis's troubled past.

"Hey, I know you done some hard time before . . ."

Theme: *You've had some hard times.*

". . . and it's obvious the thing that distresses you the most is what happened to her. As you put it, 'What I did to her. I didn't know what to do, and I needed some time to think.' Am I right?"

Echoing his words and validating his feelings was another effective tactic. Delivered in a sympathetic way, validation resembles empathy but is slightly different. You don't have to agree with someone to validate their emotions. Anyone who feels heard and validated is more likely to open up. (Some investigators who learn this in I&I class say it also helps their marriages.)

"Am I right?" Meese asked. "Is that the thing that distresses you the most?"

Davis nodded and agreed. "I fully realized when I had her in the car . . . didn't know where I was goin' or what I was gonna do."

That opened the door to ask about what happened on the Pythian hillside.

"What happened? What happened to her that made you go, 'Shit, what am I gonna do?' What'd you do to her? Was she tied up?"

"No. I had untied her when she was sittin' up on the hill. When we got up there she was untied. She was untied when I was gettin' pulled outta the ditch . . ."

"Was she awake?"

"I dunno, she mighta went to sleep, I don't know. I remember when I finally came back and found the place, she told me she thought I had left her there for the night."

Aside from the illogic—how could a frightened abducted girl possibly fall asleep alone in the darkened woods—the repetition of "I don't know" was another deceptive marker.

◌◌◌

AT THIS POINT, the pace and tone of the interview changed. The sympathetic tone and open-ended questions gave way to direct questions. Here came the shift from interview to interrogation. Time to press him on the hard details.

"Had you done anything to her?"

"I didn't do nothin' to her."

Davis answered so faintly it was hard to hear. Watching the tape later, Freyer would see a micro expression, a small shift in the facial composure. Combined with the change in volume, this struck him as a "clear deception."

"Did you try to have sex with her?"

"Uh-uh."

An innocent person would deny this with conviction. Meese asked again.

"Did you ever try to have sex with her?"

He shook his head. Again, the weak denial was a red flag. Meese pressed him.

"You sure about that?"

"I don't think so. No. I don't think so."

"You don't think so?" An innocent person would *know*.

"I don't think so . . ."

"Are you a little bit hazy about that?"

"Positive. Well, as much as I can remember, I don't think that I did."

When a question like that is repeated, an innocent person's denials should only grow stronger and more adamant. Here, the denials grew weaker and more uncertain.

"Okay. Why did you take her, then?"

"I don't know, man. I don't know. I don't, you know. I don't know why I took her."

His repetitions of "I don't know" were now numbering in the dozens. Meese was walking a fine line. He needed to probe for information now, in case Davis clammed up later. He had to ask the questions Davis most wanted to avoid. But he also needed to avoid angering the subject, who could change his mind at any moment about leading them to the body. Seeing Davis's agitation after pressing him on the question of sex, he changed directions to defuse the tension.

"She was sitting on the hill when the cops were there?"

"Yeah."

"When you left...when you came down...when did you take her up to the hill?"

"When I got stuck in the ditch."

"Okay."

"Before the lady came down from the top of the hill."

"What lady was this?"

"In the red truck or something like that. The one that said she was going to go get somebody to help me get out of the ditch. That's when two sheriff guys showed up."

"Okay, let's back up. You took her out of the car? At that point?"

"Yeah."

"Was she tied up?"

"Naw, naw, she was untied at that point."

"Okay. You remember tying her up?"

"Not really. I don't remember all that count to a thousand and shit like that."

"You don't remember any of that?"

"Uh-uh. Why would I ask, you know, you said I asked 'em for valuables, why would I ask, you know? I don't remember."

"Are there any houses up there on that hill?"

"Don't know. I remember driving up the road seein' a dirt road, turning up that, kept on goin' till I passed that gate, realized I was on private property."

"What made you realize that?"

"When I passed the gate then, uh, I tried to turn around and got stuck. I tried to head 'bout on outta there and got stuck."

"Where's Polly at this time? Where is she?"

"Oh, she was in the car when I got stuck."

"Front seat? Back seat?"

"Front seat."

Most of these direct questions were answered without delay. He was probably telling the truth.

"Okay. Was she tied up then? When you first got stuck?"

"No. I had untied her...before that."

"When did you untie her?"

"Driving down the road...I guess."

"How did you tie her?"

"Just hands behind the back."

"What did you tie her hands [with]?"

"I dunno, I don't remember what I used."

"Did you tie her feet?"

"I don't think I tied her feet."

Davis lit another cigarette, body language still open, eye contact strong.

"Did she say anything to you at any time?"

"Yeah."

"What did she say to you?"

"She wanted to go home."

THE PACE OF the questions picked up. Meese was watching the clock and wanting to get to the body before dark. But he still needed a clearer answer to the question of sexual assault. It was the one thing Davis continued to deny—albeit weakly—that could make a profound difference in a potential sentence. First-degree murder usually meant life in prison without parole. Paired with a "special circumstance"—such as sexual assault—it could open the door to the death penalty.

"Why did you turn off Highway 101 when you got to Cloverdale?" Meese asked.

"I have no idea," Davis said. "Pulled over to think and figure out what the fuck to do, you know, and what I'd done so far."

"What had you done so far?"

"I got this girl in the car. What the fuck, you know?"

"Had you done anything to her?"

"On my skin, I didn't do nuttin' to her," Davis said. He glanced down briefly, took another drag on his cigarette.

"Did you slap her or hurt her or anything?"

"No."

"Did you touch her in any place?"

"No, not that I remember," Davis said, shaking his head. His voice rose in tone and inflection—a departure from his regular monotone. "I don't think I did anything to her. You guys'll soon find that out."

This noncommittal response was not a direct answer. But it was telling. And possibly useful in court.

"That's probably true," Meese said. "But I'm asking *you*, because you've come this far clean, and you're the one that called me and wanted to talk, right?"

"Yeah." Davis wiped his forehead again, then swabbed at his mouth with the tissue.

"And I'd like to just get everything out and get it in the open."

"I'm trying as much as I can remember, you know, what was going on. All I basically remember at that point was that I fucked up..."

"Mm-hmm."

"Fucked up big time." He stubbed out his cigarette, eyes downcast at the table. His voice sank into a whisper. "Yeah, I fucked up..."

After Pythian, with Polly in the car, Davis admitted that he thought for a long time about what to do next. A sign of premeditation.

"I sat there for about an hour, I guess, and I wondered what the fuck I was going to do. Shit I had gotten myself into, what the fuck was I gonna do now? The only thing I could think of was try to cover my tracks, I guess."

"Okay. Why did you want to cover your tracks?"

"Because I knew I had fucked up." He pressed his right thumb to his temple, cigarette poised between two fingers.

"Okay. So what'd you think covering your tracks meant?"

"I couldn't send her back home. I'd be right back in the joint."

"Okay."

"She asked to go to the bathroom. I told her yeah. Got out. She went over to the bathroom."

"Where did she go?"

"I don't know, somewhere right around where the car was parked."

"Okay."

"And she came back…" He sighed, paused, and pulled a cigarette from the second pack. "I figured, well, I gotta…"

He paused to light it.

"Gotta what?"

"Gotta do something."

"Okay. So whadja figure on doin'?"

"Coverin' my tracks. Tryin' to. About the only thing I had to do was get rid of her…"

"Okay…"

"'Cause I didn't know what I had really done in the house, you know?"

"What did you think you had done in the house that made you think you had to get rid of her?"

"Well, I had her in the car. And I had to figure out what the fuck was I going to do. A person in my position…"

Meese sat in silence, letting it ride.

"She was gettin' ready to get back in the car," Davis said. "That's when I…"

"That's when you what?"

Davis's voice grew high and soft. "That's when I strangled her with a piece of cloth."

"Where did you get the piece of cloth?"

"I dunno. I had it."

"Didja have it on you? Didja have it in your pocket? Did it come from the car? Did you take it from her?"

"I had it in the car, 'cause I had to open the door for her to get out. She had to open the door 'cause the latch don't work on the outside."

"Where was she when you strangled her?"

"Gettin' ready to get back in the car."

"Were you standing there? Were you sitting?"

"No, I was standing behind her. She didn't know what hit her."

"She didn't suffer?"

"No. I figured..."

"Figured what?"

"I had faked a suicide attempt one time to escape outta county jail. I made a noose and stepped off the shitter. [I knew] how quick it was that I went out. Was the quickest thing I know. Couldn't see beatin' her with anything."

"How'd you strangle her?"

He crossed his fists and pulled them apart. "Like that. Hand over hand."

"Okay."

"And when I let loose, I tied that piece of cloth on her. Tied it in a knot."

"Why'd you tie it in a knot?"

"Because I didn't know how long it would really take. I never done anything like that before."

"So you didn't know how long it would take?"

"No."

"And so you wanted to make sure it worked?"

A good question to emphasize intent.

"Yeah. Then I got another piece of cord, tied it around her neck, cinched the knot up, tightened it up, just to make sure."

"What kind of cord was that?"

"Little piece of white cord that was laying there."

"So after you...after...after that, what'd you do then, after you'd put the second cord on?"

"I started wondering where I was gonna put her, and I looked around, saw these bushes. That's when I drug her over there..."

Earlier in the interview, he had said he "laid" her there.

"Tried to toss her in the bushes as far as I could go. Then I went and got a piece of plywood, put it over her."

"Mmm-hmm."

"Got some more chunks of wood. Tried to make it look like a garbage area or whatever."

"Okay."

"Then got in the car and drove to San Mateo."

"You're willing to take us down there and show us where you were? Why don't you hang tight just half a second. I'll be right back."

Agent Taylor, who had been listening quietly, asked Davis if he needed more coffee.

"A bullet in my brain is what I need," Davis said.

As Meese left the room, Davis slumped in his chair. Head down, shoulders hunched, a posture of defeat. Genuine remorse? An act? Hard to tell. Taylor listened and didn't respond. Silence is uncomfortable, so people keep talking to fill it.

"Don't know how I fucked up like that," he said, again wiping his brow. "Man, I used to look at dudes who did shit like that and think it was...you know? And here I found myself doin'...And I kept telling myself every day that it wasn't I that did it. Me, myself, you know?"

In court, this statement could be used as an admission. He doesn't confess to the crime, not exactly. But a jury could be asked to interpret that statement as a logical inference of guilt.

"Why do you think she didn't run away?" Taylor said. "When she was up there on that hill?"

"I don't know. I thought she was gonna come walkin' down when the sheriffs were there."

WHEN MEESE RETURNED to the room, the tone of the interview changed again. It was time to press him again and now lock down further details.

"Rick, you know I'd like to try to get everything you have to say here and just get it out in the open. I think after this we'll probably take a ride down and let you show us where she is. And I appreciate that gesture because I think that's important to the family."

"Yeah, I know."

Davis's body language changed. He rotated away, turning a shoulder to Meese and slumping on the table. His eyes were glued to the coffee cup clutched in both fidgeting hands.

"You know, I asked you before if you did anything to her," Meese said. "And you said, we'll know soon enough."

Davis shook his head and began to deny it.

"Hang on a second, for me, okay?" Meese said, reaching out and touching Davis lightly on the arm. "Hang on. Please. Please? Okay?"

The light touch was a skill, a nonverbal cue that can stop an emerging lie.

"You've come this far," Meese said. "And you're right, we will probably know soon enough. But if something did happen, maybe it'd be better if just you and I talked about that. You can tell me—"

It was another theme: *You're better off if you tell the truth now.* He might have developed it further into: *There are always two sides of the story. If you get your side of the story out now, it will be better for you in the long run.*

"I don't remember do[ing] anything to her," he said, pitch rising again. "On my skin, I don't remember!"

"I know you were a little worried about being labeled with a…" Meese stopped himself from using the term *child molester.* "…labeled with *that* if you went back to the joint. You know I appreciate the fact that you called and wanted to talk to us and wanted to get it out in the open. I'd like to get it all out in the open and be done with it. And let you get on, you know, with what's going on."

"Not much is gonna be goin' on. My life's over and done with now."

"Well, not necessarily. I mean…"

"Shit." He knew the stakes.

"I don't know that you'll necessarily ever see the outside."

"I'll never see the outside again. Even if I just got a life sentence, they'd never let me out again."

"You're probably right about that. You're probably right about that."

Taylor jumped in with a new theme: "But you sure got a chance to do something big right now."

Davis straightened his spine and opened his shoulders again.

"I wanted to do it awhile back, you know, when they showed her picture and everything. But then I thought, fuck, I'm going back to the joint. Fucked up. Fucked up."

"But at least you came forward," Meese said, continuing Taylor's theme: *It takes a man to do the right thing.* They had landed on the right theme. Davis abruptly changed his tune, acknowledging that intoxication wasn't an excuse for culpability.

"I used to hear dudes that did shit and said they were drunk or doped up. And I used to always tell myself, man, motherfucker, it doesn't matter, you're still liable for your actions no matter what," he said now. "And there I go do the same fuckin' stupid shit like that."

This was a huge admission and a major change from earlier in the interview, when Davis repeatedly emphasized that he was too "toasted" from the laced joint to be accountable for his actions.

"You're doing the best thing now," Taylor said. "I deal a lot with the families, and they always ask questions. What happened? They want to know what happened to their daughter."

They made plans to drive to Cloverdale in an unmarked car, so they wouldn't be as visible to the media. Davis said he didn't want to face the cameras and offered to lie down in the seat. Taylor assured him there were no camera crews outside—they were all at Pythian, covering the search.

Meese went over some of the details again, and the answers remained more or less consistent. Davis said that he had worked alone—"Just me, myself, and I"—and maintained that Polly had been alive, sitting up on the hillside, during the encounter with the sheriffs.

"You absolutely sure of that?" Meese pressed.

"Yeah," Davis said. "I went and parked back up there, walked back up there, she was asleep or whatever."

"What makes you think she was asleep?"

"How she was laying there."

"How was she laying there?"

"Laying on the hillside, curled up."

"How'd she wake up?"

"I don't remember."

"When you came back down off the hill, are you absolutely sure she's alive?"

"Yeah."

The interview concluded at 5:02 p.m. Only once in the nearly two-hour conversation did Davis ever refer to his victim by her name.

He said that when he returned to Pythian Road, he had called out to her in the dark. He claimed she'd responded and said she thought he was going to leave her there.

"What was her name?" Meese asked.

"She had told me then that her name was Polly."

chapter thirty-seven

CLOVERDALE

◠◠◠

December 4, 1993, 5:30 p.m.

THE SUN HAD SET BY THE TIME MEESE AND TAYLOR WRAPPED UP THE INTERVIEW. Dusk was fading into night as they loaded Davis into an unmarked car that Meese would later describe as "an old rat-trap Chevrolet." Neither of them had a cell phone, and Meese didn't have his glasses or his gun. Agent Taylor slid behind the wheel, and Meese climbed into the back seat with Davis. They pulled out of the Mendocino sheriff's office and drove south on the 101.

Taylor drove with his left hand on the steering wheel, his right hand holding a tape recorder, aiming the microphone at the back seat. It was 5:31 p.m.

"So, you didn't know this girl from before, Richard?" Meese said.

"Nah." A pause. "No."

"We talked about getting in the house. Let's go back to smoking this joint. Tell me some more about this joint."

"Got a good buzz off it."

"Remember getting in the house?"

"I'm pretty sure I think I went through the window."

"You remember where the window was?"

"Out front, I guess."

This could not have been possible.

"Did you ever go around the back of her house?"

"I don't remember."

As he had in the interview room, Davis provided vague answers peppered with classic deceptive markers. *I'm pretty sure...I think...I guess...I don't remember...*

"Did you get any dinner yet?" Meese asked.

"No."

"Well, I tell you, after we get done with this...I think my stomach is hurting. Larry, is yours?"

"Yeah," Taylor said from the front seat. It was right around six p.m. "It is."

"How's yours?" Meese asked Davis. "Maybe let's stop and get a burger or something. Go through a drive-thru. How's that?"

"Doesn't matter," Davis said.

"Cool," Meese said. "You're all right." After a long pause, he tried again to elicit some connection, some reason this guy chose Polly.

"So you didn't know this girl before then, huh?"

"No."

Davis wanted to smoke, so Meese lit a match.

"So you said something about a kitchen knife. You thought you got it in the house."

"Yeah."

"You remember picking up the knife in the house?"

"No. Not really."

"What made you think you got it there?"

"Because I didn't take one with me. I've been on parole."

"You remember where you threw your sweatshirt out of the car that night?"

"Driving down the freeway like this, and shoving it out the window."

"Why did you do that?"

"Just trying to get rid of everything."

"What did you do with the stuff you tied Polly up with?"

"I guess I threw that out the window too."

Taylor was still holding the tape recorder and worried about dying batteries. Meese dug around to find fresh ones.

"Do you remember tying Polly up?" Meese asked Davis. "Do you remember untying her?"

"Yeah."

"When did you untie her?"

"When we were driving down the road. [Highway] 116 or whatever."

"In relation to when you met the cops, when did this happen? When did you untie her?"

"Before I met them."

"Where was she in the car?"

"Passenger seat up front," Davis said. "She was never in the back."

"Remember what kind of clothes she was wearing?"

Davis sighed.

"Need you to think hard, buddy."

"I don't know."

"You don't know?"

"She had this, uh, long nightgown on."

He did remember.

"Do you remember what color the nightgown was?"

"Red striped."

Meese asked him what he remembered about meeting the deputies that night. Davis recounted the interaction: getting stuck, freeing the car, parking on the roadside for ten minutes or so, then going back for Polly. He parked in front of Dana Jaffe's gate, which was closed but unlocked. He got out of the car and walked up the road toward the embankment.

Davis said he called out to Polly, who answered that she thought he had left her there. He said she walked out of the woods and got back in his Pinto. He backed down the driveway, turned back onto Pythian Road, and pulled onto the two-lane highway. He said he pulled over at a gas station, where he asked a female attendant how to get to San Francisco. He followed her directions to the 101 and headed north, toward Ukiah.

As they neared the town of Cloverdale, Davis asked for another Camel. Then another. Meese cracked the window to let in fresh air.

"Getting close," Davis said between drags.

They exited the highway on Dutcher Creek Road, just south of Cloverdale, a rural farming community about forty-five minutes north of Petaluma. The two-lane frontage road ran parallel to the 101. On the east side of Dutcher Creek Road, semi trucks roared up and down the interstate. On the other side, there was darkness. No streetlights, no buildings, nothing but empty fields. He told them to look for "a shed."

The headlights swept across the roof of a dilapidated building. The "shed" was an abandoned sawmill. They pulled over on the side of the road. They squinted into the darkness, trying to make out any detail.

"You want me to get out and show you?" Davis said.

"Why don't you hang tight just a half a second," Meese replied.

"It's right over to the left," Davis said. "By the bush. Keep going."

"Right there," Taylor said. "Straight in front of us?"

"Yeah. I piled a bunch of brush on top."

They all got out of the car. Davis nodded at a lonely oak tree across the field. Under the tree, he said, they would find a large sheet of plywood. Under the plywood, they would find Polly. Davis asked for another smoke. Taylor reached for a match.

Taylor had worked more kidnappings than anyone on this case. Barely a year ago, he'd opened a closet door to find Charles Geschke, the kidnapped CEO of Adobe Systems, blindfolded and chained to the floor. But this was different. He looked at Davis leaning against the car, the cherry of his cigarette arcing to his lips in handcuffed hands.

"How long we gonna sit here for?" Davis asked.

Why don't you run? Taylor thought. *I wish you'd run—so I'd have to stop you.*

Eddie Freyer and Vail Bello pulled up in an unmarked Plymouth. David Alford was shortly behind.

"Get eyes on the body," Freyer's boss had said. "You have to confirm it's Polly."

Marc and Eve had been told about the arrest and called into the Petaluma PD. The media was standing by. Anyone aware of what was happening found it difficult to breathe.

Freyer and Alford waded into the knee-high grass. Headlights lit the empty field, and their shadows lurched before them. Alford marked their path with small flags. They found the sheet of weathered plywood beneath the silhouette of an oak tree.

As Freyer reached down, a series of images flashed through his mind. Ligatures. Fibers. Twelve-year-old witnesses. The palm print.

He lifted a corner of plywood. His eyes didn't need to linger. The smell betrayed what lay beneath, but the body was too far gone by now to determine anything further without forensic tests. Freyer couldn't tell if it was male or female, adult or adolescent. All he knew was that it was human.

In this moment, he felt so helpless that he tipped back his head, closed his eyes, and did something very rare: He prayed. Freyer wasn't a very religious man. He'd been raised in a large Catholic family, but he hadn't been to mass in years. He was rather out of practice in requesting divine intervention. Instead of a Hail Mary, he said the purest prayer he knew:

Help!

<hr>

FREYER WALKED BACK to the car and told Bello what he had seen. Sixty-five days ago, they had started this thing together. Even after Bello was pulled off the case, he had never stopped being a loyal friend and de facto partner.

"It has to be her, Eddie," Bello whispered. "It has to be her."

Prudence would call for a careful answer. Something about the need to do some forensic tests to confirm the identity. But his boss was demanding an answer. The family was waiting to know.

Every cell in his body seemed to tilt in one direction. If he was wrong, this would terminate his career. Freyer took a deep breath and sighed deeply.

"Call the family," he said. "Tell them we found Polly Klaas."

chapter thirty-eight

FOUND

⌒⌒

December 4, 1993, 8:30 p.m.

RICHARD ALLEN DAVIS LEANED CASUALLY AGAINST THE CHEVY, SMOKING, FACE empty of emotion.

Vail Bello glared at that face.

Fuck it, Bello thought. *I'm going to kill him. He's cuffed in front. I'll say he reached for Meese's gun. No jury in the world would convict me.*

Bello's hand crept toward the shoulder holster under his jacket.

Freyer saw him reaching and understood. He caught Bello's eye and shook his head almost imperceptibly. He uttered the words softly enough that no one else could hear.

"It's not worth it, man."

Then he turned to Meese and Taylor, and jerked his chin at the man in orange.

"Get him out of here."

⌒⌒

ONE HUNDRED MILES south in Danville, ASAC Mark Mershon and his wife were hosting a Christmas party. The phone rang, and he excused himself to take the call. Receiver pressed to his ear, his face fell. He hung up and pulled his wife aside.

"It's Pat Parks," he said. "Davis confessed."

He glanced at the guests laughing by his Christmas tree. He looked at his wife. She smiled sadly, knowing what this meant.

She nodded and whispered: "Go."

Mershon and Parks had spent two months working in lockstep, an ASAC and a captain paired up on the case as supervisory equals. Such partnerships were often fraught, with feds and cops butting heads. But these two had seen a lifelong friendship start to germinate. Mershon was especially grateful that Parks had reached out to him to share the burden of breaking the news to Polly's parents. In all his years in the Bureau, he had never had to do this.

Eve Nichol and Marc Klaas were waiting at the station. They'd been told that the suspect was talking. They might finally learn where Polly was.

Before going in to face them, Agent Mershon turned to Captain Parks.

"I'm not going to be able to sit there and talk to them," he said. "I won't hold up."

Parks nodded solemnly. He was the kind of leader unafraid to show emotion. He wasn't too manly to cry.

"I need you to minister to them," Mershon said. "You're going to lean in and help them."

They ushered Marc and Eve into Parks's office and told them to sit down. Marc and Eve leaned forward, eager to hear the news. Parks could tell from their expressions they expected the news to be good.

"I'm sorry, but I have the worst possible news to tell you," Mershon said. He paused a moment to let it sink in. "Richard Allen Davis has confessed. Polly is dead."

The agent and the captain wept with them.

⁀⁔⁀

IN CLOVERDALE, UNDER a rising gibbous moon, FBI agents, detectives, and cops converged in a lonesome field. From the vantage point of the road, the field was framed by stands of oak on the left and the abandoned sawmill on the right. In the back of the clearing, through blackberry bushes, a small creek trickled by a rusty-red conical tower—a defunct charcoal kiln. The field was flat, filled with knee-high grass and tangles of berry brambles. Here and there in the grass lay heaps of scrap metal, discarded tires, and rotting plywood. Dumped.

The ERT members had pulled on their white Tyvek suits while staging at the winery, and now they moved through the dark like astronauts, slowly and methodically, unspooling crime scene tape across the field. They discussed their plans and roles. Tony Maxwell would lead the evidence collection. David Alford would oversee body removal. Frank Doyle would ensure they had all the supplies and equipment that they needed.

Investigators at the heart of the search were offered the chance to view the body. This was unorthodox, a break from protocol. But some of these cops and agents needed to see it, for closure. Many wept. Some prayed. A few declined. Mershon knew that if he looked, he would never be able to unsee it. Parks and Andy Mazzanti, both men of deep Christian faith, chose to be two fewer gawkers. These men would all grieve privately. They would struggle to make sense of it all and find closure in singular ways. They would compartmentalize the trauma and carry it for decades, unconscious of its weight until it spilled out years later through the portal of a question.

The sixty-five-day investigation had been a race against time and deteriorating odds. That blistering pace downshifted to meticulous. Every act, every movement, had to be deliberate and precise, fastidiously documented to serve as evidence in a trial. To bring the killer to justice, they had to work flawlessly. A single error could cause a piece of evidence to be thrown out of court. Time was no longer of the essence. Thoroughness was.

But there was pressure from above to hurry. A directive shuttled down the chain of command: Move the body—*tonight*. Get it out of here before the media arrives with the light.

"No," Maxwell said. "It's too risky."

The stakes were too high. Trace evidence would be lost. To do the job right, they had to be able to see. They needed daylight, not flashlights.

But there was something else. Maxwell had indigenous blood and justice in his DNA. His grandfather, a sheriff, had been shot and killed in a gunfight on New Year's Eve in 1933 while trying to arrest two fugitive robbers. His grandmother, a member of the Red Willow tribe in New Mexico, had taught him to lean on faith and yield to spiritual callings. Maxwell had faith in science. He also believed in angels.

Maxwell's father had told him: *Life is somewhere between what you want and what you are capable of doing. What you are capable of doing is what you were meant to be.* He had worked on terrorism, bombings, ballistics, bank robberies, and weapons of mass destruction. Fate had led him to this night and this field. But something else brought him to his knees in the dark, beside this small body on a bed of thorns.

As Maxwell bent over Polly Klaas, he thought of his two young boys at home and how he would want them to be treated. With dignity and respect. Rushing and doing sloppy work in the dark would be the antithesis. Polly deserved his finest work.

Maxwell rose and approached Lillian Zilius, the supervisory senior agent who oversaw the ERT. She had always backed them up.

"We're not going to move her tonight," Maxwell told her.

He was told that moving the body wasn't a suggestion. It was an order.

"Then fire me," Maxwell said calmy. "We're not moving her tonight."

Zilius agreed to go to bat for them. As she picked up her bricklike phone and dialed a higher-up, Maxwell carefully crossed the field, following Alford's flags, and sat down next to Polly. He just wanted to keep her company for a little while in the moonlight. It was cold. He knew that Polly was afraid of the dark and hated being alone.

"We found you, Polly," he whispered. "We're going to bring you home."

⌒⌒⌒

As THE FIRST light slid over the ridge lines and illuminated the valley, the ERT members zipped up their Tyvek suits and began their clockwork. They cordoned off the path that Alford had flagged as he and Freyer had crossed the field, identifying this corridor as potentially contaminated. From here on, everyone would enter the crime scene from a point in the back, to avoid trampling trace evidence in the areas where Davis might have walked. SWAT team members had guarded the crime scene overnight, and now they controlled access to three concentric perimeters set up around Polly's body. No one was authorized to enter the innermost circle but Maxwell and Alford.

Before anything was touched or moved, they carefully measured and diagrammed the crime scene, triangulating the position of Polly's body in relation to fixed reference points—the road or a tree or the edge of the field. They called the medical examiner's office, but told them not to send a van just yet. They had hours of work to do.

As expected, the media began to swarm. TV trucks parked beside Highway 101, raising their antennas and positioning satellite dishes. Photographers with telephoto lenses scrambled up a hill across the freeway. Helicopters thundered overhead, close enough for the investigators to see cameramen leaning out, bracing their feet on the skids. Charter planes circled and banked to give photographers a better shot.

Anticipating this, Frank Doyle had brought two white pop-up tents to shield Polly from the cameras. Adding walls of white tarps, he created

Aerial photo of the Dutcher Creek Road crime scene near Cloverdale.
(COURTESY OF TONY MAXWELL)

a bright little room where Maxwell and Alford could work out of sight of the telephoto lenses.

The field was divided into quadrants that could be systematically searched. White-suited searchers crawled on their hands and knees, parting the grass in search of a hair, a drop of blood, or a single fiber. The berry brambles surrounding Polly were cut and painstakingly pulled apart on an examination table, in hope of finding evidence that might eliminate any shred of doubt in a future juror's mind.

As media helicopters hovered overhead, the rotor wash blasted the field and threatened to blow away fragile trace evidence. Someone called the Federal Aviation Administration to close the airspace over the crime scene.

Working discreetly inside the white tent, Maxwell moved with equal parts skill and prayer. His mother would later inquire why he hadn't called her today, on her birthday. He thought about how much things had changed since he started this line of work. It was no longer about murders and abstract bodies. It was about people.

At 2:40 p.m. on Sunday, December 5, the medical examiner drove a van into the field. Alford and another agent solemnly lifted the tiny body, shrouded in white plastic, and bore it to the van. On a nearby hill, a crowd of citizens watched and wept. Everyone present paused in a spontaneous moment of silence.

∽

IT HIT THEM all at different times, in different ways.

Driving home, alone in his car, Maxwell finally let go. The interstate blurred through tears. They had finally found Polly. But not the way they had hoped.

The previous night, after breaking the news to Marc and Eve, Mark Mershon and Pat Parks had driven to Cloverdale. Satisfied that the crime scene was secure, the team was well equipped, and the engine running smoothly, they had ridden back to Petaluma in silence. At the station, they walked toward the back door, where Parks paused, turned to Mershon, and held up a key.

"This is my master key to the station house," he said. "It will get you in and open any door. Now it's yours."*

Sunday afternoon at the crime scene, the last few agents were rolling up yellow tape. Eddie Freyer was exhausted. Sixty-five days of hope and despair were visible on his face. The search was over, but that would take some time to sink in. He had kept a tight lid on his emotions. Now he walked around the perimeter, checking on his guys.

JC Steiner, a fellow SWAT team member and a longtime friend, caught his eye.

"I'm sorry, Freyer."

Three kind words uncorked two months of emotion. The two men embraced and cried.

The crime scene cleared out just as the light began to fade. Freyer and Bello lingered. It was hard to know what to do now that the search was over.

"We started this together," Freyer said. "Let's finish it together."

Bello drove into town on one last mission. He stopped at a local hardware store and loaded his patrol car with poinsettias. One by one, they placed them in the field, encircling the spot where Polly was found with a perimeter of flowers.

---

* Mershon still carries that key today.

chapter thirty-nine

POSITIVE IDENTIFICATION

◠

December 6, 11:30 a.m.—Santa Rosa

ON MONDAY MORNING, FIFTEEN PEOPLE FROM SIX AGENCIES GATHERED AT THE Sonoma County Medical Examiner's Office, a small yellow building in the shade of a redwood. It was an unusually large number for an autopsy, but everyone had a different role to play. Wearing white rubber gloves and a white apron over blue medical scrubs, coroner Tom Siebe began the examination in the morgue. As everyone else in Sonoma County was going about their midday routine, they began the process of identifying the body and determining the cause of death.

Even for seasoned investigators who had seen some terrible things, this part was hard to witness. Even distilled to only the details essential for the trial, it is horrifying to fathom. What follows is very difficult to read. In order to evaluate the killer's claims, it's necessary to understand the position of clothing and ligatures, the condition of the body, and the geometry of its posture.*

---

* Out of respect for Polly and her family, many gratuitous details have been omitted. However, the position of her body and the disposition of her clothing are essential for considering Davis's claim that he did not rape her—a story he continues to assert today and a matter unresolved by the trial. Because certain crucial details are unavoidably graphic, this chapter uses clinical language.

The autopsy report noted that the skull had separated from the body and was found in the trees a short distance away. This was believed to be caused by "animal activity." The hair had separated from the skull in the process of decomposing. Two knotted ligatures were tangled in it. The first was a ragged-edged piece of cloth. The second was a thin piece of rope. Both were double-knotted, forming a loop with a diameter of three inches.

The torso was partially covered by a long-sleeved flannel nightgown. Much of the cotton was stained black, but the white sleeves had retained their visible pattern: red stripes and tiny hearts. It was the nightgown that Gillian had packed for the sleepover. The thigh-length garment was pushed up over the hips and gathered under the arms.

Examiners noted the disposition of the clothing. Under the nightgown was the hot pink samba top and white denim miniskirt that Gillian and Kate had described. The samba top had a decorative tie at the waist, and the double-knot was undone. The white mini skirt was inverted over the torso, flipped up and inside out.

At the crime scene, they had sketched the body's position, measuring the angles of its repose. The legs were bare. Knees bent, pointed out. Heels twenty-nine inches apart. One hand covered the pelvis.

David Alford and county medical examiner Dr. Jay Chapman photographed each detail, documenting every step of the three-and-a-half-hour procedure. Nothing could be left to chance or memory.

The garments were removed and placed on a table for a preliminary exam. They would need a week to dry out in a locked and sanitized storage unit before being transported to the FBI lab.

The medical examiner x-rayed the bones with the help of an assistant and an employee from the Bay Area Portable X-Ray Company. Tony Maxwell and forensic odontologist Dr. Jack Davies painstakingly examined the skull and jaw, using special magnification glasses and the ALS. They collected a number of hairs to be sent to Chris Allen in the FBI lab.

Mike Stapleton examined the hands to determine whether fingerprinting was possible. The tissue was no longer pliable enough to be flattened against a fingerprint card. He could see that the left index finger had a whorl-type pattern, consistent with the victim's known prints. But this observation was not enough to confirm a positive identification.

Stapleton called the FBI lab, which requested the hands be surgically removed and transported to DC for lab examination.

David Alford loaded a roll of film into a Mamiya 645 camera for closeup photos of the fingertips. These photographs would be essential if attempts to rehydrate the hands in the lab were insufficient to produce an inked print. The medium-format SLR camera had some tricky manual settings, and the image he saw in the viewfinder didn't look quite right. He began to sweat.

In order to capture the ridge detail of the fingerprints, he needed a perfect exposure and an image in sharp focus. Alford peered through the viewfinder and frowned. Because one of the manual settings was off, the image was too dark, and he couldn't tell if the ridge detail was in focus. He held his breath to guard against camera shake and heard the shutter click. He wouldn't know until later, when he developed the film, whether he had gotten the shot.

The body identification would also hinge on forensic odontology, the study of the teeth. The lower mandible had detached from the skull and was found nearby in the grass. Most of the teeth were still present, and they were unique in their shape and the absence of fillings. The upper jaw had permanent canine teeth emerging, on the cusp of pushing out the baby teeth.

Forensic odontologist Dr. Davies took the skull and lower jaw to be x-rayed. Comparing the X-rays to the victim's dental records, he stated that without a doubt he recognized fifteen different points of identification. This was the body of Polly Hannah Klaas.

Dr. Chapman, the medical examiner, said that "no determinate cause of death could positively be made," but stated for the record that the remains were consistent with a victim of strangulation. Further examination by a forensic paleoanthropologist would be needed to determine whether the skeletal remains showed evidence of traumatic injury.

The state of decomposition prevented serological examinations that could verify the presence of seminal fluid in or on the body. However, Maxwell had found something while scanning the body and the clothing with the ALS. On the panties, near the left side seam that would have covered the hip, a small stain fluoresced.

In the FBI lab, hair and fibers expert Chris Allen heard about the fluorescing stain and discussed it with a serologist.

"So it's semen?" Allen asked.

"All that glitters is not gold," the serologist said dryly. "All that fluoresces is not semen."

Fluorescence under the ALS didn't prove that it was semen. It *might* be semen. But it could also be another bodily fluid—possibly urine, saliva, vaginal fluid—all of which fluoresce under an ALS. Or, as unlikely as it might seem, it could have been a non-human substance like hamburger grease or laundry detergent. Tide was famous for leaving chemical markers that lit up under an ALS.

After finding the stain on the panties, Maxwell had stepped out of the morgue to call Mike Meese and share the information. Using the qualifying language of science, he said that the stain had fluoresced under the ALS in a manner "consistent with semen."*

Meese was juggling several urgent tasks when he took the call. He was gathering evidence to deliver to the district attorney's office in preparation for the following day's arraignment. And he was gearing up for another interview with Richard Allen Davis in just a few hours. This information would be useful.

THE AUTOPSY WAS still underway as Mike Meese and Larry Taylor began the interview in the Sonoma County Jail, where Davis was being held without bail.

Davis admitted cleaning his car shortly after the abduction. He threw away the seat covers and vacuumed the Pinto three or four times "to clean out any good evidence." He was particularly worried about hairs. He was right to be worried.

"You took a good look at some of the stuff we found on the hill," Meese said.

---

* Examiners would later study the panties under a microscope, and they wouldn't find any sperm. Given months of exposure to nature and proximity to a decomposing body, it was possible that bacteria could have digested any sperm—if there were any present in the first place. It wasn't possible to conclude anything with certainty.

After leading Meese and Taylor to Cloverdale, Davis had been taken to Petaluma PD and interviewed a third time. There, Meese had shown him the black men's sweatshirt they'd found on Pythian. Davis had acknowledged that yes, that was his sweatshirt. Now Meese had more findings to share.

"One of the things we found in the examination of Polly's remains is the presence of semen," Meese said.

"Where?" Davis asked.

"On the body."

"Not in her, though."

Meese asked, straight up, if Davis had molested her.

"I don't think so," was the reply. "I don't think so."

A truthful answer from an innocent person would be adamant and specific. "No!" Vague and waffling answers signal deception.

"We've got the presence of semen or what we believe to be semen on the body."

Davis continued to deny it.

"If we find semen there...or with the semen, you get a DNA reading and if it comes back to you..."

"Then hey, I'm guilty of it. That's all there is to it."

Meese pressed him on how it got there. Davis demurred, saying he could only tell him what he could remember. And there was a lot he didn't seem to remember. He blamed it on the joint he'd smoked, a joint he claimed was laced with something that must have fogged his memory and compromised his judgment.

"Hum, okay," Meese said. "But I'm also aware that you may be afraid that if something like that happened...or I should say if you're the one that was involved in something like that, that might make life a little hard for you when you go back inside."

"Life's gonna be hard as it is," he said.

Meese pressed him again on the semen. At some point, he mentioned Davis's mother, which seemed to trigger him.

"I don't give a shit no more! As far as I'm concerned, I'm pushing it out of my mind."

"Why push it out of your mind?"

"I don't wanna know."

If he was sure he didn't do "that other thing," Meese probed, "Why strangle her, then?"

"Cover my tracks. I didn't want to go back to prison. Fuck. I just panicked."

Meese asked if he had ever committed any sex crimes. Davis admitted trying to kidnap Frances Mays, who grabbed his knife and escaped after he tried to kidnap her at a BART station. There was a pattern here that might suggest a motive for choosing a twelve-year-old victim: Davis had tried to rape grown women—and failed. Repeatedly.

Larry Taylor jumped in.

"What are you going to do if the forensic evidence comes in and the autopsy and all that indicates that she had been raped. What then?"

"Tell them give me the gas, and fuck it. They can gas my ass."

In the FBI lab in Washington, DC, the evidence began connecting, like dots, to form a bigger picture: the portrait of a solid case.

The silky white bindings had already linked three crime scenes: Polly's room, the woods off Pythian Road, and the field in Cloverdale. Hair and fibers examiner Chris Allen had lined up their matching edges on November 29, the day David Alford delivered the new evidence from Pythian. There was no question in Allen's mind that they'd been cut from the same piece of cloth.

When he'd flown to Petaluma to help the ERT process the white Pinto, Allen had vacuumed the center console and rear passenger floor. It had yielded a number of tiny white fibers. The length and shape of these fibers indicated they were created when the cloth was cut, most likely with a pair of scissors. No such matching fibers had been found in Polly's house.

Such fibers were, however, stuck to the packing tape found on the Pythian hillside. And they were consistent with the nylon fibers that comprised the silky bindings. The jagged edges of the bindings suggested the nylon had been bunched when cut. Based on the jagged edges and the fibers found in the Pinto, Allen deduced that the slip had probably been cut in Davis's car.

Other fibers—red printed cotton—were scraped from the black men's sweatshirt found in the Pythian woods. Those fibers had the same microscopic, physical, and chemical characteristics as the fibers from Gillian's nightgown, which had been removed from the body during the autopsy. The element of transfer indicated physical contact between the nightgown and the black men's sweatshirt.

The scraping of the black sweatshirt also released a brown polyester fiber. That fiber was consistent with fibers vacuumed from the driver's seat of the Pinto.

The hair recovered from Cloverdale was examined with an alternate light source. It revealed pink acrylic fibers tangled in the locks. They were consistent with fibers vacuumed from the Pinto's front passenger floor. The Locard Exchange Principle suggested this transfer could have occurred through contact between the victim's head and the vehicle's floor well.

⌒⌒⌒

A WEEK AFTER Davis's arraignment, ERT members boarded another red-eye flight to DC. The clothing had been dried in the locker and was in better condition for transport. In one carry-on bag was a sterile plastic container with Polly's hands.

In the lab, fingerprint specialist Michael Smith studied them. Two fingers on the left hand—the index and the middle finger—retained enough ridge detail to compare with the ten-print card for Polly. But the fingers were not in shape to be rolled for fresh prints. He used David Alford's photos, which had turned out to be razor-sharp and perfectly exposed. Comparing these photos to the inked prints that Marc Klaas had provided in the early days of the case, Smith declared a positive identification.

When it was time to look under her fingernails for a bit of skin or fiber that could further implicate her killer, this part hit Chris Allen the hardest. He had a son around Polly's age. His child might have poured a glass of milk from a carton with Polly's picture.

Most agents and forensic experts possess a solid capacity for compartmentalizing their work. Some days thrust horrible things into view.

They develop the ability to put these horrors in a box and leave them at work so they can walk through their own front door and be a spouse or a mother or father. Moments like this seep through the box. No matter how long you've done this job, you're still human.

Staring at fibers under a microscope was one thing. But these were a little girl's hands. Hands that would never hold a diploma, wear a wedding ring, or lift a grandchild.

chapter forty

AMERICA CRIES

ON THE NIGHT THAT POLLY WAS FOUND, CHIEF DENNIS DeWITT FACED A WALL of TV cameras that had assembled outside the police station in Petaluma.

"I'm here to tell the world," he said. "Polly Klaas is dead."

Marc Klaas left the police station, numb, and staggered across the street to the volunteer center. He wouldn't break down until later, at home, surrounded by friends and family. He held himself together now to personally tell the volunteers—strangers once, now friends—who had searched and toiled and hoped.

His announcement sucked the oxygen out of the air. Everyone leaned on one another as the world seemed to tilt. How could this be?

Eve went home to 427 Fourth Street, where a white candle had burned in the window for sixty-four nights.

That night, the flame was extinguished.

⌒⌒

CANDLES AND BOUQUETS accumulated outside the volunteer center until the sidewalk was transformed into a garden of flowers and light. Children wrote letters, left dolls and gifts. One boy brought a manzanita branch adorned with lavender ribbons.

As the residents of other towns were caroling at tree-lighting events, Petalumans were singing hymns at candlelight vigils. On Sunday night, three hundred people gathered at Lucchesi Park to mourn and pray. They left their candles burning on the edge of the lake as they returned to their homes and families.

Joanne Gardner prepared a public statement for Marc to deliver. "My beautiful child is dead," he said. "America's child is dead."

Gardner's words—America's child—would appear in the *People* magazine cover story and in news broadcasts around the world. The sadness rippled across oceans. A headline in Munich, Germany, read: *America Cries: Polly Is Dead.*

Eve had written a letter to everyone who had helped and asked Gardner to read it. On Monday night, just hours after Polly's body was positively identified, Gardner stood in front of seventy-five mourners outside the volunteer headquarters. She took a deep breath, steadied herself, and tried to read it without breaking down.

"Dearest friends," Gardner began. "It is with unspeakable sorrow that I must let go of the dream we all shared—the dream of our sweet Polly coming home again..."

Polly was safe now, "in a place filled with light and love." Though Eve's heart was broken, she found solace in the community spirit forged from all the horror and pain, comparing it to the rejuvenation and growth that follows a devastating forest fire.

Eve wished she could be here to grieve with her community. But she needed to mourn in seclusion, encircled by her family and closest friends. "Your miraculous outpouring of love brings me comfort," she wrote. "And time will bring us peace."

She had feared the worst when she first heard the name Richard Allen Davis and learned of his criminal record. That's when the hope she had worked so hard to sustain gave way to her deepest fears. In the past week, she'd given only one interview—to John Walsh, the only member of the media who could possibly understand her pain. And also because "I couldn't imagine living with myself if anything I said would impair the investigation or prosecution of those responsible."

She expressed her heartfelt gratitude to the volunteers, police, FBI, and media. "Without your magnificent efforts, this case might never have been solved." The agony would have been so much worse if she had felt alone or if investigators hadn't made this case their top priority. She acknowledged that not every case receives this kind of response. "I know there have been many child kidnapping cases where families felt abandoned, and my heart goes out to them," she wrote. "Now we know what a community can and must do."

Eve described the four main outcomes she hoped for now. First, the prosecution of Richard Allen Davis, so he could never again inflict this pain on another family or community. Second, efforts to end child abuse and neglect. "Davis was an abused child, and the cycle has repeated itself in the most horrible way possible." Third, the establishment of kidnapping protocols that ensured an immediate response, "since every moment counts." Fourth: "Change our laws regarding habitual crimi-nals. Davis should never have been free to walk the streets of Petaluma, looking for an innocent child to kill."

Why had Polly's case so profoundly touched the nation and the world? Eve didn't know. She realized not every family receives this kind of support. But she hoped that what had been learned from Polly's case would help galvanize some other community in the future. If Polly's fate could change laws or inspire efforts to prevent child abuse, perhaps "something good can come out of this horror."

As Gardner read Eve's letter, the crowd before her was struck by the fierce love of this gentle mother. "When we can, let's open our hearts to for-giveness and healing. Focus on the changes we can and must effect, rather than torturing ourselves with 'what ifs.' Human errors were made, but no one is to blame except Richard Allen Davis. We must have mercy ourselves. And Polly would want us to thrive on the love we have created, not the hate."

Everyone wept and leaned on one another as Joanne read Eve's final words.

"Polly won't be coming home, but her spirit will be with us always."

⌒⌒

JOANNE GARDNER HAD been a lifeline for the media. She had given them new stories, day after day, to keep them engaged for more than two months of "no solid leads." Now she went home and hugged her daughter Jessica, who'd tagged along most days at the volunteer center. Thirteen, she bore a striking resemblance to Polly, and Gardner would watch Polly's grandmother brushing Jessica's hair, hoping it provided a moment of catharsis.

Gardner and Gaynell Rogers were feeling the same things that everyone else in Petaluma felt. But they didn't have time to fall apart. They had a funeral to plan.

"How are we going to do this?" Rogers said.

"We're gonna do it," Gardner replied.

Gardner and Rogers mined their Rolodexes, again, this time to curate the most unforgettable memorial they could imagine. They called Robin Williams. Joan Baez. Linda Ronstadt, the singer of Polly's favorite song. A musician from Peter Gabriel's band. Eve was a follower of spiritual leader Baba Ram Dass, so they asked him to come too.

All of them said yes.

Then the politicians started calling. California governor Pete Wilson wanted to speak. So did Senator Dianne Feinstein. Congresswoman Lynn Woolsey wanted to read a letter from the White House. Gardner and Rogers found themselves "juggling people's needs." They argued with press secretaries, saying things like, "No, you can't have ten minutes. You can only have one." And: "This isn't a press conference. This is a little girl's funeral." They got pushback from folks in high places. But they fought it, intent on preventing the memorial from being politicized. "We kept trying to make it about music and love and comfort," Rogers said. "I was the *no* machine."

They booked the biggest church in town: St. Vincent de Paul, a Roman Catholic church with soaring twin spires and a capacity of 1,500. Three days before the funeral, someone predicted they'd run out of room. They needed to set up screens outside the church so people outside could watch, and also find a way to televise it around the Bay Area.

One day before the memorial, CNN called. They wanted to broadcast the funeral live—an honor typically reserved only for heads of state. They needed a satellite feed. Gardner realized another need almost as

346 | IN LIGHT OF ALL DARKNESS

important: beautiful light. As a music video director, she knew the challenge of filming in low-light conditions. The church was beautiful, with soaring vaulted ceilings and stained-glass windows. It was also dim. If she didn't find a way to light up that church, the funeral would look dark and somber on TV. Everyone present—or watching at home—needed a moment of transcendent beauty.

So she cold-called Industrial Light & Magic, the division of Lucasfilm that designed lighting for movies. It was then based in nearby San Rafael. They would have the equipment and experts. But could they help on such short notice? And what would they charge?

Nothing.

"Hi, my name is Joanne Gardner..." was all she had time to say.

"Oh, yeah, we know you!" came the reply. "What do you need?"

"I need to light this church tomorrow for the funeral," she said.

"Give me half an hour."

Within the hour, the problem was solved.

"We've got two crews in here shooting movies," Gardner recalled hearing. "We're going to cancel production on those. We're going to send you our five-ton grip trucks and our lighting package and crew."

When the crew showed up, many brought their kids. "They wanted their kids to see what they were doing," Gardner said. "They were doing this for Polly."

⌒⌒⌒

THE DAY OF the memorial was cold and rainy. Seven hours before the service, people began lining up around the church, its twin spires glowing white against the steel-wool sky. Satellite trucks had infiltrated downtown. Outside of CNN's live broadcast, Gardner and Rogers gave the rest of the media limited access to the service. They could film a bit of Joan Baez, and then they had to leave.

Because several high-ranking politicians would be there, the FBI had to clear the church. Rogers was with them when her cell phone rang. She dug her blocky Motorola out of her purse to see if she knew the number. The caller ID said: the White House. She excused herself and stepped into the vestry to take the call.

"President Clinton would like to speak to Marc Klaas," said the caller, who claimed to be one of the president's handlers.

"How did you get my number?" Rogers asked.

"This is the White House."

"I'm going to have to call you back and verify that on a land line."

Rogers called from the pastor's office. Someone at the White House answered.

A LIGHT RAIN was falling when the memorial began at six p.m. As expected, the crowd spilled out of the church, onto the sidewalk, and into three square blocks. As many as 5,000 people showed up, many wearing purple ribbons. Outside the church, they clustered under umbrellas, holding candles and photos of Polly.

Joan Baez opened the service with an a cappella performance of "Amazing Grace." Polly's aunt closed her eyes and sang along. Baez personalized one of the lyrics:

> ... as when you took my own sweet child
> my child, my joy, my star ...

Eve Nichol sat next to Pat Parks and Mark Mershon. Marc Klaas sat in another pew with Mike Meese, Violet Cheer, and family. Eddie Freyer and Vail Bello stood in the back of the church. Tony Maxwell and the rest of the ERT did not attend. "We're never invited to the funerals," Maxwell said sadly. "We're invisible at that point—until the trial."

"Tonight, we continue to remember Polly, whose life and death have brought our community to an all-new height of caring and love for one another," said Reverend George Risden. "A mighty legacy for a twelve-year-old to have given us."

Governor Pete Wilson gave the eulogy and read a personal message from President Bill Clinton. Senator Dianne Feinstein said Polly was a national symbol of "every family's nightmare" and a reminder of "the awful brutality of the world."

Michael Groves, a family friend, read a line from "Ode to Joy," one of Polly's favorite songs. "Oh, you millions, let me embrace you, let this kiss be for the whole world."

Annette Schott wrote a poem that described how she went to bed hugging a picture of Polly, who "makes the stars twinkle." "I want you to know, Polly, how much I care."

Mike Meese choked back tears as he said, "Polly showed us the power of love . . ." He read a poem written by Pat Parks:

> It's not the first time God above
> Has sacrificed innocence to reveal love
> For sweet Polly when you died
> Your love by millions was multiplied.

Linda Ronstadt closed the service by calling nine of Polly's friends and siblings to stand beside her at the front of the church. Famously shy, Ronstadt began singing Polly's favorite song.

> Somewhere out there, beneath the pale moonlight
> someone's thinking of me, and loving me tonight

Her voice began to waver. Polly's sister, six-year-old Annie, ran up and reached for her hand.

chapter forty-one

THE TRIAL

⌒⌒⌒

April 17–June 18, 1996—San Jose, California

ON MAY 3, 1996, TWELVE JURORS LUGGED THEIR OVERNIGHT BAGS ONTO A private charter bus at the courthouse in San Jose. Sixteen days into the three-month murder trial of Richard Allen Davis, it was the start of a two-day "jury view"—an in-person visit to three crime scenes. The two-hour bus ride would be a scenic one, gliding north along Highway 101 through Silicon Valley, into the heart of San Francisco, across the Golden Gate Bridge, past the Marin Headlands, and into Sonoma wine country. Behind them, Davis rode in a sheriff's van. Behind him was a caravan of lawyers.

Because of the trial's high profile, the bus had a full police escort. Other drivers on the 101 must have thought it was filled with dignitaries—not jurors and a sheriff. "It was like a presidential motorcade," jury foreman Brian Bianco recollected decades later. "Lights were flashing in front of us and behind us. The side streets were blocked so there was no cross traffic."

Greg Jacobs, the assistant district attorney for Sonoma County in charge of the prosecution, rode in one of the cars. Jacobs had made a motion for the trip, so the jury could get a feel for the landscape. They needed to see the location of Wickersham Park and Polly's house, the ditch where the Pinto had gotten stuck. They needed to walk up the Pythian hillside to feel the steepness of the embankment and stand in the woods in the dark to imagine how frightened Polly must have been. It set the stage for all the witnesses' stories. "It brings the testimony to life," Jacobs said.

Defense attorney Barry Collins had strongly objected to the field trip. He felt it would be prejudicial for the jury to see the memorial garden, a manifestation of public grief beneath a live oak tree in Cloverdale. He also worried about the safety of his client. Davis had been getting death threats, so having him out in public—even with deputy escorts—seemed risky. That said, he had to be there: A defendant has the right to be present in every moment of his jury trial.

Judge Thomas Hastings overruled the objection, citing the distance between crime scenes as a factor the jurors needed to grasp. But the judge agreed that the Cloverdale memorial—a cluster of flowers, stuffed animals, painted rocks, and other gifts from anonymous visitors—could be prejudicial. So the bus would drive the jurors to Dutcher Creek Road, staying out of sight of the memorial but close enough to get a feel for the geography and distance from Pythian.

Davis's proximity to the jury raised some concerns. He had the right to see and hear every proceeding in his trial. But to do that, he would have to be within earshot. Would they feel unsafe? If someone came after Davis—a not-unlikely scenario if he was spotted in Petaluma—it would put everyone around him in danger. Collins offered a solution: Get his client a pizza and a Pepsi. If they could grant him this small but not insignificant indulgence, Davis would stay in the sheriff's car during the visit to Polly's house.

The trial had gone through three years of fits and starts before finally beginning on April 17, 1996. The original venue, Sonoma County, was rejected after jury selection failed. They summoned 8,500 prospective jurors—an astronomical number—yet nearly all had been ruled out. A thirty-five-page questionnaire and lengthy interview process had made it clear it would be impossible to find impartial jurors in Polly's county. The majority of those summoned voiced an unequivocal prejudice against Richard Allen Davis. Many had joined the search.

The trial had been postponed twice and moved to San Jose, in Santa Clara County. Which is why the jurors found themselves aboard a charter bus for a two-hour ride to Sonoma.

☙❧

THE TRIAL WAS being overseen by Superior Court Judge Thomas Hastings, a former defense attorney known for controlling his courtroom with intelligence and authority. He had good rapport with juries and little patience for attorneys who second-guessed his rulings or failed to follow courtroom decorum.

The prosecutor, Greg Jacobs, was a self-described "worrier" who obsessed over every detail. A graduate of Stanford, Jacobs had grown up enamored with Perry Mason, the fictional criminal defense lawyer played by Raymond Burr in the TV show. As an adult, Jacobs's suits and comportment echoed Perry Mason's style. He took notes with a Parker Duofold Centennial fountain pen, a replica of the pens his grandfather used in the 1920s. Jurors liked him and found him approachable. "You have this aw-shucks country-boy thing—I could see the straw coming out of your collar," an instructor once told him in prosecutor school. "Don't ever change."

The trial began just five months after the end of O. J. Simpson's murder trial, in which the jury had acquitted the former pro football star on charges of murdering his wife, Nicole Brown Simpson. The verdict had caused a national stir, and some of the public had lost faith in the justice system. Cameras had been allowed in the courtroom, and the trial would forever be known as a "media circus." Jacobs wanted the antithesis: a straightforward and orderly due process, a professional prosecution with no showboating or theatrics. A fair trial with no major screw-ups.

The media was saying Jacobs had "a slam-dunk case," which made him worry all the more. He abated his anxiety with exercise. Every morning before court, he went on a run with Eddie Freyer, assigned full-time to support him for the duration of the trial. They were sharing a condo in San Jose, where every night they would have a beer and recap the day's events. Then Jacobs would calm his racing mind by swimming laps in the condo pool.

Defending Davis was Long Island native Barry Collins, a public defender who talked like Robert De Niro and looked a bit like John Goodman. A former cab driver, he rode a Harley and would one day enjoy a retirement job as a casino blackjack dealer. Collins worked on the Serious Felonies Team (SFT), and people assumed he had drawn the short straw to get stuck with this dreadful case. But Collins liked a challenge, and he loved being the center of attention in the courtroom. He took cases no one else wanted. "I'm like Mikey," he joked, referring to the kid in the LIFE cereal commercials, the one who would eat anything. When the *People vs. Richard Allen Davis* trial came up in the Sonoma County Public Defender's Office, everyone said: "Give it to Barry!"

In his opening statement, Collins was very clear. "The evidence in this case will be overwhelming that Mr. Richard Allen Davis did, in fact, kill Polly Klaas. The defense in this case will not dispute that." What the defense would dispute—the matter that Davis seemed to be most concerned about—was sexual assault. It was one of the four "special circumstances" that would factor into a sentence: kidnapping, robbery, burglary, and an attempted lewd act upon a child under the age of fourteen.

If the jury found Davis guilty of any one of these special circumstances in the first phase of the trial (the guilt phase), it would put the death penalty on the table as they deliberated in the trial's second phase (the penalty phase). This was exactly what Davis had tried to avoid when he called Mike Meese from jail on December 4 and asked for "life without." Meese had then spoken with district attorney Gene Tunney, Jr., who approved an offer of life without parole as a bargaining chip to get Davis to lead them to the body. When the interview later began, Davis asked Meese, "What did the DA say?" Before Meese could answer, Larry Taylor diverted Davis's attention to signing the Miranda rights waiver. They never offered the "life without" deal because Davis never asked again.

∽

IN THE FORM of evidence, Greg Jacobs possessed an embarrassment of riches: physical evidence, trace evidence including a palm print linking

Davis to the crime scene, two eyewitnesses, a recorded confession, and a team of expert witnesses. He had too much to succinctly summarize in an opening statement, which typically presents an overview of the main facts of the case. Instead, he began with a portrait of Polly and the life that had been stolen.

Eve Nichol took the stand for the first and only time in the trial. At once fragile and strong, she described the events of the evening. Jurors were visibly shaken when they listened to her voice on the 911 tape, awaking into a nightmare. After testifying, Eve left the courtroom and couldn't bear to return.

Kate and Gillian, now fifteen, were growing into young women, but they were still nervous about facing Davis. Judge Hastings allowed each of them to choose a trusted adult to accompany them on the witness stand. Both of them chose forensic artist Jeanne Boylan. She sat next to each of them in turn as they told the jury their story, giving silent support with her presence and a gentle hand squeeze. This time, there was absolutely no doubt in the room.

Dana Jaffe and her daughter, Kelila, who was also fifteen years old, described seeing the Pinto stuck in the ditch as they fled into town for safety. Mike Rankin and Thomas Howard recounted their thirty-eight-minute encounter. Davis sat, expressionless, staring flatly through plastic-framed spectacles.

Various neighborhood witnesses described their Davis sightings. The jury, having visited the neighborhood, was able to imagine it clearly. One young boy, eleven years old at the time, recalled a brief encounter with Davis while playing in Wickersham Park. When he dropped his ball, it rolled toward a man who was drinking something from a paper bag and vomiting. "Are you okay?" the boy asked. Davis snarled, "Get away from me, you stupid kid!"

The FBI's forensic experts presented their evidence. Tony Maxwell described lifting the latent print, and Michael J. Smith explained the science of matching points in the ridge detail. Hair and fibers expert Chris Allen showed the jury how two hairs and a number of fibers linked Davis to Polly and four crime scenes: Polly's room, Pythian Road, Cloverdale, and the Pinto. Juries could be put to sleep by some expert witnesses, but

Allen's charisma and seven-foot photographic display were so impressive that even a bailiff said, "He was the best I've ever seen."

Larry Pelton and Mike Meese described their interviews with the subject, but it was the confession tape that truly moved the jury. They cringed and looked like they might be sick as Davis described the act of strangling Polly. When he crossed his fists and jerked them apart to show Meese how he had done it, one juror began to cry.

When the medical examiner described Polly's autopsy, photographs of her remains were passed around the jury box. One woman shook her head as silent tears fell. A man swallowed hard and took deep breaths.

The defendant's main point of contention was that he hadn't molested Polly. The photographs of her body told a different story. The geometry of her posture spoke for her.

The photos answered many questions. But it was a horrible thing to see, an image that can never be unseen. Marc Klaas closed his eyes and grimaced before running out of the courtroom.

"My lord..." he said, gasping. "I've got an image of Polly in my mind and I can't let that go. I can't let that go." Throughout the trial, he processed his thoughts and emotions by writing daily in a "cyber-space diary"—a published online journal that might qualify as one of the world's first blogs.

In his six-hour closing statement, Greg Jacobs hammered hard on evidence of sexual assault—the main count Davis seemed most desperate to refute. Even though the evidence was insufficient to prove rape, "all we have to do is prove that there was some physical touching with the intent to gratify sexual desire." He pointed to Davis's black sweatshirt. In the scraping room of the FBI lab, Chris Allen had found Polly's hair affixed to it. Thanks to Locard's Exchange Principle—every contact leaves a trace—this hair was evidence of physical touch. The condom found next to the sweatshirt provided evidence of sexual intent.

The jury deliberated for twenty hours, scrutinizing every instruction. Their verdict found Davis guilty on all counts, including murder, kidnap, robbery, burglary, false imprisonment, assault with a deadly weapon, and attempted lewd act on a child.

Upon hearing the verdict, Richard Allen Davis responded with a

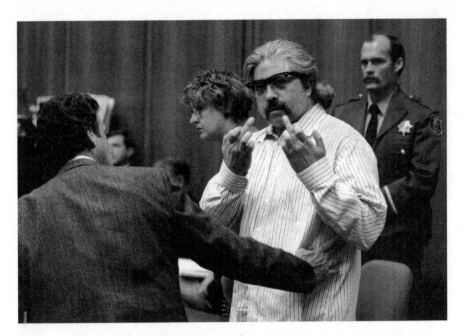

Richard Allen Davis after hearing the verdict.
(PHOTO CREDIT: JOHN BURGESS, *SANTA ROSA PRESS DEMOCRAT*)

gesture most of the jury missed—they were looking at the judge—but the cameras would capture and broadcast in perpetuity. Davis turned directly toward Marc Klaas and the media. With a menacing wink, Davis blew a kiss, raised both hands, and extended two middle fingers.

The guilty verdict triggered the "penalty phase," a second mini-trial that recapped the evidence and added character and expert witnesses to review the bigger context of the crime—Davis's childhood, past crimes, and victim impact.

This is when he'd pay—with interest—for the Kennewick robberies with Susan Edwards. He was never charged for those crimes, and probably never would have been caught. But when he ratted out his ex-girlfriend to punish her for breaking her promises, he implicated himself.

One by one, the women he'd tried to kidnap and rape took the stand and described how he'd hurt them. Marjorie Mitchell, who still suffered head and neck pain from being struck with a fireplace poker. Hazel Frost, who had personality changes and problems at work after Davis had tried to kidnap her. Frances Mays, who would never again walk through a parking lot or BART station without fear. Selina Varich, who had to sleep with the lights and the radio on and was still afraid to answer the door years after he'd bludgeoned and robbed her.

Eve Nichol couldn't bring herself to come back to the courtroom, so her father, Eugene Reed, took the stand to describe the impact on him and Polly's grandmother. "We have survived a number of traumatic situations—the Nazi Holocaust in Vienna, the blitz in London, the end of World War II," he said, "only in our old age to be hit by the devastating nightmare and catastrophe of the death of our beloved granddaughter."

Marc had spent three years "running from one death and pursuing another," and now he unleashed three years of vitriol. He referred to Davis as "that jangled bundle of nerve endings in human form" who had singlehandedly ended one life and ruined numerous others. "He has made innocent people suffer, and, truly, the honorable way out would be for him to commit suicide. It's the least he could do to alleviate our pain...And Mr. Davis, when you get to where you are going, say hello to Dahmer, and say hello to Bundy. Good riddance. The sooner you get there, the better we all are."

Davis was then given a chance to make a statement. He took the opportunity to accuse Mike Meese and Larry Pelton of making an investigative "error" that violated his Miranda rights. "If the investigators of this case had provided me a lawyer as I had asked for during the [first] interrogation...my lawyers would not have had to admit to the guilt of certain charges against me." If it hadn't been for that "error," he said, "my lawyers and I could and would have presented a regular jury trial scenario claiming no guilt to all the charges against me."

He ended by addressing Polly's family. "To Eve Nichol and her family, for what it's worth, I do offer my sincere apology. To certain members of the Klaas family, I also offer the same. I would also like to state for the record that the main reason I know that I did not attempt any lewd act that night was because of the statement the young girl made to me when walking her up the embankment: 'Just don't do me like my dad.'"

Marc lunged at Davis. "Burn in hell, Davis!" he screamed. "You fucker! *Fucker!*"

"Well," Judge Hastings said, "you've just made my job a lot easier."

The jury sentenced Davis to death by lethal injection. The judge upheld their decision. He would spend the rest of his life on Death Row in San Quentin State Penitentiary, awaiting his turn in the green room.*

---

* In 2019, California governor Gavin Newsom imposed a moratorium on executions and closed the death chamber at San Quentin. The death penalty technically still exists in the state, but no executions have taken place there in seventeen years.

chapter forty-two

POLLY'S LEGACY

AWAY FROM THE CAMERAS, OFF THE COAST OF MONTEREY, POLLY'S FAMILY SAID goodbye as her ashes sank into the sea.

Her maternal grandparents paid for a memorial bench on a seaside bluff not far from their home in Pacific Grove, where Polly had loved to play in the surf. The bench overlooked Monterey Bay, where the ashes of her paternal grandparents would one day be scattered. Her father would come here to sit and think, his back resting against the weathered wood inscribed in lieu of a tombstone.

That first summer without Polly, Marc Klaas married Violet Cheer not far from here. As they said their vows in an outdoor ceremony, a pod of dolphins crossed the bay. Marc and Violet planned to have more children, but wouldn't. Polly's room would become a sanctuary of artifacts—stuffed animals, books, clothes, swim goggles hanging from a nail. Violet would come to this room to pray—not praying *for* Polly, but *to* her—asking for consolation and guidance. In some moments, Violet felt a presence that assured her Polly was listening.

Violet kept her administrative job at a real estate agency so Marc would never have to go back to work at his rental car franchise. Instead, he devoted his life to the child-safety movement. Whenever news of a kidnapping broke, he would be there—comforting the victim's parents, talking to the media, and demanding better laws. As David Collins had shown up for Marc, Marc would show up for the next stricken parents, offering the insight and empathy of someone who knew how they felt. Searching for missing children became his therapy and his religion.

Marc didn't believe in God, but he believed in Polly. "Daddy," she had told him, "one day when I'm famous, I'm going to take care of you." Her prediction would, in the saddest way, come true. Because Polly was famous, Mark became famous. Though his fame would never eclipse that of John Walsh, Marc would use it as a platform to fight for change. "The main emotion in my life became rage," he said, and he channeled that rage into action, pushing for laws and policies that he hoped would prevent another Richard Allen Davis from victimizing another Polly. Nearly a year after Polly was "taken," he stood by President Bill Clinton's side as the president signed a federal crime bill that Marc had fought to get passed. Then he went back to his hotel and cried. "I thought I'd have this great feeling of accomplishment," Marc said, "but I didn't. Polly was still dead."

Nothing could bring Polly back, but living with purpose could ameliorate the pain of living without her. Marc wanted Polly to be remembered as "the girl who changed the world." His wish, too, would come true. America's Child would change the world—in ways he could never imagine, in the lives of people he would never meet. As Kate put it just months after losing her friend, "Polly's become a symbol. She's not just our Polly anymore. She's everybody's Polly."

While Marc broadcast his pain and anger, Eve Nichol grieved inwardly and privately, practicing meditation and yoga, retreating from the public eye. She and Allan had gotten back together, and they moved from Petaluma to a small community in Napa Valley. They had two dogs to comfort Annie, who was terrified of sleeping alone and often asked if she would live to be a grown-up. Annie rigged her room with a system of ropes and bells designed to detect intruders.

Their new home was filled with reminders—Polly's drawings, Polly's blanket, and photographs of a dimpled brown-eyed girl with shoulder-length curls. Even on the hardest days, when every breath she took seemed to burn with pain and longing, these mementos brought Eve comfort. Some days, even a sense of peace and lightness.

Instead of working for harsher punishment for criminals like the man who murdered her daughter, Eve directed her energy into programs for kids. She volunteered for Lifeworks Children's Ranch, a nonprofit where abused children could learn to grow plants, take care of animals, and get along with others. "I believe that kids who are well nurtured don't grow up to be violent grown-ups," she said without bitterness, "like Richard Allen Davis."

Eve would begin to write a book about her personal journey, hoping her story would help someone out there wrestling with despair.

"I want to reach out to others in similar situations and try to relieve their suffering, to encourage people to leave the world a little better than it was when they found it."

Not everything happens for a reason. Some horrors reach behind meaning. And yet, beautiful things emerge in spite of the horrors, and sometimes even because of them.

"I never knew there was so much goodness in the world until I came face-to-face with the kind of evil that struck us," Eve reflected. "The spirit of a remarkable child sparked the reunification of a family and a community."

Like Marc, Eve faced a lifetime without Polly. Like Marc, Eve would struggle to heal. But she would find her own way to fill the void. She'd search for light in the darkness.

"You can't grow a new heart," Eve said. "But when you have a big piece torn away, you can either fill it with anger and rage, or you can fill it with love. I just have to try and choose love."

⌒⌒⌒

Two months after Polly was found, on February 7, 1994, the investigators gathered at the Sonoma Mission Inn for a formal debriefing. They wanted to study every aspect of the case.

Post-mortem meetings were not uncommon after a major case, but an eight-hour "after action" review by both police and the FBI was unusual. The idea came from Eddie Freyer, who felt that his team had done many things right, but saw an opportunity to study and learn from what went wrong. Before everyone moved on to different cases, he wanted to record the pivotal decisions and mistakes—not only for their own closure, but for the benefit of others.

The case had been on the radar of Louis Freeh, the director of the FBI, who had stepped into the role exactly one month before Polly was kidnapped. He and other senior leaders were "intensely interested" in the case. "It became very prominent for the FBI and national law enforcement," he said nearly thirty years later. "And it remained very influential in coordinating joint federal–local law enforcement operations for child abduction."

After opening remarks by Petaluma Chief Dennis DeWitt and ASAC Mark Mershon, Freyer stepped up to a slide projector with his second partner, Sergeant Mike Meese. They played Eve Nichol's first 911 call, reviewed Petaluma PD's response to the crime scene, and flipped through slides of photographs taken in the first hours after Polly's abduction. They showed a video of TV news footage, which told the story from beginning to end.

In a series of presentations, agents and officers analyzed and appraised every cog in the investigative machine. The initial all-points bulletin and flaws in the interagency communication system. The use of Rapid Start for assigning and tracking leads. The deployment of SWAT and surveillance teams. The use of polygraph exams, profiling, and victimology. The role and handling of the media to generate tips and volunteers. Rapport with the family and the girls. Collaboration with volunteers and the need for background checks to prevent another Bill Rhodes situation. ERT tools and protocols used at every crime scene. Leadership and administration concerns in a vast and complex case.

At the end of a long day, investigators had a case study of best practices and lessons learned. Individually and sometimes in teams, they would share these insights with agencies that might one day face a kidnapping. Maybe the next child would survive.

ON JULY 2, 1994—six months after Polly Klaas was found—a twelve-year-old girl was kidnapped at knifepoint by a stranger from her home in Lodi, California. Her name was Katie Romanek.

Her parents were out of town, responding to a family emergency across the country. They had left Katie's sixteen-year-old sister, Beth, in charge. Katie had invited a thirteen-year-old friend over to play, and all three girls were home together when a stranger knocked on the door. They opened it and talked to a twenty-four-year-old man who asked about the *For Sale* sign in the yard.

Beth told the man he'd have to talk to a real estate agent. She wrote down the agent's phone number, handed him the slip of paper, then closed and locked the door.

Later, Beth left the house to drive to town and get a pizza. The man knocked again. Katie went to the door and opened it, leaving her friend, Jane,* in the kitchen. The man asked to borrow a phone book, and Katie went to get one. When Katie returned, he had stepped inside the house. As she handed him the phone book, he put a knife to her throat.

"Is this a joke?" Katie said.

"No," he said. "It's not a joke."

Katie alerted Jane, who came out of the kitchen with a knife, for self-defense. When she saw Katie with a blade to her throat, she was so startled she dropped her weapon.

The stranger took the girls upstairs. He tied up Jane with a fan cord and left her in one bedroom and took Katie into the other, where he undressed her. When Beth came home, he heard the alarm system beep. He tied up Katie and headed downstairs.

"Don't scream," he said, "or I'll kill your sister."

When Beth walked in, he put the knife to her throat and led her upstairs to the room with Katie. He undressed Beth and molested both sisters.

When a thud came from the other bedroom, he ran there and found

---

* This is a pseudonym.

it empty. Trying to get untied, Jane had fallen over, causing the thud, and had crawled into a closet.

The stranger thought she'd escaped, and panicked. He grabbed Katie, who was naked, and forced her downstairs at knifepoint. He grabbed the keys to Beth's car, put Katie on the passenger floorboard, and drove away. "Return to Innocence" was playing on her tape deck.

Beth got free and dialed 911. The Lodi police arrived in minutes. The officer called his chief and said, "We have a Polly Klaas kidnapping."

Lodi chief Larry Hansen had been to a Polly Klaas debriefing by the Petaluma PD. He had met Pat Parks and scribbled key points in his notebook:

1. *Notify all agencies and the media immediately.*
2. *Get the FBI involved right away.*
3. *Have a forensic artist sketch a composite of the suspect.*
4. *Call the Polly Klaas Foundation to create a flyer.*

Now Hansen pulled out his notebook and called Pat Parks.

"I have a case just like Polly Klaas," Hansen said. "What should I be doing?"

Parks guided him through the steps. He set up a command post outside of the station to minimize disruption. A library was soon buzzing with one hundred police officers, thirty FBI agents, and hundreds of volunteers.

Instead of relying on a teletype alert that might sit unread for hours, Hansen had an officer work the phones. The officer called every police station, sheriff's office, and fire department within one hundred miles.

A forensic artist interviewed Beth and Jane and drew a composite. Hansen sent the sketch and a photo of Katie to the Polly Klaas Foundation, which quickly designed a flyer. Within hours, 20,000 were printed and plastered around Lodi.

The local media broadcast live updates, which drew hundreds of volunteers. The Polly Klaas Foundation put them to work, first distributing flyers, and later in a ground search.

The Lodi police had a key piece of information that Petaluma police didn't have: an accurate vehicle description. The kidnapper had taken Beth's red Pontiac Fiero, so they also knew the license plate number.

Late that afternoon, a local fire department responded to a plume of smoke rising from a foothill. Thanks to the call from a Lodi cop, they knew about the kidnapping. They ran the plates and linked the car to the abduction.

The kidnapper had driven off a ten-foot cliff, stalling in a field. The catalytic converter ignited the grass, and the smoke had served as a beacon. First responders found the vehicle abandoned, but both of its doors were open: a hopeful sign that Katie was alive to open one.

Lodi had another thing Petaluma didn't have: a suspect. That evening, a Wal-Mart shopper saw a flyer and recognized the composite. The man called his neighbor and told her it looked an awful lot like her son. The mother remembered something disturbing her son had said: Sometimes he fantasized about having his way with young girls. She called the police and told them that her son might be the kidnapper.

Steven Reece Cochran had recently been paroled for arson and was staying at his mom's, about a mile from Katie's house. Lodi police obtained inked prints from the prison. They matched a latent thumbprint lifted from the scrap of paper on which Beth had written the real estate agent's number. When the kidnapper came back for Katie, he'd left it on the kitchen counter.

As dusk fell, investigators discussed a plan to keep the pressure on by searching through the night. Hansen wanted to force the kidnapper to hunker down instead of fleeing. With help from the FBI and other agencies, he unleashed every asset available, from K-9 handlers to helicopters with searchlights.

The strategy worked: The kidnapper stayed put, immersing himself and Katie in the mud of a shallow pond—a tactic he'd heard about in prison to hide from the helicopters and their infrared sensors.

Twenty hours after the abduction, the kidnapper let Katie go.

Hundreds of searchers were canvassing a camel-colored hillside when they spotted a tiny figure walking toward them through the grass.

"There she is!" someone shouted. "There she is!"

She was naked, scared, and streaked with mud. But Katie Romanek was alive.

The kidnapper was caught and arrested nearby. He was convicted on twenty-four felony counts and sentenced to 106 years in prison.

"I believe in my heart the insights they gave me played a huge part in us finding Katie when we did," said Lodi chief Larry Hansen.

Katie reunited with Hansen, who became a close friend and mentor. They began teaching classes together on child abduction. On the twenty-year anniversary of Polly's kidnapping, Katie attended the remembrance and wept. She said she wanted to help other victims of violent crime, to pay forward the efforts of all who had helped her.

"It's why I'm alive—why I wasn't murdered," she said. "That's why I'm here."

In 2018, Katie became a mother. Holding her daughter, she thought about Polly Klaas. In her jewelry box, she kept a button with Polly's smiling face, a keepsake someone had given her after she was rescued. Sometimes Katie would take the button out, hold it in her palm, and look at it for a long time.

"I was found," she'd say. "Because of you."

Epilogue

ON AUGUST 22, 1997—THREE YEARS AFTER POLLY'S DEATH—A TWELVE-YEAR-old girl who had been missing for nine days was found slain in Petaluma. Georgia Leah Moses had deep brown eyes, an old soul, and a seven-year-old sister named Angel. A CalTrans worker fixing a guard rail found her body, naked and strangled, in a grove of trees off Highway 101.

Kate McLean and Gillian Pelham remember Georgia Leah Moses. They remember seeing her face on flyers posted in Petaluma, but they don't recall ever seeing her story on the news. Gillian and Kate were only sixteen, but they recognized something deeply troubling, something that haunts them still: This brown-eyed twelve-year-old girl did not receive the same attention as Polly Klaas or the same response as Katie Romanek. Georgia Leah Moses was Black.

Twenty-six years later, in 2023, Angel Turner is still searching for her sister's killer. As part of her Justice for Georgia campaign, Angel created a podcast with a family friend and advocate. The podcast is titled "They Called Her Georgia Lee." (On her death certificate, on her gravestone, and in the title of the song by Petaluman Tom Waits, her name was misspelled Georgia Lee.)

The lasting impact of the Polly Klaas investigation is overwhelmingly positive, but its legacy must be tempered with context. Consider all the missing kids and teens—before and after Polly—who became household names. Charles Lindbergh, Jr. Adam Walsh. Kevin Collins. Etan Patz. Jacob Wetterling. Amber Swartz-Garcia. Ilene Misheloff. Amber Hagerman. Molly Bish. Jaycee Dugard. Elizabeth Smart. Samantha Runnion. Natalee Holloway. All of them white.

Kate and Gillian recognized that the media are far more likely to cover the stories of missing people if they happen to be white. Especially if they're middle to upper class, female, and attractive. This phenomenon didn't have a name in 1993. Today it's known as Missing White Woman Syndrome. Coined by Sheri Parks, an American Studies professor at the University of Maryland, it was popularized by the late journalist Gwen Ifill, who remarked at a 2004 journalism conference: "If it's a missing white woman, you're going to cover *that*, every day."

Moreover, the media frame these stories in insidiously inequitable ways. Stories about missing white women focus on the lives cut short— daughters, sisters, mothers, wives—and the voids they left behind. Stories about missing people of color tend to focus on a criminal background, an abusive boyfriend, or other factors that diminish their status as victims. Books about crimes against white women tend to reinforce this narrative and this iniquity.

Every life cut short has a story that matters. Every victim deserves their own book. The purpose of this one is to chronicle a seminal investigation that has served as a valuable case study for three decades. Its insights have trained investigators in all disciplines. It has helped to prepare them for a nightmare case that happens—if they are lucky—only once in a long career. Because of what was learned from the Polly Klaas case, many missing kids have been found.

THE POLLY KLAAS investigation became a Hall of Fame case in the FBI's San Francisco division and was closely watched by headquarters. "The case was immensely important to us at the time and was followed very closely," said FBI director Louis Freeh, who implemented a bureau-wide Crimes Against Children program during his tenure. Its stated mission was "to provide a rapid, proactive, and comprehensive ability to counter all threats of abuse and exploitation to children." Members of the Polly Klaas investigative team played a key role in that nationwide effort. Profiler Mary Ellen O'Toole used insights gleaned from Polly's case and from kidnapping experts including Larry Taylor to improve the Bureau's response to child abductions. O'Toole authored the FBI's official kidnapping protocol.

The Polly Klaas investigation didn't just inform the ways we search for and find missing children, but also the way the FBI investigates many other types of crime. Investigative methods tested and proven in this case forever transformed the Bureau's approach to crime scene investigation, forensics, behavioral science, rapid response, and kidnapping protocols.

This case marked the FBI's first use of fluorescent powder and alternate light source. These tools proved their value by identifying the latent palm print, fibers linking four crime scenes, and other evidence essential to the trial. On the day of Polly's memorial, Mark Mershon got a call from Quantico with good news: Based on the results of Polly's case, FBI headquarters had earmarked money to purchase alternate light sources. At a cost of $8,000 per unit, this was a major investment and a big win for the Evidence Response Team.

The ERT concept itself was tested and proven. This was the first major case of the San Francisco ERT—the first such team in the FBI. This team was led by several pioneers who envisioned the ERT concept and fought for its acceptance within a slow-to-change bureaucracy. Tony Maxwell, David Alford, Frank Doyle, Mike Stapleton, and their colleagues proved the effectiveness of quick-responding, local teams trained to process crime scenes, gather trace evidence, and liaise with the FBI lab. The ERT model was subsequently adopted bureau-wide. Members of the San Francisco ERT would apply skills and lessons forged in this case to a number of Bureau Specials, including the Unabomber, the Oklahoma City bombing, and the 2001 World Trade Center attacks. Today, the FBI has more than 1,000 ERT members, and each geographic division has its own dedicated team.

This case also marked the first time an FBI profiler was embedded with an ERT. Mary Ellen O'Toole worked side by side with Tony Maxwell and his team to combine behavioral science with forensic science. "Prior to this case, the two worlds were separate," Maxwell said. "Evidence was sent to the lab and the behavioral scientists would look at it." This combined approach would be repeated in high-profile cases such as the kidnapping of Elizabeth Smart and the disappearance of Natalee Holloway. Tony and Mary Ellen worked together again on the serial murder case of a sexual sadist known as the Toy Box Killer.

Eddie Freyer (left) and Greg Jacobs at the FBI Academy in Quantico, Virginia, 1996.
(COURTESY OF EDDIE FREYER)

The "after-action" debriefing produced a template for case studies taught by many members of the investigative team. After the trial, Eddie Freyer and Greg Jacobs were invited to the FBI Academy in Quantico to present a case study to new FBI agents. Mark Mershon and Pat Parks taught the case on another occasion in Quantico and in several other venues.

Eddie Freyer continues to use the case in investigative interview and interrogation courses at the Behavioral Analysis Training Institute (BATI) as well as major case management classes for California's Peace Officer Standards and Training (POST). He is asked to give his Polly Klaas presentation an average of once a month, in places as far-flung as Macedonia and Iraq, to audiences as big as 300 people. In nearly three decades of doing this, he estimates he has taught the case to several thousand people.

Sergeant Mike Meese became a criminal justice instructor at Santa Rosa Junior College, where he used the confession tape in his class. Pat Parks, promoted to Petaluma chief in 1997, took the lessons learned and "shared them far and wide," over the years to a collective audience of thousands. Tony Maxwell, Frank Doyle, David Alford, and Mike Stapleton use elements of the case in forensic classes. Mary Ellen O'Toole* retired from the FBI in 2009 and became director of the forensic science program at George Mason University, where she incorporates parts of this case and others into her courses.

Some of the tragic twists of the case were used to spur big changes. Communication between federal and local law enforcement officials was streamlined and improved. Computers were put in patrol cars, so officers could look up a suspect's prior arrests and convictions in real time.

One of the biggest lessons of the case—the handling of child witnesses—inspired major changes. Today, child witnesses and victims are interviewed by trained experts, a major investigative change that accelerated after this case. In 1996, the American Professional Society on the Abuse of Children (APSAC) held the nation's first child forensic interviewing clinic. A new kind of specialist emerged: child and adolescent forensic interviewers (CAFIs). Though they work closely with law enforcement agencies, CAFIs are typically civilians trained through an internationally recognized, research-based curriculum developed by the National Children's Advocacy Center.

CAFIs use research-based protocols for interviewing young witnesses and victims. The interviews take place in "soft rooms" with cozy love seats, child-sized coloring tables, and artwork on the walls. Their protocols emphasize free narratives—"Start at the beginning and go all the way to the end..."—instead of interrogation-style questions and interruptions for clarification. Their policy prohibits polygraph tests and starts with the assumption that the witness is being truthful.

Today, the FBI has a Child Victim Services program (part of the greater Victims Services Division) that supports child victims and witnesses of federal crimes and also trains local law enforcement in how to

---

* Mary Ellen O'Toole recently established a "body farm" at George Mason University, where forensic science students study decomposing human remains in an outdoor forensic lab. She frequently appears in the news, providing expert commentary on psychopathy and serial killers.

treat them properly. Their coordinators work to ensure that any interviews and interactions are tailored to minimize additional trauma and appropriate for the child's developmental stage. The FBI program has grown from three CAFIs in 2001 to twenty-two CAFIs and three supervisors nationwide in 2023. The unit chief has conducted more than 10,000 interviews.

⌒‿⌒

POLLY'S KIDNAPPING ALSO influenced changes outside of law enforcement. Suburban America was starting to feel unsafe, a trend that started before Polly Klaas and escalated after her death. "Stranger danger"—real and perceived—triggered a major shift in social behavior in the 1990s and beyond. Neighborhood parks and playgrounds began to see fewer kids. Families installed alarm systems or adopted a guard dog. Children were kept inside on sunny days, no longer allowed to walk a few blocks to the corner store or a friend's house. Staying home and playing video games felt like a safer alternative. The days of free-range childhood were vanishing.

"This used to be a good little town," said a twelve-year-old girl who had acted with Polly in a local production of *Annie*. "Now it's...I don't know what." Whether she was parroting her parents or truly aware of this major shift, her sentiment reflected what people were feeling in Petaluma—and nationwide. As one local high schooler put it, "All the kids around here, they're scared to go out and play."

The day after Polly's memorial, in a suburb of St. Louis, a group of children stumbled upon the body of a slain ten-year-old girl. Cassidy Senter was the second victim of a suspected child serial killer, and parents were terrified. They started patrolling neighborhood streets that had once felt safe. Kids were afraid. Parents were afraid. One twenty-one-year-old woman was afraid to take out the trash. "We're all in a quiet state of panic," said a mother of two. "I don't know how much more of this we can take."

This atmosphere of public fear became an incubator for public policies that would change the nature of crime and punishment in America.

IT'S IMPOSSIBLE TO talk about Polly's legacy without talking about three-strikes laws.

The day after Polly was found, California governor Pete Wilson called for tougher sentences for child molesters and sex offenders as "a fitting memorial for Polly Klaas." Wilson proposed life sentences for a second conviction for rape, child molestation, and other violent sex crimes. He argued that if his proposal had already been in effect, Richard Allen Davis would not have been paroled, and Polly would still be alive. "Child molesters should get automatic prison time," Wilson said. "Repeat sex offenders should spend the rest of their lives behind bars."

That same day, in a separate news conference in another part of Sacramento, Attorney General Dan Lungren announced his support for an anti-crime initiative called "Three Strikes, You're Out." The law would imprison repeat offenders after three felonies.

These tough-on-crime initiatives and harsher sentencing laws were supported by people across the political spectrum. Fueled by public outrage and fear, they addressed the mounting cries from citizens who felt that the system had failed Polly. They didn't feel safe, and they demanded change. Here are just a few comments from Petaluma residents in the days after Polly was found:

"I'm angry at that man, angry at the system, angry at the laws of this state. Why was he out there? Why was he ever released from prison? Why wasn't he caught?"

"I have a lot of anger at the criminal justice system. This should never have happened and we're going to work to see if we can't change some of these things."

"I've got a twelve-year-old daughter. You think about those people being allowed to get to the point to be free and do it over and over again."

"That makes no sense to me, especially because he has two prior kidnappings. I think it's obscene that a person like that was out on the streets."

Polly's fate was a catalyst for the passage of three-strikes laws, which imposed severe mandatory sentences for repeat offenders. The laws varied some from state to state, but generally mandated a life sentence upon conviction of a third felony. The first three-strikes law was passed in Washington state in 1993. The second was passed in California in 1994, right after Polly's death, when California voters passed it with a 72 percent majority. The concept spread. By 2004, similar laws had been passed in twenty-four states, although none with consequences as harsh as in California.

Under California's three-strikes law, defendants who have been convicted of two or more violent felonies were required to be sentenced to an "indeterminate term of life imprisonment." In other states, there remains much variability in the application of three strikes, not only at the state level, but also county to county, courtroom to courtroom. For example, Maryland dictates that any person who receives a fourth "strike" will automatically be sentenced to life in prison without parole. Some states include lesser offenses as strikes even if they are not necessarily seen as violent. Other instances of "strike" offenses in California include, but are not limited to, firearm violations, simple robbery, and drug possession.

The original intent of these laws was to lock up violent repeat offenders for good, with the hope of preventing tragedies like the murder of Polly Klaas. The initial three-strikes law proposed to California voters mandated a minimum twenty-five-year* sentence that perpetrators would have to serve before potentially becoming parole-eligible, although the majority of those incarcerated would remain behind bars for life.

However, the initial changes in the legislature did not bring about the desired change when the three-strikes law was first envisioned. A 1997 review found that the three-strikes law did not decrease the

---

* Prior to California's initial three-strikes law, an existing habitual offender statute was in effect. Under this law, offenders convicted for a third violent offense (and who had served separate prison terms for the first two convictions) were given a mandatory life sentence, with the first parole eligibility after twenty years. Upon a fourth conviction (if three separate prison terms were served) the offender received a mandatory sentence of life without parole. The three-strikes law did not require the offender to serve prison time in order for a first or second felony to count as one of the three strikes. It also did not require that the third strike be a violent felony.

rates of serious crime (or even the rates of petty crime). A 2001 study corroborated these findings, emphasizing the lack of discrimination of cases on the basis of "dangerousness." As a result, under three strikes, more people than ever were being incarcerated, and for less severe crimes.

The American Civil Liberties Union argues that repeat offenders who might have committed lesser crimes—but know they're on their third strike—might resort to more escalated, violent means when faced with law enforcement. In a 2015 study, the three-strikes law was confirmed as being "associated with a 33 percent increase in the risk of fatal assaults on law enforcement officials."

In 2003, the Justice Policy Institute found that almost two-thirds of individuals sentenced to life in prison under California law were sentenced for nonviolent offenses. Additionally, it reported that America's incarceration rate increased more in the 1990s than in any other previous decade of American history. California incarcerated roughly four times the number of individuals under its application of the three-strikes law when compared to all the other states using some variation of three strikes. According to Stanford Law's Three Strikes Project, this application of the law in California is believed to not only fuel the problem of mass incarceration in America, but also contribute to the disproportionate number of people of color in prison.

Statistics from the California Department of Corrections show that the law has been disproportionately applied not only to people of color, but also to mentally ill and physically disabled defendants. California's state auditor also estimated that the implementation of the three-strikes law added more than $19 billion to the state's prison budget alone. For the most part, criminologists agree that public safety is not improved by removing nonviolent repeat offenders from society, and the cost is more than just financial.

Over the past several years, changes have been made to the law at both the state and federal level to standardize the usage of the law more than in the past. With the passage in California of Proposition 36 in 2012, defendants may now plead "cruel and unusual punishment" in some instances where three strikes may not be appropriate sentencing.

Marc Klaas initially fought for the passage of three-strikes laws. "We believe that people at this point have had enough!" he said in 1994. "They don't want to see this kind of thing happen to the children anymore, and Polly has become a symbol of some of the things that are wrong with this country." Over time, he distanced himself from the original language of the three-strikes law and has been a strong advocate of revisions to help keep the initial intentions of the legislation while also addressing some of its unwanted impact.

Meanwhile, Polly's sisters, Annie and Jess Nichol, recently emerged, after decades out of the spotlight, to publicly and respectfully disagree. In October 2020, Annie and Jess published an op-ed in the *Los Angeles Times* that articulated their position.

"As Polly's sisters, it is difficult to fathom how these laws became our sister's legacy," they wrote. "The beauty of Polly's life shouldn't be overshadowed by this pervasive injustice." Noting that people incarcerated under three strikes "are overwhelmingly Black and Latino," they argued such laws "have significantly contributed to mass incarceration...and have exacerbated the systemic racism inherent in our justice system." Annie and Jess made a case for prevention: programs that help underserved communities through job training, support, rehabilitation, and reintegration into society. "Clearly," they wrote, "incarcerating our way to safety doesn't work."

The three-strikes law has many nuances and amendments attached to its thirty-year history. As a result, there are many books dedicated specifically to understanding it both within the context of its inception and how it is currently applied. Two that expound upon the highlights mentioned here are Joe Domanick's *Cruel Justice: Three Strikes and the Politics of Crime in America's Golden State* and Franklin E. Zimring's *Punishment and Democracy: Three Strikes and You're Out in California*.

Two ENDURING POSITIVE examples of Polly's legacy are the Polly Klaas Foundation and the KlaasKids Foundation, two distinct nonprofit organizations that support the families of missing children.

Marc Klaas was on the founding board of directors for the Polly

Klaas Foundation, a 501(c)(3) organization created in November 1993, when Polly was still missing. Marc and the PKF parted ways when he established the KlaasKids Foundation in 1994. With a mission of stopping crimes against children, KlaasKids advocates for stronger sentencing laws for violent criminals, prevention programs for at-risk youth, and governmental accountability.

Thirty years later, the Polly Klaas Foundation continues to thrive. The founders and original board members have mostly moved on after serving years in those roles. But they take great pride in what they created. "It's one of the most significant things I've ever done in my life," said Jay Silverberg, the former newspaper editor who worked closely with Joanne Gardner and Gaynell Rogers, and who later sat on the board of the Polly Klaas Foundation. "Aside from my kids, there's nothing else I could do with that much impact, that kind of legacy."

Funded predominantly by donations, the Polly Klaas Foundation is never "closed." Parents and law enforcement officials can call their hotline any hour of the day, any day of the week, 365 days a year to receive live and real-time assistance in responding to the disappearance of a child. Caseworkers provide ongoing support to families, from instructions on searching for their children, designing missing-child posters, and working with local businesses and law enforcement. Their Rapid Response Team volunteers provide a nationwide network of "feet on the street," able to quickly print and hang missing-child posters in towns and cities nationwide. They support some families for years or even decades. As executive director Raine Howe likes to say, "There's no such thing as false hope."

Over the past three decades, the Polly Klaas Foundation estimates it has helped the families of 10,000 missing children. They handle an average of 300 missing-child cases a year, which include runaways and parental custody struggles as well as the rarer stranger abductions. According to caseworker Cindy Rudometkin, 95 percent of their cases are resolved with a missing child located safely.

At Polly's twenty-year remembrance in 2013, Eve Nichol told the foundation she didn't want another event that focused on how Polly died. If they wanted to honor Polly's memory, why not celebrate how she lived? The foundation members took this to heart. In 2022, after decades of planning and fundraising, they opened the Polly Klaas Community Theater, a 110-seat theater housed in a renovated 1911 church in Petaluma.

"We're never going to forget what happened to Polly," Howe said, "but we can start shifting our minds toward her life instead of toward the tragedy of her [death.]"

Eddie Freyer, who now sits on the board of directors, attended the grand opening in 2022. Polly's family was not present, but Polly's spirit was, in the twirling skirts of young dancers and the song of a local chorus. The stage's curtains are purple, Polly's favorite color.

One of the foundation's veteran employees is Jenni Thompson, the college student who, at twenty-two, volunteered to answer phones in the first days after Polly's abduction. After the case, Jenni was hired by the Polly Klaas Foundation as a full-time caseworker. She later became an FBI agent assigned to child trafficking, but ultimately returned to the foundation to continue her work to find missing kids.

Jenni Thompson was the driving force behind getting the Amber Alert law passed in California. The bill kept sitting on the governor's desk and then expiring. After several frustrating rounds of this, she told the governor, "Sign this bill before the next kid goes missing." The very next day, a child went missing. Jenni recruited a TV news crew to film her standing in front of the Capitol and sharing this information, calling the governor out. The bill was signed the next day. Jenni went on to get the Amber Alert system passed in all fifty states. Now, at age fifty-two, Thompson is getting a law degree so she can keep working on laws to protect kids. On the course of her life and work, she says: "It's all because of Polly."

Acknowledgments

No book gets written without a constellation of supporters. At the center of it is family. My husband, Eddie Freyer, Jr., encouraged me to tackle this story, then helped me to survive it, picking up the slack whenever I had to leave town to report or write. My father-in-law, Eddie Freyer, Sr., entrusted me with his legacy and unlocked countless doors to make this book possible. My mom, Joyce Cross, feeds me, supports me unconditionally, and never questioned my goal of making words for a living. My late father and first editor, Ken Cross, taught me: *If you're going to be a writer, you need a callus on your psyche an inch thick.* My son, Austin, gifted me with unbidden hugs, noise-cancelling headphones, and unquestioned understanding when I needed to disappear for weeks-long writing retreats. Sue Freyer is always there to listen and talk. Sandy Freyer-Ashe and Dan Ashe remind me it's important to stop working and make memories. Tina, Lauren, Jason, Aleshia, Ashley, and Carrie taught me how to be a sister.

I'm grateful for the insights and efforts of my editorial team: my editor, Colin Dickerman; my agent, Leslie Meredith of Dystel, Goderich & Bourret; and Rachael Kelly, Ian Dorset, and Roxanne Jones at Grand Central. I can never adequately thank my research director, Meg Levi, for scanning and organizing tens of thousands of documents, joining me for eleven days of intense reporting, and keeping me laughing and sane. I was so fortunate to have research/reporting and fact-checking support from Naheed Attari, Bronwen Dickey, Josh Sharpe, Allison Baggott-Rowe, Alex Baggott, Lynn Dickey, and Augusta Jones. Michael Hicks and Art Meripol helped me with image scanning and prep.

I don't know how I would get through any story without the help, advice, and emotional support of my narrative tribe: Bronwen Dickey, Elisabeth Sharp McKetta, Kelly Myers, Amy Wallace, Glenn Stout, Leah Flickinger, Kathryn Miles, Latria Graham, Rocky Barker, Cort Conley, Tommy Tomlinson, Josh Sharpe, Mike Wilson, Kelley Benham French, Ben Montgomery, Thomas Lake, Michael Kruse, Melissa Segura, Jacqui Banaszynski, Chip Scanlan, Rick Bragg, Tanner Latham, Kim Girard, Naheed Attari, Jim Daly, George Getschow, J. Reuben Appelman, and the entire Auburn Chautauqua crew.

This book would not be comprehensive, accurate, or possible without the many detectives, police officers, sheriff's deputies, and other law enforcement agents who worked hard to help me get it right. Special thanks to Eddie Freyer, Greg Jacobs, Tony Maxwell, and Vail Bello for sticking with me for seven years, guiding me through the complicated world of investigations, explaining technical matters (over and over), and unlocking doors to other sources. A special eagle-eye editing award goes to David Alford and Mark Mershon, who caught many, many [sic] repetitions, typos, errors, and highly nuanced inaccuracies. Andy Mazzanti and Pat Parks provided thoughtful feedback, prayer support, and mental-health check-ins. Barry Collins, Brian Bianco, and Greg Cahill provided insights and essential, hard-to-find documents.

I am grateful for the candor and rigor of FBI agents Mary Ellen O'Toole, Tom LaFreniere, Frank Doyle, Mike Stapleton, Larry Taylor, Lillian Zilius, Ron Homer, Ron Hilley, Phil Buvia, Doug Deedrick, Bruce Burroughs, Phil Sena, Joe Davidson, John "JC" Steiner, Dominic Gizzi, Joe Hisquierdo, Elisabeth Castaneda, Chris Allen, Denise Ballew, Tina Jagerson, and Louis Freeh.

In addition to those listed above, the members of Petaluma PD have my deep respect and gratitude, especially Larry Pelton, Dennis

Nowicki, Dave Long, Mike Kerns, Danny Fish, Gene Wallace, Matt Stapleton, Eric Greenband, Roy Loden, and Peggy Swearington. I never got to meet the late Mike Meese, but I did meet his wife, Michelle Meese, and his son, Frank Meese, who helped me learn more about him. I'm also thankful for help from Mike Rankin, Larry Hansen, Tom Letras, Scott Long, Jim Gong, and Mike Percuoco.

Outside of law enforcement but central to the story were many wonderful individuals who enriched the narrative and my experience: Gillian Pelham and Kate McLean; Jeanne Boylan; Dana and Kelila Jaffe; Jay Silverberg, Joanne Gardner, and Gaynell Rogers; Larry Magid, Gary Judd, Bill Gabbert, Brian Sobel, Trisha Stretch, and Scott Morrison.

The Polly Klaas Foundation supported me fully, especially Raine Howe, Jenni Thompson, and Cindy Rudometkin. Fellow journalists generously helped me: Greg Cahill from the *Petaluma Argus-Courier*; Mary Callahan and Randi Rossman from the *Santa Rosa Press Democrat* (whose daily news coverage of the kidnapping and trial was exceptional); Anne Belden, a journalist, author, and college journalism instructor who provided me with a hard-to-find copy of the confession tape; Michelle Hord, and Phil Lerman, who worked for *America's Most Wanted*; Paul Payne, Paige St. John, and Paula Harris.

I am deeply thankful to Ruth and David for hosting me on many writing retreats in the mountains, and to my mountain-town friends who looked after me when I was away from my family: Jesse and Emily Dwyer, Ronda and Jim Bishop, and Heidi and Matt Galyardt.

Notes

Every scene, conversation, and narrative element in this book is based on meticulously reported facts verified and corroborated with reliable sources. Nothing is made up. There are no liberties, no flourishes, no imaginative touches other than logical inferences framed with uncertainty: *maybe, suppose, perhaps.*

The majority of the dialogue—particularly interviews by agents and detectives—is based on audio recordings and transcripts recorded in 1993. I edited this dialogue as minimally as possible, mostly cutting for length and to remove redundancy and verbal tics.

In some scenes the dialogue was recollected by sources who said it or overheard it. Recollected dialogue is never as reliable as a recording, because human memory is highly malleable and erodes with the passage of time. That said, the content of the conversation can still be highly accurate, even if the wording isn't verbatim.

When multiple sources recollected the same dialogue (such as the trial testimony of Eve, Kate, and Gillian recounting things said in Chapter 1), I corroborated and intertwined their memories. I favored memories recorded as closely as possible to the event, for example, 1993 interviews versus 1996 trial testimony. In some cases, I had no other source but interviews conducted decades after the event. Whenever possible I corroborated with multiple sources or looked for consistency when a source recounted a conversation consistently in multiple interviews.

The timeline and specific details came largely from primary-source documents, such as police reports, FD-302s (written reports used internally by the FBI), teletypes, and other dated documents originating in 1993. This timeline formed the backbone of the investigative story. On top of that I layered events and dates from secondary sources, such as newspaper articles and TV news clips. In my experience, human sources recollecting highly emotional events tend to remember the details fairly accurately but get the timing and sequence wrong. Or they merge disparate events into one moment in their memory. The timeline and documents helped me fact-check memories recounted in interviews decades later.

Most investigative journalists will be shocked to learn that I never filed a Freedom of Information Act (FOIA) request. I didn't have to, and good thing: The FBI is notorious for declining FOIA requests for case files and internal documents. I'm almost positive it would have been a waste of my time. My requests to the Santa Clara County Courthouse certainly were: Despite more than a year of requests and follow-ups, they failed to send a single requested document or exhibit from the trial—public records that require no FOIA.

Thankfully, a number of FBI agents, detectives, reporters, community members, volunteers, witnesses, and one juror did a deep dive into attics and garages. They entrusted me with cardboard boxes filled with case files, photos, videotapes, audiotapes, and other artifacts they'd been saving for nearly three decades. Some agents and detectives even let me look at their personal logbooks and handwritten notes.

District attorney Greg Jacobs granted me unrestricted access to his personal Polly Klaas archives, including 10,000 pages of trial transcripts, binders of newspaper clippings, photo albums of crime scene photos, and six or seven banker's boxes of documents from the case and the trial. He also gave me unlimited access to his memory, which proved to be one of the most accurate and comprehensive of anyone I have ever interviewed.

EPIGRAPH

"Polly, Alive in Memory." *People*, Sept. 22, 2003, 187.

Kirk, Paul Leland. *Crime Investigation: Physical Evidence and the Police Laboratory*. New York: Interscience Publishers, Inc., 1953.

CHAPTER 1: THE SLEEPOVER

Andy Mazzanti's interview with Kate and Dennis Nowicki's interview with Gillian were recorded and transcribed, preserved in police files. In the case of minor discrepancies between the official transcript and the audio recording, I used the audio recording. I corroborated the dialogue, facts, and sequence with 1996 trial testimony by Eve Nichol, Gillian Pelham, Kate McLean, and Alice McLean. Some details came from an FBI FD-302 report written by Larry Taylor, summarizing an interview with Eve Nichol.

The pizza delivery from Domino's was based on the list of people to be interviewed handwritten on the butcher paper that hung in the command center on the night of the abduction, preserved in Vail Bello's personal archives.

The character sketch of Polly was based largely on a recorded and transcribed three-hour interview with Eve Nichol by Mary Ellen O'Toole on October 16, 1993. The presence of her baby teeth was apparent in photographs of her skull and confirmed visually by FBI lab examiner Chris Allen, who worked in Hair and Fibers but who also worked as a dentist before and after his FBI career. Polly's a cappella singing of "Somewhere Out There" was recorded on an audio cassette collected as evidence and stored in police files. Based on evidence collection reports that noted only the first minutes of this song, it's not clear whether her singing was ever heard.

Gillian Pelham read and assisted in the fact-checking of this chapter and confirmed certain descriptions, such as the sadness in Eve's eyes even before Polly was kidnapped. She offered some additional details never reported, such as Polly's reaction at seeing herself in the mirror with makeup and Polly's first kiss.

Alford, David. FD-302. October 4,1993.

Butcher paper with handwritten leads, October 1, 1993. Vail Bello's personal archives.

McLean, Alice. Trial testimony. *People v. Richard Allen Davis*, April 17, 1996.

McLean, Kate. Trial testimony. *People v. Richard Allen Davis*, April 17, 1996.

Nichol, Eve. Interview by Mary Ellen O'Toole, October 16, 1993. Audio recording and transcription. Case files.

Nichol, Eve. Trial testimony. *People v. Richard Allen Davis*, April 17, 1996.

Pelham, Gillian. Trial testimony. *People v. Richard Allen Davis*, April 17, 1996.

Pelham, Gillian. Interview by Kim Cross via Zoom, Manchester, England, and Boise, Idaho, December 21, 2022.

Pendle, George. "The California Town That Was Famous for Eggs and Arm Wrestling." *Slate*, January 17, 2017.

Reed, Eugene. Victim impact statement by Polly's maternal grandfather, September 9, 1996.

Taylor, Larry. FD-302, October 2, 1993.

Taylor, Larry. FD-302, October 3, 1993.

CHAPTER 2: THE STRANGER

Just hours after the kidnapping, Kate and Gillian were interviewed separately at Petaluma PD by Dennis Nowicki and Andy Mazzanti. After the interviews concluded, the tape recorder was left running while the girls reunited and spoke to each other. This recording was the basis for the scenes and dialogue in this chapter. I corroborated this dialogue with recollected dialogue recounted by Kate, Gillian, and Eve during their trial testimony in 1996. The recollected dialogue varied slightly, but the facts, details, and sequence remained very consistent.

There were a few very small discrepancies. On the night of the kidnapping, Kate told Nowicki that Davis told them to "Get the fuck down on the floor." Interviewed in 2022, Gillian didn't remember him using profanity. Kate deferred to Gillian's memory.

A few details came from police reports and files, such as the number of rivets in the knife. Some police reports noted two rivets, but Kate's drawing of the knife featured three. In the press, it was reported that Polly offered thirty dollars in her jewelry box. An FD-302 for evidence collected said it was twenty-five dollars.

Gillian reviewed this chapter for accuracy.

FD-302, October 6, 1993.

Mazzanti, Andy. Interview by Kim Cross via phone.

McLean, Alice. Trial testimony. *People v. Richard Allen Davis*, April 17, 1996.

McLean, Kate. Interview by Dennis Nowicki at Petaluma PD, October 2, 1993. Audio recording and transcription.

McLean, Kate. Trial testimony. *People v. Richard Allen Davis*, April 17, 1996.

Nichol, Eve. Trial testimony. *People v. Richard Allen Davis*, April 17, 1996.

Nowicki, Dennis. Interview by Kim Cross via FaceTime, December 20, 2022. Audio recording.

Pelham, Gillian. Interview by Andy Mazzanti at Petaluma PD, October 2, 1993. Audio recording and transcription.

Pelham, Gillian. Trial testimony. *People v. Richard Allen Davis*, April 17, 1996.

Pelton, Larry. Interview by Kim Cross at his house in Emmett, Idaho, May 5, 2022.

Pelton, Larry. Email to Kim Cross, November 16, 2022.

CHAPTER 3: THE FIRST HOUR

As he prepared to move to another state, Vail Bello dug out of his garage a banker's box of documents and case-related paraphernalia that he'd been saving for thirty years. This box was filled with unexpected treasures, including the butcher paper that hung on the command center walls in the first hours of the investigation. From the leads handwritten on the butcher paper, I deciphered the investigators' very first instincts, thoughts, and steps.

The box also included the "possibilities chart" that Tom LaFreniere had mapped out in red pen, a logical branching-out of possible options and subsequent outcomes.

Research director Meg Levi listened to the tape repeatedly and corrected errors and unintelligible words on the transcript. That transcript was used nearly in full in this chapter and very close to verbatim, except for a few minor cuts for length and verbal tics.

The call was not audibly time-stamped, but several sources, including the *Los Angeles Times* and the *Ukiah Daily Journal* reported that the call was placed at 11:03 p.m., citing a law enforcement timeline.

When Eve put Kate on the phone with the 911 dispatcher, Kate said they were asked to count to "ten thousand," and this is reflected in the audio recording and the transcript of the call. I edited it to "one thousand," which was consistent in nearly every other interview and recollection.

Additional details were recounted in personal interviews with Danny Fish (who was the chief at Petaluma PD when we first spoke in 2016) and Vail Bello on numerous occasions between 2015 and 2023. Bello, who is working on a crime novel, served as an early reader and helped me fact-check.

Bello, Vail. Interview by Kim Cross, Sebastopol, California, February 2, 2016.

Bello, Vail. Interview by Kim Cross, via phone, May 19, 2021.

Bello, Vail. Interview by Kim Cross, via phone, February 16, 2022.

Bello, Vail. Interview by Kim Cross, Sebastopol, California, March 17, 2022.

Fish, Danny. Interviews by Kim Cross, Petaluma, California, 2015 and 2022.

"How It Happened: Timeline of Events." *Santa Rosa Press Democrat,* December 12, 1993.

Nichol, Eve. 911 call, audio recording, October 1, 1993. Cassette tape, Petaluma police files.

Nichol, Eve. Trial testimony. *People v. Richard Allen Davis,* April 17, 1996.

Paddock, Richard C., and Jennifer Warren. "Revelations in Klaas Kidnapping Spark Outrage." *Los Angeles Times,* December 3, 1993.

"Two Months: The Polly Klaas Case." *Santa Rosa Press Democrat,* December 3, 1993.

CHAPTER 4: THE TRESPASSER

This scene was based on the trial testimony of Dana Jaffe and her daughter Kelila, Shannon Lynch, Mike Rankin, and Tom Howard. I took no liberties with the dialogue, though it may not be verbatim: It was 1996 when they took the witness stand and quoted dialogue spoken three years earlier.

On the night of the trespassing call, Sonoma County sheriff's deputies Tom Howard and Mike Rankin filled out an "FI" (field incident report), a brief documentation of their contact with Davis. Because there was no citation or arrest, a full police report was not required. Two months later, when Dana Jaffe reported the suspicious items found on her property, Howard and Rankin were asked to write a supplemental report, based on their memories of that night. Some of the details in this chapter came from those reports.

A number of 1993 newspaper stories incorrectly reported that the All Points Bulletin was broadcast over law enforcement Channel One and the deputies did not hear it because they were tuned to Channel Three. The *New Yorker* and the *New York Times* reported the situation accurately: The APB had not been broadcast at all by the Sonoma County Sheriff's Office dispatcher, who read the "Not for Media Release" instructions on the APB and interpreted it as instructions not to broadcast the APB over the radio. Mike Rankin confirmed this with me.

Howard and Rankin were excoriated in the press after the media learned of their encounter with Davis on the night of Polly's abduction. Few or none of the news reports addressed the legal constraints that prohibited them from arresting Davis.

The most widely misunderstood element of the encounter was the legal requirement of a citizen's arrest. As the law was written, officers could not arrest an offender for a misdemeanor crime they had not witnessed. This begs the question: Was he not in the act of committing a misdemeanor (trespassing) when they encountered him on Dana Jaffe's property? Not exactly. In order to arrest a trespasser (a misdemeanor that by nature takes place on private property), the property owner must first issue a citizen's arrest. Only then can law enforcement officers legally arrest the trespasser. Dana Jaffe did not want the stranger arrested for trespassing. She just wanted him off her property.

Mike Rankin explained this to me in a phone call from his home in Oregon. He agreed to speak to me "on background," preferring not to be quoted but willing to answer questions and help me fact-check my account to ensure it was accurate and fair. I later confirmed my understanding of the situation and law with at least five other law enforcement officers (both related and unrelated to this case) as well as district attorney Greg Jacobs. Dana Jaffe told me in 2023 that she doesn't recall any mention of a citizen's arrest being explained to her in 1993.

"Abducted Girl Found Dead Is Mourned in California." *New York Times*, December 6, 1993.

Howard, Thomas. Trial testimony. *People v. Richard Allen Davis*, April 24, 1996.

Jaffe, Dana. 911 call, October 2, 1993. Transcript in police files.

Jaffe, Kelila. Trial testimony. *People v. Richard Allen Davis*, April 23, 1996.

Jaffe, Dana. Trial testimony. *People v. Richard Allen Davis*, April 23–24, 1996.

Jaffe, Dana. Interview by Kim Cross at Pythian site, March 20, 2022.

Jaffe, Dana. Fact-checking call with Kim Cross by phone, April 4, 2022.

Jaffe, Kelila. Interview by Kim Cross via Zoom from Auckland, New Zealand, April 12, 2023.

Lynch, Shannon. Trial testimony. *People v. Richard Allen Davis*, April 23, 1996.

McManus, Mike. Trial testimony. *People v. Richard Allen Davis*, April 29, 1996.

Nichol, Eve. Message to Community. *Santa Rosa Press Democrat*, December 6, 1993.

Rankin, Mike. Trial testimony. *People v. Richard Allen Davis*, April 24, 1996.

Rankin, Mike. Interviews (on background) by Kim Cross via phone from his home in Oregon, March, 2022; January 15, 2023.

Toobin, Jeffrey. "The Man Who Kept Going Free." *New Yorker*, February 27, 1994.

"Two Months: The Polly Klaas Case." *Santa Rosa Press Democrat*, December 3, 1993.

"We Should Grieve All Victims." Editorial, *Ukiah Daily Journal*, December 6, 1993.

CHAPTER 5: THE CASE AGENT

The timing of certain events on October 1–2, 1993, was difficult to verify, even with case files. In most instances, if a police report or other document authored in 1993 conflicted with an individual's memory decades later, I deferred to the document. However, I encountered many instances when different documents contained conflicting information, which may be the result of typos, inaccurate estimations, or human error.

For example: An FBI teletype dated October 4, 1993, summarized the events of October 1, 1993, and stated, "FBI was notified at 2 a.m. and arrived on scene at 3 a.m. FBI ERT arrived at approximately 3:30 a.m." Interviews with Eddie Freyer, Vail Bello, Tom LaFreniere, Tony Maxwell, David Alford, Danny Fish, and other agents and officers present on scene collectively disputed the times noted on the

FD-302. Freyer and LaFreniere recall arriving at Polly's house around 1:30 a.m., and Vail Bello's memory supports this. Tony Maxwell's trial testimony indicated he arrived around 5:30 a.m., but another document said 4:30 a.m. All he could remember for certain was that it was not yet light outside.

The character sketch of Eddie Freyer came largely from seven years of formal (recorded) interviews and two decades of informal conversations with Eddie Freyer, my father-in-law for twenty years. I also interviewed a number of his colleagues from the FBI and Petaluma PD. Vail Bello, Tom LaFreniere, Mary Ellen O'Toole, Jeanne Boylan, Ron Hilley, JC Steiner, Phil Sena, and others helped to paint a portrait of him in 1993.

The dialogue in this chapter was largely recollected in interviews conducted two to three decades after it was spoken, so it likely isn't verbatim. However, I tried to "triangulate the truth" by interviewing people multiple times, independently and together, and corroborating the most consistent recollections. In many cases, certain lines and anecdotes were repeated many times to me in different interviews over seven years. Vail Bello in particular was surprisingly consistent in recollecting dialogue: His recitation in 2016 was almost an exact match for his recollection in 2023.

The 1993 abduction statistics in this chapter were tricky to fact-check. The estimate of 200 to 300 stranger abductions a year was published in a 1993 *New York Times* article and attributed to Ernie Allen, then head of the National Center for Missing and Exploited Children, the authority on such figures. The same story said that there had been thirty-seven stranger abductions (including Polly and others) between August and December 1993. A current NCMEC spokesperson was unable to verify the source of Allen's statistics, but offered the following figures for 1993: Of 3,124 missing children reported to NCMEC between 1990 and 1993, 65 percent were endangered runaways, 30 percent were family abductions, and 2 percent were nonfamily abductions. Of those seventy-six nonfamily abductions, sixty-one were taken from their homes; fourteen were found dead; seventy-three were missing for more than twenty-four hours, and fifteen were recovered more than fifty miles from the place where they were abducted.

Exact numbers of child abductions have always been controversial, and often are dramatically inflated due to multiple reporting systems.

2006 Child Abduction Murder Study. Washington State Office of the Attorney General, 2006.

Analysis of Nonfamily Abductions Reported to NCMEC 2016–2020. National Center for Missing and Exploited Children, 2022.

Bello, Vail. Interview by Kim Cross in Sebastopol, California, February 2, 2016.

Bello, Vail. Interview by Kim Cross in Dillon, Montana, June 30, 2022.

Best, Joel. "Rhetoric in Claims-Making: Constructing the Missing Children Problem." *Social Problems*, April 1987.

Best, Joel. *Damned Lies and Statistics*. University of California Press, 2001.

Brown, Elizabeth Nolan. "Enough Stranger Danger! Children Rarely Abducted by Those They Don't Know." *Reason*, March 31, 2017.

Children Reported Missing 1990–1993. National Center for Missing and Exploited Children.

"The Federal Bureau of Investigation's Efforts to Combat Crimes Against Children" (Audit Report 09-08). Office of the Inspector General, January 2009. FBI teletype, October 4, 1993.

Klaas, Marc. Trial testimony. *People v. Richard Allen Davis*, July 3, 1996.

LaFreniere, Tom. Interview by Kim Cross in Santa Rosa, California, February 5, 2016.

National Incidence Studies of Missing, Abducted, Runaway, and Thrownaway Children (NISMART) 1, 2, 3. Office of Juvenile Justice and Delinquency Prevention, April 1, 2020.

"Psychologist Offers Chilling Profile of Girl's Kidnapper." *St. Louis Post-Dispatch*, October 8, 1993.

Shutt, J. Eagle, J. Mitchell Miller, Christopher J. Schreck, and Nancy K. Brown. "Reconsidering the Leading Myths of Stranger Child Abduction." *Criminal Justice Studies*, April 2016.

Ta, Linh. "Johnny Gosch: An Iowa Kidnapping that Helped Change the Nation." *Des Moines Register*, September 4, 2017.

Terry, Don. "A Town in Terror as Children Disappear." *New York Times*, December 10, 1993, A18.

CHAPTER 6: THE EYEWITNESSES

Kate and Gillian were first interviewed briefly by Danny Fish, the young lieutenant who was the first officer to arrive at Polly's house. Their signed, handwritten statements, with seventh-grade penmanship and misspellings, were detailed and touching. Kate's statement included a drawing of the knife she saw in the kidnapper's hand. It had a wooden handle with three metal brads. Three decades later, she would be able to recall that drawing clearly in her mind's eye, but not the actual knife.

The girls' written statements and recorded interviews formed the backbone of this chapter. The dialogue is verbatim, with no additions but some cuts for length and clarity. I shared the audio recordings and transcriptions with Gillian. After listening to the audio recording of her twelve-year-old voice, she told me she was surprised at how calm she and Kate sounded, and said, "It's no wonder they didn't believe us."

I also let Andy Mazzanti listen to the interview, and he enriched the scene with details and insights not apparent on the tape. He also helped me correct a few inaccuracies in the written transcription.

Connell, Katie. Interview by Kim Cross, February 14, 2023.

Freyer, Eddie. Interview by Kim Cross, Windsor, California, November 11, 2016.

Freyer, Eddie. Interview by Kim Cross, Petaluma, California, November 16, 2016.

Freyer, Eddie. Interview by Kim Cross, Santa Rosa, California, November 16, 2016.

Freyer, Eddie. Interview by Kim Cross, Ukiah, California, November 16, 2016.

Mazzanti, Andy. Interview by Kim Cross via Zoom, April 25, 2022.

McLean, Kate. Interview by Dennis Nowicki, Petaluma, California, October 2, 1993. Recording and transcription in case files.

McLean, Kate. Written and signed statement to police, October 2, 1993. Police files.

Nowicki, Dennis. Interview by Kim Cross via FaceTime, December 20, 2022.

Pelham, Gillian. Interview by Andy Mazzanti, Petaluma, California, October 2, 1993.

Pelham, Gillian. Written and signed statement to police, October 2, 1993. Police files.

Pelham, Gillian. Interview by Kim Cross via Zoom, December 21, 2022.

CHAPTER 7: THE CRIME SCENE

Mike Meese died from pancreatic cancer in 2009, before I started this project. His lines of dialogue in this chapter came from his interviews on *The FBI Files* (Season 1, Episode 1: Polly Klaas), which I found on YouTube. To get a glimpse of his personality and investigative style, I interviewed a number of his colleagues at Petaluma PD as well as his colleagues and students at Santa Rosa Junior College, where he taught criminal justice for years. I also met with his third wife, Michelle Meese, in Napa, California, and his son, Frank Meese, in Reno, Nevada. Michelle entrusted me with a hard drive of his files as well as several PowerPoint presentations he used when teaching the Polly Klaas case. Those PowerPoint slides and the notes therein were one of the most useful sources in understanding his thought process as an investigator.

Some of the dialogue in this scene was recollected by Tony Maxwell in a number of recorded interviews as well as a number of emails and essays. (He liked writing out his thoughts on paper.) I later corroborated the dialogue with Lillian Zilius, who died not long after we spoke.

Alford, David. Memo from his personal files, December 6, 1990.

Alford, David. Interview by Kim Cross, January 5, 2023.

Craig, Christine, and Jason Byrd. "How Does Fingerprint Powder Work?" *Scientific American*, September 2, 2022.

FD-302, October 5, 1993.

Illsely, C. Trial testimony. *People v. Richard Allen Davis*, April 23, 1996.

Kelly, John F., and Phillip Wearne. *Tainting Evidence: Inside the Scandals at the FBI Crime Lab*, Free Press, June 2, 1998.

Kirk, Paul Leland. *Crime Investigation: Physical Evidence and the Police Laboratory*. New York: Interscience Publishers, 1953.

Maxwell, Tony. Trial testimony. *People v. Richard Allen Davis*, April 23, 1996.

Maxwell, Tony. Interviews by Kim Cross via phone, 2015–2023.

Maxwell, Tony. Written notes to Kim Cross, May 7, 2021.

McLean, Kate. Interview by Dennis Nowicki, Petaluma, California, October 2, 1993. Case files.

Meese, Mike. Trial testimony. *People v. Richard Allen Davis*, April 30, 1996.

Meese, Mike. Trial testimony. *People v. Richard Allen Davis*, May 7, 1996.

Meese, Mike. Interview in *FBI Files*, accessed in 2023 on YouTube. https://www.youtube.com/watch?v=gw-fhsIN7ZA (5:35).

Pelton, Larry. Trial testimony. *People v. Richard Allen Davis*, April 23, 1996.

CHAPTER 8: DOUBTS

This chapter uses many of the same sources and approaches as Chapter 6. The complication of this chapter was that memories didn't always line up about who was most dubious about the girls' accounts and when those doubts changed into belief that the girls were telling the truth. Investigators often remembered their colleagues being more skeptical.

Until I charted the various interviews of Kate and Gillian on a timeline, I was under the impression that the doubt lasted for several weeks. It was more like a matter of days to a week.

Kate, who agreed to speak with me strictly "on background," helped me verify facts in question, check my own assumptions, and consider alternative points of view that I had not fully considered. I promised Kate I would not quote her, but she gave me permission to acknowledge her role and participation, and what I learned from it.

Boylan, Jeanne. *Portraits of Guilt: The Woman Who Profiles the Faces of America's Deadliest Criminals*. Atria, September 29, 2012.

LaFreniere, Tom. Possibilities chart, October 1, 1993. Police files.

Mazzanti, Andy. Interview by Kim Cross via Zoom, April 25, 2022.

McLean, Kate. Interview by Dennis Nowicki, Petaluma, California, October 2, 1993.

Nowicki, Dennis. Interview by Kim Cross via FaceTime, December 20, 2022.

Pelham, Gillian. Interview by Andy Mazzanti, Petaluma, California, October 2, 1993.

Pelton, Larry. Interview by Kim Cross at his house in Emmett, Idaho, May 5, 2022.

CHAPTER 9: LEADS

The details about the potential suspect at Fairwest Market and Bar came from case files that showed how a lead would be followed until it produced a suspect or turned into a dead end. It was also an example of how coincidental details can align awfully closely. I omitted the name of the individual, since he wasn't related to the kidnapping.

The dialogue of Hank Mar answering a prank call was recounted by Hank to police and documented in a written report shortly after the call. The brief scene of Marc at the end is from a blog post he wrote on KlaasKids.org.

Bush, Sean. Written and signed statement to police. October 2, 1993. Police files.

Bush, Sean. Trial testimony. *People v. Richard Allen Davis*, April 18, 1996.

Butcher paper with handwritten leads, October 1, 1993. Vail Bello's personal archives.

Composite sketch.

FD-302, October 5, 1993.

FD-302, October 12, 1993.

FD-302, October 28, 1993.

Floor plan of Polly's house. From PowerPoint presentation created by Mike Meese.

Freyer, Eddie. Interviews by Kim Cross.

Georges, Thomas. Trial testimony. *People v. Richard Allen Davis*, April 18, 1996.

Hart, T. A. Police report with details from interview with Kamika Milstead. October 1, 1993, 2330 hours. Police files.

Hilley, Ron. FD-302, 1993.

Klaas, Marc. "Sierra LaMar: Anatomy of a Search Day 80." Blog post on KlaasKids.org, June 26, 2012. http://www.klaaskids.org/blog/sierra-lamar-anatomy-of-a-search-day-80/.

Mar, Henkin "Hank." Statement to police. October 2, 1993. Police files.

Miller, Taleah. Trial testimony. *People v. Richard Allen Davis*, April 18, 1996.

Milstead, Kamika. Trial testimony. *People v. Richard Allen Davis*, April 18, 1996.

Pata, Ralph. Initial police sketch and missing poster. Case files.

CHAPTER 10: THE VOLUNTEERS

The scene of Bill Rhodes is from a profile written about him in the *Petaluma Argus-Courier*. The scene and dialogue of the volunteer leaders coming together was based on a number of news accounts and interviews with volunteers. The dialogue was recollected in several interviews with Joanne Gardner, Gaynell Rogers, and Jay Silverberg. The scene of *America's Most Wanted* was from an interview with Michelle Hord.

Early accounts of the number of volunteers who came out that first day ranged from 600 (*Santa Rosa Press Democrat*) to 1,000 (*Oakland Tribune* and others). The number of flyers printed and distributed the first two days also varied from 50,000 (*FBI Files*) to 300,000 (*Petaluma Argus-Courier*, quoting Sherry Rhodes, wife of PIP printing owner Bill Rhodes).

Allen, Keith. "Polly's Song." https://www.castaliapub.com/williamscottmorrison/scotty-the-skeptics/pollys-song.html.

Caballo, Frances. "At the Helm Again: Bill Rhodes Started Effort to Find Polly, Now He's Leading It." *Petaluma Argus-Courier*, November 16, 1993.

Cahill, Greg. "Community Gets Involved." *Petaluma Argus-Courier*, October 6, 1993.

Digitale, Robert. "Massive Search for Petaluma Youngster." *Santa Rosa Press Democrat*, October 4, 1993.

"Ex-Uniontown Man to Edit Calif. Paper." *Baltimore Sun*, September 11, 1993.

Fimrite, Peter. "600 Search for Kidnapped Girl." *San Francisco Chronicle*, October 4, 1993.

Gardner, Joanne. Interview by Kim Cross, November 18, 2021.

Goldston, Linda. "Grim Petaluma Hunts Missing Girl." *San Jose Mercury News*, October 4, 1993.

Hord, Michelle. Interview with Kim Cross by phone, December 13, 2022.

Klineman, Eileen. "A Mother's Plea." *Santa Rosa Press Democrat*, October 10, 1993.

"The Legacy of Polly Klaas," *Santa Rosa Press Democrat*, December 10, 1993.

Lewis, Gregory. "Petaluma Unnerved by Girl's Kidnapping." *San Francisco Examiner*, October 4, 1993.

Mason, Elizabeth. "Police Still Seek Lead in Abduction." *Oakland Tribune*, October 4, 1993.

McConahey, Meg, and Eileen Klineman. "Petaluma's Grief, Hope, over Polly's Abduction." *Santa Rosa Press Democrat*, October 6, 1993.

McLean, Kate. Interview by Special Agent Janet Bery, October 3, 1993.

Rogers, Gaynell. Interviews by Kim Cross, December 7, 2021; March 14, 2022; August 11, 2022.

Silverberg, Jay. Interviews by Kim Cross, February 3, 2016; October 20, 2021; April 1, 2022; July 19, 2022; December 7, 2022.

Smith, Chris. "Petaluma Girl, 12, Abducted." *Santa Rosa Press Democrat,* October 3, 1993.

TV news coverage. Various outlets. DVD compilation shared with me by Anne Belden.

CHAPTER 11: SEVENTY-TWO HOURS

Details in this chapter came from a number of news stories, layered with perspective from investigators and participants, expressed in interviews decades after the event. Kidnapping stats reflect what was reported at the time, and the National Center for Missing and Exploited Children assisted in verifying those stats. Quotes from David Collins came from various news stories.

Joanne Gardner and Jenni Thompson both shared their personal stories in multiple interviews with me, as did Larry Magid, who also shared a column that he wrote at the time for the *San Jose Mercury News*.

Baker, K. C. "A Family Shattered: Mom of Missing Kevin Collins, 10, Still Thinks of Him Decades After He Vanished." *People*, November 18, 2019.

Cahill, Greg. "Collins Hopeful about Polly." *Petaluma Argus-Courier*, October 6, 1993.

Fimrite, Peter. "600 Search for Kidnapped Girl." *San Francisco Chronicle*, October 4, 1993.

Goldston, Linda. "Grim Petaluma Hunts Missing Girl." *San Jose Mercury News*, October 4, 1993.

Klineman, Eileen. "A Mother's Plea." *Santa Rosa Press Democrat*, October 10, 1993.

LaFreniere, Tom. Interview by Kim Cross via Zoom, April 5, 2022.

Locke, Michelle. "Kidnapping Shatters Community Calm." Associated Press, October 6, 1993.

Magid, Lawrence J. "On-line Services Unite to Help Find Abducted Girl." *San Jose Mercury News*, October 10, 1993.

Martinez, Don. "Sharing Heartache Helps Father of Kidnapped Girl." *San Francisco Examiner*, October 5, 1993.

Mershon, Marc. Interview by Kim Cross via Zoom, May 6 and 9, 2022.

Paddock, Richard. "All-Out Search for Missing Girl: Kidnapping: A Community Is Galvanized in Its Efforts to Locate 12-Year-Old Polly Klaas. She was abducted from her bedroom during a slumber party." *Los Angeles Times*, October 6, 1993.

"Psychologist Offers Chilling Profile of Girl's Killer." *St. Louis Post-Dispatch*, October 8, 1993.

Rojas, Aurelio. "Kevin Collins Foundation to Shut Its Doors / 12 Years, Sluggish Donations Take Toll on Boy's Dad." *San Francisco Chronicle*, April 2, 1996.

"San Francisco Police Link Deceased Criminal to Kevin Collins Case." CBS Bay Area, February 6, 2013. Online.

Smith, Chris. "Petaluma's Grief, Hope over Polly's Abduction." *Santa Rosa Press Democrat*, October 6, 1993.

Smolowe, Jill. "A High-Tech Dragnet: A California Kidnapping Spurs a Novel Use of the Information Superhighway." *TIME*, November 1, 1993.

Sonenshine, Ron. "Petaluma Kidnap Baffles Parents, Authorities." *San Francisco Chronicle*, October 5, 1993.

Special to the *New York Times*. "Kidnapping Summons City to Action." *New York Times*, October 15, 1993.

"Stolen Children: What Can Be Done about Child Abduction." *Newsweek*, March 19, 1984.

Thompson, Jenni. Interview by Kim Cross in Sacramento, California, March 15, 2022.

Vasquez, Daniel. "Parents in Tearful Plea for Daughter's Return." *Oakland Tribune*, October 5, 1993.

CHAPTER 12: AMERICA'S MOST WANTED

The biographical sketch of John Walsh was based largely on his book *Tears of Rage*, in which he recounts the tragic kidnapping and murder of his son, Adam, and how his rage evolved into the creation of the National Center for Missing and Exploited Children and his role as host of *America's Most Wanted*. Additional details and quotes came from an October 1993 profile by Julie Winokur in the *San Francisco Examiner*.

Scenes of Marc and Eve watching the episode came from a compilation of TV news stories shared with me by Anne Belden. After months of searching for the *America's Most Wanted* episodes on Polly, I was given a VHS tape featuring all of them by Michelle Meese, the widow of investigator Mike Meese, who used the tape in his criminal justice class, along with the confession tape. Scenes and quotes from David Collins came from various news stories.

America's Most Wanted. Compilation of episodes featuring Polly. VHS tape. Archives of Mike Meese.

Bellafante, Ginia. "Child in Need." *TIME*, July 21, 2008.

Cahill, Greg. "Collins Hopeful about Polly." *Petaluma Argus-Courier*, October 6, 1993.

Harris, Paula K. "TV Show Triggers New Tips." *Petaluma Argus-Courier*, October 1993.

Klineman, Eileen. "Town Rallies behind Search for Young Girl." *Santa Rosa Press Democrat*, October 6, 1993.

Lopez, Rob. "Just Keep Her Safe." *Petaluma Argus-Courier*, October 6, 1993.

Miller, Edwin. "In the Spotlight—Winona Ryder." October 1988. winona-ryder .org.

Nakeo, Annie. "Media Blitz Could Bring Polly Home." *San Francisco Examiner*, October 24, 1993.

Paddock, Richard. "All-Out Search for Missing Girl: Kidnapping: A Community Is Galvanized in Its Efforts to Locate 12-Year-Old Polly Klaas. She Was Abducted from Her Bedroom during a Slumber Party." *Los Angeles Times*, October 6, 1993.

Smith, Chris. "Actress Offers $200,000 for Polly." *Santa Rosa Press Democrat*, October 10, 1993.

TV news coverage. Compilation of various 1993 news stories about Polly Klaas. VHS tape from personal archives of Anne Belden.

Walsh, John. *Tears of Rage: From Grieving Father to Crusader for Justice, the Untold Story of the Adam Walsh Case.* Atria, October 1, 1997.

Winokur, Julie. "The Violent World of 'Most Wanted's' Host." *San Francisco Examiner*, October 19, 1993.

CHAPTER 13: THE CELEBRITY

Winona Ryder, through her handlers, declined to speak with me for the book, so the quotes and scenes involving her came from several stories published in newspapers and magazines in 1993 and years later. Her conversation with Joanne Gardner was recounted by Gardner to me in an interview and was consistent with what she told Jeffrey Giles in 2003 for a *Rolling Stone* profile on Ryder. Some sources (*Argus-Courier*) say she attended Petaluma Junior High as well as Petaluma High; others say she went to junior high at an arts school.

Scenes of David Alford's search for evidence came from a review of his FD-302s, which detail his actions and listed the items collected, and interviews with him.

Some of the information about Polly's habitat and habits came from Mary Ellen O'Toole's victimology interview with Eve Nichol.

Alford, David. FD-302 documenting investigation on October 9, 1993.
Allen, Jenny. "Little Women, Big Star." *LIFE*, December 1994.
Bellafante, Ginia. "Child in Need." *TIME*, July 21, 2008.
Blistein, Jon. "Songwriters Remake Soul Asylum's 'Runaway Train' for Video's 25th Anniversary." *Rolling Stone*, May 22, 2019.
Cahill, Greg. "Collins Hopeful about Polly." *Petaluma Argus-Courier*, October 6, 1993.
Commons, Jamie N., and Skylar Gray featuring Gallant. "Runaway Train" music video remake, May 2019. Video online at http://smarturl.it/RunawayTrain.
Frantz, Annie. "Parents Share Their Fears, Hope." *Petaluma Argus-Courier*, October 8, 1993.
Frantz, Annie. "Winona Boosts Search Efforts." *Petaluma Argus-Courier*, October 12, 1993.
Gardner, Joanne. Interview by Kim Cross, November 2022.
Giles, Jeff. "Interview: Winona Ryder." *Rolling Stone,* March 10, 1994.
Handleman, David. "Winona Ryder: Hiding High." *Vogue*, October 1993.
Klineman, Eileen. "Town Rallies behind Search for Young Girl." *Santa Rosa Press Democrat*, October 6, 1993.
Nichol, Eve. Interview by Mary Ellen O'Toole, October 18, 1993.
Smith, Chris. "Actress Offers $200,000 for Polly." *Santa Rosa Press Democrat*, October 10, 1993.
Sonenshine, Ron. "Kidnap Recreated, Videotaped." *The San Francisco Chronicle*, October 9, 1993.
TV news coverage. Compilation of various 1993 news stories about Polly Klaas. VHS tape from personal archives of Anne Belden.
Winokur, Julie. "The Violent World of 'Most Wanted's' Host." *San Francisco Examiner*, October 19, 1993.

CHAPTER 14: THE POLYGRAPHER

The opening scene of Marc Klaas in the parking lot was reported by Tim Keown in a *San Francisco Magazine* story in 1997, but he has recounted this moment several times in a number of interviews. Eddie Freyer recounted this moment several times to me from his perspective. He may have grabbed Marc by the shirt cuffs or shoulders, but he's not sure. His internal thoughts and shift came from "The Grim Reaper," an excellent profile of Marc by Tom Junod in *GQ* magazine.

The bulk of this chapter came from a series of interviews with polygrapher Ron Hilley. I also interviewed Homer, who taught me a great deal about the craft. Unfortunately, because their names were so similar, I worried that alternating between Ron Hilley and Ron Homer would be very confusing for the reader. Because Ron Hilley worked so closely with Mary Ellen O'Toole and conducted many of the pivotal examinations in this case, I chose to focus on him. It is my understanding that Ron Homer was equally involved in this case.

Hilley reviewed the chapter and helped correct inaccuracies in my language, which is very particular. For example: Don't call it a polygraph "machine." It's an "instrument." And the person being polygraphed is not a "subject" (a term the FBI uses for a prime suspect); they're an "interviewee."

Bello, Vail. Handwritten notes in case files, October 1, 1993.

Bello, Vail. Interview by Kim Cross, January 21, 2023.

Burgess, Ann Wolbert. *Killer by Design: Murderers, Mindhunters, and My Quest to Decipher the Criminal Mind.* Hachette Books, 2021, 139.

Cohen, Laurie P. "The Polygraph Paradox." *Wall Street Journal*, March 22, 2008.

"Connolly, Francis 'Frank' Marlin." SFGate.com, June 11, 2003.

Digitale, Robert. "Massive Search for Petaluma Youngster." *Santa Rosa Press Democrat*, October 4, 1993.

Hilley, Ron. FD-302 documenting his examination of Kate on October 10, 1993; the report was written on October 12, 1993.

Keown, Tim. "B228 The Grim Reaper: Why Does Marc Klaas Still Feel Compelled to Relive His Daughter Polly's Death in Public?" *San Francisco Magazine*, November 1, 1997.

Klaas, Marc. "Polly Klaas—Jan. 3, 1981–Oct. 1, 1993." Blog post on KlaasKids, October 1, 2013. http://www.klaaskids.org/blog/1248/.

O'Toole, Mary Ellen. Interview by Kim Cross, February 19, 2016.

CHAPTER 15: THE FORENSIC ARTIST

Finding Jeanne Boylan was one of the great triumphs of my reporting adventure for this book. I interviewed her by phone several times and asked her many questions via email. But it was her excellent memoir, *Portraits of Guilt*, that provided so many of the key details, scenes, and dialogue that I needed for this narrative. She wrote it a decade earlier, while those details were fresher, so I drew heavily upon the book for this and a subsequent chapter.

I tried to reach producer Debbie Alpert to fact-check her role in bringing Boylan into the case. She didn't respond. Based on Boylan's memory, I wrote in an earlier draft that Alpert had reached out to Mark Mershon to tell him about Boylan's work and convince him to bring her in. Mershon (who took meticulous notes and referenced them to answer my questions), did not recall being contacted by Alpert. His recollection is that Jeanne Boylan simply showed up. Either way, Alpert's role in getting Boylan to Petaluma was pivotal, not only because of the sketch she produced, but because she was instrumental in "rehabilitating the girls," as Eddie Freyer put it, after the girls were traumatized by interviewing and interrogation.

I also asked Gillian Pelham to review this chapter and "The Composite." She found them accurate and shared an interesting personal observation. When she'd first read Boylan's book a decade ago, Gillian felt a bit put off at how she was portrayed—as a goofy, immature kid. But her 2022 self felt a bit differently, and she felt Boylan's portrait of her at that age was probably more accurate and fair than she originally thought.

Boylan, Jeanne. *Portraits of Guilt: The Woman Who Profiles the Faces of America's Deadliest Criminals*. Atria, September 29, 2012.

Boylan, Jeanne. Email to Kim Cross, December 18, 2022.

Boylan, Jeanne. Interviews by Kim Cross via phone, 2022–2023.

Mershon, Mark. Emails to Kim Cross, 2022–2023.

Mershon, Mark. Interviews by Kim Cross via Zoom and phone, 2022–2023.

Pelham, Gillian. Interview with Kim Cross via Zoom from Manchester, England, December 2022.

Pelham, Gillian. Emails to Kim Cross, 2022–2023.

CHAPTER 16: THE PROFILER

Mary Ellen O'Toole is an incredibly busy woman. In her current position as director of the forensic science program at George Mason University, she serves as a program administrator as well as a professor teaching courses in the program.

Because most of her profiling and victimology work was done while Polly was still missing, there was no formal written profile (which generally requires a body, a murder weapon, a homicide crime scene, and so forth). And she didn't leave a paper trail like other investigators, because most of her work was advisory, as an ongoing presence in investigative meetings where her psychological insights informed group decisions about how to approach various interviews.

Most of the information about her role in the case came from my correspondence with O'Toole as well as interviews with Eddie Freyer, Tony Maxwell, Ron Hilley, Larry Taylor, Frank Doyle, David Alford, Mark Mershon, and a number of other FBI agents who worked with her on this case and others. Her name came up in so many interviews that I won't list them all below, but I will note that she was highly regarded and universally respected by everyone I spoke with.

Her book, *Dangerous Instincts*, is well written and informative, though it is more focused on reader service than biographical information about O'Toole. I interviewed her co-author, Alisa Bowman, to get more of a sense of her presence and personality.

Bowman, Alisa. Interview by Kim Cross via phone, October 13, 2022.

Burgess, Ann Wolbert. *Killer by Design: Murderers, Mindhunters, and My Quest to Decipher the Criminal Mind*. Hachette Books, December 7, 2021.

"Criminal Investigative Analysis: Sexual Homicide." National Center for the Analysis of Violent Crime, Critical Incident Response Group, FBI Academy, Quantico, Virginia, 1990. Accessed online at https://vault.FBI.gov.

Douglas, John E., with Mark Olshaker. *Mindhunter: Inside the FBI's Elite Serial Crime Unit*. Scribner, November 26, 1998.

FBI teletype, October 14, 1993.

Medina, Eduardo. "Idaho Man Convicted in 1984 Murder of 12-Year-Old Colorado Girl," *New York Times*, October 31, 2022.

Neighborhood questionnaire, no author cited, used in the neighborhood canvassing efforts in early October 1993. Copy found in case files.

Osborne, Margaret. "Forensic Scientists Are Testing Whether Honey Bees Can Help Locate Human Bodies." *Smithsonian Magazine,* April 4, 2022.

O'Toole, Mary Ellen. Bio and background info on website: maryellenotoole.com.

O'Toole, Mary Ellen. Interview with Kim Cross by phone, February 19, 2016.

O'Toole, Mary Ellen. Interview with Kim Cross by phone, December 28, 2021.

O'Toole, Mary Ellen. Violent offenders class, attended by Kim Cross via Zoom, March 31, 2022.

O'Toole, Mary Ellen. Email to Kim Cross, September 25, 2022.

O'Toole, Mary Ellen. Email to Kim Cross, January 10, 2023.

O'Toole, Mary Ellen. Email to Kim Cross, January 28, 2023.

O'Toole, Mary Ellen, and Alisa Bowman. *Dangerous Instincts: How Gut Feelings Betray Us—Fear Can't Help You. An FBI Profiler Shows You What Can.* Hudson Street Press, October 13, 2011.

Ramsland, Katherine. "Criminal Profiling: How It All Began—An Unsolved Kidnapping Proved the Value of Psychology in Crime Solving." *Psychology Today* blog post, March 23, 2014.

Udell, Erin. "Steve Pankey Found Guilty of Kidnapping, Felony Murder in Jonelle Matthews Case." *Fort Collins Coloradoan*, October 31, 2022.

CHAPTER 17: THE COMPOSITE

Notes on Chapter 15 apply here as well. To understand more about the effects of trauma on memory, I interviewed Dr. David Diamond, a University of South Florida psychology professor. With a PhD in cognitive and neural sciences, Diamond specializes in the neurobiology of memory and the disturbance of brain and behavior by stress.

His review article (cited below) nearly broke my brain, but he explained its concepts to me in layman's terms during an interview. I wanted to understand what was likely occurring, cognitively, as Kate misremembered certain details (such as the yellow bandana).

Without knowing anything about the case, Diamond told me, "Go look at the crime scene photos. My guess is that you'll find something yellow in the room." I went back to the dozens of photos taken in Polly's room by the ERT and saw something I'd never noticed before: a giant yellow parasol, designed to resemble a sunflower, in one corner of a photo. It appears to be hanging from the top corner of Polly's bunk bed.

From where Kate was sitting on the floor, it's plausible that when the kidnapper walked through Polly's doorway and instructed the girls not to look at him, Kate's eyes swept across the yellow parasol in a moment that must have been charged with extreme adrenaline and stress. It would have been one of the last things she saw before he pulled a pillowcase over her head.

Marc's and Eve's reactions to the sketch came from quotes in newspaper stories.

Aviv, Rachel. "How Elizabeth Loftus Changed the Meaning of Memory." *New Yorker*, March 29, 2021.

Diamond, David, Adam M. Campbell, Colin R. Park, Joshua Halonen, Phillip R. Zoldaz. "The Temporal Dynamics Model of Emotional Memory Processing: A Synthesis on the Neurobiological Basis of Stress-Induced Amnesia, Flashbulb and Traumatic Memories, and the Yerkes-Dodson Law." Hindawi Publishing Corporation, *Neural Plasticity*, Volume 2007, Article ID 60803.

Dougan, Michael. "Kidnap Shatters Family's World: Polly's Parents Bound by Tragedy." *San Francisco Examiner*, October 15, 1993.

Kovner, Guy. "New Sketch Nets Calls." *Santa Rosa Press Democrat*, October 16, 1993.

Lopez, Rob. "New Sketch of Suspect Released." *Petaluma Argus-Courier*, October 15, 1993.

Rossman, Randi. "New Sketch of Polly's Abductor." *Santa Rosa Press Democrat*, October 15, 1993.

CHAPTER 18: VICTIMOLOGY

The heart of this chapter is the three-hour interview with Eve by Mary Ellen O'Toole, which was preserved on audio cassettes and a 126-page transcript found in the case files. This information has never before been publicly available.

I edited it as minimally as possible, only making cuts for length and redundancy. That said, I had to make considerable cuts, given the length of the interview.

Because Polly's family opted not to participate in this book, I struggled with how to present Polly as a real, three-dimensional person, not just a victim. I wanted readers to appreciate who she was to the people who loved her most. This interview helped me provide depth and nuance far beyond a collection of quotes by Polly's family to the press.

That said, I agonized over whether this interview would violate their privacy. (I would have asked them if they'd agreed to speak with me.) In the absence of their guidance, I tried to read this with the eye of a mother, omitting personal details that I wouldn't want published if this were about my daughter. There wasn't much of that nature to omit, but there were a few things.

I shared with Mary Ellen O'Toole copies of the audio interviews and the written transcript. I'm not sure if she had time to review them, but she did review this chapter for accuracy and insights.

Alford, David. FD-302 on evidence collection. October 8, 1993.

Nichol, Eve. Interview by Mary Ellen O'Toole, October 16, 1993. Audio recording and transcription.

O'Toole, Mary Ellen. Interview with Kim Cross by phone, February 19, 2016.

O'Toole, Mary Ellen. Interview with Kim Cross by phone, December 28, 2021.

O'Toole, Mary Ellen. Violent offenders class, attended by Kim Cross via Zoom, March 31, 2022.

O'Toole, Mary Ellen. Email to Kim Cross, September 25, 2022.
O'Toole, Mary Ellen. Email to Kim Cross, January 10, 2023.
O'Toole, Mary Ellen. Email to Kim Cross, January 28, 2023.

CHAPTER 19: RAPID START

Very little has been documented about Rapid Start, despite the role it played in cases including Polly Klaas and UNABOM.

The FBI agents who were trained to operate Rapid Start in the Polly Klaas case were Steve Donohue and Gary Joseph. Both are still alive, but I wasn't able to speak with them. So I was thrilled when FBI agent Phil Buvia, the creator of Rapid Start, agreed to speak. Most of the history of this then-state-of-the-art system came from our interview. He reviewed the chapter for accuracy.

Echoing a theme from earlier chapters—the susceptibility of memory to the power of suggestion—it's worth noting that witness Daryl Stone recalled seeing a yellow bandana. Pretty much everyone inside the investigation believes that the yellow bandana never existed. Davis never admitted to having or wearing one, and there was no evidence in any of the files I saw that one was ever found or collected into evidence (aside from the yellow headband collected in a search of Garcia Garcia's residence). Daryl Stone didn't remember the man he encountered in Wickersham Park until he saw Jeanne Boylan's sketch. But because he had seen the earlier composite—the one with the yellow bandana—it's plausible that he merged the two images in his memory.

Buvia, Phil. Interview by Kim Cross via phone, August 10, 2022.
Buvia, Phil. Email to Kim Cross, March 9, 2023.
Cox, Rhonda. Letter to DEA, October 18, 2023.
Department of Motor Vehicles records, October 15, 1993.
Farrow, Connie. "Police Arrest Three in Girl's Killing." AP News, February 3, 1994.
FBI teletype, January 13, 1992.
FBI teletype, October 4, 1993.
FBI teletype, October 14, 1993.
FBI teletype, October 16, 1993.
FBI teletype, October 23, 1993.
Freyer, Eddie. Interviews by Kim Cross on various occasions, 2015–2023.
Google Maps estimation of car chase length based on start and ending address.
"Kidnapping Summons City to Action." New York Times, October 15, 1993.
Kramer, Staci D. "FBI Computer Team Ties Clues Together." Chicago Tribune, December 17, 1993.
"A Look Back on the Brown's Chicken Massacre—25 Years Ago." CBS News Chicago, January 8, 2018.
Privacy Impact Assessment Violent Criminal Apprehension Program (ViCAP), FBI, July 18, 2003.

Sander, Libby. "Murder Trial to Begin in Illinois, 14 Years after 7 Died." *New York Times*, April 13, 2007.

Stone, Daryl. Witness statement given to Petaluma police. November 5, 1993. Case files.

Stone, Daryl. Trial testimony. *People v. Richard Allen Davis*, April 18, 1996.

CHAPTER 20: THE ERT TEAM

Tony Maxwell, David Alford, Frank Doyle, and Mike Stapleton were among my most engaged sources. I talked to them repeatedly for this chapter, in phone calls recorded and unrecorded. To my (and their) knowledge, a comprehensive history of the founding of the FBI's ERT program hasn't yet been written.

Their interviews were the main source for this chapter. The history of the PSA plane crash was recounted to me by Maxwell and Alford in interviews. The Crime on the High Seas case in Half Moon Bay was shared by Alford in an interview. And the backstory of the 1984 Summer Olympics in Los Angeles was corroborated by Maxwell, Alford, and Doyle. I corroborated the dates of the ERT's founding with internal FBI memos shared by David Alford.

Chris Allen initially agreed to participate in my research, and consented to one interview, but later opted out. I sourced his quotes, thoughts, and analysis from his trial testimony and his interviews in the Polly Klaas episode of *FBI Files*. In our one interview, he told me he had opened the fridge one day to see Polly's face on a milk carton.

What I would have liked to have asked Allen I obtained from David Alford, who worked in the FBI lab and the Kentucky State Police Crime Lab, doing work very similar to Allen's. He walked me through the basic procedures of hair and fibers analysis. I also interviewed Doug Deedrick, Allen's supervisor and the unit chief, who further explained how the science works and added the story of the automotive carpet database, which I've never read elsewhere.

Alford, David. Interview by Kim Cross, January 8, 2023.

Allen, Chris. Trial testimony. *People v. Richard Allen Davis*, May 15, 1996.

Deedrick, Doug. Interview by Kim Cross, January 24, 2023.

Doyle, Frank. "Crime Scene/Evidence Response Team San Francisco Division." Memo to SAC, San Francisco, December 28, 1987.

Doyle, Frank. Interviews by Kim Cross, May 19, 2021; June 15, 2021; June 18, 2021; July 6, 2021; November 7, 2022.

FBI lab specimen report, December 8, 1993. Case files.

The FBI Laboratory: A Brief Outline of the History, the Services, and the Operating Techniques of the FBI Laboratory. United States: U.S. Department of Justice, Federal Bureau of Investigation, 1980. https://hdl.handle.net/2027/uc1.c025525893.

FBI website: https://www.fbi.gov/history/history-of-fbi-headquarters.

FBI website: https://archives.fbi.gov/archives/news/stories/2007/november/major-fbi-laboratory-milestones.

Hsu, Spencer S. "Justice Department, FBI to Review Use of Forensic Evidence in Thousands of Cases." *Washington Post*, July 10, 2012.

Hsu, Spencer S. "FBI Admits Flaws in Hair Analysis over Decades." *Washington Post*, April 18, 2015.

Jacobs, Greg. Statement of Evidence. *People v. Richard Allen Davis.*

Kelly, John F., and Phillip Wearne. *Tainting Evidence: Inside the Scandals at the FBI Crime Lab.* Free Press, June 2, 1998.

Mack, Gerald. "Crime Scene/Evidence Response Team San Francisco division." Memo to SAC, San Francisco Division, June 25, 1990.

"Polly Klaas: Kidnapped." *FBI Files*, Season 1, Episode 1, September 22, 1998. Accessed on YouTube: https://youtu.be/9G9oWPowwMA?t=2064.

Reikes, John. "Crime Scene Response Team (CSRT) San Francisco Division." Memo to SAC, San Francisco Division, February 15, 1988.

Shafaieh, Charles. "The Ugliest Building in Washington: Students Navigate Federal Pressures and Local Values in Rethinking FBI Site." Harvard University Graduate School of Design, blog post, September 21, 2020.

Zilius, Lillian. Interview by Kim Cross, December 16, 2022.

CHAPTER 21: THE SWAT TEAM

I found few documents related to the SWAT team operations in this case, so most of the information in this chapter came from interviews with SWAT team members, including the FBI's Tom LaFreniere, Eddie Freyer, Phil Sena, Bruce Burroughs, Joe Davidson, and John "JC" Steiner; Petaluma PD's Vail Bello, Danny Fish, Gene Wallace, Matt Stapleton, and Larry Pelton. Some historical information came from these interviews, particularly from Bruce Burroughs, who was present at the Wounded Knee Occupation. Other historical asides came from an interview with SWAT team member, historian, and author Lieutenant Dan Marcou, and other literature on crimes involving FBI special operations.

Bay, John. Letter to Atomic Safety & Licensing Board Panel, April 28, 1983. Re: "A Terrorists' Guide to the 1984 Olympics," *Playboy*, May 1983. https://www.nrc.gov/docs/ML2002/ML20023B427.pdf.

Bello, Vail. Interviews by Kim Cross, January 21, 2023.

Burroughs, Bruce. Interviews by Kim Cross, January 18, 19, 20, 2023.

Castaneda, Elizabeth. FD-302.

Chertoff, Emily. "Occupy Wounded Knee: A 71-Day Siege and a Forgotten Civil Rights Movement." *The Atlantic*, October 23, 2012.

Davidson, Joe. Interviews by Kim Cross, March 11, 2022.

Domonoske, Camila. "Dennis Banks, Native American Activist and Wounded Knee Occupier, Dies at 80." NPR, October 30, 2017.

Doubek, James. "50 Years Ago, the Munich Olympics Massacre Changed How We Think about Terrorism." NPR, September 4, 2022.

"The FBI Will Take the 'Lead Role' over Local . . ." UPI, December 19, 1982.

FD-302, October 19, 1993.

Fish, Danny. Interviews by Kim Cross, April 5, 2022.

Freyer, Eddie. Interviews by Kim Cross, January 16, 2020; January 19, 2023.

Homer, Ron. FD-302.

Jacobs, Greg. Statement of Case, *People v. Richard Allen Davis*, April 1993.

Koletar, Joseph W. *The FBI Career Guide: Inside Information on Getting Chosen for and Succeeding in One of the Toughest, Most Prestigious Jobs in the World.* Ukraine: AMACOM, 2006.

LaFreniere, Tom. Interviews by Kim Cross, February 5, 2016; April 5, 2022; February 4, 2023.

LaFreniere, Tom. FD-302. October 18, 1993.

Lewis, Sherwood. Application for affidavit for search warrant.

Marcou, Dan. Interview with Kim Cross, January 18, 2023.

Sena, Phil. Interview by Kim Cross, January 26, 2023.

Stapleton, Matt. Interview by Kim Cross, January 18, 2023.

Steiner, John "JC." Interview by Kim Cross, January 29, 2023.

Wallace, Gene. Interviews by Kim Cross, January 21, 2023.

CHAPTER 22: TROUBLE WITHIN

This chapter was very difficult to report because much of the matter is subjective and influenced by strong emotions. But I felt it was important to include a portrait of the complex dynamics that exist within probably every law enforcement department. This kind of conflict is largely invisible to anyone outside of an investigation. But it shows the human cost of these cases, in which people have to make decisions with incomplete (and sometimes erroneous) information, under the unrelenting pressure of time and deadly stakes. This seemed relevant for readers to understand.

I interviewed people in both camps—many of them repeatedly—including Pat Parks, Dave Long, Andy Mazzanti, Dennis Nowicki, Larry Pelton, Vail Bello, Gene Wallace, Danny Fish, and Mike Kerns. I also interviewed people outside the department who were involved in the case and observed some of the tension, including Eddie Freyer, Mark Mershon, Lillian Zilius, and others.

The dialogue was recollected in these interviews, and I corroborated it with as many sources as I could, and some discrepancies caused me to make cuts. Some of the facts are disputed based on what different sources remembered. For example, Pat Parks feels 100 percent confident in his memory that Dennis Nowicki did participate in the videotaped reenactment with Kate and Gillian, while Dennis Nowicki and Vail Bello insist that Nowicki was not present. I omitted facts that were in dispute from the chapter and tried to write around the gaps in a way that felt honest and as accurate as possible.

The reporting and fact-checking of this chapter was difficult from a psychological perspective, because it stirred up past blood and opened old wounds. It was such a low point for Dennis Nowicki that he initially declined to speak with me.

At the urging of colleagues Larry Pelton and Andy Mazzanti, he changed his mind, and he spoke very candidly about the lasting emotional impact.

As a side note, Gillian doesn't remember Eddie bringing her and Kate flowers but believes it is true. Eddie Freyer relayed it in an interview and said the idea may have come from Jeanne Boylan, who also recounted the story in her memoir, *Portraits of Guilt.*

Bello, Vail. Interviews by Kim Cross, February 2, 2016; March 31, 2022; April 4, 2023; April 12, 2023.

Bentell, Carol. "City Reaches into Reserves for Polly Hunt: Police Following Hundreds of Tips." *Santa Rosa Press Democrat*, October 17, 1993.

"Key Dates in Polly Case." *Marin Independent Journal*, December 1, 1993.

"Kidnapping Summons City to Action." *New York Times*, October 15, 1993.

Long, David. Interviews by Kim Cross, October 18 and 21, 2022.

Mazzanti, Andy. Interviews by Kim Cross, January 22, 2023.

Mazzanti, Andy. Email to Kim Cross, February 14, 2023.

Nowicki, Dennis. Interviews by Kim Cross, December 20, 2022; April 12, 2023.

Parks, Pat. Interviews by Kim Cross, April 29, 2022; April 12, 2023.

Parks, Pat. Emails to Kim Cross, March 15, 21, 26, 27, 30, 2023; April 12, 2023.

Shafaieh, Charles. "The Ugliest Building in Washington: Students Navigate Federal Pressures and Local Values in Rethinking FBI Site." Harvard University Graduate School of Design, blog post, September 21, 2020.

Sonenshine, Ron. "Kidnap Recreated, Videotaped." *San Francisco Chronicle*, October 9, 1993.

"Two Months: The Polly Klaas Case." *Santa Rosa Press Democrat*, December 3, 1993.

Zilius, Lillian. Interview by Kim Cross, December 16, 2022.

CHAPTER 23: THE FOUNDATION

So much of the community story in this book can be traced back to help from Jay Silverberg, who has helped and supported me since my 2016 pre-reporting for the book proposal. One of the leaders of the volunteer effort, Jay was the former editor-in-chief of the *Marin Independent Journal,* and later the founder of a PR company specializing in crisis management, so he understood what I needed as a journalist writing about a crisis.

In addition to giving extensive interviews in person and by phone and Zoom, Jay provided me with scans of newspaper clips and primary sources germane to the volunteer and community story. He also introduced me to Joanne Gardner and Gaynell Rogers, who came to be prominent characters. Joanne and Gaynell spoke with me repeatedly and shared candid perspectives on some of the more sensitive parts of the community story, including regarding Bill Rhodes and Marc Klaas. Bits of dialogue in the chapter were corroborated between the three, individually and in at least one group Zoom chat.

Many of the news stories sourced in this book were unavailable in online databases. I relied heavily on print newspaper clippings preserved by various sources. Greg Jacobs, Barry Collins, Andy Mazzanti, Jay Silverberg, Greg Cahill, Eddie Freyer, Vail Bello, Larry Taylor, and jury foreman Brian Bianco sent dozens of boxes of clips to me.

Several local reporters who covered the kidnapping and foundation in 1993 generously provided information, perspective, and clips: Greg Cahill of the *Petaluma Argus-Courier*; Randi Rossman and Mary Callahan at the *Santa Rosa Press Democrat*.

Cahill, Greg. "Volunteers Launch Their Own Probe." *Petaluma Argus-Courier*, November 2, 1993.

Cahill, Greg. "Police, FBI Reject Offer of Outside Help." *Petaluma Argus-Courier*, November 16, 1993.

Cahill, Greg. "Polly's Dad: We've Tried Everything." *Petaluma Argus-Courier*, November 19, 1993.

Cahill, Greg. "Polly Funds Won't Go to City Police." *Petaluma Argus-Courier*, November, 1993.

Gabbert, Bill. Interview by Kim Cross in Petaluma, California, March 21, 2022.

Gardner, Joanne. "Polly Klaas Search Fund." Polly Klaas Foundation, press release, October 21, 1993.

Gardner, Joanne. Interviews by Kim Cross, November 18, 2021; August 11, 2022; November 20, 2022.

Junod, Tom. "America's Most Haunted." *GQ*, September 1, 1997.

"Key Dates in Polly Case." *Marin Independent Journal*, December 1, 1993.

Klineman, Eileen. "Polly Fund Offers City $50,000." *Santa Rosa Press Democrat*, November 16, 1993.

Kovner, Guy. "Polly Hunt Gets Experienced Hand." *Santa Rosa Press Democrat*, October 23, 1993.

Kovner, Guy. "Investigator: Likely Someone Hired Abductor." *Santa Rosa Press Democrat*, November 5?, 1993. Print clipping incomplete and undated.

Kovner, Guy. "Funds for Polly Searcher Refused." *Santa Rosa Press Democrat*, November 16, 1993.

Kovner, Guy. "Rhodes Turned Down Calls for Investigations." *Santa Rosa Press Democrat*, November 25, 1993.

McConahey, Meg. "Volunteers Helping with Police Work." *Santa Rosa Press Democrat*, November 8, 1993, B1.

McConahey, Meg. "Waiting for Polly." *Santa Rosa Press Democrat*, November 8, 1993, B1.

Neill, Alex. "Polly's Dad Wants More Private Eyes: Says That's Best Use for Donated Money." *Marin Independent Journal*, November 12, 1993.

Patel, Roxanne. "Celebrities Play Benefit Concert." *Santa Rosa Press Democrat*, October 26, 1993.

Patel, Roxanne. "Polly Funds to Go to Family." *Santa Rosa Press Democrat*, November 4, 1993.

Rogers, Gaynell. Interviews by Kim Cross, December 7, 2021; March 14, 2022; August 11, 2022.

Rossman, Randi. "Ryder, Polly's Parents to Lead Non-profit Search Foundation." *Santa Rosa Press Democrat*, October 25, 1993.

Rossman, Randi. "Polly Group Hurries to Go Non-profit," *Santa Rosa Press Democrat*, November 1993.

Rossman, Randi. "Polly Klaas Foundation Wants to Hire Expert." *Santa Rosa Press Democrat*, November 13, 1993.

Silverberg, Jay. Interviews by Kim Cross, February 6, 2016; October 20, 2021; April 1, 2022; July 19, 2022; December 7, 2022.

Sonenshine, Ron. "Private Detective Joins Search for Missing Girl: SF's Hal Lipset Hired to Try to Find Polly." *San Francisco Chronicle*, November 2, 1993.

Sridhar, Priya. "Heidi Search Center Closing after Nearly 30 Years." KENS5 News, January 12, 2018.

CHAPTER 24: THE INSIDER

The timeline and external point of view for this chapter came largely from published newspaper reports, supplemented with interviews with insiders including investigators and volunteers. *Santa Rosa Press Democrat* reporter Randi Rossman and *Petaluma Argus-Courier* reporter Greg Cahill also allowed me to interview them to understand the community and media perspective. Their news coverage was particularly useful. Cahill shared that the reporter who wrote the glowing profile of Bill Rhodes was so upset by the timing of the story and the truth that came out days later that she left journalism entirely. Her story, however, gave me useful details with which to show Rhodes's character and reputation in the community.

"Bill Rhodes." *Santa Rosa Press Democrat*, February 25, 2012.

Caballo, Frances. "At the Helm Again." *Petaluma Argus-Courier*, November 16, 1993.

Cahill, Greg. "Search Center Settles into New Headquarters." *Petaluma Argus-Courier*, November 16, 1993, 3A.

Cahill, Greg. Interviews with Kim Cross, September 29, 2022; October 6, 2022.

Freyer, Eddie. Interviews with Kim Cross, 2015–2022.

Gardner, Joanne. Interviews by Kim Cross, November 18, 2021; August 11, 2022; November 20, 2022.

Klineman, Eileen. "A's a Hit at New Polly Center." *Santa Rosa Press Democrat*, November 17, 1993.

Kovner, Guy. "Polly Center Moving to Bigger Office." *Santa Rosa Press Democrat*, October 25, 1993.

Mershon, Mark. Interviews with Kim Cross, May 6, 9, 2022; January 1, 2023.

"Pitching for Polly." *Petaluma Argus-Courier*, November 19, 1993.

Rhodes, Bill. Statement from lawyer.

Rogers, Gaynell. Interviews by Kim Cross, December 7, 2021; March 14, 2022; August 11, 2022.

Rossman, Randi. Interview with Kim Cross, October 23, 2022.

Rossman, Randi, and Meg McConahey. "Leader in Polly Search Resigns among Allegations." *Santa Rosa Press Democrat*, Saturday, November 20, 1993.

Silverberg, Jay. Interviews by Kim Cross, February 6, 2016; October 20, 2021; April 1, 2022; July 19, 2022; December 7, 2022.

Sommer, Skip. "Wrist by Wrist, Wrestlers Captivated Petaluma." *Petaluma Argus-Courier,* August 28, 2016.

Sonenshine, Ron. "Polly Searcher Is Sex Offender." *San Francisco Chronicle,* November 23, 1993.

"Wrist Wrestling Capital and Statue." http://www.RoadsideAmerica.com /story/202096.

CHAPTER 25: THE SUSPECT

To my knowledge, the story of Xavier Garcia Garcia never appeared in the press and has never been documented publicly. While this was a major red herring that didn't advance the investigation, I felt it was important to include as an example of the difficulty of making decisions with incomplete (and sometimes inaccurate) information. Considering Garcia Garcia's criminal history, the timing of his arrest for breaking into the home of a twelve-year-old girl, and the items found in searches, I could see for the first time how it could be possible to arrest the wrong suspect.

Most of the information in the chapter came from internal documents found in the case files and from interviews with insiders.

Alford, David. FBI teletype, October 11, 1993.

FD-302, October 26, 1993. Search of Xavier Garcia Garcia's vehicle.

FD-302, November 6, 1993.

FD-302, November 12, 1993. Items taken from bedroom.

FD-302, November 12, 1993. Re: Search of Xavier Garcia Garcia's vehicle.

FD-302, November 28, 1993.

Freyer, Eddie. Memo to SAC San Francisco Division, October 26, 1993.

Freyer, Eddie. Interviews by Kim Cross, 2015–2023.

Jacobs, Greg. Statement of Facts. *People v. Richard Allen Davis*, 1993.

Mazzanti, Andy. Interview with Linda Dabbs, November 8, 1993.

Mershon, Mark. Handwritten notes on November 9, 1993.

Nation, Nancy Isles. "Volunteers for Polly Rebound." *Marin Independent Journal,* November 21, 1993.

Statement of Facts. *People v. Garcia.*

CHAPTER 26: PYTHIAN ROAD

I am not alone in my belief that if it hadn't been for Dana Jaffe, this case might not have been solved. But she was also part of a "perfect storm" of factors: the media coverage, the investigators' use of tips from the public, the internal organization to prioritize such tips (among 60,000 others), the collaboration between local and federal agencies, and the involvement of the FBI lab and the newly formed ERT team.

Over the past thirty years, Jaffe had given only two interviews about her role in solving this case. She not only granted me hours of interviews but led me (along with research director Meg Levi, who assisted me with research and reporting) on a three-hour hike across the property. We tried to retrace the route she walked the day she found the suspicious items. "I've always felt like Polly led me here," she told me, "like she wanted me to bring her home."

That walk with Jaffe was one of the most important on-the-ground moments of reporting I could do. I stood on the spot where Davis said Polly was waiting and was surprised at how close it was to the road (about thirty paces) and how close that spot on the road was to the gate where the deputies parked. Much of the property burned during the 2017 Tubbs Fire, and the 2020 Glass Fire consumed the house. "It feels clean now," Jaffe told me as we hiked in 2022.

While writing this book, I felt it was important to withhold my own opinions, preferring to present the facts—along with a relative degree of uncertainty—and let readers draw their own conclusions. Several early readers desired an informed opinion, wanting to know if I thought Polly was alive—or not—when the deputies were there.

With Jaffe's permission, Meg and I returned on a night with a nearly full moon (much as it was on the night of Polly's abduction). We parked my car in the location and position of the patrol cars, left the headlights on and car running, and stood for a while on the hill. Then Meg turned the car and the headlights off (and locked the doors). I was left alone in the dark on that hill, trying to imagine Polly's terror.

Based on the pitch of the terrain and the proximity to the patrol cars, the deputies' presence would have been bright—even through a blindfold and thick underbrush—and loud, with the radio chatter. Why would she not have screamed for help or, if gagged, rustled to make a noise? She could have been unconscious or incapacitated with fear.

I later attended a talk by Elizabeth Smart, who explained how her fear and her tender age prevented her from calling for help when her captors took her out in public, disguised under a veil. Jeanne Boylan, who wrote about (and sketched) her rapists in her memoir, *Portraits of Guilt*, told me that while she's a confident, capable woman, comfortable enough to travel the world solo, she found herself, too, incapacitated by fear.

No amount of empathy can allow us to know how Polly felt. It's also impossible to know how we would react if ever put in such a circumstance. Michelle Hord, a journalist who covered true crime and later was the mother of a murdered child, cautioned me not to speculate or wonder, in a salacious way, in the book. Other journalist friends advised that I couldn't dodge this important question. So I've decided to answer it here, rather than in the chapters.

Like the majority of investigators to whom I posed this question, I believe that Davis killed Polly after babysitter Shannon Lynch saw him and before the deputies arrived.

FBI teletype. October 1993.

Freyer, Eddie. Interviews with Kim Cross, 2015–2023.

Jaffe, Dana. 911 call, October 2, 1993. Transcript in police files.

Jaffe, Kelila. Trial testimony. *People v. Richard Allen Davis*, April 23, 1996.

Jaffe, Dana. Trial testimony. *People v. Richard Allen Davis*, April 23–24, 1996.

Jaffe, Dana. Interview by Kim Cross at Pythian site, March 20, 2022.

Jaffe, Dana. Fact-checking call with Kim Cross by phone, April 4, 2022.

Jaffe, Kelila. Interview by Kim Cross via Zoom from Auckland, New Zealand, April 12, 2023.

Lynch, Shannon. Trial testimony. *People v. Richard Allen Davis*, April 23, 1996.

Mazzanti, Andy. Interviews with Kim Cross, April 25, 2022.

McManus, Mike. Sonoma County Sheriff's report on evidence gathered at Dana Jaffe's property, November 28, 1993.

McManus, Mike. Trial testimony. *People v. Richard Allen Davis*, April 29, 1996.

Pelton, Larry. Interviews by Kim Cross, May 10, 2022; November 15, 2022.

"Polly Klaas: Kidnapped." *FBI Files*, Season 1, Episode 1, September 22, 1998. Accessed on YouTube: https://youtu.be/9G9oWPowwMA?t=2064.

Rankin, Mike. Interviews (on background) with Kim Cross, March 2022; January 15, 2023.

CHAPTER 27: THE SUBJECT

An individual's rap sheet—Record of Arrests and Prosecutions—is generally a document available only to law enforcement and not accessible to the public—unless that rap sheet is part of the public record. Because it's in the police files and trial exhibits, it is. Andy Mazzanti helped me decipher Davis's rap sheet, which is peppered with abbreviations and technical language new to me. He helped me read it through the eyes of an investigator using it as a tool to begin "a full workup." Brief aside for researchers: A number of 1993 newspaper stories mentioned an "11-page RAP sheet," but Mazzanti and I together counted eight pages.

The background on Davis's past crimes came from Greg Jacobs's personal archives, which included copies of the original police reports on those crimes as well as information obtained later for the trial, some of it by Mike Meese, who left Petaluma PD to take a job as an investigator for the DA's office. Meese was instrumental in helping Jacobs prepare for trial.

Alford, David. Interview by Kim Cross, 2023.

Bello, Vail. Interview by Kim Cross, October 14, 2022.

Berns, Thomas. Trial testimony. *People v. Richard Allen Davis*, May 28, 1996.

Cochran, K. Trial testimony. *People v. Richard Allen Davis*, May 16, 1996.

Davis, Richard Allen. RAP sheet. Case files.

Doyle, Frank. Interview by Kim Cross, May 19, 2021.

FD-302, March 18, 1985.

Fischer, David. *Hard Evidence: How Detectives Inside the FBI's Sci-Crime Lab Have Helped Solve America's Toughest Cases*. Simon & Schuster, 1995.

Frost, Hazel. Trial testimony. *People v. Richard Allen Davis*, May 16, 1996.

Gong, Jim. Interview by Kim Cross, November 28, 2022.

Griffith, Mike. Supplemental report, January 11, 1995.

Jacobs, Greg. Interviews by Kim Cross, November 11, 2015; November 18, 2021; January 1, 2022; March 18, 2022; May 14, 2022; November 27, 2022.

Kennewick PD and FBI reports on robberies, December 4, 1989.

Krieger, J. Trial testimony. *People v. Richard Allen Davis*, May 16, 1996.

Ladd, Thomas. FD-302, November 29, 1989. Interview with Richard Allen Davis in San Luis Obispo Men's Colony.

Ladd, Thomas. Trial testimony. *People v. Richard Allen Davis*, July 2, 1996.

Letras, Tom. Fact-checking phone call by Kim Cross, June 8, 2022.

Mazzanti, Andy. Personal logbook from October to November 1993.

Mazzanti, Andy. Interviews by Kim Cross, June 8, 2022; November 10, 2022; November 11, 2022.

Miller, Douglas B. Trial testimony. *People v. Richard Allen Davis*, May 16, 1996.

Mitchell, Marjorie. Trial testimony. *People v. Richard Allen Davis*, May 16, 1996.

O'Rourke, Lois. "Kidnap Suspect Arraigned: Clothing Linked to Kidnap Found." *Ukiah Daily Journal,* December 2, 1993.

"Polly Klaas: Kidnapped." *FBI Files*, Season 1, Episode 1, September 22, 1998. Accessed on YouTube: https://youtu.be/9G9oWPowwMA?t=2064.

Stanley, Pat. "'Primetime Live' Visits Napa." *Petaluma Argus-Courier,* January 21, 1994.

Sweeney, James, and Chris Smith. "At Age 12 Davis Began Crimes." *Santa Rosa Press Democrat*, December 2, 1993.

Toobin, Jeffrey. "The Man Who Kept Going Free." *New Yorker*, February 27, 1994.

CHAPTER 28: THE LAB

Lab examiner Chris Allen granted me one interview, then opted out of subsequent participation. Most of his scenes, dialogue, and quotes came from his trial testimony and from his interview in the Polly Klaas episode of *FBI Files*.

David Alford recollected scenes he witnessed in the lab, when he was interacting with Allen. Alford also provided the technical information about lab procedures such as the scraping room. Prior to joining the ERT, Alford had worked in the Kentucky State Police Crime Lab and later the FBI lab as a hair and fibers examiner (among other things). Alford spent hours with me on the phone, and any time I emailed a question, he emailed back a thoughtful and thoroughly detailed answer. His expertise is behind the descriptions of hair and fiber analysis, though when he was working as an examiner he refused to do hair analysis because it was so fraught with subjectivity.

Alford had moved on to other work by the time news broke about the FBI lab's hair and fibers controversy. In 2012, the US Department of Justice and the FBI began a review of all criminal cases in which FBI hair and fibers expert witnesses testified prior to 2000. The review found that in the "vast majority" of cases, they had overstated the certainty with which two similar hairs could be considered "a match." I dug into this, and this case does not appear to be one of them.

Frank Doyle shared the hair-plucking story in an interview with me before he died. The condom examination scene came from trial testimony by Thomas Lynch.

Researchers Meg Levi and Allison Baggott-Rowe and he also reviewed and helped me fact-check the chapters containing ERT history and forensic science to help me get the language right.

The scene of Greg Jacobs being called into the DA's office was described to me in an email from Greg.

Alford, David. Email to Kim Cross, September 30, 2022.
Alford, David. Interviews by Kim Cross, October 20, 2022; January 8, 2023.
Allen, Chris. Trial testimony. *People v. Richard Allen Davis*, May 15, 1996.
Deedrick, Doug. Interview by Kim Cross, January 24, 2023.
Doyle, Frank. Interview by Kim Cross, June 15, 2021.
Guy, Brian. Interview with Kim Cross, March 8, 2022.
Hsu, Spencer S. "Justice Department, FBI to Review Use of Forensic Evidence in Thousands of Cases." *Washington Post*, July 10, 2012.
Hsu, Spencer S. "FBI Admits Flaws in Hair Analysis over Decades." *Washington Post*, April 18, 2015.
Jacobs, Greg. Email to Kim Cross, March 11, 2023.
Lynch, Thomas. Trial testimony. *People v. Richard Allen Davis*, May 14, 1996.
"Polly Klaas: Kidnapped." *FBI Files*, Season 1, Episode 1, September 22, 1998. Accessed on YouTube: https://youtu.be/9G9oWPowwMA?t=2064.

CHAPTER 29: SWAT RAID

I found few internal documents related to the SWAT raid on Darlene and Richard Schwarm's house on the reservation. Most of the details and dialogue in this chapter's scenes were recounted in interviews decades later with the SWAT team members who participated. Mike Kerns recounted the diversionary tactic of hosting a press conference to provide cover for the SWAT team's departure from the station. The scene of the arrest was corroborated between Pat Parks and Mark Mershon.

Interestingly, no one was able to remember who the snipers were, so I was unable to talk to one. Because the snipers positioned themselves out of sight, perhaps they didn't get embedded in the memory as deeply as assault team colleagues in full view and close proximity.

Almost all of the SWAT team members who participated in this raid remembered Bruce Burroughs's radio transmission consistently: "He's not here." The subsequent radio transmission was recollected consistently in content but inconsistently in language. Most people agreed that "Hey, I think your guy is waiting in line here" sounded true.

Nearly everyone attributed that quote to "a young rookie deputy stationed on the outer perimeter, at a checkpoint" who spotted Richard Allen Davis and called it in. No one could remember his name.

I felt it was important to credit this person for recognizing Davis and triggering the sequence of events that led to his arrest. It took a surprising amount of effort to figure out the name of that deputy (Rusty Noe), and a ridiculous amount of time to track him down to verify the story. Months.

It turns out that Rusty Noe was not a rookie and did not recognize Davis at all, which to me made the story even better. However, he said he was not the one who made that radio transmission. It was the FBI radio tech. No one remembered much about him, except that his first name was "Ernie."

Alford, David. Interview by Kim Cross, April 21, 2022.

Bello, Vail. Interview by Kim Cross, January 21, 2023.

Burroughs, Bruce. Interviews by Kim Cross, January 18, 19, 20, 2023.

Davidson, Joe. Interview by Kim Cross, March 11, 2022.

Doyle, Frank. Interview by Kim Cross, June 15, 2021.

Fish, Danny. Interviews by Kim Cross, April 5, 2022.

Freyer, Eddie. Interviews by Kim Cross, January 16, 2020; June 20, 2021; January 12, 19, 2023.

Gizzi, Dominic. Interview by Kim Cross, February 7, 2023.

Hisquierdo, Joe. Interview by Kim Cross, December 13, 2022.

Jacobs, Greg. Statement of Case, *People v. Richard Allen Davis*, April 1993.

Kerns, Mike. Interview by Kim Cross, August 2, 2022.

LaFreniere, Tom. Interviews by Kim Cross, February 5, 2016; April 5, 2022; February 4, 2023.

Marcou, Dan. Interview by Kim Cross, January 19, 2023.

Meadows, K. C. "Coyote Valley Tribe Meets with Lawyer for Davis's Kin." *Ukiah Daily Journal,* December 7, 1993.

Mershon, Mark. Interview by Kim Cross, May 6, 2022.

Noe, Rusty. Interviews by Kim Cross, January 21, 22, 2023.

Parks, Pat. Interviews by Kim Cross, April 29, 2022.

Pelton, Larry. Email to Kim Cross, November 16, 2022.

Schwarm, Richard. Trial testimony. *People v. Richard Allen Davis*, May 20, 1996.

Sena, Phil. Interview by Kim Cross, January 26, 2023.

Sonenshine, Ron. "Prime Suspect Held in Abduction of Girl, 12." *San Francisco Chronicle,* December 2, 1993.

Stapleton, Matt. Interviews by Kim Cross, January 18, 21, 2023.

Steiner, John "JC." Interview by Kim Cross, January 29, 2023.

Wallace, Gene. Interview by Kim Cross, January 21, 2023.

CHAPTER 30: THE FIRST INTERVIEW

Rusty Noe recounted the first scene in this chapter, which surprised most of the people involved in the raid. Dialogue in the interview scene is from a written transcript of the recorded interview. (I did not have access to an audio or videotape of this interview.) A few lines of dialogue (such as Davis's comment, "I've helped kill people like that,") were redacted in the trial exhibits. Greg Jacobs gave me the unredacted version with permission to include the redacted parts.

Davis, Richard Allen. Interview by Larry Pelton and Larry Taylor at Mendocino County Jail, November 30, 1993. Transcript from Larry Pelton's archives.

Jacobs, Greg. Statement of Case, *People v. Richard Allen Davis*, April 1993.

Noe, Rusty. Interviews by Kim Cross, January 21, 22, 2023.

Pelton, Larry. Interview by Kim Cross, November 16, 2022.

Taylor, Larry. Interviews by Kim Cross, June 13, 2021; July 6, 2021; November 15, 2021.

CHAPTER 31: THE PALM PRINT

FBI lab fingerprint specialist Michael J. Smith was deceased by the time I began this book, so I turned to his trial testimony for facts and quotes. Other experts provided the rest.

David Alford currently teaches forensic investigation classes for Sirchie, a company that provides crime scene investigation tools and training. I lost track of the hours we spent on the phone, going over the intricate details of forensic science, and on one occasion he spent more than an hour on Zoom with me, demonstrating fingerprint dusting techniques with standard and fluorescent powder and ALS. Alford sometimes co-instructs with Mike Stapleton, a certified fingerprint specialist who has taught at the FBI Academy (among many other places). Alford and Stapleton reviewed this and other chapters to help me get the terminology and science right.

The source of the inked palm print was one of the greatest mysteries—and most exciting moments of reporting—in this project. No one could tell me who found it, or where. I spent weeks re-interviewing sources and scouring the case files, and everyone I talked to believed or guessed a different source. Greg Jacobs recalled something about Stanislaus County, and I scribbled that down.

Finally, I found one photograph of the inked print in Tony Maxwell's personal archives. To confirm its provenance, I reached out to the Stanislaus County Sheriff's Office. Because cold calls from reporters don't always prove fruitful, I asked Tony Maxwell to call ahead and let them know I was legit. Tony agreed to "grease the skids."

Lieutenant Tom Letras called me immediately after talking to Tony. He found notes in the file that documented who made the request (Andy Mazzanti) and when it was faxed to the Petaluma command center. In the Stanislaus files was a copy of the actual inked prints along with a note that said the originals had been sent to the FBI. (I never could find out how the originals were transported.)

While Lieutenant Letras was not allowed to send me any new documents, he was able to confirm the provenance of documents I already had in my possession.

I immediately called Andy, who had spent hours trying to help me figure out who tracked down the palm print.

"Andy!" I said. "I figured out who found the palm print."

"Really?" he said. "Who?"

When I told him it was him, he was quiet for a long time.

Then Andy checked his personal logbook from 1993, which confirmed he was out on bereavement leave when it rolled in.

Alford, David. Interview by Kim Cross, April 5, 2022.

Doyle, Frank. Trial testimony. *People v. Richard Allen Davis*, May 7, 1996.

FBI teletype. "Palm print identified." Undated.

Fischer, David. *Hard Evidence: How Detectives Inside the FBI's Sci-Crime Lab Have Helped Solve America's Toughest Cases*. Simon & Schuster, 1995.

Letras, Tom. Fact-checking phone call by Kim Cross, June 8, 2022.

Maxwell, Tony. Trial testimony. *People v. Richard Allen Davis*, April 23, 1996.

Maxwell, Tony. Trial testimony. *People v. Richard Allen Davis*, May 6, 1996.

Mershon, Mark. Email to Kim Cross, October 15, 2022.

Smith, Michael J. Trial testimony. *People v. Richard Allen Davis*, April 29, 1996.

Smith, Michael J. Trial testimony. *People v. Richard Allen Davis*, May 7, 1996.

Smith, Michael J. Trial testimony. *People v. Richard Allen Davis*, May 8, 1996.

Stapleton, Mike. Email to Kim Cross, December 20, 2022.

CHAPTER 32: THE LINEUP

The scenes and dialogue in this chapter came from a police report written by Andy Mazzanti, who included dialogue and details such as Kate lying down on the floor. I also found a lineup schedule and documents listing which witnesses were transported to the lineup by whom.

Mazzanti, Andy. Police report documenting interview with Kate and Alice McLean after Kate's viewing of the lineup, December 3, 1993.

Pelton, Larry. Police report documenting results of the lineup, December 1, 1993.

Pelton, Larry. Trial testimony. *People v. Richard Allen Davis*, April 23, 1996.

Pelton, Larry. Trial testimony. *People v. Richard Allen Davis*, April 29, 1996.

"Polly Klaas: Kidnapped." *FBI Files*, Season 1, Episode 1, September 22, 1998. Accessed on YouTube: https://youtu.be/9G9oWPowwMA?t=2064.

CHAPTER 33: SYSTEM FAILURES

Much of this chapter was sourced from news stories written in 1993. Some of the details about Davis's interactions with his parole agent came from Thomas Berns's trial testimony. Marc Klaas's quotes and reactions came from published stories.

Berns, Thomas. Trial testimony. *People v. Richard Allen Davis*, May 28, 1996.

Hunt, Karyn. "Suspect Has Long Criminal History." Associated Press, December 2, 1993.

Meadows, K. C., and the Associated Press. "High Hopes and Low Times at Petaluma Search Center." *Ukiah Daily Journal*, December 2, 1993, A1.

O'Rourke, Lois. "Kidnap Suspect Arraigned." *Ukiah Daily Journal*, December 2, 1993, A1.

O'Rourke, Lois. "Kidnap Suspect Pleads Guilty to Drunken Driving." *Ukiah Daily Journal*, December 3, 1993, A1.

Paddock, Richard C., and Jennifer Warren. "Revelations in Klaas Kidnapping Spark Outrage." *Los Angeles Times*, December 3, 1993, A1. Accessed online.

Shonenshine, Ron. "'Prime Suspect' Held in Abduction of Girl, 12." *San Francisco Chronicle*, December 2, 1993, syndicated in *San Diego Union-Tribune* and accessed online.

Vasquez, Daniel. "Suspected Kidnapper's Neighbors Seek Answers." *Oakland Tribune*, December 2, 1993, A11.

CHAPTER 34: THE WILD CARD

The scenes and dialogue of Marvin White came from 1996 trial testimony by Marvin White, Mike Meese, Troy Furman, and Daniel Lockart.

The conversations between Richard Allen Davis and Mike Meese—both in the hallway at the jail and later on the phone—were recounted by Meese several times: in a police report he wrote in 1993, in his 1996 trial testimony, and in TV interviews for *American Justice* and *The FBI Files*.

Some snippets of dialogue came from interviews with Eddie Freyer. The anecdote about the dog came from an interview with David Alford. I corroborated the facts and dialogue with Frank Doyle, Tony Maxwell, and Lillian Zilius, who were also present.

Alford, David. Interview with Kim Cross, March 9, 2022.

Fagan, Kevin. "Palm Print Links Man to Missing Polly Klaas." *San Francisco Chronicle*, December 4, 1993.

"Free to Kill: The Polly Klaas Murder." *American Justice*, Season 5, Episode 26, October 23, 1996. Accessed on VHS tape but also available on YouTube.

Freyer, Eddie. Interview by Kim Cross, November 16, 2015.

Furman, Troy. Trial testimony. *People v. Richard Allen Davis*, April 30, 1996.

Lockart, D. Trial testimony. *People v. Richard Allen Davis*, April 30, 1996.

Meese, Mike. Police report, December 5, 1993.

Meese, Mike. Trial testimony. *People v. Richard Allen Davis*, April 30, 1996; May 1, 1996; May 7, 1996; May 13, 1996; May 20, 1996; May 28, 1996; July 2, 1996.

"Polly Klaas: Kidnapped." *FBI Files*, Season 1, Episode 1, September 22, 1998. Accessed on YouTube: https://youtu.be/9G9oWPowwMA?t=2064 (see 40:01).

Stapleton, Mike. Email to Kim Cross, March 9, 2022.

Stapleton, Mike. Email to Kim Cross, October 10, 2022.

Taylor, Larry. Interviews by Kim Cross, June 13, 2021; July 6, 2021; November 15, 2021.

White, William Marvin. Trial testimony. *People v. Richard Allen Davis*, April 29, 1996.

Zilius, Lillian. Interview by Kim Cross, December 16, 2022.

CHAPTER 35: THE CONFESSION

The confession tape was extremely hard to find. Not even case agent Eddie Freyer was able to obtain a copy. He had requested one for educational use in his

Investigative Interview and Interrogation class for the Behavioral Analysis Training Institute (BATI). The current district attorney denied his request.

I obtained a copy legally and serendipitously. At the wedding of my brother-in-law, Jason Freyer, I found myself discussing the confession tape with his new bride, Aleshia Sbragia. I mentioned I'd been searching for a copy for years. "I've seen it!" Aleshia said.

Her college journalism instructor had played the confession tape in class at Santa Rosa Junior College. Aleshia put me in touch with her professor, journalist and author Anne Belden, who was friends with Mike Meese, who also taught at SRJC. Meese used the tape in his criminal justice class.

Meese died in 2009. He was known to save a lot of files, but his wife, Michelle, had purged them by the time I contacted her in 2021. But he had made Belden a copy of the confession tape to use in her class. Belden made two copies of the tape: one for me, and one for Eddie Freyer, who now uses it in his course. His students—detectives and FBI agents—say it's one of the highlights of the class.

Davis, Richard Allen. Interview by Mike Meese and Larry Taylor, December 4, 1993. Videotape and transcript.

Freyer, Eddie. Interviews by Kim Cross, January 1, 2021; June 20, 2021; October 22, 2021.

Lee, Patrick (student of Mike Meese). Interview by Kim Cross, February 18, 2023.

Loden, Roy. Interview by Kim Cross, January 1, 2020.

Meese, Frank. Interview by Kim Cross, March 22, 2022.

Meese, Michelle. Interviews by Kim Cross, November 21, 2021; March 19, 2022.

Meese, Mike. Trial testimony. *People v. Richard Allen Davis*, April 30, 1996; May 1, 1996; May 7, 1996; May 13, 1996; May 20, 1996; May 28, 1996; July 2, 1996.

Swearington, Peggy (Petaluma PD colleague who gave Mike Meese's eulogy). Interview by Kim Cross, May 13, 2022.

Taylor, Larry. Interviews by Kim Cross, June 13, 2021; July 6, 2021; November 15, 2021.

CHAPTER 36: ANATOMY OF A LIE

To my knowledge, this is the first time the transcript of the confession tape has been made publicly available. I initially wanted to publish an unabridged transcript as an addendum to the book, but it was simply too long. The version in this chapter is abridged because of length and it contained too many extraneous asides. What appears in the chapter is very close to verbatim, with edits/additions made in brackets and minor cuts for length and clarity.

I first watched the confession tape with Eddie Freyer at his home in Sonoma on New Year's Day 2021. We were there for a family visit over the holidays. Eddie Jr., our son, and the rest of the family left the house, having no desire to watch it with us. I recorded Eddie's commentary as he analyzed the interrogation techniques and interpreted Davis's verbal and physical responses.

On June 13, 2021, Tony Maxwell and Larry Taylor came to my house in Boise, and we watched the tape together, pausing it repeatedly to talk about what they saw. I recorded this conversation as well.

In March 2023, as I was writing the chapter, Andy Mazzanti watched it at his new home in Oregon and provided additional insights.

I wove all of their insights into the chapter. All of them, as well as Greg Jacobs (who thought it was too long) reviewed my additions for accuracy.

Freyer, Eddie. Interview/analysis with Kim Cross, January 1, 2021.

Jacobs, Greg. Interview by Kim Cross, May 24, 2022.

Jacobs, Greg. Email to Kim Cross, February 18, 2023.

Maxwell, Tony, and Larry Taylor. Joint interview/analysis of confession tape with Kim Cross, June 13, 2021.

Mazzanti, Andy. Email to Kim Cross, January 2023.

Mazzanti, Andy. Interviews by Kim Cross, January 2023.

CHAPTER 37: CLOVERDALE

The dialogue in this chapter comes from a transcript of the audio recording of the drive to Cloverdale. Greg Jacobs shared the unredacted transcript.

While some sources note that Mike Meese and Larry Taylor were driving with Davis in a patrol car, journalism professor Anne Belden had notes from a talk Meese gave to her class in which he recalled them driving an "old rat-trap Chevrolet." Logic suggests that they would be driving an unmarked vehicle to avoid being followed by the media.

The scene and dialogue of Eddie viewing Polly's body was recounted to me in numerous interviews with Eddie Freyer and Vail Bello.

Belden, Anne. Notes taken during a lecture by Mike Meese to her journalism class.

Davis, Richard Allen. Interview by Mike Meese and Larry Taylor. December 4, 1993. Transcript of audio recording.

Paddock, Richard C., and Jennifer Warren. "Suspect's Palm Print Found in Klaas Home; Kidnapping: Evidence Discovered in Bedroom on Night of Girl's Abduction Shows Parolee Was There, FBI Says. Richard Allen Davis Could Be Charged Next Week." Los Angeles Times, December 4, 1993.

Paddock, Richard C., and Jennifer Warren. "Suspect's Tip Leads to Body of Polly Klaas." Los Angeles Times, December 5, 1993.

"Polly's Body Found in Woods near Cloverdale." Associated Press, December 5, 1993.

CHAPTER 38: FOUND

This chapter was based on exhaustive interviews with all the individuals present. Much of the dialogue was recollected in these interviews some decades later, so it may not be verbatim. I corroborated the dialogue with as many sources as possible and in some cases asked the speakers to recount it on several occasions.

Vail Bello and Eddie Freyer shared the dialogue and scene at the beginning of the chapter. Mark Mershon and Pat Parks recounted the scene in which they had to notify Marc and Eve.

The scene and dialogue of Tony's pushback against pressure to remove Polly's body before daybreak is one scene where not everyone's memory lines up. Tony Maxwell vividly remembers this moment because it was so pivotal—not only for the case but personally, as he felt his job was on the line. He recounted the dialogue in several interviews spanning seven years, and while the wording changed slightly, the content remained consistent.

Tony's supervisor, Lillian Zilius, recalled the conversation with Tony during an interview with me before she died. I read her the dialogue Tony recollected, and she said, "That sounds about right." She confirmed Tony's perception that his job was on the line.

David Alford and Frank Doyle did not join or overhear the conversation between Tony and Lillian, but in separate interviews they both recollected the pressure from "higher ups" to move the body. Vail Bello also said it was his impression that they were under that directive.

The scene was questioned by Eddie Freyer, Mark Mershon, and Pat Parks, who don't recall any such orders to remove the body. Eddie was present at the crime scene, but wasn't part of the conversation between Tony and Lillian. It was his leadership style to stay out of the way and let them decide as experts. At the time of the conversation, Mark Mershon and Pat Parks were in Petaluma notifying Polly's parents of her death.

FD-302 (read to me on Zoom by Mark Mershon) noted the time.
Freyer, Eddie. Interviews by Kim Cross, 2015–2023.
Maxwell, Tony. Trial testimony. *People v. Richard Allen Davis*, May 6, 1996.
Maxwell, Tony. Interviews by Kim Cross, 2015–2023.
Meese, Mike. PowerPoint presentation on Polly Klaas.
Mershon, Mark. Interviews by Kim Cross, 2022–2023.
Parks, Pat. Interviews with Kim Cross, 2022–2023.
"We Should Grieve All Victims." *Ukiah Daily Journal*, December 6, 1993.

CHAPTER 39: POSITIVE IDENTIFICATION

I agonized over this chapter. I wanted to avoid sensationalizing or appealing to salacious curiosity by including lurid and gratuitous details. However, to hold Davis fully accountable, it was important to include some key facts that were unavoidably graphic. I felt that withholding these details would let Davis off too lightly.

The one thing he seems to care most about is avoiding the label of child molester. That was his main point of contention in the trial. The evidence was insufficient to prove in the trial he sexually assaulted Polly. Some details and facts suggest another story.

In consideration of Polly's family, these descriptions and details were minimized and distilled to what I felt was absolutely necessary for readers to know in order to come to their own conclusions about Davis's assertions.

Many of the details came from internal documents and ERT photos of the crime scene and autopsy. Every participant in the autopsy was listed in the report: Charles K. Wilcox, David Alford, Anthony Maxwell, Frank Doyle, Michael Stapleton, and Lillian Zilius from the FBI; Dr. Jay Chapman, SC Medical Examiner, and David Nahunan from the Sonoma County Medical Examiner's Office; Tom Siebe from the Sonoma County Sheriff's Office; Chief Deputy Coroner John Birrer; Dennis Nowicki and Margaret Paulson from the Petaluma PD; Tom Kessler from the Bay Area Portable X-Ray Company; forensic odontologist Dr. Jack Davies and odontology assistant Debbie Anderson.

Alford, David. Email to Kim Cross, October 17, 2022.

Autopsy photos from the files of Greg Jacobs, Tony Maxwell, Mike Meese.

FD-302, December 6, 1993. Autopsy report.

FD-302 (read to me on Zoom by Mark Mershon) noted the time of the autopsy.

Jacobs, Greg. Facts of the Case. *People v. Richard Allen Davis*, 1996.

Meadows, K. C. "Coyote Valley Tribe Meets with Lawyer for Davis' Kin." *Ukiah Daily Journal*, December 7, 1993.

Meese, Mike. PowerPoint presentation on Polly Klaas.

Meese, Mike. Trial testimony. *People v. Richard Allen Davis*, May 7, 1996.

Stapleton, Mike. Email to Kim Cross, October 3, 2022.

CHAPTER 40: AMERICA CRIES

Joanne Gardner, Gaynell Rogers, and Jay Silverberg provided a number of personal anecdotes and dialogue in this chapter. A video clip of 1993 news coverage by NBC is posted on Joan Baez's YouTube page. Other details came from news stories.

"Eve Nichol's Message to Community," *Santa Rosa Press Democrat*, December 7, 1993.

Gardner, Joanne. Interviews by Kim Cross, November 18, 2021; August 11, 2022; November 20, 2022.

Hart, Steve. "Cloverdale: 'An Angel Rested Here': Memorial Grows Where Polly Was Found." *Santa Rosa Press Democrat*, December 14, 1993.

Locke, Michelle. "Davis Says He Murdered Polly." Associated Press, December 6, 1993.

Minton, Toni, Susan Yoachum, and Kevin Fagan. "Tears and Prayers for Polly." *San Francisco Chronicle*, December 10, 1993.

Parks, Pat. Interviews with Kim Cross, April 29, 2022.

Polly Klaas memorial service. Video clip of Joan Baez singing. Accessed via YouTube: https://youtu.be/G37i3MoU5n4?t=109.

Rogers, Gaynell. Interviews by Kim Cross, December 7, 2021, March 14, 2022; August 11, 2022.

Rose, Bleys W. "Polly Klaas Memorial Service." *Santa Rosa Press Democrat*, December 9, 1993.

Silverberg, Jay. Interviews by Kim Cross, February 3, 2016; October 20, 2021; April 1, 2022; July 19, 2022; December 7, 2022.

"With Song and Poetry, a Farewell to a Kidnapped Girl Named Polly." *New York Times*, December 11, 1993.

CHAPTER 41: THE TRIAL

This chapter weaves together facts and details from the 12,000 pages of trial transcripts loaned to me by Greg Jacobs, who gave me no limits on interviews, phone calls, emails, and questions. He talked with me for hours, on many occasions, by email, text, phone, and in person, and loaded at least six banker's boxes of documents, trial exhibits, photos, videos, and other primary source materials into my car. It would have been impossible for me to obtain even a fraction of this with Freedom of Information Act requests. I did request a number of records from the Santa Clara Courthouse, but in more than a year of waiting I did not receive a single page. They were that busy.

Richard Allen Davis still sends Christmas cards to public defender Barry Collins, who spent many hours with me, both at his house not far from Pythian Road and on the phone. He let me visit him at the casino where he works as a blackjack and baccarat dealer so I could witness the theatrical personality that surely played out in the courtroom. Barry lent me the original folder he was handed when he accepted the case, and it contained documents that I didn't find elsewhere. As Meg Levi and I interviewed him in his living room, his wife, Grace, baked us cookies and retrieved the orange prison jumpsuit worn by Davis during his sentencing, and set it up on a dress form in the living room. He let us hold his three pet tortoises.

Press clips covering the trial were abundant, though there are considerable gaps in online archives during the 1990s. The vast majority of the newspaper stories sourced in this book came from print clippings preserved by Greg Jacobs, Andy Mazzanti, Brian Bianco, Greg Cahill, Vail Bello, and Larry Taylor, who shared them with me. Meg Levi, director of research for this project, scanned, logged, and archived hundreds of them. Reporter Mary Callahan of the *Santa Rosa Press Democrat* covered the trial comprehensively and skillfully, and she let me interview her to understand the media's point of view.

Jury foreman Brian Bianco granted me interviews and sent me a box of documents, including a binder of newspaper articles they were admonished not to read during the trial. Judge Thomas Hastings had made a copy for each juror. He helped me imagine what it was like to view the trial from the jury box and gave me a glimpse of the personality of the jury.

An unexpected source was reporting on a "cyber diary" written by Marc Klaas, who journaled throughout the trial and published it on what may be one of the internet's first blogs. I was unable to find the cyber diary online, but there were excerpts in a newspaper story.

Victim impact statements from the trial transcripts were used to shape the emotional perspective of those affected by the crime.

Bianco, Brian. Interview by Kim Cross, December 1, 2021.

Callahan, Mary. "Pain of Polly's Kidnap on Tape." *Santa Rosa Press Democrat*, April 20, 1996.

Callahan, Mary. "Davis' Gesture Points to Trouble." *Santa Rosa Press Democrat*, May 6, 1996.

Callahan, Mary. "Davis Jurors View Graphic Photos." *Santa Rosa Press Democrat*, June 20, 1996.

Ceppos, Jerry. "1,248 Readers Respond to Davis Photo." *San Jose Mercury News*, June 23, 1996.

Collins, Barry. Interviews by Kim Cross, March 5, 2022; in Sonoma March 16, 2022.

"Davis Jury Hears DNA testimony." Associated Press, May 9, 1996.

Halstead, Richard. "Davis Tells How He Killed Polly." *Marin Independent Journal*, April 24, 1996.

Hoover, Ken. "Klaas Prosecutor's Final Arguments." *San Francisco Chronicle*, June 11, 1996.

Hoover, Ken. "Polly's Killer Guilty on All Counts." *San Francisco Chronicle*, June 19, 1996.

Hourel, E. Dean. "Inmate: Davis Has Never Shown Remorse." *San Jose Mercury News*, June 23, 1996.

Jacobs, Greg. Interviews by Kim Cross, November 11, 2015; November 18, 2021; March 18, 2022; May 14, 2022.

Lafferty, Shannon. "Hastings Leaves No Doubt Who's in Control of His Court." Law.com, March 13, 2001.

Locke, Michelle. "Videotaped Confession Played in Polly Klaas Trial." Associated Press, May 1, 1996.

Locke, Michelle. "Jurors Relive Journey to Find Polly's Body." Associated Press, May 2, 1996.

Locke, Michelle. "Details Emerge in Polly Case Testimony." Associated Press, May 8, 1996.

Lum, Rebecca Rosen. "Davis Jury Sees Crime Scene." *Petaluma Argus-Courier*, May 3, 1996.

"Marc Klaas' Cyberspace Diary." Associated Press, May 27, 1996.

Mead, Tyra Lucille. "Polly Klaas' Death Changed Lives, Laws." *San Francisco Chronicle,* April 11, 1996.

Rossman, Randi. "Davis No Longer Alone—Hate Mail Pours In." *Santa Rosa Press Democrat*, December 14, 1993.

Victim Impact Statements. *People v. Richard Allen Davis*, September 9, 1996, p 25.

CHAPTER 42: POLLY'S LEGACY

The scenes, quotes, and thoughts of Polly's family came from published stories reported by others, acknowledged below, from TV news coverage recorded on VHS tapes shared by Greg Jacobs and Andy Mazzanti, and from the trial transcripts. The scene and details of the case debriefing came from interviews and a memo of the itinerary.

The scenes of Katie Romanek's abduction and rescue came from interviews with Katie and Larry Hansen, supplemented by news articles and TV interviews.

Larry, Katie, and her sister, Beth, were featured in "22 Hours of Terror," an episode of *On the Case with Paula Zahn* in 2016.

"106 Years for Lodi Abduction / Drifter Raped and Kidnapped 12-Year-Old Girl." *SF Gate*, April 25, 1995.

"12-Year-Old Found Muddy but Safe." Associated Press, July 4, 1994.

"22 Hours of Terror." *On the Case with Paula Zahn*, Season 14, Episode 1, August 28, 2016.

Freyer, Eddie. Interviews with Kim Cross, 2015–2023.

Hansen, Larry. Interviews by Kim Cross, June 5, 2022; March 7, 2023; April 5, 2023.

Junod, Tom. "America's Most Haunted." *GQ*, September 1997.

"Lodi Kidnap Victim Opens Up 21 Years Later: 21 Years Later, Katie Romanek Is Talking about What Happened, How She Struggled in the Years Following, and How She Wants to Help Other Victims of Violent Crime." KXTV: ABC 10, Lodi. October 11, 2015.

Mershon, Mark. Interviews with Kim Cross, 2022–2023.

"Monterey Wedding for Klaas and Cheer." *Petaluma Argus-Courier*, July 19, 1994.

Parks, Pat. Interview with Kim Cross, April 10, 2023.

"Polly, Alive in Memory." *People*, September 22, 2003, 187.

Polly Klaas Case Debriefing schedule, Sonoma Mission Inn, February 7, 1994. Internal memo from Vail Bello's personal archives.

Romanek, Katie. Interviews by Kim Cross, March 7, 12, 2023.

Sheehan, Susan. "Life After Polly." Publication unknown, date unknown (circa 1994). Magazine tearsheet from Greg Jacobs's personal archives.

EPILOGUE

"10 Reasons to Oppose '3 Strikes, You're Out.'" American Civil Liberties Union, March 17, 2002. https://www.aclu.org/other/10-reasons-oppose-3-strikes-youre-out.

California's Three Strikes Sentencing Law. California Courts. https://www.courts.ca.gov/20142.htm.

Chiesa, James. "California's New Three-Strikes Law: Benefits, Costs, and Alternatives." Santa Monica, CA: RAND Corporation, 1994. https://www.rand.org/pubs/research_briefs/RB4009.html.

Crifasi, C. K., K. M. Pollack, and D. W. Webster. "Effects of State-Level Policy Changes on Homicide and Nonfatal Shootings of Law Enforcement Officers." *Injury Prevention*, 2016.

"Does the Three Strikes Law Still Exist, and What Is It?" H Law Group. https://www.thehfirm.com/blog/does-the-three-strikes-law-still-exist-and-what-is-it.

Greene, Robert. "Opinion: Polly Klaas' Murder Accelerated the Tough-on-Crime Movement. Her Sisters Want to Stop It." *Los Angeles Times*, October 17, 2021.

Howe, Raine. Interviews by Kim Cross, November 18, 2015; November 19, 2021; March 16, 2022.

Jacobs, Greg. Interviews by Kim Cross, 2015–2023.

Levin, Sam. "Polly Klaas's Murder Fueled the '90s Crime Panic. Her Sisters Fear 'We're Repeating History.'" *Guardian*, October 22, 2022.

Macallair, Dan, and Mike Males. "Striking Out: The Failure of California's 'Three Strikes and You're Out' Law." (1999) *Stanford Law & Policy Review*.

McLean, Kate. Interview (on background) by Kim Cross, January 9, 2023.

Mershon, Mark. Interview by Kim Cross, May 6, 2022.

Nichol, Jess, and Annie Nichol. "Polly Klaas Was Our Sister. We Don't Want Unjust Laws to Be Her Legacy." *Los Angeles Times*, October 18, 2020.

Parks, Pat. Interviews by Kim Cross, April 29, 2022; September 29, 2022.

Pelham, Gillian. Interview by Kim Cross, December 21, 2022.

Rose, Bleys W. "Tough Anti-crime Initiatives Gain New Momentum." *Santa Rosa Press Democrat,* December 7, 1993.

Schiraldi, Vincent, Jason Colburn, and Eric Locke. "Three Strikes and You're Out: An Examination of the Impact of Strikes Laws 10 Years After Their Enactment." Policy brief from the Justice Policy Institute.

Spolar, Christine. "California Town Cries as Polly Klaas Is Found." *Washington Post,* December 6, 1993.

Stein, Sarah, as told to Adrienne Frank. "3 Minutes on Missing White Woman Syndrome." *American University Magazine*, August 2022.

Stolzenberg, Lisa, and Stewart J. D'Alessio. "Three Strikes and You're Out: The Impact of California's New Mandatory Sentencing Law on Serious Crime Rates." *Crime and Delinquency* (1997) vol. 43, pp. 457–469.

Terry, Don. "A Town in Terror as Children Disappear." *New York Times*, December 10, 1993, A18. Accessed online.

Thompson, Jenni. Interviews by Kim Cross, February 11, 2016; March 15, 2022.

Three Strikes. Cornell Law School: Legal Information Institute website. https://www.law.cornell.edu/wex/three_strikes.

"Three Strikes Basics." Stanford Law School: Three Strikes Project. https://law.stanford.edu/three-strikes-project/three-strikes-basics/.

Victim Impact Statements. *People v. Richard Allen Davis*, September 9, 1996. See pp. 29, 35.

"Wilson Proposes Tougher Molesting Law as Memorial for Polly Klaas." Associated Press, December 7, 1993.

Bibliography

"$316,000 Raised for Search Fund; More Events Scheduled." *Santa Rosa Press Democrat*, October 27, 1993.

Allen, David. "Police Offered $50,000 by Polly Center." *Petaluma Argus-Courier*, November 12, 1993.

Anima, Tina. "Haircuts, Air Searches in Effort to Find Polly." *Santa Rosa Press Democrat*, October 18, 1993.

Anima, Tina. "Polly Foundation Names New Chief: French to Take Place of Rhodes." *Santa Rosa Press Democrat*, November 22, 1993.

Baker, K. C. "A Family Shattered: Mom of Missing Kevin Collins, 10, Still Thinks of Him Decades After He Vanished." *People*, November 18, 2019.

Baker, K. C. "What Happened to 10-Year-Old Kevin Collins, Who Vanished from a Bus Stop in 1984?" *People*, November 15, 2019.

Becker, Ingrid. "FBI Pulls 6 Agents off Polly Case." *Marin Independent Journal*, October 21, 1993.

Becker, Ingrid. "Police Pull 8 Officers off Polly Case." *Marin Independent Journal*, October 29, 1993.

Becker, Ingrid. "Polly Effort Is Big Business: As Money Pours In, Volunteers Look Ahead." *Marin Independent Journal*, October 5, 1993.

Becker, Ingrid. "Polly Group to Run Background Checks on All Its Top Leaders." *Marin Independent Journal*, November 30, 1993.

Becker, Ingrid. "Winona Ryder Comes Home to Join Search for Polly." *Marin Independent Journal*, October 10, 1993.

Becker, Ingrid, and Alex Neill. "Woolsley Makes Plea for Polly." *Marin Independent Journal*, October 14, 1993.

"Before Being Sentenced to Die, Killer Disrupts a Courtroom." *New York Times*, September 27, 1996.

Bellafante, Ginia. "Child in Need." *TIME*, October 25, 1993

Benfell, Carol. "City Reaches into Reserves for Polly Hunt: Police Following Hundreds of Tips." *Santa Rosa Press Democrat*, October 17, 1993.

Benfell, Carol. "Pythian Rd Resident Says He Suspected Davis." *Santa Rosa Press Democrat*, December 3, 1993.

Boylan, Jeanne. *Portraits of Guilt: The Woman Who Profiles the Faces of America's Deadliest Criminals.* Atria, September 29, 2012.

Caballo, Frances. "At the Helm Again: Bill Rhodes Started Effort to Find Polly, Now He's Leading It." *Petaluma Argus-Courier*, November 16, 1993.

Cahill, Greg. "Collins Hopeful about Polly." *Petaluma Argus-Courier*, October 6, 1993.

Cahill, Greg. "Community Gets Involved." *Petaluma Argus-Courier*, October 6, 1993.

Cahill, Greg. "Five Stories: The Selling of Marc Klaas." *Bohemian*, August 19, 1999.

Cahill, Greg. "The Longest Year." *Sonoma County Independent*, September 22–28, 1994.

Cahill, Greg. "Police, FBI Reject Offer of Outside Help." *Petaluma Argus-Courier*, November 16, 1993.

Cahill, Greg. "Polly Funds Won't Go to City Police: But Volunteers, City Officials Will Pool Resources." *Petaluma Argus-Courier*, November 2, 1993.

Cahill, Greg. "Polly's Dad: We've Tried Everything." *Petaluma Argus-Courier*, November 19, 1993.

Cahill, Greg. "Polly's Parents Waiting, Hoping: Month-long Search for Daughter Takes Its Toll." *Petaluma Argus-Courier*, October 29, 1993.

Cahill, Greg. "Search Center Settles into New Headquarters." *Petaluma Argus-Courier*, November 16, 1993.

Cahill, Greg. "Volunteers Getting Little Rest: They Juggle Home Life and Work with Efforts to Help Find Polly Klaas." *Petaluma Argus-Courier*, October 19, 1993.

Cahill, Greg. "Volunteers Launch Their Own Probe: Private Investigator Joins Search." *Petaluma Argus-Courier*, November 2, 1993.

Callahan, Mary. "20 Years Later, Petaluma Remembers Polly Klaas." *Santa Rosa Press Democrat*, September 29, 2013.

Close, Sandy. "'America's Child,' Polly, Perplexes Other Teenagers." *Pacific News Service*, December 26, 1993.

Cohen, Laurie P. "The Polygraph Paradox." *Wall Street Journal*, March 22, 2008.

Del Vecchio, Rick. "Grief and Fear Are Painful Legacy for Polly's Peers." *San Francisco Chronicle*, December 6, 1993.

Digitale, Robert. "Massive Search for Petaluma Youngster." *Santa Rosa Press Democrat*, October 4, 1993.

Digitale, Robert. "Polly's Friends Look for Answers." *Santa Rosa Press Democrat*, October 5, 1993.

Dougan, Michael. "Deputies Tried to Save Polly." *San Francisco Gate*, April 25, 1996.

Dougan, Michael. "Kidnap Shatters Family's World: Polly's Parents Bound by Tragedy." *San Francisco Examiner*, October 15, 1993.

Dougan, Michael. "Movie Star Offers Reward for Child's Return." *San Francisco Examiner*, October 13, 1993.

Dougan, Michael. "Polly Search Effort Now International." *San Francisco Examiner*, November 5, 1993.

Dougan, Michael, and Janet Kornblum. "Klaas 'Hero' Tried in '68 Molest Case: Jury in Peninsula Case Acquitted Bill Rhodes; He Organized Petaluma Search for Polly." *San Francisco Examiner*, November 24, 1993.

Dougan, Michael, and Seth Rosenfeld. "Kidnap Extortion Suspect Arrested: Wanted $10,000 to Lead to Polly." *San Francisco Chronicle*, October 19, 1993.

Dugard, Jaycee. *A Stolen Life: A Memoir*. New York: Simon & Schuster, July 2001.

Elliott, Steve. "Investigation Reveals Ties to Modesto Crimes." *Modesto Bee*, December 2, 1993.

Fagan, Kevin. "20 Years after Polly Klaas Killing, Attitudes Change." *San Francisco Gate*, October 2, 2013.

Fagan, Kevin. "Palm Print Links Man to Missing Polly Klaas." *San Francisco Chronicle*, December 4, 1993.

Fagan, Kevin, and Michael Taylor. "Amber, Kevin—Other Bay Kidnaps Unsolved." *San Francisco Chronicle*, December 2, 1993.

Fernandez, Elizabeth. "Slumber Party Kidnap Shocker." *San Francisco Examiner*, October 3, 1993.

Fernandez, Elizabeth, Marsha Ginsburg, and George Rainer. "Suspect Palm Print Found in Bedroom: Search for Polly Expanding." *San Francisco Examiner*, December 4, 1993.

Fimrite, Peter. "600 Search for Kidnapped Girl." *San Francisco Chronicle*, October 4, 1993.

Frantz, Annie. "Winona Boosts Search Efforts." *Petaluma Argus-Courier*, October 12, 1993.

Gardner, Joanne. "Live Auction Lots." Polly Klaas Foundation, press release, October 25, 1993.

Gardner, Joanne. "Media Advisory: PKF Leadership Team." Polly Klaas Foundation, November 15, 1993.

Gardner, Joanne. "Oakland As T-shirt with Names of Missing Kids." Polly Klaas Foundation, November 2, 1993.

Gardner, Joanne. "Polly Klaas Search Fund." Polly Klaas Foundation, press release, October 21, 1993.

Gardner, Joanne. "Press release: Polly Memorial." Polly Klaas Foundation, December 5, 1993.

Gardner, Joanne. "Shop for Polly." Polly Klaas Foundation, press release, October 19, 1993.

Gelman, David, Susan Agrest, John McCormick, Nikki Finke Greenberg, Holly Morris, Tessa Namuth, and Marsha Zabarsky. "Stolen Children." *Newsweek*, March 19, 1984.

Geniella, Mike. "CHP, Mendocino Jailers Say They Followed Policy on Davis." *Santa Rosa Press Democrat*, 1993.

Geniella, Mike. "Davis Kin's Return to Reservation Blocked: Pomos, FBI in Tense Standoff." *Santa Rosa Press Democrat,* December 4, 1993.

Giles, Jeffrey. "Winona." *Rolling Stone,* March 10, 1994.

Ginsburg, Marsha. "Bay Area Has More than Its Share of Child Kidnappings." *San Francisco Examiner,* October 17, 1993.

Goldston, Linda. "Grim Petaluma Hunts Missing Girl." *San Jose Mercury News,* October 4, 1993.

Goldston, Linda. "Man Steals Polly, 12, during Sleep-Over." *Calgary Herald,* October 8, 1993.

Grabowicz, Paul, and Diana Williams. "Palm Print Matches: Bedroom Clue Links Suspect to Polly." *Oakland Tribune,* December 4, 1993.

Grammys, 1994 PSA. https://www.youtube.com/watch?v=2CYjbyNtOtc, January 1994.

Haeseler, Rob. "Suspect Gets Glow." *San Francisco Chronicle,* December 2, 1993.

Hall, Dee J. "State Used Flawed Hair Evidence to Convict Innocent People." *Wisconsin Law Journal,* May 11, 2017.

Handelman, David. "Winona Ryder: Hiding High." WinonaRyder.org. Winona Forever, October 1993. https://winona-ryder.org/articles/winona-ryder-hiding -high/.

Harris, Paula K. "Psychiatric Evaluation Ordered: Man Faces Extortion Charges in Polly Case." *Petaluma Argus-Courier,* October 19, 1993.

Harris, Paula. "Tangled Web: Child Killer Richard Allen Davis Gets a Home Page of His Own." *Sonoma County Independent,* February 24, 2000.

Harris, Paula K. "TV Show Triggers New Tips." *Petaluma Argus-Courier,* October 6, 1993.

Hart, Steve. "Cloverdale: 'An Angel Rested Here': Memorial Grows Where Polly Was Found." *Santa Rosa Press Democrat,* December 14, 1993.

Hord, Michelle. *The Other Side of Yet: Finding Light in the Midst of Darkness.* Atria Books, March 2022.

Horowitz, Donna. "Novato Father Offers His $20,000 Corvette as Reward for Polly." *Marin Independent Journal,* October 14, 1993.

"How It Happened: Timeline of Events." *Santa Rosa Press Democrat,* December 12, 1993.

"How to Help the Search for Polly Klaas." *Petaluma Argus-Courier,* October 6, 1993.

Hsu, Spencer S. "FBI Admits Flaws in Hair Analysis Over Decades." *Washington Post,* April 18, 2015.

Hsu, Spencer S. "Justice Department, FBI to Review Use of Forensic Evidence in Thousands of Cases." *Washington Post,* July 10, 2012.

Isles, Nancy Nation. "Volunteers for Polly Rebound." *Marin Independent Journal,* November 21, 1993.

Jowers, Andrew. "Mothers Gather for Support in Wake of Kidnapping." October 1993.

Junod, Tom. "America's Most Haunted." *GQ,* September 1, 1997.

Kataoka, Mike. "Tip about Suspect Gets Little Notice." *Riverside Press Enterprise,* December 1, 1993.

Kelly, John F., and Phillip Wearne. *Tainting Evidence: Inside the Scandals at the FBI Crime Lab*, Free Press, June 2, 1998.

Keown, Tim. "The Grim Reaper: Why Does Marc Klaas Still Feel Compelled to Relive His Daughter Polly's Death in Public?" *San Francisco Magazine,* November 1, 1997.

"Kevin Collins Foundation to Shut Its Doors / 12 Years, Sluggish Donations Take Toll on Boy's Dad." *San Francisco Gate*, April 2, 1996.

"Kidnapping Galvanizes Petaluma." *Oakland Tribune*, October 7, 1993.

"Kidnapping Summons City to Action." *New York Times*, October 15, 1993.

Klineman, Eileen. "$200,000 Offered to Polly's Abductor." *Santa Rosa Press Democrat*, October 13, 1993.

Klineman, Eileen. "A Mother's Plea." *Santa Rosa Press Democrat*, October 5, 1993.

Klineman, Eileen. "A's a Hit at New Polly Center." *Santa Rosa Press Democrat,* November 17, 1993.

Klineman, Eileen. "Experts: Parents Must Ease Own Anxieties before Easing Their Child's." *Santa Rosa Press Democrat*, October 17, 1993.

Klineman, Eileen. "Napa Volunteer Fields Psychic Tips." *Santa Rosa Press Democrat*, October 21, 1993.

Klineman, Eileen. "Petaluma Man Held in Polly Extortion." *Santa Rosa Press Democrat*, October 20, 1993.

Klineman, Eileen. "Polly Center Looks for New Home." *Santa Rosa Press Democrat*, October 19, 1993.

Klineman, Eileen. "Polly Fund Offers City $50,000: Petaluma Pleased, but Cautious." *Santa Rosa Press Democrat,* November 5, 1993.

Klineman, Eileen. "Polly Klaas Fund $250,000." *Santa Rosa Press Democrat*, October 27, 1993.

Klineman, Eileen. "Polly Quilt 'Therapy' for Kids: Klaas' School Patches Caring Messages Together." *Santa Rosa Press Democrat*, October 5, 1993.

Klineman, Eileen. "Sen. Marks' Request for State Reward in Polly's Case in Limbo: Petaluma Police Approval Sought." *Santa Rosa Press Democrat,* November 10, 1993.

Klineman, Eileen. "Town Rallies behind Search for Young Girl." *Santa Rosa Press Democrat*, October 6, 1993.

Kovner, Guy. "Buffet Auction for Polly." *Santa Rosa Press Democrat,* November 2, 1993.

Kovner, Guy. "Funds for Polly Search Refused." *Santa Rosa Press Democrat*, November 16, 1993.

Kovner, Guy. "High Tech Polly Hunt May Help Others." *Santa Rosa Press Democrat*, October 1993.

Kovner, Guy. "Investigator: Likely Someone Hired Abductor." *Santa Rosa Press Democrat,* November 5, 1993.

Kovner, Guy. "Kidnapping Brings Media Mob to Petaluma." *Santa Rosa Press Democrat*, October 16, 1993.

Kovner, Guy. "New Sketch Nets Calls." *Santa Rosa Press Democrat*, October 16, 1993.

Kovner, Guy. "No Free Postage for Polly Fliers." *Santa Rosa Press Democrat*, October 14, 1993.

Kovner, Guy. "Polly Center Moving to Bigger Office." *Santa Rosa Press Democrat*, October 25, 1993.

Kovner, Guy. "Polly Hunt Gets Experienced Hand." *Santa Rosa Press Democrat*, October 23, 1993.

Kovner, Guy. "Private Eye Lipset Joins Polly Case." *Santa Rosa Press Democrat*, October 5, 1993.

Kovner, Guy. "Rhodes Turned Down Calls for Investigations." *Santa Rosa Press Democrat,* November 25, 1993.

Kovner, Guy. "Stars Come Out to Help Find Polly." *Santa Rosa Press Democrat*, October 22, 1993.

Kovner, Guy, and Bony Saludes. "Fewer FBI Agents in Polly Hunt: Petaluma Police Team Remains at Full Strength." *Santa Rosa Press Democrat*, October 21, 1993.

Kramer, Staci D. "FBI Computer Team Ties Clues Together." *Chicago Tribune,* December 17, 1993.

Lafferty, Elaine. "Final Outrage: Facing Execution, Polly Klaas' Killer Lashes Back." *TIME*, October 7, 1996.

Levin, Sam. "Polly Klaas's Murder Fueled the '90s Crime Panic. Her Sisters Fear We're Repeating the Same History." *Guardian*. October 22, 2022.

Lewis, Gregory. "Petaluma Unnerved by Girl's Kidnapping." *San Francisco Chronicle*, October 4, 1993.

Locke, Michelle. "Davis Says He Murdered Polly." Associated Press, December 6, 1993.

Locke, Michelle. "Kidnap Probe Turns Up More Links with Polly." Associated Press, December 3, 1993.

Lopez, Rob. "2 Girls Talk about Friend's Kidnapping." *San Francisco Chronicle*, October 9, 1993.

Lopez, Rob. "Just Keep Her Safe: Parents of Kidnapped Girl Plea for Her Return." *Petaluma Argus-Courier*, October 6, 1993.

Lopez, Rob. "New Sketch of Suspect Released." *Petaluma Argus-Courier*, October 15, 1993.

Lopez, Rob. "Police Chief Pleads for Help: More Officers Needed to Relieve Burden of Kidnap Case." *Petaluma Argus-Courier,* October 29, 1993.

Magid, Larry. "App Helps Guard Kids from the Unthinkable." *San Jose Mercury News*, November 6, 2016.

Magid, Lawrence. "On-Line Services Unite to Help Find Abducted Girl: Electronic Poster Makes Photograph of Polly Klaas Available Worldwide." *San Jose Mercury News*, October 10, 1993.

Martinez, Don. "Search Goes On for Missing Petaluma Girl." *San Francisco Examiner*, October 5, 1993.

Martinez, Don. "Sharing Heartache Helps Father of Kidnapped Girl." *San Francisco Examiner,* October 5, 1993.

Mason, Clark. "Winona Ryder Joins Search." *Santa Rosa Press Democrat,* October 25, 1993.

Mason, Elizabeth. "Police Still Seek Lead in Abduction." *Oakland Tribune,* October 4, 1993.

McConahey, Meg. "3 Airplanes Aid Effort to Find Girl." *Santa Rosa Press Democrat,* October 20, 1993.

McConahey, Meg. "Ex Polly Search Chief Style Draws Criticism." *Santa Rosa Press Democrat,* November 21, 1993.

McConahey, Meg. "Waiting for Polly: It's 'When,' not 'If,' for Girl's Mom." *Santa Rosa Press Democrat,* November 8, 1993.

McConahey, Meg, and Eileen Klineman. "Petaluma's Grief, Hope over Polly's Abduction." *Santa Rosa Press Democrat,* October 6, 1993.

McCoy, Mike, R. Rossman, and Mike Geniella. "Polly Kidnap Suspect Held." *Santa Rosa Press Democrat,* December 1, 1993.

Meadows, K. C. "Coyote Valley Tribe Meets with Lawyer for Davis' Kin." *Ukiah Daily Journal,* December 7, 1993.

Meadows, K. C. "Tension Runs High during Coyote Valley Standoff: FBI Plows through Tribal Roadblock." *Ukiah Daily Journal,* December 5, 1993.

Meadows, K. C. "Tribal Power Remains a Complicated and Confusing Issue to Many." *Ukiah Daily Journal,* December 5, 1993.

Minton, Toni, Susan Yoachum, and Kevin Fagan. "Tears and Prayers for Polly." *San Francisco Chronicle,* December 10, 1993.

"Monterey Wedding for Klaas and Cheer." *Petaluma Argus-Courier,* July 19, 1994.

Nakeo, Annie. "Media Blitz Could Bring Polly Home." *TIME,* October 25, 1993.

Neill, Alex. "New Song Reinforces Search for Polly." *Marin Independent Journal,* November 12, 1993.

Neill, Alex. "Polly's Dad Wants More Private Eyes: Says That's Best Use for Donated Money." *Marin Independent Journal,* November 12, 1993.

Nichol, Eve. "Eve Nichol's Message to Community." *Santa Rosa Press Democrat,* December 7, 1993.

Nichol, Eve, and Marc Klaas. "Parents' Plea: Please Send Polly Back to Us." *San Francisco Examiner,* October 17, 1993.

"Odyssey of Violence." *People,* May 13, 1996.

Olmstead, Marty. "Friends Play for Polly: Concert Raises $15,000 for Kidnap Fund." *Marin Independent Journal,* October 22, 1993.

O'Rourke, Lois. "Kidnap Suspect Arraigned: Clothing Linked to Kidnap Found." *Ukiah Daily Journal,* December 2, 1993.

Paddock, Richard C. "All-out Search for Missing Girl: Kidnapping: A Community Is Galvanized in Its Efforts to Locate Polly Klaas. She Was Abducted from Her Bedroom during a Slumber Party." *Los Angeles Times,* October 6, 1993.

Paddock, Richard C. "Internet Aids Hunt for Polly: Missing-Child Team, beyond Milk Cartons, Taps into Cyberspace." *Los Angeles Times,* October 17, 1993.

Paddock, Richard C., and Jennifer Warren. "Revelations in Klaas Kidnapping Spark Outrage." *Los Angeles Times,* December 3, 1993.

Paddock, Richard C., and Jennifer Warren. "Suspect's Tip Leads to Body of Polly Klaas." *Los Angeles Times,* December 5, 1993.

Patel, Roxanne. "Celebrities Play Benefit Concert." *Santa Rosa Press Democrat,* October 26, 1993.

Patel, Roxanne. "Polly's Family Thankful for Help." *Santa Rosa Press Democrat,* November 26, 1993.

Patel, Roxanne, and Eileen Klineman. "Polly Funds Go to Family." *Santa Rosa Press Democrat,* November 4, 1993.

Patel, Roxanne, and Chris Smith. "Kidnap Fund Hits $300,000." *Santa Rosa Press Democrat,* October 31, 1993.

Pendle, George. "The California Town That Was Famous for Eggs and Arm Wrestling." *Slate,* January 17, 2017.

"Police Say Polly Kidnap Case Still on Front Burner." *San Francisco Chronicle,* October 21, 1993.

"Polly, Alive in Memory." *People,* September 22, 2003.

"Polly Search Center Profile of Volunteer Effort." *Santa Rosa Press Democrat,* October 16, 1993.

Price, Richard. "For the Love of Polly / Calif. Town Rallies for Abducted Girl." *USA Today,* October 15, 1993.

"Psychologist Offers Chilling Profile of Girl's Kidnapper." *St. Louis Post-Dispatch,* October 8, 1993.

Reber, Diane. "Coping with Fears and Anxieties." *Petaluma Argus-Courier,* October 6, 1993.

Reed, Christopher. "Computers Link to Hunt Kidnapper." *The Age,* October 18, 1993.

"Review of FBI Forensics Does Not Extend to Federally Trained State, Local Examiners." *Washington Post,* December 22, 2012.

Rist, Curtis, and Laird Harrison. "No Surrender: As a Jury Recommends Death for Daughter Polly's Killer, Marc Klaas Carries on His Fight for Kids." *People,* August 19, 1996.

Rose, Bleys W. "Polly Klaas Memorial Service." *Santa Rosa Press Democrat,* December 9, 1993.

Rose, Bleys W. "Tough Anti-crime Initiatives Gain New Momentum." *Santa Rosa Press Democrat,* December 7, 1993.

Rossman, Randi. "Davis No Longer Alone—Hate Mail Pours In." *Santa Rosa Press Democrat,* December 14, 1993.

Rossman, Randi. "Hundreds of Tips, Nothing Concrete." *Santa Rosa Press Democrat,* October 7, 1993.

Rossman, Randi. "New Sketch of Polly's Abductor." *Santa Rosa Press Democrat,* October 15, 1993.

Rossman, Randi. "Petaluma Cuts Back on Polly Search." *Santa Rosa Press Democrat,* October 29, 1993.

Rossman, Randi. "Police Check Out Rhodes." *Santa Rosa Press Democrat,* November 27, 1993.

Rossman, Randi. "Polly Group Hurries to Go Non-profit." *Santa Rosa Press Democrat*, November 5, 1993.

Rossman, Randi. "Polly Klaas Foundation Wants to Hire Expert." *Santa Rosa Press Democrat*, November 13, 1993.

Rossman, Randi. "Polly's Dad Says Family Cleared by Lie Tests." *Santa Rosa Press Democrat*. October 8, 1993.

Rossman, Randi. "Ryder, Polly's Parents to Lead Non-profit Search Foundation: PTSA Cuts Ties by Noon Today." *Santa Rosa Press Democrat*, October 25, 1993.

Rossman, Randi. "Satellite May Aid Search." *Santa Rosa Press Democrat*, November 19, 1993.

Rossman, Randi. "Suspect Posed as Kidnap Victim." *Santa Rosa Press Democrat*, November 5, 1993.

Rossman, Randi, and Meg McConahey. "Leader in Polly Search Resigns." *Santa Rosa Press Democrat*, November 20, 1993.

Rossman, Randi, and Bleys W. Rose. "Davis Twice Convicted of Kidnapping." *Santa Rosa Press Democrat*, December 2, 1993.

Rossman, Randi, and Bleys Rose. "Rhodes Cleared in '68 Sex Crime: Incident Had Similarities to Polly Case." *Santa Rosa Press Democrat*, November 25, 1993.

Rossman, Randi, and Chris Smith. "Winona Ryder Offers Reward for Polly's Return." *Santa Rosa Press Democrat*, October 9, 1993.

"Routine Lie Detector Tests Eliminate Family as Suspects in Kidnap Case." *Ukiah Daily Journal*, October 8, 1993.

Royner, Guy. "Abduction Strains Family Relationships." *Santa Rosa Press Democrat*, October 20, 1993.

Saludes, Bony. "Guilty Plea in Klaas Extortion Attempt." *Petaluma Argus-Courier*, October 19, 1993.

Saludes, Bony. "Ito Says He'll Take On Davis Trial." *Santa Rosa Press Democrat*, September 27, 1995.

"San Francisco Police Link Deceased Criminal to Kevin Collins Case." CBS News Bay Area, February 6, 2013.

Schevitz Wills, Tanya. "Not Guilty, Says Klaas Suspect." *San Francisco Examiner*, December 22, 1993.

Schrag, Peter. "Exploitation of Polly Shows Politicians' Hypocrisy." McClatchy News Service, December 26, 1993.

Seligman, Katherine. "Marc Klaas, Polly's Dad, to Urge Child Safety in Session with the President." *San Francisco Examiner*, December 16, 1993.

Sheehan, Susan. "Life After Polly." Publication unknown, date unknown (circa 1994). Magazine tear-sheet from Greg Jacobs personal archives.

"Shopping, Fill-Ups, Sweets Help Fund Search Efforts: 'Polly Day' Could Raise $10,000." *Santa Rosa Press Democrat*, October 20, 1993.

Sinberg, Stan. "Hunt for Polly Captivates Town." *Marin Independent Journal*, October 17, 1993.

Smith, Chris. "Actress Offers $200,000 for Polly." *Santa Rosa Press Democrat*, October 10, 1993.

Smith, Chris. "Decision on Polly Detective." *Santa Rosa Press Democrat*, November 14, 1993.

Smith, Chris. "Petaluma Girl, 12, Abducted." *Santa Rosa Press Democrat*, October 3, 1993.

Smith, Chris. "Polly's Friends Thought It Was 'Joke.'" *Santa Rosa Press Democrat*, October 9, 1993.

Smith, Chris. "Still Only Questions in Abduction." *Santa Rosa Press Democrat*, October 6, 1993.

Smith, Chris, and Randi Rossman. "Print Links Davis, Polly: Police Say They'll Seek Charges; Big Search Today." *Santa Rosa Press Democrat*, December 4, 1993.

Smith, Harry. "Marc Klaas, Eve Nichol and Allan Nichol, Parents of Polly Klaas, Discuss Their Daughter's Kidnapping in California." *CBS This Morning*. CBS, October 18, 1993.

Smolowe, Jim. "A High-Tech Dragnet." *TIME*, November 1, 1993.

Sonenshine, Ron. "FBI Questions Father of Kidnapped Girl." *San Francisco Chronicle*, October 6, 1993.

Sonenshine, Ron. "Kidnap Recreated, Videotaped." *San Francisco Chronicle*, October 9, 1993.

Sonenshine, Ron. "Kidnap Search Runs Up Big Tab: Photo of Polly Klaas on 7 Million Flyers Faxed and Mailed Out." *San Francisco Chronicle*, October 17, 1993.

Sonenshine, Ron. "Petaluma Kidnap Baffles Parents, Authorities." *San Francisco Chronicle*, October 5, 1993.

Sonenshine, Ron. "Polly Searcher Is Sex Offender: Ex-chairman of Foundation Foiled Background Check." *San Francisco Chronicle*, November 23, 1993.

Sonenshine, Ron. "'Prime Suspect' Held in Abduction of Girl, 12." *San Francisco Chronicle*, December 2, 1993.

Sonenshine, Ron. "Private Detective Joins Search for Missing Girl: SF's Hal Lipset Hired to Try to Find Polly." *San Francisco Chronicle*, November 2, 1993.

Sonenshine, Ron. "Some Officers to Be Pulled off Polly Kidnap Case: Man Held on Extortion Charge—Official Says Wide Search Goes On." *San Francisco Chronicle*, October 21, 1993.

Spolar, Christine. "California Town Cries as Polly Klaas Is Found." *Washington Post*, December 6, 1993.

Spolar, Christine. "Kidnapping Search Focuses on a Mysterious Intruder." *Kansas City Star*, October 16, 1993.

"Stolen Children: What Can Be Done about Child Abduction." *Newsweek*, March 19, 1984.

Sulzberger, Arthur Gregg. "Marc Klaas Joins Utah Search." *Santa Rosa Press Democrat*, June 6, 2022.

Sweeney, James. "Police Liaison Undaunted by Coverage." *Santa Rosa Press Democrat*, October 18, 1993.

Sweeney, James, and Chris Smith. "At Age 12 Davis Began Crimes." *Santa Rosa Press Democrat,* December 2, 1993.

Terry, Don. "A Town in Terror as Children Disappear." *New York Times,* December 10, 1993.

Thomas, Karen. "Ryder Pulls for Abducted Girl." *USA Today,* October 12, 1993.

Thurman, Maura. "Polly Postage Needed: 1 Million Fliers Wait for Mailing." *Marin Independent Journal,* October 15, 1993.

Toobin, Jeffrey. "The Man Who Kept Going Free." *New Yorker,* February 27, 1994.

"Two Months: The Polly Klaas Case." *Santa Rosa Press Democrat,* December 3, 1993.

Vasquez, Daniel. "Parents in Tearful Plea for Daughter's Return." *Oakland Tribune,* October 5, 1993.

Vasquez, Daniel. "Suspected Kidnapper's Neighbors Seek Answers." *Oakland Tribune,* December 2, 1993.

Wallace, Danny. "Polly," poem by eighth grade student at Cotati Middle School, October 26, 1993, author's archives.

Walsh, John. *Tears of Rage: From Grieving Father to Crusader for Justice, the Untold Story of the Adam Walsh Case.* Atria, October 1, 1997.

Warren, Jennifer, and Richard C. Paddock. "Suspect's Palm Print Found in Klaas Home; Kidnapping: Evidence Discovered in Bedroom on Night of Girl's Abduction Shows Parolee Was There, FBI Says. Richard Allen Davis Could Be Charged Next Week." *Los Angeles Times,* December 4, 1993.

Winokur, Julie. "The Violent World of Most Wanted's Host." *San Francisco Examiner,* October 10, 1993.

"Winona Ryder Offers $200,000 to Help Find Missing Girl." Associated Press, October 9, 1993.

"With Song and Poetry, a Farewell to a Kidnapped Girl Named Polly." *New York Times,* December 11, 1993.

Witt, Linda. "Sad Case of Another Missing Child." *USA Today,* November 1, 1993.

Wohl, James P. "A Terrorist's Guide to the 1984 Olympics." *Playboy,* May 1983.

Zamora, Jim Herron. "Emotional Plea to Return Daughter." *San Francisco Examiner,* October 5, 1993.

Zamora, Jim Herron, and John Finn. "FBI Experts Grill Petaluma Kidnap Victim's Family." *San Francisco Examiner,* October 6, 1993.

Index

Note: *Italic page numbers* indicate photographs.

About the Author

KIM CROSS is a *New York Times* best-selling author, journalist, and historian known for meticulously reported narrative nonfiction. Her stories have been recognized in "best of" lists by the *New York Times*, the *Columbia Journalism Review*, the Sunday Long Read, Longform, Apple News Audio, and *Best American Sports Writing*. She lives in Boise, Idaho.